A Bibliography

of

The Periodical Works of Charles Dickens

BIBLIOGRAPHICAL
ANALYTICAL
AND
STATISTICAL

By

THOMAS HATTON and
ARTHUR H. CLEAVER

With 31 Illustrations and Facsimiles

LONDON:
CHAPMAN & HALL, LTD.
1933

TYPESETTING AND PRINTING
BY
DE MONTFORT PRESS, LEICESTER, ENG.

PRINTED IN GREAT BRITAIN.

Dedicated
To the Memory of
JOHN FURBER DEXTER.
A great collector of
A great man's works.

John Furber Dexter.

MY Father—who was born in 1847—was essentially a
"Londoner," and London was the only home he knew
during a long life of eighty years. On the rare occasions
when he was persuaded to take a holiday, he left with the
apparent reluctance of one who was a staunch believer in
Dr. Johnson's dictum :—

"For there is in London all that life can afford."

At the end of his school-days, part of which had been spent
in Paris, he successfully resisted parental pressure to adopt
a career and deliberately chose the freer existence of a critic
and collector. He inherited a taste for collecting from both
sides of his family, but instead of following in the footsteps
of his father, who had acquired an important and valuable
collection of old silver, he turned his attention, at an early age,
to books and engravings.

Illustrated books with literary merit had a special attraction
for him, but no author appealed to him more strongly than
Charles Dickens, whose writings soon claimed his interest
and provided him with a congenial task for the rest of his
life. Surely, no man was better qualified to become an
expert ! He was born at the right moment, he lived in the
Dickens atmosphere, the material was at hand, and he had the
necessary leisure for the uninterrupted pursuit of his hobby.

He was quick to take advantage of these opportunities and
his "Hints to Dickens Collectors," written in 1884, shows
clearly that he soon won recognition as an expert. In that
book he indicated that his own collection was started not later
than 1868, and of this there is ample evidence in my possession,
consisting of numerous sales catalogues, showing that in the

early "seventies" he was already dealing extensively in the first editions of Charles Dickens and other contemporary writers.

An unfailing memory and an exceptionally keen eye for detail served him in good stead during the years he spent searching the shelves of old and second-hand bookshops for material that would add to or improve his collection. He was seldom absent from any book auction sale of importance, and was a well-known figure at "The Rooms," where he was recognised as the leading authority on all matters connected with the works of Charles Dickens. On one occasion he was caricatured for a London daily, with five other well-known bibliophiles, while attending a sale at Sotheby's. When the cartoon appeared in the paper, this inscription had been added: "Mr. Dexter has nothing to learn about the value of rare Dickens editions."

The result of his prolonged research is reflected in copious notes, clearly intended for a bibliography, and these together with his complete collection of Charles Dickens' works, remain intact in my possession. It has given me great satisfaction to be able to perpetuate my father's life work by placing both collection and notes at the disposal of so keen a student and collector as Mr. Thomas Hatton, who has collaborated with my husband in the preparation of this volume. Prior to this, no person other than the late H. G. Child, who assisted my father in the compilation of his catalogue, has, with my knowledge and consent, had access to any part of the Dexter collection.

DOREEN CLEAVER.

December 12th, 1933.

CONTENTS.

LIST OF FACSIMILE ILLUSTRATIONS.

Also a facsimile Title-page precedes each of the 13 works.

Introductory Chapter

WHEN the authors decided upon the production of this work, it was agreed that it should contain every bibliographical detail known to them, relating to the first issue of the first editions of the thirteen important books written by Charles Dickens, and published in periodical form. The object was to present these details in such a manner that the student, as well as the experienced collector, might have, at long last, a standard book of reference, which could be relied upon to put an end to the uncertainty still associated with the expression—"original parts as issued." If this object has been achieved, it is due to the actual possession of thousands of the original parts, from the study and microscopic examination of which, an abundance of new evidence has been brought to light; and more especially because it has been made possible to verify this evidence, by constant reference to the collection, notes, and records, in the John F. Dexter library, where confirmation was invariably to be found.

The year 1936 will see the centenary of the publication of the greatest and most popular book of modern times, "The Pickwick Papers," which has been read and re-read by millions of people in our own language, and in that of almost every foreign tongue; it appeals to a larger circle of collectors than possibly any other known book and, in its original form of issue, possesses more interesting typographical and physical problems than even the great folios of Shakespeare.

Yet, with all its intriguing features, the collector has never been presented with the comprehensive bibliography

[xi]

which is warranted by the importance of the subject. The value of the great effort by John C. Eckel is fully recognised, but unfortunately, and perhaps unwittingly, Mr. Eckel leaves the collector still groping in the dark, when he comes to consider the very essence of "Pickwick"—the text, or letterpress. This sin of omission or commission, applies in an even greater degree to the other periodical works. Why not commute the sentence passed 20 years ago on "Nicholas Nickleby," for being uninteresting to the collector? Again, where can a printed record be found of the details which go to make up "Our Mutual Friend,"—to name but one of the least important in the series?

A collector, whether of old silver, china or furniture, has no use for the individual piece which cannot be authenticated as original and complete. So with the first editions of Charles Dickens—he is entitled, when he buys a bibliography, to feel certain that it furnishes the essential data, which will enable him to recognise the exact constituents of each of the 215 monthly parts contained in the thirteen books.

The magnitude of the material contained in the thirteen works, may surprise those not well versed in the subject, and the statistics set out in the table below may even give food for thought to experienced collectors. The numbered columns denote the nature of the material, and the figures beneath indicate the number of pages. Front and Back wrappers, as well as plates, are considered as two pages each.

Column 1 Outer Wrappers. (215 parts.)
,, 2 Official Advertising Sheet. (166 insets.)
,, 3 Other Front Insets and Slips. (81 items.)
,, 4 Addresses by Author or Publishers. (9 items.)
,, 5 Back Insets and Slips. (460 items.)
,, 6 Plates. (417.)
,, 7 Text or Letterpress.
,, 8 Preliminary Leaves.

INTRODUCTION.

PHYSICAL FORMAT.

Works.	1	2	3	4	5	6	7	8	Total.
Pickwick Papers	76	188	16	16	178	86	610	16	1186
Sketches by "Boz"	80	16	4	4	26	80	528	8	746
Nicholas Nickleby	76	296	2	2	208	80	624	16	1304
M. Humphrey's Clock	80	—	12	—	86	—	1038	20	1236
Martin Chuzzlewit	76	288	6	—	330	80	624	16	1420
Oliver Twist	40	16	2	—	—	48	312	12	430
Dombey and Son	76	244	32	—	220	80	624	16	1292
David Copperfield	76	188	30	—	130	80	624	16	1144
Bleak House	76	264	54	—	334	80	624	16	1448
Little Dorrit	76	244	34	—	248	80	626	14	1322
Tale of Two Cities	28	56	6	—	36	32	254	10	422
Our Mutual Friend	76	320	26	—	282	80	640	20	1444
Edwin Drood	24	138	—	—	80	28	192	8	470
Totals	860	2258	224	22	2158	834	7320	188	13864

The wrappers, which clothe the monthly parts of the various issues, are a striking feature of the finished production. The front covers consist mainly of designs illustrative of the text, by artists who, with one exception, also illustrated the books. These are, Robert Seymour (one); George Cruikshank (two); Hablot K. Browne (seven); George Cattermole (one); Marcus Stone (one); G. A. Collins (one). All cover designs were engraved on wood, by the most eminent wood-engravers of the day.

Although the front design for each individual work is actually uniform, there are, nevertheless, variations in the cover as a whole, which are not always apparent at first glance and, for this reason, call for close scrutiny when proof of a complete part is desired. Each front cover has its numerical reference which might be considered sufficient for the purpose but, unfortunately, experience has shown that corroborative evidence is essential, in order to prove that the serial number has not been tampered with. By comparing the advertisements printed on the covers, with the authentic details

INTRODUCTION.

shown in the collations, it will be readily seen whether any change has been made in the "Part No." by erasure and substitution.

In the case of "Pickwick," however, there is no printed matter on the inside covers of Parts I, II, and III; consequently the clues are confined to the outer covers of these three parts. The reproductions in this book are taken from the John F. Dexter original parts, and are within one millimetre of the exact size, so that they afford, in themselves, a comparatively accurate standard of security against the spurious reproductions of these parts, which are known to exist.

The all-important question of "Text" has been approached from an entirely new angle, which can be relied upon, to either settle or dispose of many hitherto unprofitable sources of argument, speculation, and misconception. This subject is dealt with more appropriately, and at length, in the chapter on "Pickwick," pp. 6–16.

In order to carry out the object to the fullest extent, no advertising matter has been considered too insignificant for inclusion in the various collations. For the first time, advertisement insets have received recognition, when proved to be part of an original issue. However unimportant some bibliophiles may regard these, and other apparently extraneous material, there can be but one originality of "make-up," viz. :—the first copy of any particular monthly part emanating from the publishers, bound up to a pre-arranged programme, and not thrown together in haphazard manner at the whim of the binder.

The mass of advertising matter is of exceptional interest, if only for the light it throws on the times when Charles Dickens was making his name. During the publication of "Pickwick," there were no great dailies willing to sell their front pages; the prohibitive price of the better class newspapers, prevented them from becoming a practical medium for successful advertising ; the Press actually paid Chapman & Hall for space in the shilling numbers, in order to make the circulation of their papers known. Such famous weeklies as "Punch" and "The Field," made their initial bow to the public in the "green leaves" of Charles Dickens. Tradesmen, whose names are still household words to-day, Insurance Companies, and Banks, were regular patrons of the monthly numbers.

The majority of collectors will agree, that the Illustrations have so far failed to receive, from bibliographers, the serious notice to which they are justly entitled, and that nothing approaching adequate recognition has been given to the labour entailed in their production. Prior to about 1850, when the electrotype process for duplicating on a large scale from etched and engraved plates became known, the illustrations were produced entirely by hand ; a slow and laborious task, which accounts for the numerous difficulties met with in the earlier publications.

Ten of the books, now under review, were illustrated with etchings on steel plates, and the remaining three with engravings on wood blocks. The etchings, with a few exceptions, were issued in pairs of octavo size : one pair to each monthly part. For the earlier books, each pair was etched on one steel plate of quarto size, and it is not uncommon to find the individual octavo impressions in "undivided state," examples of which have frequently afforded valuable clues to what, otherwise, would be puzzling points.

Owing to the necessity for frequent use from now on, of the terms "Etchings," "Plates," "Steels" and "Woodcuts," the present opportunity is taken to state, that individual illustrations etched on steel plates, are referred to as either Plates or Etchings ; those engraved on wood blocks as Woodcuts ; while the steel plates themselves will be designated as Steels.

INTRODUCTION.

CENSUS OF PLATES.

Works.	Date.	Plates.	Artists.	Steels
Pickwick Papers	1836–7	7	Robert Seymour ..	11
,, ,, ...	,,	2	R. W. Buss	2
,, ,, ...	,,	34	Hablot K. Browne ..	60
Sketches by "Boz" ..	1837–9	40	George Cruikshank ..	40
Nicholas Nickleby ..	1838–9	40	Hablot K. Browne ..	129
Martin Chuzzlewit ..	1843–4	40	,, ,, ..	90
Oliver Twist	1846	24	George Cruikshank ..	24
Dombey and Son ..	1846–8	40	Hablot K. Browne ..	80
David Copperfield ..	1849–50	40	,, ,, ..	80
Bleak House	1852–3	40	,, ,, ..	50
Little Dorrit..	1855–7	40	,, ,, ..	49
Tale of Two Cities ..	1859	16	,, ,, ..	16
		363		631

CENSUS OF WOODCUTS.

Works.	Date.	Artists.	Wood-cuts.
Master Humphrey's Clock ..	1840–1	Hablot K. Browne ..	157
,, ,, ,, ..	,,	George Cattermole	39
,, ,, ,, ..	,,	S. Williams	1
,, ,, ,, ..	,,	Daniel Maclise ..	1
Our Mutual Friend	1864–5	Marcus Stone	40
Edwin Drood	1870	Luke Fildes	14
			252

Hablot K. Browne was responsible for 554 of the steels in eight out of the thirteen books, but his full name did not appear on the front wrappers until "Dombey" was reached. For the first two steels (Pickwick, Part 4), he adopted the pseudonym of "NEMO"; afterwards he signed himself "Phiz," and continued to do so to the end of the chapter. Although he achieved remarkable success in faithfully copying his own designs, in such books as "Nicholas Nickleby," he seldom failed to make a variation in his signature, sufficient to provide a clue to the identification of duplicate plates.

INTRODUCTION.

The duplication of steels, as shown above, has caused much confusion in the past, also constant misinterpretation of the terms "Plates" and "States." The facts are, that every plate, whether it be an impression from a duplicate steel or not, can be found in varying "states," and these states may be divided into two classes :

(a) *Major* variations, due to actual additions or alterations effected by the artist himself.

(b) *Minor* variations, due to either retouching, or extra cross-hatching, by the artist; or to mechanical work, such as re-biting, done by an assistant.

When "Phiz" came on the scene, he knew nothing about the mechanical side of etching, and it is well known that all the original "biting-in" with acid, of his own steels, was done by his friend and assistant, Robert Young, who was also responsible for any re-biting that subsequently became necessary. For this reason, it is extremely unlikely that "Phiz" ever did any work on the Seymour and Buss steels, and it may be taken for granted that, after Seymour's death and after Buss was superseded, any additional "work," which resulted in the production of "second states," was done, not by "Phiz," but by other artists employed by the Publishers for that purpose.

In the detailed collations, major variations have been described in the briefest possible manner. With a few exceptions, however, no attempt has been made to record early and late states, due solely to mechanical work, which accentuated original lines, and thus increased the strength or depth of the impression.

A case in point is furnished by the Dexter specimens of the two Buss illustrations ; there are no major variations to be noted in these two plates, but there is abundant evidence of additional "work," as time went on, in the deterioration of the available impressions.

The first example of "The Arbour Scene" is in "proof" state. It once belonged to Edward Chapman, and bears

[xvii]

the following inscription in his handwriting :—"This was the first impression taken from the plate by Buss himself." Every line, light and heavy, stands out clearly ; the two coats, the fat boy's left leg, and the bottom of the watering can, resemble perfectly ruled trellis work with clean cut white centres. The seat, the framework of the arbour, and the branches above, stand out boldly but not heavily. The background is light and airy.

The second example is in "first state," and is perceptibly darker than the first example, but shows no sign of new "work."

The third example is in "second state"; this is darker again than the first state, and shows clear evidence of re-biting, as well as strong cross-hatching on the coats and bottom of the water-ing can. The framework of the arbour, the branches above, and the background, are considerably heavier than is the case in the other two specimens. Further unclassified examples are progressively darker and heavier.

Minor variations of the same character are in evidence in "The Cricket Match" plate, and could be described in a similar manner.

There has been a suggestion made quite recently, that Seymour did not sign "The dying Clown" plate in Part II of Pickwick, but that the signature was added later by "Phiz" ; and for this reason, impressions bearing the signature "Seymour Del," are of later state than those without the signature. The only unsigned specimen, so far produced, is a cut copy extracted from a bound volume ; and a careful examination shows clearly, that it is later in "state" than signed examples to be seen in authentic copies of the first issue of this part. Up to the present time, not one example of the original 500 copies of the first issue, containing an *un-signed* plate, has been recorded, and no reference of any kind is made by John F. Dexter to the existence of such a plate. Therefore, until one of the 500 excessively rare copies of Part II, in untouched condition, containing a plate without

INTRODUCTION.

Seymour's signature, comes to light, the authors decline to endorse the suggestion.

After due consideration, all reference to values has been omitted from these pages, on the ground that such information belongs rightly in dealers' catalogues, where any particular item can be described and priced on its merits ; moreover, the prices of yesterday and to-day are mere history to-morrow.   In looking back, however, to the earlier days of collecting, one may be excused a feeling of envy towards those pioneers, who were able to assemble the monthly parts at less than the published price of one shilling each.   This is what John F. Dexter was able to do ; he was actually collecting these parts several years before the death of Charles Dickens. In his library was discovered a fully-priced catalogue of a sale of his books, which took place in 1875 at Sotheby's. It is hardly believable that three complete copies of "Sketches by Boz," in the original parts, were sold for £15 ; they cost him altogether exactly £8. A set of Pickwick fetched no more than forty-three shillings. Complete sets of Nickleby, Chuzzlewit, Dombey, Bleak House and Our Mutual Friend, ranged in price from twenty-six down to five shillings. Poor Edwin Drood could command no more than one florin, although it had cost the owner double that amount.

The authors are indebted to many collectors and friends for information and assistance ; particularly Mr. W. H. Collis, of Liverpool, and Dr. Hablot Browne, of Hoylake. They are especially under obligation to Mr. Walter Dexter, the editor of *The Dickensian*, for important data in connection with the chapter on "Sketches by Boz."   They desire also to thank Mr. Arthur E. Calkin for valuable advice in the matter of binding ; and Messrs. Raithby, Lawrence & Co., Ltd., of Leicester, for facilities afforded, and consideration shown, during the progress of printing.

On the 31st of March will be published, to be continued Monthly, price ONE SHILLING, the First Number of

THE POSTHUMOUS PAPERS

OF

THE PICKWICK CLUB;

CONTAINING A FAITHFUL RECORD OF THE

PERAMBULATIONS, PERILS, TRAVELS, ADVENTURES, AND SPORTING TRANSACTIONS OF THE CORRESPONDING MEMBERS.

EDITED BY 'BOZ.'

And each MONTHLY PART embellished with FOUR ILLUSTRATIONS by SEYMOUR.

The PICKWICK CLUB, so renowned in the annals of Huggin-lane, and so closely entwined with the thousand interesting associations connected with Lothbury and Cateaton-street, was founded in the year One Thousand Eight Hundred and Twenty-two, by Samuel Pickwick—the great traveller—whose fondness for the useful arts prompted his celebrated journey to Birmingham in the depth of winter; and whose taste for the beauties of nature even led him to penetrate to the very borders of Wales in the height of summer.

This remarkable man would appear to have infused a considerable portion of his restless and inquiring spirit into the breasts of other members of the Club, and to have awakened in their minds the same insatiable thirst for Travel which so eminently characterized his own. The whole surface of Middlesex, a part of Surrey, a portion of Essex, and several square miles of Kent, were in their turns examined, and reported on. In a rapid steamer, they smoothly navigated the placid Thames; and in an open boat they fearlessly crossed the turbid Medway. High-roads and by-roads, towns and villages, public conveyances and their passengers, first-rate inns and road-side public houses, races, fairs, regattas, elections, meetings, market days—all the scenes that can possibly occur to enliven a country place, and at which different traits of character may be observed and recognized, were alike visited and beheld, by the ardent Pickwick and his enthusiastic followers.

The Pickwick Travels, the Pickwick Diary, the Pickwick Correspondence—in short, the whole of the Pickwick Papers, were carefully preserved, and duly registered by the secretary, from time to time, in the voluminous Transactions of the Pickwick Club. These transactions have been purchased from the patriotic secretary, at an immense expense, and placed in the hands of 'Boz,' the author of 'Sketches Illustrative of Every Day Life, and Every Day People'—a gentleman whom the publishers consider highly qualified for the task of arranging these important documents, and placing them before the public in an attractive form. He is at present deeply immersed in his arduous labours, the first fruits of which will appear on the 31st March.

Seymour has devoted himself, heart and graver, to the task of illustrating the beauties of Pickwick. It was reserved to paint, in colours that will never fade, the Decline and Fall of the Roman Empire—to Hume to chronicle the strife and turmoil of the two proud houses that divided England against herself—to Napier to pen, in burning words, the History of the War in the Peninsula—the deeds and actions of the gifted Pickwick yet remain for 'Boz' and Seymour to hand down to posterity.

From the present appearance of these important documents, and the probable extent of the selections from them, it is presumed that the series will be completed in about twenty numbers.

CHEAP AND ENTERTAINING PERIODICAL.

On the 31st of March will be published, price ONE SHILLING, to be continued Monthly, containing 56 pages of letter-press Octavo, and Two Illustrations, No. I. of the

LIBRARY of FICTION, or FAMILY STORY-TELLER,

CONSISTING OF

TALES, ESSAYS, AND SKETCHES OF CHARACTER, ORIGINAL AND SELECTED.

CONTENTS: The Tuggs's at Ramsgate, by 'Boz' (original)—The Castle of Cleves, or the Witness Hand, translated for this work from the German of Castelli—Mr. Firedrake Fidget—A Tale (original)—The Last Words of Charles Edwards, Esq.—Ginevra.

One volume, small 8vo. elegantly bound, gilt leaves, price 6s.; or in silk, 7s.

A GARLAND OF LOVE,

WREATHED OF CHOICE FLOWERS,

GATHERED IN THE FIELD OF ENGLISH POETRY.

With a beautiful Frontispiece, from a Design by HARVEY, printed in Sepia by BAXTER.

"A charming collection of love verses, gathered from the English poets, who understood more about the matter than the minnesingers themselves. The book is its own commendation. It is a sort of lover's commonplace-book, in which the most elevated imagination may look, 'like the deer in the water,' and find itself reflected."—Atlas.

"A choice selection of amatory verses from the English poets, beginning with Wyatt and Surrey, and ending with Wordsworth and Moore, and quaintly entitled 'A Garland of Love,' will make a pretty present from a lover to his mistress: for the poems are free from the voluptuousness which too frequently characterizes these passionate effusions; the sentiment is pure and refined, and its tone exalted. The frontispiece—a pair of lovers, designed by Harvey—is a beautiful specimen of Baxter's printing in sepia, from wood blocks."—Spectator.

One volume, royal 16mo. neatly bound, price 5s. 6d.

CHESS FOR BEGINNERS

IN A SERIES OF PROGRESSIVE LESSONS,

Showing the most approved Methods of beginning and ending the Game, together with various Situations and Checkmates.

By WILLIAM LEWIS,

AUTHOR OF SEVERAL WORKS ON THE GAME.

With TWENTY-FOUR DIAGRAMS PRINTED in COLOURS.

"A neat and prettily got up work. Mr. Lewis has already produced several works of merit on Chess; but he has contributed nothing more valuable in reality than the present unpretending book of rudiments. His observations on the different openings, and on various points of nicety, are distinguished by great clearness."—Metropolitan Magazine.

"We recommend this work, because it is handsome, portable, and scientifically good."—Metropolitan Magazine.

One volume, foolscap, handsomely bound in embossed cloth, gilt edges, price 12s.; or in morocco, 16s.

THE ARTIST;

OR,

YOUNG LADIES' INSTRUCTOR IN ORNAMENTAL PAINTING, DRAWING, &c.

CONSISTING OF LESSONS IN

GRECIAN PAINTING, JAPAN PAINTING, ORIENTAL TINTING, MEZZOTINTING, TRANSFERRING, INLAYING,

AND

MANUFACTURING ARTICLES FOR FANCY FAIRS, &c.

By B. F. GANDEE, Teacher.

Embellished with a beautiful Frontispiece and Title-page, printed in Oil Colours by BAXTER, and Seventeen other Illustrative Engravings.

In one volume, square 16mo. neatly bound, price 3s. 6d.

THE JUVENILE PIANIST;

OR,

A MIRROR OF MUSIC FOR INFANT MINDS.

By ANN RODWELL,

TEACHER OF THE PIANOFORTE.

Illustrated by upwards of One Hundred Musical Diagrams, and embellished with Engravings printed in Colours.

"This instructive little work, which is illustrated with numerous engravings and diagrams, explanatory of its interesting art, is truly what it professes to be, a Mirror of Music for Infant Minds, constructed with such simplicity and clearness, that it would be impossible, even for a very young child, to read without deriving the wished-for instruction. It is admirably calculated to render the early practice of the piano easy and attractive."—Morning Post.

Price 5s. 6d. cloth boards,

A SUMMER'S TOUR

THROUGH BELGIUM, UP THE RHINE, AND TO THE LAKES OF SWITZERLAND;

ALSO

TO CHAMOUNI, AND OVER THE COL-DE-BALME TO MARTIGNY, &c

With a Table of Routes, Distances, Course of Exchange, Fares by Diligences, Boats, &c.

Square 16mo. neatly bound in cloth, price 2s. 6d.

CAROLINE;

OR,

THE PLEASURES OF A BIRTHDAY.

By M. M. RODWELL.

Illustrated by Six Engravings on Wood.

Square 16mo. neatly bound in cloth, price 2s. 6d.

THE SPOILED CHILD RECLAIMED.

By M. M. RODWELL.

Illustrated by Six Engravings on Wood.

"Two very excellent little school story books in dialogue, embellished with tasteful engravings. The latter is a tale devoted to the illustration of the advantages of good instruction; and the former volume is a little birthday conversazione, into which pretty stories are introduced. Miss Rodwell, who, we believe, is herself a teacher, has produced two works that may be consigned to the young with advantage."—Atlas.

Square 16mo. neatly bound, price 2s. 6d.

POETRY FOR CHILDREN,

SELECTED BY THE LATE WM. BURDON.

A NEW EDITION.

Embellished with Four Engravings printed in Colours.

One volume, 12mo. neatly bound in cloth, gilt edges, price 4s,

FLEURS DE POESIE MODERNE;

CONTAINING

THE BEAUTIES OF

A. DE LAMARTINE, VICTOR HUGO, DE BERANGER, C. DELAVIGNE.

"A selection made in the spirit of the day. Instead of a collection from other and old collections, the compiler has chosen the best of modern French writers, and presented us with the very best of their thoughts. The volume is about the size of a handsome pocket-book, and it is got up as beautifully as one of the Annuals."—Spectator.

LONDON: CHAPMAN & HALL, 186, STRAND.

London: JAMES HOLMES, Took's Court, Chancery Lane. Published every Saturday at the ATHENÆUM OFFICE, No. 2, Catherine-street, Strand, by J. FRANCIS, and sold by all Booksellers and Newsvenders.—Agents: for SCOTLAND, Messrs. Bell & Bradfute, Edinburgh; for IRELAND, W. F. Wakeman, Dublin; for the CONTINENT, M. Baudry, 9, Rue du Coq, near the Louvre, Paris.

The earliest advertisement announcing the forthcoming publication of "The Pickwick Papers," as it appeared in *The Athenaeum* for March 26, 1836. The 33-line address is written by Charles Dickens. Reduced to exactly three-fifths of the original, the type area of which measures $9\frac{7}{8}'' \times 7\frac{1}{8}''$ (251 × 181 mm.)

(From the John F. Dexter Library.)

THE

𝕻𝖔𝖘𝖙𝖍𝖚𝖒𝖔𝖚𝖘 𝕻𝖆𝖕𝖊𝖗𝖘

OF

THE PICKWICK CLUB.

BY CHARLES DICKENS.

WITH

FORTY-THREE ILLUSTRATIONS, BY R. SEYMOUR AND
PHIZ.

LONDON:
CHAPMAN AND HALL, 186, STRAND.

MDCCCXXXVII.

The Pickwick Papers

in

19/20 Monthly Parts
April, 1836, to November, 1837.

THE Posthumous Papers of the Pickwick Club—to give the work its extended title—was originally published in twenty numbers, bound in nineteen monthly parts, priced at one shilling per number; the last two (19 and 20) forming a double-number at two shillings. The first part appeared in April, 1836, and continued to completion with Part 19/20, in November, 1837, except for a lapse of one month—June, 1837—when publication of Part 15 was deferred by a bereavement in the Author's family.

The original plan of the issue allowed for three half-sheets of 8 pages, making a total of 24 pages of text to each monthly number, with four etchings on steel; but commencing with Part 3, this was modified by increasing the amount of letterpress to two sheets of 16 pages—or 32 pages in all—and reducing the number of plates from four to two.

For Part 1, Dickens had over-estimated by 18 lines of text, the amount of subject matter required for the allotted 24 pages, and in consequence, the printer was obliged to supply a single extra leaf, carrying page numbers 25 and 26.

This unusual procedure not only caused inconvenience to both printer and binder, but forced Dickens to supply additional matter in order to complete the two extra pages. He thus had no option but to commence his "Chapter III" on page 25, and leave it unfinished on page 26, to be continued

A 2

in Part 2 ; with the result that we have, in the original setting, two headings of Chapter III : one on page 25 of Part 1, and the other on the opening page of Part 2.

Whilst Part 1 contained the requisite four plates, only three appeared in Part 2, owing to the death of the artist—Robert Seymour—who had been unable to prepare the fourth etching prior to his demise.

With regard to the constitution of a perfect "Pickwick," i.e., one which may be designated as one hundred per cent. perfect, no attempt has previously been made to place the requirements on record in such detail as is warranted by the intricate nature of the components of each individual part. The Bruton copy, which was used by John C. Eckel as a basis of comparison with other "prime" copies, is undoubtedly an extremely fine one, and at the time of its sale at Sotheby's in 1921, John F. Dexter said,—"it is absolutely right from beginning to end with regard to text and plates, and is the purest copy that has appeared in these rooms up to the present time." Mr. Eckel's collation as presented is a simple statement of the facts, but notwithstanding its excellent qualities, it does not follow that this particular copy achieves complete perfection.

Since the appearance of the "Mary Hogarth" copy at public auction in 1899, about fifteen copies of the highest merit have been noted either through the sale rooms or in private collections, and it is a fact, in so far as detailed collations are available, that not one of these fifteen copies combines all the points which, taking them collectively, are in evidence and in accordance with the collation submitted in the following pages. The original method of production, with an interval of one month between the issue of each part, determines the principle now adopted, of dealing with each individual part as a separate unit, as opposed to consideration of the nineteen parts as a completed book. It would be stretching the imagination too far to suggest that an original subscriber in 1836–7, found himself in possession of the earliest issue of each number upon completion of the work. In the light of present-day knowledge, we should term him an exceedingly fortunate person, or the subject of a miracle. It should follow that, although no one known set (with the possible exception of the Dexter copy) may be said to be perfect to the last detail, there is no insuperable obstacle to achieving perfection, if the collector recognises that he is collecting not one, but nineteen books ; and that a complete set, conforming to the requirements of first issue throughout, can only be acquired by replacing inferior units with those of superior character, whenever the opportunity presents itself.

The essentials of earliest text, plates, and wrappers are well known and generally agreed upon—the advertisements which should be present in the first issue of any part are equally well known, but not so generally agreed as essential : at least in respect to the early numbers. The collations of many of the "big" copies have to confess the lack of some particular advertisement leaf or inset ; and it has been contended that its absence, or otherwise, does not necessarily disqualify a copy as being of the earliest issue. With that contention we most emphatically disagree, however disdainfully advertisement material may be regarded in some quarters ; and it is submitted that the publication of a particular number with all its material matter as planned by the publishers, and put together by the binder, is the one which carries the official hall-mark, and must decidedly take precedence over another falling short of this standard. The circulation of the earlier parts of "Pickwick" was too insignificant to permit of the assumption that possibly only later copies from the binder contained a particular inset. On the contrary, we take the stand that the supplies of insets were delivered to the binder in lesser quantities than the number of copies printed of the periodical itself, and on the principle of first come, first served, the earlier copies were more likely to carry the inset than those coming later. The absence of advertisement material may easily be accounted for by the passage of time, and the utter disregard and indifference of the average reader to the presence of what, to him, was extraneous matter, unworthy of preservation and treated accordingly. Briefly, it is simple enough to evolve an explanation for the absence of advertisement insets, but not so easy to explain away their presence.

TEXT.

It is now a fairly well-established fact, that 1000 copies of Part 1 were printed from the original set-up of type, of which only 400 were issued on the day of publication. The sale of these was slow in the beginning, and the Publishers not anticipating any greater sale of the next number, only printed 500 copies of Part 2. These 1000 copies of Part 1, and 500 of Part 2, which constitute the first issue of the first edition, were eventually sold out, and it then became necessary with an increased demand, to reprint both parts, which was done before the publication of Part 3. These facts account for the extreme rarity of the text to Part 2 in its original setting, also of the wrapper in which it was bound, and make it the keystone to all copies of "Pickwick" which aspire to perfection. The text to all the monthly parts, from 1 to 8, was actually reprinted many times at very early dates, and in so doing, notable replacement of textual matter was made in Part 2, as well as alterations of a lesser degree in the others; all tending to show in these eight numbers, far greater evidence of differences between the various issues of each, than is shown by the sequence of parts which followed.

With "Pickwick" the most difficult "points" to substantiate in regard to earliest issue, by comparison with those immediately following, are those of the text or letterpress. Until quite recent times, no recognition appears to have been accorded to what should rightly be considered, the essential feature of a printed book—the impressed subject matter as conceived by the Author of the work. From the viewpoint of collectors in a generation anterior to the present, the question of text in any work was not of the same paramount

6

importance. No book emanating from any of his predecessors or contemporaries, was ever of sufficiently large circulation to contain within its covers, the number of textual problems which have to be faced in this, the "First Octavo" of Charles Dickens. Early bibliographers of our particular Author, covered the subject by giving us a more or less simple chronological list of his writings—we were not enlightened to the fact that "Pickwick" was reprinted scores of times; that these printings were impressions from practically the same standing type or reproductions of that type; and that whilst the year 1836 saw the issue of the first copy, the original handiwork of the compositor is still to be seen in an edition published so late as 1888. As with bibliographers, so with bibliophiles. Text was accepted at face value; if the known correct wrappers of the periodical issues were present, and contained the requisite number of pages, all was well—it was a "Pickwick." It remained with John F. Dexter and a few others, to realize the importance of this feature of the longest run in publishing history; and although, during his lifetime, he seldom divulged the results of his research, his voluminous records leave to us ample evidence, that he was in possession of all the facts connected with the typography of "Pickwick."

In "Pickwick" we have many visible proofs that some particular monthly part is, or is not, the earliest to issue from the press, and, with the first eight parts especially, well-defined clues of correction, omission, or defects in type can with facility be conveyed. With the majority of later parts however, no very definite or outstanding differences in text are disclosed, and in consequence, it is not easy to convey in words an intelligible description of them.

Before touching upon the alternative method of authenticating pages of text, which expose no striking and immediate evidence of printing errors or type blemishes, a word or two may not be out of place in deprecation of the practice of compiling long lists of clues: such as dropped letters,

7

broken or smudged type, misprints, and additional or deleted text; which claim to distinguish between the first impress of type-face and reprints of later date. Such indications of careless, inferior, or accidental press-work do not always fulfil the object in view—some may, but the majority are misleading: for, as Mr. George W. Davis, in his admirable though all too modest booklet (of bibliographical discoveries), very rightly points out: typographical errors "continued for a considerable time, and although, of course, they occur in the earliest issue, do not distinguish them from later ones."

The standard tests to be found in the collations of the various monthly parts in the following pages, are purposely limited to those which have emerged successfully as a result of most exhaustive investigations, and, it is claimed, they will prove reliable in any test to which they may be put. On the other hand, a few notable examples from a formidable list compiled from various sources, which in practice have proved veritable pitfalls, should once and for all be ruled out, as having no significance whatever in indicating priority or otherwise of text.

Part 1. Page 1, line 1.—	First letter "T" is not sufficiently defective to class as "*broken*" in later issues.
,, ,, line 4 up.—	The final "*s*" *continues* unbroken in many later issues than the first.
,, Page 9, footnote.—	This was *never* suppressed in the original text and all reprints of it. It was stereotyped and appears as late as 1888.
,, Page 10, last line.—	"*r*" in "rum" does *not* always have a dot between the first two letters in all later issues.
,, Page 16, line 9 up.—	"*unheeded*" is *not* always followed by a dot in all later issues.
,, Page 17, last line.—	Final "*e*" is *not* necessarily perfect in first issue, but is often slightly smudged, whilst in some later issues it is much more perfect.

8

THE PICKWICK PAPERS.

Part 1. Page 18, line 1.—   *"loud knocking."* Although perfect in first issue, and later became damaged ; at a still later date the words were re-set and made good.

   „   Page 23, line 30.—   "W" in "What" is *not* always imperfect in later issues.

   „   Page 24, line 1.—   "*o*" in "not" is *not* broken in all later issues.

   „   Page 26, heading.—   The misprint "&c" is seen in quite late printings, as well as in first issues.

   „   „   7 line up.—   Two faint quad marks between the words *"you begin"* do *not* denote the earliest impression. The first issue should have *one* very pronounced quad mark only, just below the "*u*" of "you."

Part 2. Page 27.—   The duplication of "Chapter III" is no indication of early issue, as it appears in all issues of the original text.

Part 3. Page 53, line 1.—   The dot of letter "*i*" in "rousing" is *not* always missing in later issues.

   „   Page 60, line 1.—   The dot of letter "*i*" in "promises" is *not* always missing in later issues.

Part 4. Page 107, line 13.—   "*i*" in "its" is *not* always missing in later issues.

Part 5. Page 119, line 9 up.—The inverted comma before first letter "P" is *not* always missing in later issues.

   „   Page 146, line 3.—   "*a*" in "all" is perfect in some later issues as well as the first.

Part 8. Page 211, at foot.—   Sig. "*S*" in first issue is clean and perfect—it also appears so in some later issues.

Part 13. Page 375, heading.—*"Picwkick."* This error appears in all issues of the original text, down to 1888.

It must be conceded that the earliest printed text is one which discloses a clean, bold, and perfect impression—the product of newly-cast and unworn type ; in contradistinction to an uneven, sickly and imperfect impression—the result of long usage and consequent type deterioration. But how—it may reasonably be demanded—is anyone unversed in the subject, able to discriminate between these varying qualities ? —a very pertinent though fair question. If Nature had given to every pair of eyes uniform perception for the obvious ; if every mind was endowed with the same characteristics for the reception of sight impression ; if the material matter for comparison was equally available to all would-be seekers of the truth : then no such question would of necessity arise. The bloom of "virgin" type, which hall-marks an initial type impression, cannot be confounded with the "faded" results of long and continuous, though possibly faithful service. Being but human, we realize the impossibility of arriving at a consensus of opinion by actual sight of the printed page, and it becomes obligatory to find other and more practical means of placing the merest tyro, and the expert bibliophile, upon an equal footing in ability to authenticate any page of text, as being of the first or later issue.

We have already endeavoured to illustrate that examples of errors or damaged type, are not always to be relied upon in arriving at a conclusion ; and even those which may be considered dependable, are not in themselves sufficient in the aggregate, to cover adequately each of the 609 pages of text, which go to make up the twenty monthly parts of "Pickwick." When outstanding evidence of type inferiority and typographical errors is not available, the most conclusive proof of first printing is to be obtained by close page measurement. In this manner it is possible, owing to con-traction in type-area, to verify each page of the book for pre-cedence in order of issue. Let it first be appreciated that the gradations of type-area throughout the run of monthly parts, have a very considerable and varied range of measurements ; and although the differences between the maximum (i.e. of the earliest issue), and the minimum (representing the latest known issue), may be a matter of only a few millimetres, yet each fractional reduction in depth or width of page points to a progressively later issue.

It would be a reflection on the intelligence of any who may read these notes, to propound the principle of type-area on the evidence and analysis of a few copies, chosen at random, as being representative of a circulation running into tens of thousands of each of the twenty parts. The necessary scope for analysis of the early parts (e.g. 1, 2, 3, 4) is not even absent, for they were reprinted on twenty different occasions during the first eighteen months of publication. This principle of type-area and page-measurement, so far as it applies to "Pickwick," is based upon an exhaustive examination of at least 4,000 copies of original "Pickwick" parts—equal to about 200 complete sets—and in addition many scores of volumes have passed under review, each page of which has been tested for quality of impression cum type-area. The results disclosed are very definite, and consistently show that the poorer the type-impression, the more contracted becomes the type-area of the page.

The collation proper sets out the easily recognisable and established typographical errors, and other obvious variations, between the first and next immediate issues ; but in addition, is appended, a tabulation of maximum page-depth measurements for every page of the book, which are claimed to represent the first issue of text, and any copy which can be found to "exceed" these quoted figures, may surely take a high place in the order of printing.

The original text for Parts 1 to 8, and many succeeding re-issues of these early numbers, was in the first place printed from the actual movable type, made up into formes containing eight pages of type-matter. Although the first issues of all succeeding numbers (9–19/20) were *also* printed from movable type, it was not until a time coincident with the first printing of Part 9, that the practice of stereotyping was brought into use, to cope with the ever-increasing circulation : and from that time onwards all reprints of back numbers were effected

11

by this process. The stereotype plates continued in use for very long periods, and even so late as the year 1888, they were responsible for an edition printed by Richard Clay & Sons, of Bungay, and published by Chapman & Hall. These plates represent the same actual type-setting of the original publication of the monthly parts in 1836–7, although before the transference to stereos, hundreds of worn or damaged letters and page-numbers had been replaced with new type : in many instances of a slightly different fount.

We have therefore two processes of printing by which to account for contraction in type-area : movable type, and stereotype plates.

Although, whilst in use, the movable type was never fully "distributed," yet it was frequently released to effect small textual alterations, and to make good, broken or dropped letters, as well as the replacement of many page-numbers. Knowing the "furniture" of the printing shop in those earlier days was not so standardised as that now in common use, it is quite conceivable when again making-up the forme, some extra "furniture" was inserted which would bring more leverage to bear on the type-page, and result in a closer combination of the mass of individual loose type.

The process of stereotyping—presumably as nowadays—involved an impression of the type-face upon a sheet of papier maché, and the running of hot metal over the transferred type impression. The metal sheet, or "stereo" thus formed, would, in cooling off, assume a natural shrinkage ; not readily perceptible, but sufficient on a close measurement to disclose a difference in page-depth, to the extent sometimes, of six or seven millimetres.

The method adopted (unless otherwise stated) in arriving at text-measurements is as follows :

(1) Depth of page is taken from the topside of running headline, to the underside of last line, or of the printer's "signature" where

12

appearing ; disregarding the tail-pieces of projecting letters : g, j, p, or y.

(2) Width of headline, "Posthumous Papers of," is taken from top-left of "P" to top-right of last letter "F."

(3) Width of headline, "The Pickwick Club." is taken from left foot of "T" to the "period" at end of line.

(4) It is not deemed necessary to quote page-width.

Part 1. *Pages* 25 *and* 26. It cannot be too strongly emphasised, that to pass the test of earliest issue, copies must contain the single leaf which was printed without signature "E" at foot of page 25. The best proof of this contention is again that of superior quality of printing, in comparison with later issues bearing the signature, and which is confirmed by page-measurements. The first few copies printed were undoubtedly run off *without* the signature, but in the first reprint, a return to normal practice was adopted by the inclusion of this very necessary signification mark. When making good this omission in the first reprint (or second issue), a further error was created by accidentally failing to set-up the pagination of the opposing page 26. By the known scarcity of the leaf in the latter state, it may be assumed the correction was quickly made. The second reprint (or third issue) has both signature and page-number, but still retains the misprinted headline on page 26—common to all three issues—"Posthumous Papers, &c." Altogether, this single sheet appears to have had a most unfortunate history, and possibly was a source of annoyance and irritation to everyone who had to do with the printing of an odd leaf such as this. The table below (quoted in millimetres) will, at a glance, prove the order in issue of the three printings ; leaving only to be noted that, of the third issue (C), copies will be found which do not pull the maximum measures given ; and these of course, come still later in order of printing. For better comparison with the first issue, the page-depth of page 25 in the second and third issues is taken to the foot of text only, and does not include the signature "E."

CHARLES DICKENS.

(A) First Issue.   *Without* sig. "E" on page 25.
(B) Second Issue.   *With* sig. "E" and *without* pagination on page 26.
(C) Third Issue.   *With* sig. "E" and *with* pagination on page 26.

	Page 25. Depth.	Page 25. Width.	Page 25. Headline.	Page 26. Depth.	Page 26. Width.	Page 26. Headline.
A	174½	97	31	150½	97	37¼
B	172	95½	30	148½	95½	37
C	171½	95½	30	148	95½	36½

Part 12, *pages* 341 *and* 342. A curious typographical conundrum of the first importance is presented by these two pages, in which three errors appear, and of which there are three versions or variant issues. They may be summarised thus :—

Variant A. Correct spelling of two words *"inde-licate"* and *"inscription"* in page 341, lines 1 and 5 ; and the misnomer "S. Veller" for "Tony Veller" in page 342, line 5.

Variant B. With the two errors introduced, *"inbe-licate"* and *"inscriptino"* in page 341 ; and "S. Veller" uncorrected in page 342.

Variant C. With one error corrected, leaving still uncorrected the word *"inscriptino"* in page 341 ; and "S. Veller" replaced with "Tony Veller" in page 342.

These misprints, which appear in a large proportion of the "part" issues and volume editions, are common knowledge to most students and collectors of "Pickwick," and the generally accepted opinion gives preference to the correct spelling in page 341, as an indication of the original setting. It is not, however, so generally appreciated, that another school of thought, including as it does, many well-informed and expert bibliophiles, is genuinely serious in the advocacy of the mis-spelt words (Variant B) as denoting the original make-up of these pages. Only seven years ago, the present writer, upon this subject, had many a long tussle with a highly esteemed Dickensian, who knew and understood his "Pickwick" as few others did ; but who was adamant in his contention that the placing in order of issue should read : B.C.A.

This implies that the errors were progressively corrected, as opposed to the prevailing opinion that they were progressively made. The principle of page-measurements would alone be all-sufficient to solve the riddle, but there are so many other and more apparent features available, that it might be as well to bring them forward and finally dispose of whatever "optical delusions" yet prevail.

Variant A. Printed from movable type. First issue of text shows on page 341, a page-depth of 175 mm., with a reducing figure for later issues. This variant bears every indication of original setting by its clean and perfect impression, and an almost entire lack of defective letters or any evidence of type wear. It is never seen without the stab-holes of a "parts" issue, even when bound up in volume form.

Variant B. Also printed from movable type. Earliest printing of this text on page 341 has a maximum page-depth of 173 mm., whilst a later issue has been noted measuring no more than 168 mm. Whatever the circumstances were which necessitated a replacement of certain words, and the creation of the two errors on page 341, the fact remains, that the whole north-east corner of the page was entirely reset with eighty letters and the page-number "341." The affected letters are at the end of the first five lines, and in a close scrutiny they are seen to be most carelessly composed, with many out of alignment—in fact the type impression of this replaced matter stands out unmistakably from the rest of the adjoining text. The figures "341" proclaim themselves as a distinctly different type to the opposing page 342, also the pagination of the conjugating pages, 351 and 352 : an arrangement which logically would not be permitted in the original setting. This variant is to be seen in very late reprints of the "parts" issue, and contains a great many defects in type when compared with Variant A.

Variant C. Printed from stereotyped plates, and was never used for the publication in original monthly parts, but only in volume form on completion of the periodical issue. In page 341, the letter *"d"* replaces *"b"* in *"inbe-,"* thus correcting the word *"inbe-licate,"* and the page-number "341" is again reset with a new and slightly different fount of type, showing the figure "3" as distinctly smaller than "41." The word *"inscriptino"* still remains uncorrected, and actually was never altered in any reprints of the original setting, even down to the previously mentioned 1888 edition. Although other changes are effected in page 342, "Tony Veller" replaces "S. Veller." When making this correction, spacing had to be adjusted, which altered the balance of more than one line of text. The whole of the first

15

seven lines have been reset, together with headline and page-number, and this was done with new type of a different fount, and sufficiently distinctive as to require no microscopical assistance. We may assume there was none of the original fount of type on hand or available when the correction came about, and as the resetting of a single line would have been too apparent, a disguise was attempted by resetting the entire upper portion of the page with a uniformly new type.

Analysing the facts so noticeable in the printed page, we can, by a reasonably sound deduction, place the three variants in order of issue as A.B.C., and not B.C.A.

PLATES.

The dramatic story of the "Pickwick" illustrations has been told so many times, and the names of the three principal actors are so well known, that it seems hardly necessary to repeat the names of Robert Seymour, Robert William Buss and Hablot Knight Browne, or, as he signed himself, "Phiz."

These three artists etched, in all, 92 plates for the completed work ; of which, 43 are the "Originals" as they appeared in the first issue of the monthly parts, 4 are "Replacements," 2 are "Substitutes," and 24 are "Duplicates" of the originals : total 73. The remaining 19 are not dealt with in this bibliography, for they appeared only in the one volume (1837), and later editions, but never in the parts. As a matter of record, the 19 plates in question are those with inscriptions for Parts 1 and 2, and Parts 4 to 9 inclusive, viz.:—Plates 1 to 7 and 10 to 21 inclusive.

THE ORIGINALS.

Part 1.	Seymour	Subjects	-	-	-	-	4
„ 2.	„	„	-	-	-	-	3
„ 3.	Buss	„	-	-	-	-	2
Parts 4 to 18.	Phiz	„	-	-	-	-	30
Part 19/20	„	„	-	-	-	-	2
„ „	„	Frontispiece and Vignette					2
							— 43

THE PICKWICK PAPERS.

THE REPLACEMENTS.

Part 1.	Seymour	Subjects - - - -	4	
				— 4

THE SUBSTITUTES.

Part 3.	Phiz	Subjects - - - -	2	
				— 2

THE DUPLICATES.

Parts 10 to 18.	Phiz	Subjects - - - -	18	
Part 19/20	,,	,, - - - -	2	
,, ,,	,,	,, - (triplicates)	2	
,, ,,	,,	Frontispiece and Vignette	2	
				— 24
				73

When John F. Dexter wrote his "Hints to Dickens Collectors" in 1884, he undoubtedly held the view that the second set of plates to Part 1 was etched by "Phiz," and his opinion on this point had apparently undergone no change in 1899, for he was then closely associated with F. G. Kitton in the production of the latter's well-known book—"Dickens and his Illustrators"—in which the same view is expressed.

In this connection it is pertinent to point out that, in his "Life of Hablot K. Browne" (1884), David Croal Thomson says : "The seven plates by Seymour for Pickwick were, like all the others, executed in duplicate after the success of the book was certain, and they were probably etched by Hablot K. Browne at the time he did the second series of his own, but on this point there is no evidence, although it is usually taken for granted that such was the case." This statement coming from Croal Thomson, who had assumed the responsibility of writing at length on "Phiz" and his works, is both curious and misleading, for the three plates by Seymour to Part 2 were never duplicated until November 1837, when "Phiz" reproduced the 19 plates previously referred to as bearing inscriptions.

CHARLES DICKENS.

It therefore seems clear that, up to 1899, these three authorities—Thomson, Kitton, and Dexter—were largely responsible for attributing the authorship of the second plates of Part 1 to "Phiz."

Some time after 1899, however, Dexter's opinion on this point underwent a radical change, for, in his extensive as well as emphatic notes on this subject, he strongly contends that Seymour etched a second set of plates to Part 1, and his specimens of these four etchings, which he terms the "second" Seymour plates, are those which have heretofore been recognised as the first "Phiz" plates.

Taking as an example the notes which accompany his own copy of "Pickwick," the following statement clearly indicates the decided views he held up to the time of his death in June, 1927 :—

> "This copy of 'Pickwick' contains in a separate wrapper, the second set of etchings by R. Seymour for Part 1. Seymour etched two sets of plates, and says so in his diary. The copies by 'Phiz' of these four plates were never issued in the parts, and all of them carried the inscriptions. They were neither etched nor published until the book was completed."

A further comment appears in the margin of one of his many bibliographies :—

> "There are three or four different states of the first set of Seymour plates. Seymour etched a second set of plates to Part 1, for, after much cobbling and re-biting of the first plates, the whole of the cross-hatching on the men's coats absolutely collapsed, which gave an effect of aquatinting in the hiatus thus made."

Again, in his copy of J. C. Hotten's "Life of Dickens" (1870), some exceptionally interesting notes exist. The author says on page 49 : "It should here be stated that the original designs were in some degree modified, as it is certain from an entry in the artist's books, that the first four plates were re-etched." Dexter's comment on this is as follows :—

> "No ! The original designs were in no wise modified. The reason for the plates to Part 1 being re-etched, was that, the original plates

18

had been etched on steels which were hard on the surface, but very soft underneath. The consequence was, that, the shading on the men's coats absolutely collapsed and disappeared entirely (even to the back of the Secretary's chair in the Club scene), leaving only a blank space. I have seen evidence of Seymour's attempt to repair these etchings, but they constantly gave way, and he was forced to etch a second set of the four plates. I very much doubt whether more than 50 impressions in first state were obtained from the first set of steels,—which indeed are 'rare birds.' I have only come across two sets in the whole of my life.

"More than sufficient evidence that Seymour etched two sets of plates was afforded to me in a sale at Sotheby's, which took place on May 2, 1919 ; when a tin deed box came up on offer. It contained, among other things, a 'Life of Robert Seymour' by R. D. Morewood, a manuscript on about 340 quarto sheets (unpublished) ; a number of letters from Robert Seymour to his wife ; from Mrs. Seymour to her Son ; and from Robert Seymour Junr. to R. D. Morewood ; also an album containing a miscellaneous collection of etchings and engravings. Among the etchings I noticed three of the first four plates—one of which (Dr. Slammer) was worn to a shadow ; also three of the second set of plates. It is not a little curious that, some few years before I had, with the help of my old friend F. W. Pailthorpe (who was a past-master in everything connected with the technical details of etching), discovered that there were undoubtedly two sets of the four plates for Part 1 by R. Seymour, and was more than glad when I found the varying plates in the above mentioned album."

Revolutionary though it may appear to be, this overwhelming evidence, coming as it does from such an authoritative source, cannot be disregarded, and there is no option but to refer to the duplicate plates for Part 1, as being the "Second Seymour Plates" instead of the "First 'Phiz' Plates."

It is abundantly evident that Seymour, profiting by his disastrous experience with the steel used for his earliest plates, was able to secure satisfactory material for the Part 2 plates and the Part 1 duplicates—both of which were etched at about the same time. These two sets of plates stood the test of constant usage so well, that there are fewer signs of re-touching and re-biting than in almost any other plate throughout the series.

The original plan for the illustrations to "Pickwick," provided for four plates in each monthly part by Robert

Seymour, who executed the first four plates for Part 1, but had only completed three for Part 2 up to the time of his death on April 20th, 1836.

When the Author and Publishers had solved this new problem by appointing R. W. Buss as successor to Seymour, they also decided to reduce the number of illustrations to two, which plan remained in effect until completion of the book.

Buss supplied two plates for Part 3 :—
The Cricket Match, and
The Arbour Scene,

neither of which gave satisfaction to Dickens, and at a later date they were withdrawn from publication. These two plates are generally spoken of as the "suppressed plates," which is an incorrect term, for they were in active circulation not only in the original issue of Part 3, but in all reprints up to November, 1836, and, notwithstanding persistent efforts to create the impression that they are rare or scarce, it can be safely said that a comparatively large number are in existence to this day. They were never copied for official circulation, although a very fine reproduction on India paper by F. W. Pailthorpe of "The Cricket Match" was made about the year 1880. There are few points of difference to distinguish early and late "states" in the original plates, except those due to strength or depth of impression.

The association of Buss with "Pickwick" terminated on the publication of Part 3, and Hablot K. Browne, who was then engaged as his successor, remained to complete the work.

From the foregoing, a comparatively clear chronological sequence of events in the production of plates up to Part 9, can thus be constructed :—

1. Mch.,1836   Seymour etched 4 plates to Part 1.
2.   ,,   ,,   ,,   many times re-touched these plates.

3. Apl., 1836 Seymour etched a *second* set of plates to Part 1.
4.   ,,   ,,   ,,   etched 3 plates to Part 2.
5. May, ,, Buss   ,, 2 ,, ,, ,, 3.
6. June, ,, "Phiz"   ,, 2 ,, ,, ,, 4.
7. July, ,,   ,,   ,, 2 ,, ,, ,, 5.
8. Aug., ,,   ,,   ,, 2 ,, ,, ,, 6.
9. Sept., ,,   ,,   ,, 2 ,, ,, ,, 7.
10. Oct., ,,   ,,   ,, 2 ,, ,, ,, 8.
11.   ,,   ,,   ,,   ,, 2 ,, ,, ,, 3 (substitutes).
12. Nov., ,,   ,,   ,, 2 ,, ,, ,, 9.

Onwards, from this time (Nov., 1836) the course was comparatively clear, and no further mishaps of importance have to be recorded. In anticipation of a considerably greater demand for the monthly parts, "Phiz" etched duplicates for all remaining parts, 10–19/20, and a third set of plates for the two subjects of Part 19/20. As the latter point has never previously been brought to notice, the distinguishing features between the three plates of the two subjects are noted below. The third steel of Plate No. 40 is not all etched by "Phiz," but probably by R. Young, his partner. These triplicated etchings of Nos. 40 and 41 are exceptionally rare and previously unrecorded.

Plate 40. "The Fat Boy and Mary."

First Plate.   The knife in Fat Boy's hand points downwards.

Second ,,   The knife points upwards. The back of chair behind Mary is fully shaded, and artist's signature varies from the third plate.

Third ,,   The knife points upwards. The top rail of chair is unshaded.

21

Plate 41. "Coachmen drinking the Toast."

First Plate. A small bottle stands on left corner of table.

Second „ No bottle on table. The coachman on extreme right has only three buttons on his coat.

Third „ No bottle on table. The coachman's coat has four buttons.

Many other features in respect to the illustrations of "Pickwick" are dealt with in their respective places in the collations of each monthly part. In point of rarity, however, none exceed the two plates as originally etched for Part 6. To quote again the words of J. F. Dexter, "they are the greatest rarity known to me in this book."

WRAPPERS.

The design for the Front Wrapper was executed by Robert Seymour, the artist originally engaged to illustrate the scenes and incidents of the work during its progress as a periodical. The drawing represents two scenes emblematical of fishing and shooting, the former showing Pickwick asleep in his punt, and the latter depicting Winkle with gun to shoulder, sighted apparently at a range of only a few yards from some unfortunate bird. At the sides are fishing-tackle, a gun, and other sporting emblems; these extending almost the full height of the drawing.

This design was engraved on wood by J. Jackson. The person actually responsible for the engraving, however, was Mason Jackson, who was an apprentice with his brother, where he was learning "the ancient art of engraving on wood." This "celebrated design"—the engraver's own expression— is worthy of more than passing reference, and we quote from an article contributed by Mason Jackson to "The Sketch" of April 12, 1899, under the title of : "How I engraved the cover for 'Pickwick.' "

THE PICKWICK PAPERS.

"John Jackson had been for some time employed by Chapman and Hall to do their wood-engraving, and when 'Pickwick' was in preparation, Seymour's drawing for the cover of the monthly parts was sent to Jackson to be engraved, and I was entrusted with the work. I well remember the drawing . . . The drawing was not at all elaborate, being done with a pencil in clear outline. I had engraved much more difficult things, and I was not particularly interested in the subject, so that I worked on this celebrated design with no more care or attention than was necessary to produce a faithful facsimile of Seymour's lines. This was the cut that was printed on the celebrated green covers of 'Pickwick' as it appeared in the first form of monthly numbers. If I could have foreseen how world-famous it would become, no doubt I should have taken a keener interest in the matter. I had seen sporting etchings by Seymour in Chapman and Hall's window in the Strand, and I suppose, if I thought about it at all, I must have looked upon this cover or title-page of the 'Pickwick Club' as being intended for something of the same kind."

Within the Front Cover design of the first issues of Parts 1 and 2, appeared the name of Seymour as illustrator, reading : "*With Four Illustrations | by Seymour*," which (upon his tragic death, just prior to the publication of Part 2) was subsequently deleted and replaced in Part 3 by the lines : "*With Illustrations | by R. W. Buss.*" The latter artist, having etched only two plates for Part 3, was superseded by "Phiz," and with this second change, the artist's name was omitted altogether from the wrapper ; the Author and Publishers doubtless having decided to court no further possible complications in production.

The outer-side of Back Wrappers to Parts 1, 2 and 3, were occupied with announcements of Chapman and Hall's new periodical—"The Library of Fiction"—then being issued concurrently with "Pickwick" ; whilst the inner-sides were left blank. In the remaining series of covers (Part 4 to the end) all available space was utilized for advertisements, chiefly of a literary character, varying in matter and context with each monthly issue.

Apart from the essential changes of "Part No." there were five differences in detail to the 19 Front Wrappers during the course of publication : this referring only to the actual first issue of each. The following denote the particular part with which the changes were effected :—

(1) Part 1. Two lines, reading : "With Four Illustrations | by Seymour."

(2) Part 3. With the substituted lines : "With Illustrations | by R. W. Buss."

(3) Part 4. Reference to the artist's name replaced with a line : "With Illustrations," and so continued in all succeeding numbers.

(4) Part 16. An additional imprint of Bradbury and Evans, with two brackets, was added at foot.

(5) Part 19/20. "Price 1s." altered to "Price 2s." and the bracket preceding the price, was omitted. The brackets around the imprint of Bradbury and Evans were likewise dropped.

Reprints of the monthly parts were clothed in wrappers distinctly at variance with those of the earliest issues, considerable differences in detail and advertisement matter arising, and apart from the first issues of Parts 1 to 8, no less than 13 variants for re-issues of Parts 1 to 15 were printed and circulated during the first seventeen months. In other words, of Part 1 alone, 14 entirely distinct formats of wrappers can be authenticated. With the publication of each monthly part, there was consistently a reprint of all the back numbers, and often these reprinted wrappers closely followed the arrangement of the then current number. Thus, for example, the original "Buss" wrapper of Part 3 was actually used for re-issues of Parts 1 and 2 ; the "Part No." having been adjusted accordingly. Wrappers of this issue are of such rarity that their existence might conceivably be received by a majority of collectors *cum grano salis ;* but the present writer can put on record having at one time possessed a copy of the first number in this state, whilst John F. Dexter had both Parts 1 and 2 pass through his hands ; and makes the statement that in 50 years of collecting "Pickwick" parts, he had only seen

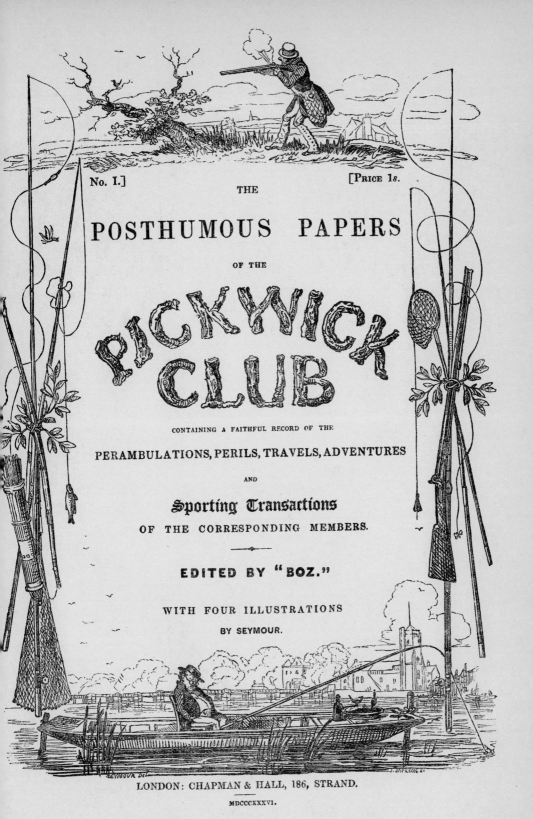

No. I.]   [Price 1s.

THE

POSTHUMOUS PAPERS

OF THE

PICKWICK CLUB

CONTAINING A FAITHFUL RECORD OF THE

PERAMBULATIONS, PERILS, TRAVELS, ADVENTURES

AND

Sporting Transactions

OF THE CORRESPONDING MEMBERS.

EDITED BY "BOZ."

WITH FOUR ILLUSTRATIONS

BY SEYMOUR.

LONDON: CHAPMAN & HALL, 186, STRAND.

MDCCCXXXVI.

The rare first issue of the Front Wrapper to Part I of "The Pickwick Papers," of which not more than 1,000 copies were printed. Inner side of wrapper is blank. In the John F. Dexter Library.

three copies of Part 1 with the "Buss" wrapper. A complete set in parts was sold in Sotheby's rooms, May, 1919, and being returned by the purchaser was again offered in November of the same year—this time fetching a lower price. This set contained Part 1, "*With Illustrations by R. W. Buss*," and on the back wrapper advertised "*No. III of the Library of Fiction.*" Again, in May, 1920, an incomplete set of 13 parts was offered in the same rooms, and a similar Part 1 appeared in this lot, although the text was of the third issue.

It would be difficult to conceive a more intriguing occupation, than an endeavour to establish a collection of all the known variant wrappers to " Pickwick " ; and an unenviable task awaits the aspirant, without the surety that the foundation can be laid with the first three parts, each bearing the name of R. W. Buss as illustrator. Any collector who has the inclination, enthusiasm and determination to persist in the chase, may find of assistance the appended schedule, setting out every state of wrappers, both original and reprinted.

Wherever "original issue" is referred to, particulars will be found in the detailed collation appropriate to that individual part. The variant wrappers are numbered in the order of publication, with the month and year when issued, or approximately so. I/S. signifies "Inside Wrapper" ; O/S. "Outside Wrapper."

(1) April, 1836.
        Part 1, original issue.

(2) May, 1836.
        Part 2, original issue.

(3) June, 1836.
        Part 3, original issue.

(4) June, 1836.
        Front, O/S. "With Illustrations by R. W. Buss."
                Dated 1836.
         „   I/S. Blank.

Back, I/S. Blank.
„ O/S. Same as Part 3, original issue.
Reprinted for Parts 1 and 2.

(5) June, 1836.
Front, O/S. "With Illustrations by Seymour." Dated 1836.
„ I/S. Same as Part 4, original issue.
Back, I/S. do. do. do.
„ O/S. do. do. do.
Reprinted for Parts 1, 2 and 3.

(6) July, 1836.
Part 4, original issue.

(7) Aug., 1836.
Part 5, original issue.

(8) Aug., 1836.
Front, O/S. "With Illustrations." Dated 1836.
„ I/S. Blank.
Back, I/S. Blank.
„ O/S. Same as Part 5, original issue, except, the word "novelties" is altered to "nouvellettes."
Reprinted for Parts 1, 2, 3, and 4.

(9) Sept., 1836.
Part 6, original issue.

(10) Sept., 1836.
Front, O/S. "With Illustrations." Dated 1836.
„ I/S. Blank.
Back, I/S. Blank.
„ O/S. Same as Part 6, original issue.
Reprinted for Parts 1, 2, 3, 4, and 5.

(11) Oct., 1836.
Part 7, original issue.

(12) Oct., 1836.

       Front, O/S. "With Illustrations." Dated 1836.
            ,,   I/S. Blank.
       Back, I/S. Blank.
            ,,   O/S. Same as Part 7, original issue.
       Reprinted for Parts 1, 2, 3, 4, 5 and 6.

(13) Oct., 1836.

       Front, O/S. "With Illustrations." Dated 1836.
            ,,   I/S. Same as Part 7, original issue.
       Back,   I/S. Same as Part 7, original issue, begin-
                 ning "Sketches"; but ending at foot
                 with "John Horner," etc., as in Part 8,
                 original issue.
            ,,   O/S. Same as Part 7, original issue.
       Reprinted for Parts 1, 2, 3, 4, 5 and 6.

(14) Nov., 1836.

       Front, O/S. "With Illustrations." Dated 1836.
            ,,   I/S. Same as No. 13 above.
       Back, I/S. Same as No. 13 above.
            ,,   O/S. Same as Part 8, original issue.
       Reprinted for Parts 1, 2, 3, 4, 5 and 6.

(15) Nov., 1836.

       Part 8, original issue.

(16) Nov., 1836.

       Front, O/S. "With Illustrations." Dated 1836.
            ,,   I/S. Same as Part 8, second issue.
       Back, I/S.   do.   do.   do.
            ,,   O/S.   do.   do.   original issue.
       Reprinted for Parts 1, 2, 3, 4, 5, 6 and 7. Identical with
       Part 8 second issue throughout, except for change in "Part
       No."   See collation for details of second issue.

(17) Nov., 1836.

       Front, O/S. "With Illustrations." Dated 1836.
            ,,   I/S. Blank.

Back, I/S. Blank.
 ,, O/S. Same as Part 8, original issue.
Reprinted for Parts 1, 2, 3, 4, 5, 6 and 7.

(18) Dec., 1836.
  Front, O/S. "With Illustrations." Dated 1836.
   ,, I/S. Blank.
  Back, I/S. Blank.
   ,, O/S. "Cheap & Entertaining Periodical. |
     This day is published, | price 8s.
     | ... | ... | The First Volume of |
     The Library of Fiction."
Reprinted for Parts 1 to 11 inclusive.

(19) Jan., 1837.
  Front, O/S. "With Illustrations." Dated 1836.
   ,, I/S. Blank.
  Back, I/S. Blank.
   ,, O/S. "New and Splendid Volume | This
     day is published, | . . . | The
     Pictorial Album, | ... | ... | For the
     year 1837."
Reprinted for Parts 1 to 13 inclusive.

(20) May, 1837 (about)
  Front, O/S. "With Illustrations." Dated 1836.
   ,, I/S. "The Pictorial Album"; "The Library
     of Fiction"; "Edward, the Crusader's
     Son."
  Back, I/S. "Travelling and Hunting Maps." Be-
     low: "A Garland of Love"; "The
     Poetic Wreath"; and "The Artist."
   ,, O/S. "Popular Juvenile Books"; with seven
     works in half column measure; fol-
     lowed by, "Fleurs de Poesie Moderne"
     and "Nursery Government" in full
     measure.

Reprinted for Parts 1 to 13 inclusive.
The set-up of advertisements on both sides of Back Wrapper is identical with the first appearance in Part 13 "Pickwick Advertiser," pp. 8 and 9.

(21) Aug., 1837 (about)
Same as No. 20 above, except, the Front Wrapper is dated 1837, and has the additional imprint at foot: "Bradbury and Evans, Printers, Whitefriars."
Reprinted for Parts 1 to 15 inclusive.

The first issue wrappers to Parts 9 to 19/20 were never reproduced for reprinted back numbers, but always retained their numerical individuality. Although re-issues of Parts 9 to 15 were published with reprinted wrappers, only the original wrappers were ever used for Parts 16 to 19/20. Original wrappers for Parts 9 to 13 are never found other than with date 1836, but Parts 14 to 19/20 are in two states, one dated 1836, and the other 1837. Dexter states that there was no priority of publication of Parts 14 to 19/20, with wrappers dated 1836 over those dated 1837—the old stereotype block of the wrapper dated 1836, being used concurrently with the new stereotype blocks dated 1837, of which there must have been several.

Part	9	Dec.,	1836	Original	Issue	Dated	1836		
,,	10	Jan.,	1837	,,	,,	,,	,,		
,,	11	Feb.,	,,	,,	,,	,,	,,		
,,	12	Mch.,	,,	,,	,,	,,	,,		
,,	13	Apl.,	,,	,,	,,	,,	,,		
,,	14	May,	,,	,,	,,	,,	1836 & 1837		
,,	15	July,	,,	,,	,,	,,	,,	,,	,,
,,	16	Aug.,	,,	,,	,,	,,	,,	,,	,,
,,	17	Sept.,	,,	,,	,,	,,	,,	,,	,,
,,	18	Oct.,	,,	,,	,,	,,	,,	,,	,,
,,	19/20	Nov.,	,,	,,	,,	,,	,,	,,	,,

Variant wrappers numbered in foregoing schedule, 8, 10, 12 and 17, are without any inside printed advertisements.

These represent editions totalling 1500 copies, and were specially printed for A. Tilt, the publisher and bookseller, and circulated by him ; the sales averaging only about fifty copies per number.

"PICKWICK ADVERTISER."

What may be termed the official advertising sheet, issued by, and printed for the Publishers, and consequently an integral unit of the periodical, was introduced with Part 4, and regularly appeared in each succeeding part until completion of the volume with Part 19/20 ; making a total of sixteen issues. It commenced its career with a modest 4 pages, working up to 16 pages in Part 10, and then fluctuated in an unaccountable degree from 8 to 24 pages. Why, when the circulation was undoubtedly bounding up from Part 4 onwards, should the advertising department permit a drop to 8 pp. in Parts 11, 12, 16 and 17, whilst in the interim Part 14 carried 24 pages ? We know circulation figures of 20,000 copies were announced in Part 14, and this very fact of what, in those days, was a phenomenal output, should have tended to increase the advertising space, instead of restricting it to 8 pages in Parts 16 and 17. One can detect as a possible solution, an every-day commercial instinct on the part of the advertising manager, for increased rates commensurate with increased circulation, and an equally well-known reticence by the purveyor of his wares to pay on an enhanced scale.

As the "Advertiser" was issued only with the earliest printed copies, and appeared in none of the reprints or later editions, it can be appreciated that those for Parts 4 to 8 are of the utmost rarity. With Part 4, for example, it would be no exaggeration to assert there does not exist to-day in the whole "Pickwickian" field, more than a few score copies containing the "Advertiser" applicable to that part.

Only three changes denoting priority of issues occur throughout the series. These are found in Parts 4, 10 and

19/20, and are duly noted in detail in the appropriate collations.

None of the pages are numbered, but each has a running headline "The Pickwick Advertiser," with the exception of page 17 of the last part—19/20.

FRONT INSETS.

These appear in only three parts throughout the run, viz., Parts 1, 3 and 13 ; and in each instance are describable as excessively rare, so much so, that very few copies have survived the passage of time. A census of all the well-known copies discloses that "Pigot's Views" in Part 13 is almost an unknown quantity. The first to be recorded was in 1921, and since that year two further copies have been noted as appearing in the New York sale rooms. The three insets essential to the perfect "Pickwick" are :—

(1) Part 1. Chapman & Hall's announcements. 8 pp.

(2) Part 3. "Sunday under Three Heads," etc. (C. & H.), 4 pp.

(3) Part 13. "Pigot's Views in the Isle of Wight," etc. 4 pp.

BACK INSETS.

The first appearance of a trade advertising inset was in Part 3, where is introduced that enterprising house of Rowlands, the purveyors of Macassar Oil, Kalydor, and Odonto. These trade advertisements are stitched in with all other material of the periodical, and placed to follow the text within the back wrapper. The perfect copy of "Pickwick" must contain a total of 34 such insets, the most illusive and difficult to trace being "Phrenology Made Easy" in Part 7, closely followed by the two called for in Part 5.

CHARLES DICKENS.

ADDRESSES.

A series of seven addresses were issued during the course of the periodical issue in monthly parts. Those applicable to Parts 2 and 3 are obviously the scarcest, and should not be found in any but the early copies bearing artist's name on outer wrapper—Seymour or Buss respectively. As noted in the collation following, facsimiles of these two addresses have been printed, and are often met with in later issued parts, for which they were never intended, either in a genuine or any other state.

Part 2.   Address by the Author.
,,   3.   Jointly by Author and Publishers.
,,   10.   By the Author.
,,   15.   ,, ,,   ,,
,,   17.   By the Publishers.
,,   18.   ,, ,,   ,,
,,   19.   ,, ,,   ,,

CHEAP & ENTERTAINING PERIODICAL.

THIS DAY IS PUBLISHED,

PRICE ONE SHILLING, TO BE CONTINUED MONTHLY,

CONTAINING FIFTY-SIX PAGES OF LETTER-PRESS OCTAVO, AND

TWO ILLUSTRATIONS,

No. I.

OF

THE LIBRARY OF FICTION,

OR

𝔉amily 𝔖tory 𝔗eller:

CONSISTING OF

TALES, ESSAYS, AND SKETCHES OF CHARACTER,

ORIGINAL AND SELECTED.

CONTENTS:

THE TUGGS'S AT RAMSGATE, by "Boz." (original.)

THE CASTLE OF CLEVES, or the Witness Hand, translated for this work from the German of Castelli.

MR. FIREDRAKE FIDGET.—A Tale (original.)

THE LAST WORDS OF CHARLES EDWARDS, Esq.

GINEVRA.

MODE OF PUBLICATION.

Each Number will contain one or more Original Tales by distinguished writers, as well as Translations from the Periodical and Romantic Literature of the Continent, which will be made expressly for this work.

The selected portion will be altogether of a higher character than has hitherto been offered to the public, and will not be extracted from publications of very recent date; but drawn from such sources as will enable the Editor to present to his readers the happiest efforts of modern genius with all the effect of novelty

Two Designs, engraved on wood, in the first style of the art, will accompany each number, and will, in most cases, illustrate the original Tales.

LONDON: CHAPMAN AND HALL, 186, STRAND,
AND SOLD BY ALL BOOKSELLERS AND NEWSMEN.

The first issue Back Wrapper to Part I of "The Pickwick Papers."
Inner side of wrapper is blank.   In the John F. Dexter Library.

THE PICKWICK PAPERS.

PART 1.

FRONT WRAPPER (OUTSIDE)

"No. I.] [Price 1s. | The | Posthumous Papers | of the | Pickwick | Club | containing a faithful record of the | Perambulations, Perils, Travels, Adventures | and | Sporting Transactions | of the Corresponding Members. | Edited by 'Boz.' | With Four Illustrations | by Seymour. | London : Chapman & Hall, 186, Strand. | MDCCCXXXVI."

The words "Pickwick Club" are embodied in, and form part of the cover design ; all other lettering is type-set. Signed in lower left corner, "Seymour Del.", and in right corner, "J. Jackson Sc."

In some copies seen, there is no bracket after "No. I."

FRONT WRAPPER (INSIDE)

Blank.

BACK WRAPPER (INSIDE)

Blank.

BACK WRAPPER (OUTSIDE)

"Cheap & Entertaining Periodical. | This day is published, | . . . | No. I. | of | The Library of Fiction." (13 lines in all). Followed by paragraph in half-column measure, of 10 lines, headed : "Contents." Below : "Mode of Publication" in three paragraphs, and at foot, imprint in two lines of Chapman and Hall.

ADVERTISEMENTS (FRONT)

Slip :—8 pp. unnumbered ($7'' \times 4\frac{7}{8}''$) announcing Works published by Chapman and Hall, and dated on first page, "March, 1836." A running headline, "Chapman and Hall" appears on pages 2 to 8 inclusive, which, together with the following book-titles, are all printed in red.

p. (1) 2 lines, "A Garland of Love," and "Chess for Beginners."

p. (2) 3 „ "The Artist," "Fleurs de Poesie Moderne," and "A Summer's Tour."

p. (3) 3 „ "The Squib," "Rambles in Northumberland," "Scenes and Recollections of Fly-Fishing."

p. (4) 3 lines, "Maps of the English Counties," "Map of the Inland Communication," and "Stanly."

p. (5) 2 „ "Topographical Dictionary" and "A Series of Fifty-four Quarto Maps."

p. (6) 2 „ "At a greatly Reduced Price," and "New British Atlas."

p. (7) 4 „ "The Juvenile Pianist," "Caroline," "The Spoiled Child Reclaimed," and "Poetry for Children."

p. (8) 2 „ "Cheap and Entertaining Periodical," and "The Library of Fiction."

PLATES (FOUR)

(No. 1) "Mr. Pickwick addresses the Club"; Page 2; signed in lower left corner, "Seymour del."

First state of first Seymour plate : All the picture frames are lightly etched; the division of Tupman's waistcoat is an open white line; Pickwick's vest buttons are on his left side; middle picture at back has double cord, and signature is legible.

Second state of first Seymour plate : The picture frames are deepened and more heavily ruled; Tupman's waistcoat is closed with a black line, and signature fainter.

First state of second Seymour plate : Pickwick's buttons are on his right side; middle picture has faint single cord.

(No. 2) "The Pugnacious Cabman"; Page 7; signed in lower left corner, "Seymour."

First state of first Seymour plate : The collar of Pickwick's coat is only $\frac{1}{16}$th inch in depth, and indicated by a white line beneath; there is no defined curve for the brim of his hat; the milkmaid on left is boldly etched; soldier in background has no moustache, and the signature is legible.

Second state of first Seymour plate : The collar is $\frac{1}{8}$th inch in depth, and white line is obliterated by cross hatching; a black line defines curve of hat brim, and signature is fainter.

First state of second Seymour plate : Milkmaid very faintly etched, and the soldier has a moustache.

(No. 3) "The Sagacious Dog"; Page 9; signed in lower centre, "Seymour del."

First state of first Seymour plate : There is a break, in between the gun barrel and the gamekeeper's hair—a white curve disconnecting it from the rest of the gun; the gun has both lock and trigger, and signature is quite legible.

Second state of first Seymour plate : The break in the gun barrel **is** closed, and signature is not so legible.

First state of second Seymour plate has no trigger to the gun.

(No. 4) "Dr. Slammer's defiance of Jingle" ; Page 17 ; unsigned.

First state of first Seymour plate : The panelling behind **Jingle's** head is not etched in ; the lines of the panels over, under, **and** between the lamps are fragmentary and not continuous ; **there** are ten floor boards only.

Second state of first Seymour plate : All the panels are very distinctly etched.

First state of second Seymour plate : Eleven floor boards, not ten ; also unsigned.

Note.—With the Dexter copy is a duplicate set of these four Seymour plates in brilliant first proof state, on plate paper.

TEXT, WITH HEADING

"Posthumous Papers | of | The Pickwick Club | Chapter I. | The Pickwickians." pp. (1)–26. (B.C.D. in eights+ E, a 2 pp. signature—unlettered in first issue).

p. (1) line 14.— "*O*" in "Observations" must be perfect.

p. 3, line 1.— "*d*" in "ardour" must be perfect.

p. 3, line 47.— "*h*" in "honourable" must be perfect.

p. 14, line 5.— "*h*" in "heavily" must be perfect.

p. 14, line 12.— "*w*" in "we" must be perfect.

p. 17, page No.—The foot of "7" is slightly raised.

p. 23, line 29.— "*s*" in "stared" must be perfect.

p. 25, there must be no signature "E" to this page.

TEXT MEASUREMENTS

Extreme depth of pages :—

pp. 10, 17, 20	=	179 mm.
p. 9 (including footnote)	=	178½ ,,
pp. 5, 7, 23	=	175 ,,
pp. 2, 3, 6, 8, 11–16, 18, 19, 21, 22, 24, 25	=	174½ ,,
p. (1) to bottom of signature "B"	=	160 ,,
p. (1) to bottom of second footnote	=	157 ,,
p. 26	=	150½ ,,
p. 4	=	141 ,,

Page 1 requires very careful testing. In some quite early issues, the sig. "B" is placed perceptibly lower down the page than in the genuine first issue, and in both cases when the page-depth is inclusive of the signature, they will show 160 mm., but if taken only to the bottom of the footnotes, a difference of 3 mm. is exposed in first issue, and in the later ones a difference of 5 mm. can be detected.

PART 2.

FRONT WRAPPER (OUTSIDE)
Same as No. I. except "No. II."

> In some copies the bracket after "No. II" does not appear, as is the case in the Dexter copy.

FRONT WRAPPER (INSIDE)
Blank.

BACK WRAPPER (INSIDE)
Blank.

BACK WRAPPER (OUTSIDE)
"Cheap & Entertaining Periodical. | This day is published, | . . . | No. II. | of | The Library of Fiction." (13 lines in all). Followed by two paragraphs in half-column measure, headed: "Contents" and "Contents of No. I." respectively. Remainder of page as Part 1.

PLATES (THREE)
(No. 5) "The Dying Clown"; Page 31; signed in lower left corner, "Seymour Del."

> The listener's hat touches his foot.

(No. 6) "Mr. Pickwick in chase of his hat"; Page 38; signed in lower centre, "Seymour Del."

> The lady on right with parasol has feathers in her hat.

(No. 7) "Mr. Winkle soothes the refractory Steed"; Page 47; signed in lower centre "Seymour Del."

> The horse in vehicle has one rein showing, not two.

THE PICKWICK PAPERS.

ADDRESS
Written by Dickens, announcing the death of Seymour ;
    dated April 27th, 1836. Single leaf of 19 lines, printed
    one side only. Depth of page 97½ mm.

There exist facsimiles of this Address, and the test of genuineness
is the measure given above, together with the fact that the first
letter "B" of first line, and the first letter "A" in "April" of last
line, should be in perfect alignment.

TEXT, WITH HEADING
    "Chapter III." pp. 27–50. (E. F. G. in eights).

p. 28 : in last line ; "*was drawn out*," not " was draw out."

p. 30 : at the end of third completed paragraph, the word
    "*wanderings*" appears instead of "murmurings."

p. 33 : line 22 ; "*by God*," not "everyman."

p. 34 : second paragraph of Chapter IV, line 3, after the word
    "Snodgrass," should contain the following in brackets :
    "(presented on the 2nd of December, 1828, and ordered
    to be bound on the same day)."

42 lines of text, which was reduced to 41 lines on revision.

p. 36 : line 15 ; there is no comma after "feet."

The "comma" was afterwards dropped in without
altering the space between the two words.

p. 37 : the figure "7" in pagination soon became slightly
    mutilated.

p. 43 : the first line under "Chapter V" ends in "Pick-" and
    the second in "and."
    The second paragraph of "Chapter V," line 1, should
    contain after the words "ruined walls" : "of the ancient
    castle."

p. 44 : line 4 up ; the word "*printed*" appears instead of "entered."

p. 47 : line 13 ; "*his horse's bridle*," instead of "the reins."
    line 20 ; "*bridle*," instead of "reins."
    line 21 ; "*it*" and "*its*," instead of "them" and "their."

p. 48 : line 3 ; "*the bridle*," instead of "his hold."

p. 50 : line 27 ; "*apartment*," instead of "room."
    line 28 ; there should be no comma after "it."

Text Measurements
  Extreme depth of pages :—

p. 27	=	178 mm.
p. 35	=	$177\frac{1}{2}$,,
p. 43	=	$176\frac{1}{4}$,,
pp. 28–30, 32–34, 36–38, 48	=	$174\frac{1}{2}$,,
pp. 44–47	=	$173\frac{1}{2}$,,
p. 31	=	173 ,,
pp. 40, 41	=	$171\frac{1}{4}$,,
pp. 39, 42, 49	=	$170\frac{1}{2}$,,
p. 50	=	$156\frac{1}{2}$,,

PART 3.

Front Wrapper (Outside)
  Same as No. I. except "No. III." and the substitution of
  "With Illustrations | by R. W. Buss" instead of "With
  Four Illustrations by Seymour."
  The bracket after "No. III." does not appear in the Dexter copy.
  It is inscribed " With the Publishers' Compliments."

Front Wrapper (Inside)
  Blank.

Back Wrapper (Inside)
  Blank.

Back Wrapper (Outside)
  "Cheap & Entertaining Periodical. | This day is published,
  | . . . | No. III. | of | The Library of Fiction." (13
  lines in all). Followed by two paragraphs in half-
  column measure, headed, "Contents of No. I." and
  "Contents of No. II." Remainder of page as Parts 1
  and 2.

Advertisements (Front)
  Slip :—"Chapman and Hall, 186, Strand." 4 pp. unnumbered, 12 mo. ($6\frac{1}{2}'' \times 4\frac{3}{16}''$).
  p. (1) "Sunday under Three Heads."
  p. (2) "The Pickwick Club."
  p. (3) "The Library of Fiction."
  p. (4) "Maps of the English Counties."

ADVERTISEMENTS (BACK)

(No. 1) "The Toilet." 4 pp. numbered (1)–4.

The first paid advertisement to appear in "Pickwick," and had reference to "Rowland's Kalydor." It should be present in any copy of the earliest issue, or alternatively by one of the three following.

(No. 1a) "Rowland's Kalydor." The same format and subject matter as above No. 1.

(No. 1b) "The Auto-Biography | of | An Oil Bottle." 4 pp. numbered (1)–4.

This has entirely different subject matter to either of above, advertising in this case, Rowland's "Genuine Macassar Oil." In addition it carries an imprint at foot of page 4 ; "Peart and Co ; Printers, 143, St.-john-street-road."

(No. 1c) A slight variant of above No. 1b, with heading : "Adventures of an Oil Bottle." First page shows difference of text in line 5 : "I was" instead of "was." Line 16 : "genuine" instead of "Original." Line 19 : "Original" for "Genuine" ; and in last line the word "kind" is the usual fount of type instead of italics.

The Dexter copy contains variant No. 1b.

PLATES (TWO)

(No. 8) "The Cricket Match" ; Page 69 ; signed in lower left corner : "Drawn & Etched by R. W. Buss."

(No. 9) "The Arbour Scene" ; Page 74 ; signed in lower centre : "Drawn & Etched by R. W. Buss."

These, known as the "suppressed plates," were five months later replaced by two others, designed and etched by "Phiz." The substituted plates, "Under the influence of the Salmon," and "The Arbour Scene," only appear in very late issues.

ADDRESS

"Address from the Publishers" ; followed by, "Postscript from the Editor " : relating to the illustrator Mr. Buss, who succeeds Seymour. 2 pp. numbered on second page, and dated May 30th, 1836.

Facsimiles of this Address have also been seen. A genuine copy should conform to these measurements :

Length of page (1)	=	156 mm.
Length of page 2, inclusive of page number	=	113½ „
Width of average full line	=	97 „

TEXT, WITH HEADING
"Chapter VI." pp. 51–82. (H. I. in sixteens).

p. 51 : in last line ; after the word "*family*," there is a kind of mis-printed semi-colon (*;*).

p. 52 : line 14 up ; the first letter "*s*" is perfect.

p. 53 : line 6 up, in first issue, the word "*snuff*" overlaps in the outer margin.

TEXT MEASUREMENTS
Extreme depth of pages :—

p. 51	=	178½ mm.
pp. 53, 56–58, 67	=	178 „
p. 55	=	176¼ „
pp. 52, 54, 59–66, 68, 69, 71, 73–80	=	174½ „
p. 78	=	173 „
pp. 70, 81	=	171¼ „
p. 72	=	166½ „
p. 82	=	163½ „

PART 4.

FRONT WRAPPER (OUTSIDE)
Same as No. I. except "No. IV." followed with bracket ; and the substitution of "With Illustrations" instead of "With Four Illustrations by Seymour."

FRONT WRAPPER (INSIDE)
"New Works | Published by Chapman and Hall, Strand." Followed by six announcements bearing titles of works :

(1) "With Illustrations . . . | Sunday, under Three Heads . . ." ; followed by a verse of four lines. (8 lines in all).

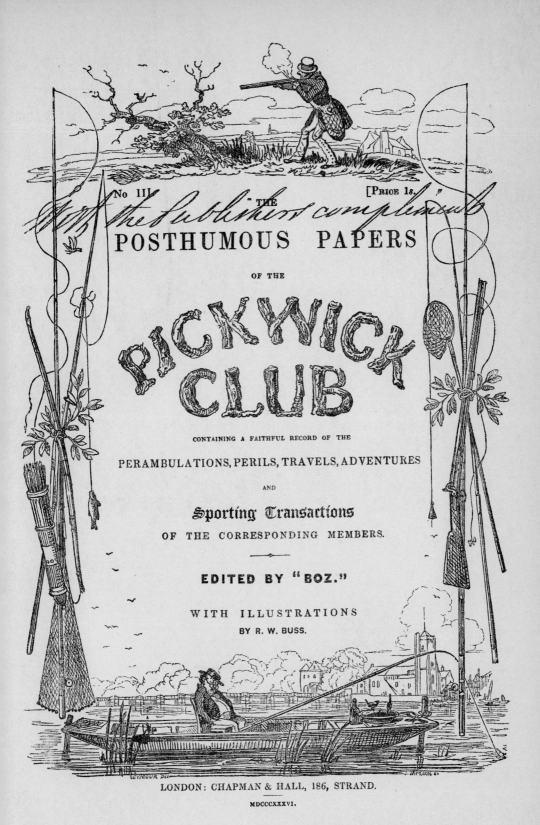

No III   [PRICE 1s.

the Publishers compliments

THE POSTHUMOUS PAPERS

OF THE

PICKWICK CLUB

CONTAINING A FAITHFUL RECORD OF THE

PERAMBULATIONS, PERILS, TRAVELS, ADVENTURES

AND

Sporting Transactions

OF THE CORRESPONDING MEMBERS.

EDITED BY "BOZ."

WITH ILLUSTRATIONS

BY R. W. BUSS.

LONDON: CHAPMAN & HALL, 186, STRAND.

MDCCCXXXVI.

The first issue Front Wrapper to Part III of "The Pickwick Papers,"
the rarest of the series, and of which not more than 500 copies were
printed. Inner side of wrapper is blank. In the John F. Dexter Library.

(2) "Price One shilling, | Nursery Government : . . ." (8 lines).

(3) "In Two Volumes, . . . | Edward, the Crusader's Son."
(3 lines).

(4) "In One Volume, . . . | The Poetic Wreath." (4 lines).

(5) "One Volume, . . . | A Garland of Love." (12 lines).

(6) "Price 5s. 6d. . . . | A Summer Tour Through Belgium . . ."
(8 lines).

BACK WRAPPER (INSIDE)
"Works Published by Chapman and Hall"; with four
announcements bearing titles of works :

(1) "One Volume . . . | Chess for Beginners . . ." (9 lines).

(2) "In one Volume foolscap . . . | Rambles in Northumberland
and on the | Scottish Border . . ." (12 lines).

(3) "Foolscap 8vo . . . | Scenes and Recollections of Fly-
Fishing . . ." (9 lines).

(4) "Sidney Hall's County Maps." (7 lines).

BACK WRAPPER (OUTSIDE)
"Cheap & Entertaining Periodical. | This day is pub-
lished, | . . . | The Library of Fiction." (11 lines in all).
Followed by an address of the Proprietors, of 14 lines ;
and three paragraphs detailing Contents of No. I,
No. II, and No. III. Below this a 2-line imprint of
Chapman and Hall ; and at foot, imprint :—"Bradbury
and Evans, Printers, Whitefriars."

ADVERTISEMENTS (FRONT)
"The Pickwick Advertiser." 4 pp. unnumbered.

p. (1) "Interesting and Amusing Books lately published by |
Charles Tilt, 86, Fleet Street." Eight titles are listed, each
numbered I–VIII.

p. (2) "3, St. James's Square, July 1. | Mr Macrone has just
published the following | New and Popular Works."
Eight titles are listed, each numbered I–VIII.

p. (3) "Albemarle Street, June 18. | Mr Murray's List of New
Works." Ten titles, each numbered I–X.

p. (4) "Mr Murray's List continued." Four titles, numbered
XI–XIV. Lower half of page is occupied with Richard
Bentley's announcements of "James' Naval History of

Great Britain," "Madame Junot's Memoirs of the Court and Family of Napoleon," and "Bourrienne's Celebrated Memoirs of the Emperor Napoleon."

Although the absence of house number "17" before Albemarle Street in page (3) is undoubtedly a sign of earlier issue, yet the presence of the number might be considered the rarer of the two. Of the many copies which have been under review, none have been seen with number "17."

PLATES (Two)

(No. 10) "The Breakdown"; Page 89; signed very faintly in lower left corner—"NEMO" (Phiz).

First state of original plate. There is a wheel on ground, of which the smaller of the two down-pointing spokes does not quite touch the rim.

Second state of original plate. Both spokes of wheel actually touch the rim.

Second plate, with inscription. This has many altered features, the main one being the absence of wheel on ground.

(No. 11) "First appearance of Mr. Samuel Weller"; Page 94; signed in lower right corner—"NEMO," but more distinctly than in previous plate.

First state of original plate. There are three darkly etched topboots; whilst to their immediate left are three others very faintly outlined, and appear to form part of the steps upon which Sam's foot is resting. Wardle's stick is almost in halves, and only held together in the middle by a hair-line.

Second state of original plate. The three top-boots on extreme left are more boldly shaded and outlined, and unmistakable for what they are. Wardle's stick has no break whatever.

Second plate, with inscription. The main feature shows a top-boot on bottom step, which does not appear in the original plate.

Both these plates (10 and 11) were re-touched and re-bitten. In the earlier states as described, they are very uncommon and not generally known.

TEXT, WITH HEADING

"Chapter IX." pp. 83–114. (K. L. in sixteens).

p. 91, line 37 : "why dont" is correctly spaced in first issue.

p. 93, headline : "The Pickwick Club" is not centrally placed, but leans to the right of page. Distance from "period" to tail of figure "9" measures 24 mm. in first issue. As corrected the space is lengthened to 29½ mm.

p. 96, line 20 : "catalogue" shows the "*e*" separated in first issue.

p. 103, line 19 : "abated" ; imperfect "*te*" in first issue.

p. 112, last line : the word "light" has "*l*" damaged in first issue.

TEXT MEASUREMENTS
Extreme depth of pages :—

pp. 83, 85, 89, 99	= 174½ mm.
p. 101	= 173 „
pp. 84, 86–88, 91, 92, 95–98, 100, 102–105, 107–113	= 171¼ „
p. 93	= 170½ „
pp. 90, 94	= 169¾ „
p. 106	= 165 „
p. 114	= 113 „

PART 5.

FRONT WRAPPER (OUTSIDE)
Same as No. IV. except "No. V."

FRONT WRAPPER (INSIDE)
"New Works | Published by Chapman and Hall, Strand." Consists of five announcements similar to Part IV ; with these differences :

(1) Omits the 4-line verse, but with 7 added lines of Press notices, now consists of 11 lines.

(2) "Nursery Government." This is identical.

(3) Has additional 7 lines, making 10 in all.

(4) Has additional 10 lines, making 14 in all.

(6) Omits 3 lines of Press notice, leaving only 5 lines.

No. 5, "A Garland of Love" is entirely omitted.

BACK WRAPPER (INSIDE)
"Works Published by Chapman and Hall." Similar to Part IV, except No. 5 "A Garland of Love" is brought

to the head of this page ; and although identically the same text, it is arranged in a slightly different manner. The page now contains five titles.

BACK WRAPPER (OUTSIDE)
"Cheap & Entertaining Periodical. | This day is published, | . . . | Number V. of | The Library of Fiction, | or | Family Story Teller" (9 lines in all). Followed by 13 lines ; and at foot, the two imprints as in Part IV.

ADVERTISEMENTS (FRONT)
"The Pickwick Advertiser." 4 pp. unnumbered.

p. (1) "14, Chandos Street, West Strand, | August 1st, 1836." "W. Kidd has just published the following | interesting Works." Follows ten titles, each of which is numbered I–X.

p. (2) Continuation of W. Kidd's announcements, listing four more books, numbered XI–XIV. Below :—"The Juvenile Every-Day Book," printed by and for John Limbird ; and "Woodhouse's Essence of Ginger and Patent Corn Plaster."

p. (3) "T. Cox Savory, Working Silversmith, 47, Cornhill, London." Three illustrations of Dish Covers, a Tea Service, and a Wall Clock.

p. (4) "Rennies Scientific Alphabets," partly in half measure. Below :—"The British Cyclopædia." All published by Orr and Smith, Paternoster Row.

ADVERTISEMENTS (BACK)
(1) Grattan's Publications, 4 pp. numbered in top centre only of page 2 ($7\frac{7}{8}'' \times 5\frac{1}{4}''$).

p. (1) "Now publishing, | In Weekly Numbers Price 1s. each, | embellished with numerous Portraits | . . . | James' | Naval History | of | Great Britain." Follows text of 26 lines, continuing to page 2.

p. (2) Continuation from page (1); text of 38 lines, ending with the words "octavo volumes." Imprint of Richard Bentley at foot : "Sold by Edward Grattan . . ."

p. (3) "Just published, size 38 inches by 19, Printed on the best Drawing Paper | Gilbert's | New Map of the World," followed by Press criticisms : five lines, Literary Gazette, April 9th ; and four lines, Court Journal, April 2nd. At foot : "Russell's | Map of London."

p. (4) "Also just published . . . | Gilbert's | New Map of Europe, | on four sheets." Lower half of page : "Russell's | Map of the Environs of London." Imprint at foot : Clarke, Printers, Silver-street, Falcon-square.

This inset varies considerably in textual matter, when compared with those noted in the Kern and Bruton copies. The latter is the more generally met with.

(2) A large sheet ($11\frac{3}{16}'' \times 8\frac{9}{16}''$) twice folded, advertising Rowland's Kalydor and Macassar Oil ; with wood-cut of a black woman. Imprint : "Printed by W. Hatfield, Independent Press Office, Cambridge.

PLATES (TWO)
(No. 12) "Mrs. Bardell faints in Mr. Pickwick's arms" ; Page 117 ; signed faintly left of centre : "Phiz del."

The glass shade on mantel-shelf covers an ornament, and not a clock.

(No. 13) "The Election at Eatanswill" ; Page 132 ; signed "Phiz del."

The Beadle's legs are straight.

TEXT, WITH HEADING
"Chapter XII." pp. 115–146. (M. N. in sixteens).

p. 121 : line 13 up ; last word "the" is printed "*th*" in first issue.

p. 133 : line 1 ; comma after "Lodge" is placed too high in first issue.

The text of the Dexter copy is partly unopened.

TEXT MEASUREMENTS
Extreme depth of pages :—

p. 133	=	178 mm.
pp. 117, 128, 131, 132, 141–146	=	$174\frac{1}{2}$ „
p. 115	=	173 „
pp. 118, 120–127, 129, 130, 134–140	=	$171\frac{1}{4}$ „
p. 116	=	172 „
p. 119	=	137 „

CHARLES DICKENS.

PART 6.

FRONT WRAPPER (OUTSIDE)
Same as No. IV. except "No. VI."

FRONT WRAPPER (INSIDE)
Same as No. V.

BACK WRAPPER (INSIDE)
Same as No. V.

BACK WRAPPER (OUTSIDE)
The first 9 lines same as No. V, except, now reads, "Number VI." Followed by 17 lines which detail contents of Nos. VI and V. At foot, the two imprints as in Parts IV and V.

ADVERTISEMENTS (FRONT)
"The Pickwick Advertiser." 8 pp. unnumbered.

p. (1) "3, St. James's Square. | Mr. Macrone's Last New Publications." Follows 12 titles, each numbered I–XII.

p. (2) "London : 14, Chandos Street, West Strand, Sept. 1, 1836. | A Select List of W. Kidd's New Publications." Follows, in half column measure, a list of nine works, six of them with Press notices.

p. (3) Continuation of Kidd's announcements, all in half column measure. Eight works on page.

p. (4) Four book announcements by John Limbird, followed below by two of Charles Tilt.

p. (5) ($\frac{1}{2}$ col.) "Under the especial patronage | of | His Most Gracious Majesty," occupying whole column of Woodhouse's remedies. Second column has three other advertisements, the first being "Mr Jesse's New Work," and the final "Ladies best Gold" (T. Cox Savory) with two woodcuts.

p. (6) "London Therapeutic Institution"; and "Brilliant Pier and Chimney Glasses, &c." (Henry L. Cooper).

p. (7) "49, Lombard-street. | Established 1784. | E. P. Doudney & Son." Two illustrations, and between them are the words "Shooting Jackets" in heavy black-faced type, $\frac{7}{16}$" deep. Full page.

THE PICKWICK PAPERS.

p. (8) "Rowland's Kalydor," nearly half-page; below: "A Certain Cure for Corns and Bunnions | Allingham's" and at foot, "To Advertisers. | The Pickwick Club."

The "Advertiser" of the Dexter copy is entirely unopened.

PLATES (TWO)
(No. 14) "Mrs. Leo Hunter's Fancy dress dejeune"; Page 169; signed, "Phiz del."

The first state is incorrectly paginated as above, and the bird-cage is shown resting in the boughs.

(No. 15) "The unexpected breaking up of the Seminary for young Ladies"; Page 154; signed "Phiz del."

The first state is incorrectly paginated as above, and there is no bell fixed on the door.

As noted earlier in this volume (p. 22), these mis-paginated plates may be considered the rarest items in the whole realm of "Pickwick." Such a fact would go to prove that the correction was quickly made, before many impressions were run-off. The artist re-etched over the original figures, thus giving the proper page-number to plates 14 and 15, "154" and "169" respectively.

TEXT, WITH HEADING
"Chapter XV." pp. 147–178. (O. P. in sixteens).

p. 148 : the words "Expiring Frog" are out of alignment with preceding line, "On a log," at end of first verse.

p. 154 : line 6; between the words "their mamma" appears two quad marks in first issue.

p. 157 : line 18; "*Te Count*" in first issue; afterwards corrected to "The Count."

p. 161 : line 29; the words "Wellerthe" are run together.

The Dexter copy is entirely unopened.

TEXT MEASUREMENTS
Extreme depth of pages :—

pp. 147, 149, 163, 165, 171, 173–176, 178	=	$174\frac{1}{2}$ mm.
p. 172	=	172 „
pp. 148, 150–152, 156, 164, 166–168, 170, 177	=	$171\frac{1}{4}$ „
p. 158	=	$169\frac{3}{4}$ „
pp. 153–155, 157, 159–162, 169	=	$167\frac{1}{2}$ „

CHARLES DICKENS.

PART 7.

FRONT WRAPPER (OUTSIDE)
Same as No. IV. except "No. VII."

FRONT WRAPPER (INSIDE)
"Cheap & Entertaining Periodical. | In the course of October will be Published, | Price 7s. 6d., | . . . | The First Volume of | The Library of Fiction, | or | Family Story Teller. | Address." Followed by 17 lines, ending here with the words :—"Original Tales or" ; and continued to the inside of Back Wrapper.

BACK WRAPPER (INSIDE)
Headline :—"Library of Fiction." Begins with word : "Sketches" in continuation of address as above ; 15 lines ; and in half measure is a list of fourteen contributors. Imprint at foot in three lines : "London : | Chapman and Hall, 186, Strand. | And sold by all Booksellers and Newsmen."

BACK WRAPPER (OUTSIDE)
"New and Splendid Volume. | In the course of November will be Published, | . . . | The Pictorial Album, | . . . | for the year 1837." Imprint : "Chapman and Hall, 186, Strand." At foot, on extreme right, imprint : "Bradbury and Evans, Printers."

ADVERTISEMENTS (FRONT)
"The Pickwick Advertiser." 8 pp. unnumbered.

> p. (1) "New and Interesting Works | recently published by | Smith, Elder, and Co., | 65, Cornhill." Follows seven titles of books, each numbered I–VII.

> p. (2) (½ col.) "Under the especial patronage | of | His Most Gracious Majesty." Occupying whole column of Woodhouse's remedies. Second column has three other advertisements.

> p. (3) "New System at Bull's Library" ; A. B. Savory and Son's "Silver Tea Services" with four illustrations ; and "Aux Voyageurs" (Palmer, Jun.)

CHEAP & ENTERTAINING PERIODICAL.

THIS DAY IS PUBLISHED,

PRICE ONE SHILLING, TO BE CONTINUED MONTHLY,

EACH CONTAINING FIFTY-SIX PAGES OF LETTER-PRESS OCTAVO, AND

TWO ILLUSTRATIONS,

THE LIBRARY OF FICTION,

OR

𝔉𝔞𝔪𝔦𝔩𝔶 𝔖𝔱𝔬𝔯𝔶 𝔗𝔢𝔩𝔩𝔢𝔯:

CONSISTING OF

TALES, ESSAYS, AND SKETCHES OF CHARACTER,

ORIGINAL AND SELECTED.

———◆———

THE Subscribers to this Work, and the Public in general, are respectfully apprised, that arrangements have been made, by virtue of which it is confidently hoped that its future Numbers will present additional claims to general approbation and patronage. Several distinguished Writers, who have already obtained the meed of high popularity, have engaged to enrich the LIBRARY OF FICTION with regular contributions. The "Original" portion of the Work, therefore, if it do not altogether supersede the "Selected," will be at once considerably increased in extent and elevated in character. While the reader will not fail occasionally to recognise, also, the hand of individuals who have so successfully contributed to the first Numbers.

The Proprietors are aware that when so many candidates for public favour are in the field, great exertions are requisite to ensure approval and support; and this consideration, together with the unequivocal success that has attended the commencement of their present undertaking, induces them to resolve on withholding neither trouble nor expense, in order to give to the LIBRARY OF FICTION a high rank among the periodicals of the day.

CONTENTS OF NO. I. THE TUGGS AT RAMSGATE, by "Boz," (original.) — THE CASTLE OF CLEVES, or the Witness Hand, translated for this work from the German of Castelli.—MR. FIREDRAKE FIDGET. A Tale, (original.)—THE LAST WORDS OF CHARLES EDWARDS, ESQ.—GINEVRA.

CONTENTS OF NO. II. SOME PASSAGES IN THE LIFE OF FRANCIS LOOSEFISH, ESQ., (original.)—THE TALE OF A CHEMIST.—THE LANDLORD OF ROYSTON, by the Author of "Scenes and Recollections of Fly-fishing," (original.)—THE IRISH LORD LIEUTENANT AND HIS DOUBLE, by the Author of the "O'Hara Tales."

CONTENTS OF NO. III. A LITTLE TALK ABOUT SPRING AND THE SWEEPS, by "Boz," (original.)—MONKWYND, a Legendary Fragment.—DESTINY, (original.) —DIARY OF A SURGEON, (original.)—MY LITTLE GREY LANDLORD. By the Author of "Scenes in Poland."

———

LONDON: CHAPMAN AND HALL, 186, STRAND.

AND SOLD BY ALL BOOKSELLERS AND NEWSMEN.

———

BRADBURY AND EVANS, PRINTERS, WHITEFRIARS.

The first issue Back Wrapper to Part IV of "The Pickwick Papers." Inner side of wrapper was printed with announcements of four book titles published by Chapman & Hall. In the John F. Dexter Library.

p. (4) "Brilliant Pier and Chimney Glasses, &c." and T. Cox Savory, Working Silversmith, with two illustrations.

p. (5) "London Therapeutic Institution"; "Without injuring the Hair or soiling the Skin" of W. Day and Co.; and "Brown Stout Porter."

p. (6) "Approved Articles for the Toilet, prepared by | Hannay and Co." Full page.

p. (7) Same as Part 6.

p. (8) Same as Part 6.

ADVERTISEMENTS (BACK)

Slip:—(to follow Text). Single leaf printed one side only. (6″×3½″). "September, 1836. | Just published | on a Card, | Price Ninepence, | A | Large Chart, | entitled | Phrenology Made Easy"; Imprint: "London: Effingham Wilson, 88, Royal Exchange."

PLATES (TWO)

(No. 16) "Mr. Pickwick in the Pound"; Page 197; signed "Phiz del."

The eave of house on left is very faintly drawn, and the larger of the two donkeys does not show hind legs.

(No. 17) "Mr. Pickwick and Sam in the attorneys' office"; Page 201; signed "Phiz del."

Sam Weller's legs are together, and the third clerk from left has no pen.

No. 16 plate is the only one in Parts 5 to 9 which has distinctive features of priority, previous to the entirely re-etched plates for the volume issue bearing inscriptions. The plates in these five parts have little or no "point" of early state in the various issues of the monthly parts.

TEXT, WITH HEADING

"Chapter XVIII." pp. 179–210. (Q. R. in sixteens).

p. 194: in line 7, the letter "*b*" is dropped in "bagginets."
p. 202: in line 30, the letter "*r*" in "for" is upside-down; and date is "Sep. 28" not "Aug. 28."

TEXT MEASUREMENTS
    Extreme depth of pages :—

p. 179	=	175 mm.
pp. 181, 197, 203, 205	=	174½ ,,
p. 190	=	172 ,,
pp. 180, 182, 185–189, 193–195, 198–202, 204, 206–209	=	171¼ ,,
pp. 183, 184, 191, 192, 196	=	168¾ ,,
p. 210	=	165 ,,

PART 8.

FRONT WRAPPER (OUTSIDE)
    Same as No. IV. except "No. VIII."

FRONT WRAPPER (INSIDE)
    Same as No. VII. except the second and third lines read :
    "This Day is Published, | Price 8s."

BACK WRAPPER (INSIDE)
    Same as No. VII. except the 3-line imprint is omitted,
    and replaced with an announcement reading :—"No. 8,
    commencing the Second Volume, contains | John
    Horner, the Man with the Plums ; | By Douglas
    Jerrold . . . | The Tempter, | By J. S. Coyne. | Mon-
    sieur Antony Bougainville, or the Petition."

BACK WRAPPER (OUTSIDE)
    Same as No. VII. except the second line reads : "Early
    in November will be Published."

A great deal of confusion and uncertainty to collectors has always
surrounded the question of the arrangement of textual matter in
the "Address" printed upon the inside of front and back wrapper
to Part 8; or to simplify the expression—on pages 2 and 3.
The tangle can now, at long last, be straightened by a reference
to the collation set out immediately above, which is the one
applicable to the Dexter copy. It represents indisputably the
earliest form of the wrapper to Part 8, announcing the publication
of the first volume of The Library of Fiction, and coinciding in

THE PICKWICK PAPERS.

the setting of the "Address" with the first issue of the wrapper
to Part 7 ; before the transference of one line of text from the
head of page 3, to the foot of page 2.   It must be apparent that
a wrapper following the same lay-out as the preceding number,
takes precedence over the subsequently re-arranged text.   When
the "John Horner" announcement was brought in at the foot of
page 3, Part 8, the page at first had an unbalanced appearance,
and to correct this, one line at a later period was transferred to
page 2 of the front wrapper.

Below, particulars are set out of the previously designated first
issue wrapper to Part 8, which can now only be referred to as a
"Second Issue."

FRONT WRAPPER (INSIDE).   SECOND ISSUE
Same as No. VII. except the second and third lines read :
"This Day is Published, | Price 8s." and an additional
line in the Address : ending the page with, "and many
of the . . ."

BACK WRAPPER (INSIDE).   SECOND ISSUE
Headline : "Library of Fiction." Same text as No. VII.
except the first line of that Part has been transferred to
Front Wrapper.   Begins : "highly-prized contributions."
The 3-line imprint is omitted, and replaced with an
announcment reading : "No. 8, commencing the Second
Volume, contains | John Horner, the Man with the
Plums ; | By Douglas Jerrold . . . | The Tempter, | By
J. S. Coyne. | Monsieur Antony Bougainville, or the
Petition."

ADVERTISEMENTS (FRONT)
"The Pickwick Advertiser." 8 pp. unnumbered.

p. (1) "Splendid Annuals for 1837. | 86, Fleet Street, October 1,
1836. | Mr. Tilt has in preparation," etc.   Seven books
are enumerated.

p. (2) ($\frac{1}{2}$ col.) "14, Chandos Street, West Strand, | November
1st, 1836. | W. Kidd's New Catalogue of nearly Two
Hundred Popular Works, is now ready."   In all eight
advertisements to the page.

51

p. (3) "Palmer's Pocket Toilets"; "Vincent's Gowland's Lotion"; and Henry L. Cooper's "Brilliant Pier and Chimney Glasses, &c."

p. (4) "Without injuring the Hair or soiling the Skin" (W. Day and Co.); "A Certain Cure for Corns and Bunnions" (Allingham); and "Gold Watches," (A. B. Savory and Sons) with woodcuts of two watches.

p. (5) "T. Cox Savory, Silversmith, 47, Cornhill, London"; with cuts of two candlesticks. Also, D. A. Doudney's "Important New Invention !—The | ANDROMETER !"

p. (6) Same as Part 7.

p. (7) Same as Parts 6 and 7.

p. (8) "Rowland's Kalydor" with date at foot, "July 10, 1836." Half-page; "Brown Stout Porter," and "To Advertisers. | The Pickwick Club."

ADVERTISEMENTS (BACK)
"Geo. Henekey and Compy. | Wine Merchants | to | H.R.H. the Duke of Sussex." 4 pp. numbered on page 3 only. Blue paper. Imprint on p. (1): Printed by W. Clowes and Sons, | Stamford-street."

PLATES (TWO)
(No. 18) "The last visit of Heyling to the Old Man"; Page 223; signed "Phiz del."

The tops of Heyling's chair are visible.

(No. 19) "The middle-aged lady in the double-bedded Room"; Page 233; signed "Phiz del."

The chair back has three vertical rails, and not cross-rail. The garment on chair is black—not white.

TEXT, WITH HEADING
"Chapter XXI." pp. 211–242. (S. T. in sixteens).

p. 225, line 34 : in word "reg'larly" the "e" is almost obliterated.

p. 233, line 8 : two faint quad marks appear after "I" in "I ever."

TEXT MEASUREMENTS
Extreme depth of pages :—

pp. 211, 212, 219, 220, 223–225, 229, 233–236	=	174½ mm.
p. 215	=	172 „
pp. 216–218, 221, 222, 226, 227, 230–232, 237–241	=	171¼ „
p. 228	=	168¼ „
p. 214	=	164¼ „
p. 242	=	160¼ „

PART 9.

FRONT WRAPPER (OUTSIDE)
Same as No. IV. except "No. IX."

FRONT WRAPPER (INSIDE)
"Tilt's | Miniature Classical Library." Imprint at foot, "Charles Tilt, Fleet Street."

BACK WRAPPER (INSIDE)
"Heath's Picturesque Annual | for 1837"; "Hints on Etiquette"; and "Short Whist"; all published by Longman, Rees, Orme, and Co.

BACK WRAPPER (OUTSIDE)
"Popular and Amusing Works, | Recently published by Charles Tilt, 86, Fleet Street." A list of Eleven works by George Cruikshank, and three other works.

ADVERTISEMENTS (FRONT)
"The Pickwick Advertiser." 12 pp. unnumbered.

p. (1) "The Imperial Classics." To be published in Monthly Parts by William Smith.

p. (2) "Published this day, by Fisher, Son, & Co., London"; detailing Seven books, each numbered I–VII.

p. (3) "Fraser's Magazine for the ensuing Year"; 13 lines, and below in half measure, W. Kidd's list of four books; "Hodgson's Library" and "Gems of Beauty" published by Longmans.

p. (4) ($\frac{1}{2}$ col.) "The Naturalist's Library" and Seven other advertisements.

p. (5) "In 17 vols. . . | The Complete Works of Lord Byron" ; "The Keepsake for 1837" ; and in half measure, Effingham Wilson's "Superior Presents for Youth," of Nine Titles.

p. (6) "3, St. James's Square, Nov. 30. | Christmas Gifts. | New Work by 'Boz.' | In a few days Mr. Macrone will publish | Sketches by 'Boz.' | The Second Series" ; "The Wit's Miscellany" edited by 'Boz' ; and "A New System of Domestic Cookery."

p. (7) "Elegant and Cheap Christmas Presents" ; Seven items published by Richard Bentley.

p. (8) "Important New Invention !—The | ANDROMETER !" (D. A. Doudney) ; below in half measure : "Annuals for 1837.—Just published" (Ackermann) ; and "Messrs. Delcroix and Co."

p. (9) "Genuine British Wine | Establishment." E. and T. Taylor. Full-page.

p. (10) "Silver Tea Services." (A. B. Savory and Sons, with four woodcuts of tea-pots) ; "Without injuring the Hair or soiling the Skin" ; and below in half measure, "The calamitous effects of Fire" and "Pierce Egan's New Work."

p. (11) Same as Parts 6, 7, and 8, page 7. (Doudney).

p. (12) "Rowland's Kalydor" ; "Vincent's Gowland's Lotion" ; and "Allingham's Corn Cure," etc.

In the Dexter copy, appears an inset of George Mann, Bookseller. It is pasted on page 12 of the "Advertiser," and although it cannot be accepted as a definite unit in the construction of Part 9, it is interesting and proper to place on record, in view of its extreme rarity, and its known presence in but one or two copies.

The leaflet, which measures $7\frac{5}{16}'' \times 4\frac{1}{2}''$ is printed on one side only, with a ruled border and scroll corner pieces, headed : "George Mann, | Bookseller, | . . . | 39 Cornhill" ; followed by nine lines of text.

ADVERTISEMENTS (BACK)

(1) Chapman and Hall's Announcements. 8 pp. unnumbered.

p. (1) "The Pictorial Album."

p. (2) "The Pickwick Papers," and "Sunday under Three Heads."

p. (3) "The Library of Fiction" : continued to p. (4).

p. (5) "The Poetic Wreath" and "Edward, | The Crusader's Son."

p. (6) "A Garland of Love" ; "Chess for Beginners" and "The Artist."

p. (7) "Fleurs de Poesie Moderne" ; "Rambles in Northumberland" etc. ; and "Scenes and Recollections of | Fly Fishing."

p. (8) "Popular Juvenile Books" ; seven books in all. Imprint at foot : "Whiting, London."

(2) Slip :—Effingham Wilson, Junior, "The Parterre" ; 4 pp. unnumbered. ($6\frac{3}{4}'' \times 4\frac{3}{8}''$).

p. (1) "Specimen of the Engravings" with 2 woodcuts.

p. (2) "The Parterre."

p. (3) Contents of Volumes I and II.

p. (4) Contents of Volumes III. and IV. Imprint at foot : "Manning and Smithson, Printers, Ivy-lane."

(3) "Works | Published by W. S. Orr and Co., London ; | and | W. & R. Chambers, Edinburgh." 8 pp. numbered (1)–8. Pages 2–8 are each headed : "Works Published by W. S. Orr and Co." Imprint at foot of p. 8 : "Bradbury and Evans, Printers, Whitefriars, London."

(4) "Speedily will be Published, . . . | Jennings | Landscape Annual, | for 1837, or | Tourist in Spain :" 4 pp. unnumbered, Yellow Paper. Imprint at foot of p. (4) : "Maurice & Co., Printers, Fenchurch Street."

(5) "Geo. Henekey and Compy." 4 pp., same as in Part 8, except on Pink paper.

PLATES (Two)

(No. 20) "Mr. Weller attacks the Executive of Ipswich" ; Page 254 ; signed "Phiz del."

Pickwick's right thumb is turned in.

(No. 21) "Job Trotter encounters Sam in Mr. Muzzle's Kitchen" ; Page 265 ; signed "Phiz del."

Clock shows ten minutes to twelve.

The present writer has in his possession, specimens of the above two plates with the "page-number" etched in a different manner to that on the generally known first impressions. It is difficult to describe the variations, but they are probably early proof copies, and not to be regarded as having precedence over the ordinary published etchings.

TEXT, WITH HEADING
"Chapter XXIV." pp. 243-274. (U. X. in sixteens).
  p. 260, line 29 : "hodling" for "holding."
  p. 261, signature at foot is misprinted "N2" instead of "X2."
    This "point" is an extremely rare one, and has not been previously recorded. Only twice has it come under writer's notice.
  p. 267, the figure "7" in pagination is slightly raised above other figures.

TEXT MEASUREMENTS
  Extreme depth of pages :—

pp. 254, 261, 270	=	$174\frac{1}{2}$ mm.
pp. 243, 259, 267, 268	=	$173\frac{3}{4}$,,
pp. 245, 253	=	173 ,,
pp. 244, 246, 249–262, 260, 262–266, 269, 271–273	=	$171\frac{1}{4}$,,
p. 248	=	$170\frac{1}{2}$,,
pp. 247, 255, 256	=	$169\frac{3}{4}$,,
pp. 257, 258	=	$166\frac{1}{2}$,,
p. 274	=	119 ,,

PART 10.

FRONT WRAPPER (OUTSIDE)
  Same as No. IV. except "No. X."

FRONT WRAPPER (INSIDE)
  "Popular Works just Published." Charles Tilt's list of Eight books.

BACK WRAPPER (INSIDE)
  "Splendid New Year's Gift. | ... | The Pictorial Album" ; and below : "No. 10 of | The Library of Fiction."

THE PICKWICK PAPERS.

BACK WRAPPER (OUTSIDE)
"Splendidly Illustrated Works, | Just Published by Charles
Tilt, Fleet Street." Followed by Seven book titles.

ADVERTISEMENTS (FRONT)
"The Pickwick Advertiser." 16 pp. unnumbered.

p. (1) "New Works, | printed for | Longman, Rees, Orme,
Brown, Green, and Longman." Eight titles, each
numbered I–VIII.

p. (2) "Edited by Theodore Hook, Esq., | . . . | Colburn's New
Monthly Magazine." Below, in half measure, three other
advertisements.

p. (3) "3, St. James's Square, December 27th, 1836. | Mr.
Macrone will speedily publish the following New Works."
Follows six titles, each numbered I–VI; and below:
"Also, just published, | . . . | Crichton"; numbered "I."

p. (4) Continuation of Macrone. Two titles, numbered "II and
III." Lower half of page: "Illustrated Edition of |
Captain Marryat's Novels." (Saunders and Otley).

p. (5) "Edited by Boz, and Illustrated by George Cruikshank.
| . . . | Bentley's Miscellany." Followed by Richard
Bentley's "Elegant and cheap Christmas Presents."

p. (6) "Travelling and Hunting Maps," and five other books.
Chapman and Hall.

p. (7) (½ col.) "Vol. XXVIII. of The Mirror of | Literature . . ."
and Eight other advertisements.

p. (8) "Popular Juvenile Books." In half measures, seven titles,
and below: "Second Edition. | . . . | Nursery Govern-
ment."

p. (9) "This day is published, . . . | Hood's Comic Annual."
Followed by: "The Complete Works of Lord Byron";
"Modern Domestic Medicine"; and "Annuals for 1837."

p. (10) "Cribbage, Chess, and Draughts," published by Sher-
wood, Gilbert, and Piper. Below: "Edited by W.
Harrison Ainsworth, Esq., and illustrated by George |
Cruikshank, Esq. | . . . No. 1 . . . of | The Lions of
London." Printed for John Macrone.

p. (11) "Corporation of the London Assurance," whole page,
signed at foot: "John Laurence, Secretary."

57

p. (12) "Mr. S. G. Taylor's | Offices for Landed and House Property"; "Gold Watches. | A. B. Savory & Sons," with two illustrations of watches; and "Allingham's Corn Cure."

p. (13) Woodhouse's "Balsam of Spermaceti" in half measure; "Beaver Hats, 21s."; and "Without injuring the Hair or soiling the Skin."

p. (14) "Genuine British Wine." Full page as in Part 9.

p. (15) "Important New Invention!—The | ANDROMETER! Followed by, in half measure: "To Invalids"; and "Messrs. Delcroix and Co."

p. (16) "New Year's Gifts" (Rowlands); and "Gowland's Lotion"; half page to each.

A definite point of priority in issue arises with Part X "Pickwick Advertiser." As noted above, page 10 carries an announcement of "No. 1 of the Lions of London," edited by Harrison Ainsworth. Difficulty was experienced in respect to the use of this title, and the Publisher was compelled to withdraw it from circulation, which entailed a withdrawal of all publicity matter. Page 10 of the "Advertiser" was reset, and "The Poetic Wreath" advertisement substituted to fill the gap thus made.

ADVERTISEMENTS (BACK)
(1) "Literary Announcement. | Omitted Stanzas of Don Juan : [Hitherto unpublished.]" These two lines are followed by five lines of supposedly bibliographical facts, and below are three verses of 8 lines each, advertising Rowland's Macassar Oil, Kalydor, and Odonto. 1 leaf, verso blank.

(2) James Fraser's Announcements. 2 pp. unnumbered.

p. (1) "Ryall's Portraits of Eminent Conservative | Statesmen"; and, "Finden's and Ryall's Portraits of the Female | Aristocracy of Great Britain."

p. (2) "Fraser's Magazine for 1837"; "The Reliques of Father Prout"; "Recollections of Sir Walter Scott, Bart."; and "Fraser's Panoramic Plan of London."

PLATES (TWO)
 (No. 22) "Christmas Eve at Mr. Wardle's" ; Page 296 ;
   signed "Phiz del."
   First plate : With Dog and Kitten in foreground.
   Second plate : No ,,   ,,   ,,   ,,
   This plate has been seen without pagination. The Dexter collection contains a specimen, and another collector has a copy. In
   the absence of further confirmation, we should regard these as
   proof impressions before the page-number was etched on the
   steel.

 (No. 23) "The Goblin and the Sexton" ; Page 301 ; signed
   "Phiz del."
   First plate : With face in the middle of tree-trunk.
   Second plate : No ,,   ,,   ,,   ,,

ADDRESS, BY THE AUTHOR
 A single leaf, printed one side only, commencing :
   "Ten months have now elapsed since the appearance
   of the first number | of the Pickwick Papers." Contains
   five paragraphs, and is dated at foot : "December 1836."
   Extreme length of Text, $6\frac{9}{16}$ inch.
   The first issue of this address is known by the omission of a
   dash (—) or any other punctuation mark, following the word
   "performance" at the end of fourth paragraph. The dash was
   afterwards inserted, and is present in the major portion of copies
   which call for the leaflet.

TEXT, WITH HEADING
 "Chapter XXVII." pp. 275–306. (Y. Z. in sixteens).

TEXT MEASUREMENTS
 Extreme depth of pages :—

pp. 275–277	=	$174\frac{1}{2}$ mm.
pp. 291, 293	=	173 ,,
pp. 280, 282, 297, 298	=	$171\frac{1}{4}$,,
pp. 278, 286–290, 300	=	$170\frac{1}{2}$,,
pp. 281, 283–285, 292, 294–296, 299, 302–305	=	$169\frac{3}{4}$,,
p. 301	=	169 ,,
p. 279	=	$166\frac{1}{2}$,,
p. 306	=	149 ,,

CHARLES DICKENS.

PART 11.

FRONT WRAPPER (OUTSIDE)
Same as No. IV. except "No. XI."

FRONT WRAPPER (INSIDE)
"New Engravings | recently | Published by Ackermann
& Co., 96, Strand." A series of 27 plates are listed.

BACK WRAPPER (INSIDE)
"In the course of this month will be published, | Weeds of
Witchery, | in a series of Poems, by Thomas Haynes
Bayly, Esq." Published by Ackermann & Co.

BACK WRAPPER (OUTSIDE)
"This day is published, price Sixpence, | The February
number (XX) of | The | Magazine of Domestic
Economy." Below :—"Cage Birds"; and titles of
Three Hand-books.

ADVERTISEMENTS (FRONT)
"The Pickwick Advertiser." 8 pp. unnumbered.

p. (1) "By Charles Dickens, Esq. | Author of | 'The Pickwick
Papers,' &c. | 3, St. James's Square, January 30." Mr.
Macrone announces "Sketches by 'Boz'" the First
Series, Third Edition ; and the Second Series, Second
Edition.

p. (2) "Valuable New Works, | Published by A. H. Baily and
Co., No. 83, Cornhill, | London." Below, in half column
measure, Twelve Titles of Works, the first Eleven
numbered I–XI.

p. (3) "Fraser's Magazine | for 1837. | Second Edition of the
January number."

p. (4) "The New Comic Periodical Work, | Edited by 'Boz,'
| . . . | Bentley's Miscellany." Below, "The Standard
Novels and Romances," with list of 57 volumes.

p. (5) "Lodge's Portraits. | A new and cheap Edition," pub-
lished by William Smith. Followed by five other announcements, the last two in half measure.

p. (6) "Eruptions on the Skin." (M. O. Wray), half-page.
Lower half : G. Minter's chairs, with three cuts.

p. (7) Half-page in half measure ; Woodhouse's Remedies, the first, "Balsam of Spermaceti." Below : Cornelius Dicker ; W. Day and Co., and Robert Wiss.

p. (8) " 'Cold blights the fairest Flowers, and Blossoms fade before it.' " (Rowland's Kalydor, etc.). Lower half of page : "The Mirror of Beauty" (Gowlands).

PLATES (TWO)
(No. 24) "Mr. Pickwick slides" ; Page 313 ; signed "Phiz del."
First plate : Has four stakes embedded in the ice.
Second plate : Has five   „   „   „   „

(No. 25) "The first interview with Mr. Serjeant Snubbin" ; page 326 ; signed "Phiz del."
First plate : Has roll of paper in centre of floor.
Second plate : No   „   „   „   „

TEXT, WITH HEADING
"Chapter XXIX." pp. 307–338. (AA. BB. in sixteens).

TEXT MEASUREMENTS
Extreme depth of pages :—

pp. 309, 323, 325, 326, 333, 336, 337	= 174½ mm.
pp. 307, 310–314, 316–322, 324, 328–332, 334, 335	= 171¼ „
p. 308	= 168¼ „
p. 315	= 157 „
p. 327	= 147 „
p. 338	= 103 „

PART 12.

FRONT WRAPPER (OUTSIDE)
Same as No. IV. except "No. XII."

FRONT WRAPPER (INSIDE)
"New Works, | printed for | Longman, Rees, Orme, Brown, Green, & Longman." Eleven titles, each numbered, I–XI. Half column measure.

BACK WRAPPER (INSIDE)

"Important Invention in the Fine Arts. | Cowen & Waring's | Newly-invented | Caoutchouc, or India-Rubber Canvas, | for Oil Painting." With four Testimonials.

BACK WRAPPER (OUTSIDE)

"Fraser's Magazine for 1837. | Contents of the January Number (Second Edition)." Below: also "Contents of the February Number."

ADVERTISEMENTS (FRONT)

"The Pickwick Advertiser." 8 pp. unnumbered.

p. (1) Same as No. XI, except date is February 28, and three lines added at foot, giving "Agents for Mr. Macrone."

p. (2) "The | Pictorial History of England. | Prospectus." 37 lines continued to p. (3).

p. (3) Continuation from p. (2), with imprint at foot :— "London : | Charles Knight and Co., Ludgate Street."

p. (4) "New Edition of Lingard's England, | in Monthly Five Shilling Volumes." Also : "Le Cameleon"; "Dublin Penny Journal"; and "Music Made Easy"; all in half measure. "Heraldry" at foot in full measure.

p. (5) "The | Monthly Magazine | of | Politics, Literature, and Science." (Sherwood & Co.). Below, in half measure are five other advertisements.

p. (6) "Woodhouse's Ætherial Es- | sence of Ginger"; "A Substitute for Sarsapa- | rilla and Colchicum"; "Balsam of Spermaceti," and "Ringworm effectually Cured"; all in half measure. At foot, in full measure : "Without injuring the Hair or soiling the Skin."

p. (7) "Argus Life Assurance Company," signed at foot :— "E. Bates, Resident Director."

p. (8) " 'Cold blights the fairest Flowers, and Blossoms fade before it.' " (Rowland's Kalydor, half-page). Below :— "Delicacy of Complexion" (Gowlands), and "Caution" (Robert Wiss).

ADVERTISEMENTS (BACK)

Slip :—"Mechi's | Catalogue | of | Cutlery, &c. | Inventor of | the Magic Strop, | & | Paste. | No. 4 | Leadenhall

Street. | London. | Fourth House from Grace- | church Street." A booklet, trimmed to $4\frac{5}{8}'' \times 3\frac{1}{4}''$; 18 pp. printed on thin paper, and bound in a wrapper of slightly stouter substance : 22 pp. in all. Outside of wrapper (back and front) is printed in two colours, with the title as described appearing on the front ; the insides and outside back are blank. Numbered (1, 2)–18 ; consisting of a 12mo sheet (pp. 1–12), and three single leaves (pp. 13–18). Imprint at foot of last page : "Whiting, London." Printed in three or four varying coloured wrappers, for this, and Part 19/20.

PLATES (Two)

(No. 26) "The Valentine," signed "Phiz del" ; no page-number (page 343).

First plate, first state : No newspaper on floor   (1).

  ,,   ,, *second state :* ,,   ,,   ,,   ,,   (2).

Second plate, first state : With newspaper on floor   (1).

  ,,   ,, *second state :* ,,   ,,   ,,   ,,   (2).

(No. 27) "The Trial," signed "Phiz del" ; no page-number (page 358).

First plate, first state : No hat on front bench   (1).

  ,,   ,, *second state :* ,,   ,,   ,,   ,,   (2).

Second plate, first state : With hat on front bench   (1).

  ,,   ,, *second state :* ,,   ,,   ,,   ,,   (2).

Figure (1) denotes no page-number on plate.

Figure (2) denotes page-number is etched on plate.

Plate 27, *second plate, second state,* has "page 353" etched in error ; this was never corrected.

The earliest state of the original and duplicate plates to this Part 12, and all which follow, should have no etched page-number. It has repeatedly been stated and published, that they must carry the pagination, but this is not so ; the earliest states exist as described above.

TEXT, WITH HEADING
"Chapter XXXII." pp. 339–370. (CC. DD. in sixteens).
p. 341, lines 1 and 2 : correct reading of "inde-licate."
p. 341, line 5 : correct reading of "inscription."
p. 342, line 5 : with uncorrected "S. Veller."

TEXT MEASUREMENTS
Extreme depth of pages :—

p. 355	=	176¼ mm.
p. 341	=	175 „
pp. 347, 348, 351–354	=	174½ „
pp. 339, 357	=	173 „
pp. 340, 342, 343, 345–350, 356, 358–364, 368	=	171¼ „
p. 349	=	169¾ „
pp. 344, 365–367	=	168¼ „
p. 369	=	167 „
p. 370	=	150½ „
p. 351	=	140½ „

PART 13.

FRONT WRAPPER (OUTSIDE)
Same as No. IV. except "No. XIII."

FRONT WRAPPER (INSIDE)
"Important Invention in the Fine Arts. | Cowen & Waring's | Newly-invented | Caoutchouc, or India-Rubber Canvas." Same as Inside Back Wrapper of Part 12, except the substitution of one testimonial for another.

BACK WRAPPER (INSIDE)
"Price 8s . . . | Manly Exercises, | by Donald Walker." Below : "Exercises for Ladies"; and "Games and Sports."

BACK WRAPPER (OUTSIDE)
"New Works, | printed for | Longman, Rees, Orme, Brown, Green, & Longman." Eleven titles, each numbered I–XI ; the first ten set in half measure.

THE PICKWICK PAPERS.

Pigot's Coloured Views.   4 pp. unnumbered.

p. (1) "Prospectus.—Pigot's Coloured Views. | On the 1st of April, 1837, will be published, price Three Shillings, | Part I. | To be continued monthly, | of | A Series of Views | in | The Isle of Wight :"

p. (2) "The Percy Anecdotes," and, "The Olio" ; half page to each.

pp. (3–4) List of Cumberland's British and Minor Theatre : detailing Plays already published, Vols. I–XXXVI, and "Minor Theatre" Vols. I–XII.

> This inset has been noted in five copies only ; the first being one sold in London, November, 1921, by Col. K. H. M. Connal of Monkton, Ayrshire ; the second was in the "Hatton" copy sold in New York, December, 1927 ; the third is in the possession of Mr. Richard Gimbel ; the fourth appeared in the "Kern" sale, whilst a fifth is owned by a Liverpool collector.

"The Pickwick Advertiser."   16 pp. unnumbered.

p. (1) "3, St. James's Square, March 30. | Mr. Macrone has just ready the following | New and Standard Works." Ten titles, in two sections of five books each, numbered I–V respectively.

p. (2) "Publishing Monthly, price Sixpence, | The | Magazine of Domestic Economy." Below : "Cage Birds" and three other titles. All published by "W. S. Orr and Co. ; and W. and R. Chambers."

> Except for the first line, this page is identical with Outside Back Wrapper of Part XI.

p. (3) "New and Popular Work | . . . | Woodland Gleanings" and two others (Charles Tilt). "Oliver Twist" (Richard Bentley) ; and "Piso and the Præfect" (Smith, Elder, and Co.).

p. (4) "Flowers and Flower Gardens." Three titles (Saunders and Otley) ; "The British Legion in Spain" (Simpkin and Co.) ; "The | Monthly Magazine" (Sherwood and Co.) ; and in half measure at foot, two other announcements.

p. (5) "Published by Mr. Murray, Albemarle Street, | London." Eleven titles, each numbered, I–XI.

p. (6) "Mr. Curtis's New Works on the Ear | and Eye." "Lodge's Portraits" ; and four other announcements, all in half measure. At foot :—"Lithography" in full measure panel, with woodcut.

p. (7) "New and Popular Works, | printed and published by A. J. Valpy, M.A." Four titles, but numbered, I. II. III.

p. (8) "Travelling and Hunting Maps" ; "A Garland of Love" ; "The Poetic Wreath" ; and "The Artist" (Chapman and Hall).

p. (9) "Popular Juvenile Books, | Elegantly Embellished." Followed by, in half measure, seven titles : "Remember" ; "The Juvenile Pianist" ; "Poetry for Children" ; "The Two Cousins" ; "Caroline" ; "The Spoiled Child Reclaimed" ; and "Rose and Anne." Below, in full measure : "Fleurs de Poesie Moderne" and "Second Edition . . . | Nursery Government" (Chapman and Hall).

p. (10) "The Imperial Classics" (William Smith) ; "Caution" (Robert Wiss) ; "Ringworm effectually Cured" ; and G. Minter, with three woodcuts.

p. (11) "Extensive Robberies of Plate" (J. J. Rippon) ; "Without injuring the Hair or soiling the Skin" ; and "How to get a good Dressing ! ! !" : the latter in nine verses.

p. (12) "The Ageracome, | Pomade" ; "Candles" ; and "Silver Tea Services" (A. B. Savory and Sons) : with four illustrations of Tea-pots.

p. (13) ($\frac{1}{2}$ col.) "New Invention !" (Frost and Co.'s Blacking) ; "Morison's Pills" ; and three other announcements.

p. (14) "The Light of other Days." (Gowland's Lotion) ; and "Tyzack's Imperial Jet Black Ink."

p. (15) ($\frac{1}{2}$ col.) "T. Cox Savory, 47, Cornhill, London" ; and five other announcements ; the last : "Outfits to India and the | Colonies."

p. (16) "Indispensable for Personal Comfort and Attraction !" Rowland's Kalydor, etc.

Pages 8 and 9. Chapman & Hall's announcements in these pages : "Travelling and Hunting Maps," and "Popular Juvenile Books," respectively, appear for the first time in this exact form. The date of the first issue of Part 13 is April 1st, 1837, and it is important to note this, because it fixes approximately the date of issue of the well-known reprint-wrapper which carried these identical pages of advertisements. The text of page 8 was reproduced for inside of Back Wrapper, and that of page 9 for the outside.

THE PICKWICK PAPERS.

Advertisements (Back)

   (1) "This day is published, | . . . | The Third Monthly Part ; | . . . | Ward's Miscellany" ; Page 4 : "Prize Essay on Sailors." 4 pp. numbered (1)–4. Imprint at foot of p. 4 :— "W. Tyler, Printer, Bolt-court, Fleet-street."

   (2) "Argyll Rooms." Printed broadside across, with two illustrations of premises ; and : "J. Turrill | Manufacturer of | Dressing Cases . . ." Verso : in half measure : "Manufacturer of | Dressing Cases, Writing Desks." Imprint : "J. Bradley, Printer, 78, Great Titchfield-street, London." 2 pp. unnumbered.

> Alternatives to the above inset vary slightly in the imprint of J. Bradley. One has the line "St. Mary-le-Bone" instead of "London" ; and another shows the "y" in "Bradley" spaced out from the rest of the name.

Plates (Two)

   (No. 28) "The Card Room at Bath," signed "Phiz del" ; no page-number (page 382).

> *First plate :* The cards on the table are very faintly etched.
>
> *Second plate :* The cards are clearly defined.

   (No. 29) "Mr. Winkle's situation when the door blew to" ; signed "Phiz del" ; no page-number (page 391).

> *First plate :* Between the hat on ground and the shadow beneath, there is a distinctly clear space.
>
> *Second plate :* There is no space between the hat and shadow.

Text, with Heading

   "Chapter XXXIV," pp. 371-402. (EE. FF. in sixteens).

> p. 389, line 7 : "wi shI was" instead of "w ishI was."
>
> > Neither of these errors in spacing were ever corrected.
>
> p. 397, line 4 up : "I think" is unspaced.
>
> p. 400, line 21 : "this friends" instead of "his friends."

CHARLES DICKENS.

TEXT MEASUREMENTS
  Extreme depth of pages :—

pp. 371, 373, 381, 387, 389	=	$174\frac{1}{2}$ mm.
pp. 372, 374–377, 382, 383, 385, 386, 390, 401	=	$171\frac{1}{4}$,,
pp. 379, 392, 397, 399	=	$168\frac{1}{4}$,,
pp. 378, 380, 391, 394–396, 398, 400	=	$167\frac{1}{2}$,,
p. 393	=	$166\frac{1}{2}$,,
p. 402	=	161 ,,
p. 388	=	130 ,,
p. 384	=	123 ,,

PART 14.

FRONT WRAPPER (OUTSIDE)
  Same as No. IV. except "No. XIV."

FRONT WRAPPER (INSIDE)
  "Lodge's Portraits," and "The Imperial Classics." Imprint : "London : William Smith, 1, Bouverie Street."

BACK WRAPPER (INSIDE)
  "51, Paternoster Row, April 29, 1837. | E. Grattan begs respectfully to inform the Public that he has | bought . . . | The Court Magazine." Follows a list of 54 numbers, set in half measure.

BACK WRAPPER (OUTSIDE)
  "New Works | Published by Charles Tilt, Fleet-Street." Ten titles, set in half measure, each numbered I–X.

ADVERTISEMENTS (FRONT)
  "The Pickwick Advertiser. No. XIV. | [20,000 of the Advertizing Sheet will be Printed and Stitched in each Monthly | Number.]" 24 pp. unnumbered.
    p. (1) "The Naturalist's Library, conducted by Sir William Jardine, | . . . | The Birds of Western Africa" ; and four more titles, published by S. Highley. Below : Simpkin, Marshall and Co.'s announcement of Two books.

p. (2) "Popular Juvenile Books"; the page identical with Part 13, page 9.

p. (3) "The Wasp (embodied in woodcut) | No. 1 will appear on the 4th of May, Price 2d. | Address." Follows subject matter of Address in half measure, small type.

p. (4) "New Works, | published by | Charles Knight & Co., 22, Ludgate Street, London." In half measure, Four Works, the first :—"The Gallery of Portraits"; each numbered I–IV ; and continued to page (5).

p. (5) Continuation of page (4) ; Eleven Works, the first being : "The Book of Human Cha- | racter"; each numbered V–XV, and all in half measure.

p. (6) "In the Press. | Sketches of Young Ladies"; partly in half measure. Below :—"Malibran"; "The Rise and Progress of | the British Power in | India"; and "Gallery of Comicalities" : these three titles are all in half measure.

p. (7) "Now publishing in Monthly Parts. | The Engineer's and Mechanic's | Encyclopædia" and two other titles, each numbered I–III; published by Thomas Kelly. Below :—"Literature of France," by Jules Janin.

p. (8) "Books Published by Mr. Murray, Albemarle | Street, London. | ... | A New System of Domestic | Cookery"; and four other titles : each one numbered I–V.

p. (9) "Just published . . . | Pictures Picked from the Pickwick Papers, | by Alfred Crowquill." In half measure below : "J. Calvert, | Worker in Ivory"; and five more advertisements.

p. (10) "In the Press. | A Visit to | The British Museum"; "Splendid New Edition of Plays ! | Webster's Acting National Drama"; Chapman and Hall. Below : in half measure, "A Portrait of Boz"; "The Court Magazine"; and "First Impressions and Stu- | dies from Nature in Hin- | dostan."

p. (11) ($\frac{1}{2}$ col.) "The only Complete Picture | of London. | Kidd's London Directory"; and eight additional advertisements.

p. (12) ($\frac{1}{2}$ col.) "Compound Microscopes"; "Important to the Public"; and four others, one with woodcut.

p. (13) ($\frac{1}{2}$ col.) "Geary's New-invented | Stay" (whole column); "Horticultural Improve- | ment"; "The Vine Inn"; and "To all our Readers."

p. (14) (½ col.) "Dr. John Armstrong's Liver | Pills"; "Magic Drops"; "Deafness. | Mr. S. Maw, Acoustic In- | strument Maker"; "Just ready, . . . | Doveton"; "C. Campanari"; "Weak Legs, Knees, and Ankles"; and "French Sultana Paper."

p. (15) (½ col.) "Mineral Magnets"; and "Morison's Pills." Below, in full measure: "Reform your Tailors' Bills ! !" (E. P. Doudney & Son).

p. (16) (½ col.) "List of Articles" (Mechi); "The Splendid New Pin"; and three others.

p. (17) (½ col.) "A Chinese Tea Party"; "Outfits to India and the | Colonies"; and four other advertisements.

p. (18) (½ col.) "Balsam of Spermaceti"; "Woodhouse's Ætherial Es- | sence of Ginger"; and below in full measure: "Labern's Botanic Cream"; "Lithography" with wood-cut in panel; and "Caution" (Robert Wiss).

p. (19) "(Illustration) Tooth-Ache"; and "Address to the Public" (Brandreth's Pills).

p. (20) (½ col.) "The Severity of the | Weather"; "Influenza"; "Millinery"; "New Italian Company for | Select Musical Parties"; "To Anglers . . . | J. Cheek"; and "Riding Whips" (J. Cheek).

p. (21) "Splendid German Asters, Stocks, &c."; "White's Preservative Tooth Paste"; and "Interior Decorations of the Newest . . ." (I. F. Isherwood).

p. (22) "May Day !" Gowland's Lotion; and "Most Important Information"; G. Minter; with three woodcuts.

p. (23) "Charles Stewart"; "Hints to the Nervous and Dyspeptic"; "Candles"; "A. B. Savory and Sons, Goldsmiths," with two cuts of plated dishes; and "Without injuring the Hair or soiling the Skin."

p. (24) "Atmospheric Influence upon the Skin." (Rowland's Kalydor, etc.).

ADVERTISEMENTS (BACK)

"New Works, | printed for | Baldwin and Cradock, | Paternoster Row, London." 8 pp. numbered (1)–8. Pages 2–8 are each headed: "Baldwin and Cradock, Paternoster-Row." Imprint in left lower corner of Page 8: "C. Baldwin, Printer, | New Bridge-street, London."

PLATES (TWO)
(No. 30) "Conviviality at Bob Sawyer's"; signed "Phiz del," no page number (page 409).

> *First plate :* There is a book lying flat on top of the book-rack to right of window.
>
> *Second plate :* No book on top of book-rack.

(No. 31) "Mr. Pickwick sits for his Portrait"; signed "Phiz del," no page number (page 434).

> *First plate :* There is no star in the top centre pane of window.
>
> *Second plate :* All the three top panes have stars.

TEXT, WITH HEADING
"Chapter XXXVII." pp. 403-434. (GG. HH. in sixteens).

> p. 432, headline : letter "F" in "OF" is imperfect.

TEXT MEASUREMENTS
Extreme depth of pages :—

pp. 403, 405, 421	=	$174\frac{1}{2}$ mm.
p. 416	=	172 ,,
pp. 404, 406, 409–415, 417–419, 422, 425, 426, 429, 430	=	$171\frac{1}{4}$,,
pp. 407, 408, 420, 423, 424, 427, 428, 431-433	=	$168\frac{1}{4}$,,
p. 434	=	$158\frac{1}{2}$,,

PART 15.

FRONT WRAPPER (OUTSIDE)
Same as No. IV. except "No. XV."

FRONT WRAPPER (INSIDE)
"Just Published, price One Shilling each, Parts I. and II., . . . | Samuel Weller's | Illustrations | to | The Pickwick Club." (E. Grattan).

BACK WRAPPER (INSIDE)
"Splendidly Illustrated Work. | Cunningham's Gallery | of Pictures, | by the first Masters of | English and Foreign Schools." Imprint : "Rayner and Hodges,] [Shoe Lane, Fleet Street."

CHARLES DICKENS.

BACK WRAPPER (OUTSIDE)

"J. Sanger's | Genuine Patent & Public Medicine Ware-house, | 150, Oxford Street, opposite Bond Street."

ADVERTISEMENTS (FRONT)

"The Pickwick Advertiser. No. XV. | [20,000 of the Advertising Sheet will be Printed and Stitched in each Monthly | Number.]" 16 pp. unnumbered.

p. (1) "Mr. Saxby | Begs to acquaint his Friends . . . of his Academy"; "Superior School Books"; and "This day is published . . . | Hints on Etiquette, and the Usages | of Society."

p. (2) (½ col.) "Just published . . . | Cobbett's Political Works"; "Thomas's Burlesque Drama"; "Yarrell's British Birds"; and Seven other advertisements.

p. (3) "New Works." Twelve titles, each numbered 1–12; published by Longman and Co.

p. (4) "Books of Entertainment and Instruction | for Young Persons." Ten titles, each numbered I–X. Below: "New Books Published by Mr. Murray." Eight titles, each numbered I–VIII. All the 18 titles published by John Murray.

p. (5) "Guide Books | for Travellers on the Continent." Fifteen titles, each numbered I–XV. John Murray.

p. (6) (½ col.) "Just published . . . | Short's System of Short- | hand"; "New Music"; and Five other advertisements.

p. (7) (½ col.) "Just published . . . | The Ladies' Science of Eti- | quette"; "Flowers of Fiction"; "Advice to Proprietors"; and "The Queer-Fish Society."

p. (8) "The Hippodrome; | at Bayswater, Near Hyde Park." Whole page.

p. (9) "Now ready . . . | The Magazine of Domestic Economy," Orr and Co.; and Five other announcements; the last, "Pictures Picked from the Pickwick Papers, | by Alfred Crowquill"; Ackermann and Co.

p. (10) (½ col.) "Now ready . . . | The Golden Rules of Life"; "The Pocket-Book of Eti- | quette"; and Four other announcements.

p. (11) (½ col.) "Court Mourning"; "French Wool Mattresses"; "Lever Watches"; and Five other advertisements.

p. (12) (½ col.) "The Original Patent Pin"; "The Splendid New Pin"; "Court Blacking"; "Watches"; and Four others.

p. (13) ($\frac{1}{2}$ col.) Royal Arms—"Important Reasons for using | Bett's Patent Brandy"; "Fine Wines"; "To Pedestrians, Sportsmen, &c."; and Six other announcements.

p. (14) "Elegancies for the Toilet. | . . . | Gowland's Lotion"; "Caution" (Robert Wiss); and "Ede's Odoriferous Compound," set in panel, with cut of Royal Arms.

p. (15) "Embroidery"; "British Consul's Office, | Philadelphia," with illustration; "How to get a good Dressing !!!" printed sideways; and "List of Articles" (Mechi).

p. (16) "Rowland's Kalydor"; "Rowland's Macassar Oil"; and "Rowland's Odonto, or Pearl Dentifrice."

ADVERTISEMENTS (BACK)

(1) "Established 1820 | John James Rippon's | Furnishing Ironmongery Warehouses," 4 pp. numbered (1)–4. Imprint at foot of p. 4: "J. Bradley, Printer, 78, Great Titchfield-street, London." Yellow paper.

(2) "Caledonia Illustrata. | New Work by Dr. Beattie." Verso with imprint: "Johnson, Printer, Lovell's Court, St. Paul's." 2 pp. together with "Specimen Plate of Dr. Beattie's 'Scotland Illustrated';" verso blank; the whole forming a 4-paged inset on thick white paper.

(3) "Prize Essay on Sailors. | . . . | Britannia." 2 pp. numbered on second page; with imprint at foot: "T. C. Savill, Printer, 107, St. Martin's Lane, Charing Cross."

(4) Allan Bell and Co.'s Publications. 8 pp., pages 4, 7, and 8 numbered.

   p. (1) "In Parts . . . | . . . | The | Artist's Portfolio."
   p. (2) "Advertisement"; partly in half measure.
   p. (3) "Literary Novelties": with Critical Notices.
   p. 4. Continuation of p. 3, in half measure.
   p. (5) "Unique Illustrated Classical Library," etc.
   pp. (6), 7, 8: "Diamond Pocket Editions | of the | Holy Bible, Common Prayer"; announcing Sixteen publications. Imprint at foot of p. 8: "Baine, Printer, Gracechurch-street."

(5) "Apsley Pellatt ; | . . . | Glass Manufacturer and Cutter." 4 pp. unnumbered, printed in blue, and with illustrations of glass-ware on each page. Imprint at foot of p. (4) : "M. & W. Collis, Printers, 104, Bishops-gate-street Within."

(6) "The Popular Works of Mr. Peter Parley, | Voyager, Traveller, and Story-Teller." Below this heading is illustration of an eye. Verso : announcement of Six works, each numbered 1–6. 2 pp. unnumbered.

(7) "Royal Beulah Spa & Gardens, | Norwood." Woodcut of Royal Arms at head of page. Verso, with imprint : "Vizetelly, Branston & Co., Printers, 76, Fleet Street." 2 pp. unnumbered. Printed on either Grey, Pink, Blue, or Green paper.

PLATES (TWO)
(No. 32) "The Wardens' Room" ; signature irregular, no page-number (p. 441).
First plate : Signed " Phiz del."
Second plate : Unsigned.

(No. 33) "Discovery of Jingle in the Fleet" ; signature irregular, no page-number (p. 453).
First plate : Signed " Phiz."
Second plate : Signed " Phiz del."

ADDRESS (TO FOLLOW PLATES)
Written by Dickens. 4 pp., numbered on pages 3 and 4.

> p. (1) "186, Strand, June 30, 1837. | Address." Contains 22 lines, and at foot : "Notice to Correspondents," six lines.

> p. (2) "New Works | published by Chapman and Hall. | In One Volume . . . | Sketches of Young Ladies" ; and below : "A few Words on a few Wines."

> p. (3) Chapman & Hall announce the Third Edition of Sketches by "Boz," First Series ; and the Second Edition of the Second Series.

p. (4) "Works in the Press"; announcing Three works: "A Visit to | The British Museum"; "Morals from the Church-Yard"; and "Tales & Stories for Young People." Two entirely different settings of this "Address" are known, varying in the fount of type used.

TEXT, WITH HEADING
"Chapter XL." pp. 435–466. (I I. K K. in sixteens).

TEXT MEASUREMENTS
Extreme depth of pages :—

pp. 437, 449, 451, 457	=	174½ mm.
pp. 435, 436, 438–443, 445–448, 450, 452–456, 458–465	=	171¼ ,,
p. 444	=	143 ,,
p. 466	=	126½ ,,

PART 16.

FRONT WRAPPER (OUTSIDE)
Same as No. IV. except "No. XVI," and an additional imprint at foot: "Bradbury and Evans,] [Printers, Whitefriars."

FRONT WRAPPER (INSIDE)
"An Important Addition to the Pickwick Papers! | Just published. . . Parts I. to III. of | Samuel Weller's | Illustrations | to | The Pickwick Club." (E. Grattan.)

BACK WRAPPER (INSIDE)
"New Works on India, | published by Wm. H. Allen & Co., 7, Leadenhall Street." Fourteen titles of Works, each numbered I–XIV.

BACK WRAPPER (OUTSIDE)
"New Works in the Press, | by A. H. Baily and Co., | 83, Cornhill." Five announcements. Imprint of Bradbury and Evans as on front cover.

ADVERTISEMENTS (FRONT)
"The Pickwick Advertiser. No. XVI. | [20,000 of the Advertising Sheet will be Printed and Stitched in each Monthly | Number.]" 8 pp. unnumbered.

CHARLES DICKENS.

p. (1) "New Works | Published by Chapman and Hall, 186, Strand. | . . . | Third Edition | Sketches of Young Ladies" ; and "A few Words on a few Wines."

p. (2) "Sketches by 'Boz'" ; announcing both the First and Second Series in two paragraphs. Below : "The Bridal."

p. (3) "Just Published . . . | Saunders' Portraits and Memoirs | of the most eminent | Living Political Reformers." Below, in half measure : "Guides for Travellers" ; and Five other announcements.

p. (4) "Seventh Edition . . . | Instructions to Young Sportsmen." Below, in half measure : "Green's Diseases of the | Skin" ; and "New Music." Set in full measure : "Circulating Expanding Dining Tables" etc. ; and again in half measure : "Ringworm effectually | Cured" ; and "Extract of Roses for | washing the Hair."

p. (5) ($\frac{1}{2}$ col.) "To Pedestrians, Sportsmen, &c." ; "The Bloom of Ninon de | l'Enclos." ; and Six other advertisements.

p. (6) "The Elections. | . . . | Gowland's Lotion" ; "French Wool Mattresses" ; and "List of Articles" (Mechi).

p. (7) ($\frac{1}{2}$ col.) "Embroidery" ; "The Original Patent Pin" ; "Dr. John Armstrong's | Liver Pills" ; and below, in full measure : "Reform your Tailors' Bills ! !"

p. (8) "Rowland's Kalydor" ; "Rowland's Macassar Oil" ; and "Rowland's Odonto," etc.

PLATES (Two)

(No. 34) "The Red-nosed man Discourseth" ; signed "Phiz del," no page number (page 484).

First plate : The legs of Sam's chair are turned, and not square.

Second plate : Legs of chair are unturned, and square.

(No. 35) "Mrs. Bardell encounters Mr. Pickwick in the prison" ; signed "Phiz del," no page number (page 498).

First plate : There is a hand-rail on left of steps, and a cockade in Sam's hat.

Second plate : No hand-rail, and no cockade.

TEXT, WITH HEADING

"Chapter XLIII." pp. 467-498. (L L. M M. in sixteens).

76

TEXT MEASUREMENTS
  Extreme depth of pages :—

p. 485	=	175 mm.
pp. 467–472, 478–481, 483, 484, 486–489, 491–497	=	171¼ ,,
pp. 473–476, 482	=	168¼ ,,
p. 490	=	158½ ,,
p. 498	=	132 ,,
p. 477	=	111 ,,

PART 17.

FRONT WRAPPER (OUTSIDE)
  Same as No. XVI. except "No. XVII."

FRONT WRAPPER (INSIDE)
  "Chubb's New Patent Detector Lock. | 57, St. Paul's Churchyard." Below : "Chubb's Patent Combination Latch."

BACK WRAPPER (INSIDE)
  "Fourth Edition. | In One Volume, . . . | Sketches of Young Ladies ; | . . . | by Quiz." Below : "Webster's Acting National Drama." (Chapman and Hall).

BACK WRAPPER (OUTSIDE)
  "The Nobility, Gentry, and their Gardeners, | are recommended to peruse the New | Horticultural Newspaper, | . . . | Gardeners' | Gazette." Imprint : "Bradbury and Evans, Printers, Whitefriars."

ADVERTISEMENTS (FRONT)
  "The Pickwick Advertiser. No. XVII. | [The impression of the Advertising Sheet is limited to 20,000—but the circulation of the Work being 26,000, that number of Bills is required.]" 8 pp. unnumbered.

  p. (1) "Popular Juvenile Books," the page identical with Part 13, page 9 ; and Part 14, page 2.

  p. (2) "Price One Shilling. | A few Words on a few Wines" ; and "Travelling and Hunting Maps" ; Chapman and Hall, half page. Below, in half measure : "Dodsley's and Rivington's | Annual Register for 1836"; "Historical and Statistical | Account of New South Wales"; and Three announcements of Scott, Webster, and Geary.

p. (3) (½ col.) "Baths"; "Grouse, Partridge, and Pheasant | Shooting"; "My Book"; and Six other advertisements.

p. (4) Illustration of Spectacles.—"Adam's Improved Spectacles"; "Prepared Metallic Labels"; "List of Articles" (Mechi); and in half measure: Three other announcements.

p. (5) (½ col.) "Important to the Nervous . . . | Harvey's Restorative Cor- | dial"; "Furs"; "Comfort to the Feet"; "Mineral Magnets"; "Extract of Roses for | washing the Hair"; and T. Cox Savory, with two woodcuts.

p. (6) "The Modern Toilette | . . . | Gowland's Lotion"; and "Crosby-Hall Wine Establishment."

p. (7) (½ col.) "Teeth"; "The Original Patent Pin"; and Four others. Below, in full measure and printed sideways: "How to get a good Dressing ! ! !"

p. (8) "To Families." (Rowland's Kalydor, and Rowland's Odonto).

An inset which has twice come under notice, is a single leaf, 8vo, entitled: "Philosophy of the Eye," printed on one side only, and preceding the "Advertiser." The Bruton copy contained it, as also did one owned by the present writer some years ago. Even with the best of intentions to establish every possible component of an ideal "Pickwick," the evidence of two copies is scarcely sufficient guarantee of the Publishers' programme or intentions at time of issue. The inset may have been a genuine and integral unit of Part 17, but the probabilities are that it is one of the many instances of the bookseller inserting after publication. Two copies in a circulation of possibly 30,000, hardly justify the right of inclusion in a definitive collation.

ADVERTISEMENTS (BACK)

(1) "To the Nobility, Families, Keepers of Hotels, Schools, | and all Large Consumers of Tea. | The Tea Establishment, | 4 & 5, King William Street, | City, London, | (near the Mansion House)."

One leaf, verso blank. (Ridgway, Sidney & Co.).

There are Two Issues, both identical in text, although slightly differing in set-up of the subject matter. The most easily perceivable difference is in the 6th line of heading, "Near the

Mansion House." One version of this line is set-up in solid-faced, the other in open letter type.

(2) John Amesbury's Patent Spine Supports, with three large woodcuts. Four leaves, printed one side only of each leaf, pages 1, 4, 5 and 8 being blank.

p. (2) Fig. 1, of deformed girl, and below, seven lines of descriptive matter.

p. (3) Fig. 2, of girl wearing support, followed by ten lines.

p. (6) Fig. 3, of girl fully dressed, followed by five lines.

p. (7) Continuation of subject matter from page (6).

(3) "Edinburgh, September 1837. | Life of Sir Walter Scott, Bart. | by J. G. Lockhart, Esq., | his Literary Executor." 16 pp. all numbered, except pp. 1, 2, 3 and 16. Imprint on last page : "Robert Cadell, Edinburgh : Whittaker & Co., London."

PLATES (Two)

(No. 36) "Mr. Winkle returns under extraordinary circumstances" ; signed "Phiz del" ; no page number (p. 504).

First plate : The top shelf on right is empty.

Second plate : Two bottles on top shelf.

(No. 37) "The Ghostly passengers in the ghost of a mail" ; signed "Phiz del" ; no page number (p. 523).

First plate : The bundle at the right of lantern is not corded. Signature in small letters.

Second plate : Bundle is corded. Signature in caps.

ADDRESS, BY THE PUBLISHERS

"New Work by 'Boz' " ; seven lines announcing an Entirely New Work, the first number to appear on the 31st of March, 1838. Lower half of page headed : "Sketches by 'Boz.' " Ten lines follow, notifying the publication in Twenty Monthly Numbers, the first to appear on the 1st of November. Dated at foot, August 26, 1837. Verso : "New Works | Preparing for Publication," with three announcements : "The

CHARLES DICKENS.

Juvenile Budget"; "Morals from the Church-Yard"; and "A Visit to | The British Museum." 2 pp. unnumbered.

Eight distinct issues of this Address have been traced, differing four times in the fount of type employed for the headlines to both sections of announcements on page (1). The length of the three sets of double-ruling which separate headlines and text, vary in every instance. The text apparently was not disturbed in any of the eight issues, although text measurements disclose many fractional differences in alignment.

TEXT, WITH HEADING
"Chapter XLVI." pp. 499–530. (N N. O O. in sixteens).

TEXT MEASUREMENTS
Extreme depth of pages :—

p. 501	=	178 mm.
p. 499	=	176¼ „
p. 515	=	175 „
pp. 502, 517	=	174½ „
p. 508	=	173 „
pp. 500, 503–507, 509–514, 516, 518–529	=	171¼ „
p. 530	=	152 „

PART 18.

FRONT WRAPPER (OUTSIDE)
Same as No. XVI. except "No. XVIII."

FRONT WRAPPER (INSIDE)
"An Important Addition to the Pickwick Papers ! | Just published . . . Parts I. to V. of | Weller's Illustrations | to | The Pickwick Club." Followed by : "Gilbert's New Map of the World" and "Gilbert's New Map of Europe." (E. Grattan.)

BACK WRAPPER (INSIDE)
"Shortly will be published, | Under the Superintendence of Mr. Charles Heath. | Gems of Beauty, for 1838." With five other announcements, all published by Longmans.

BACK WRAPPER (OUTSIDE)

"Splendid Annuals for 1838. | Mr. Tilt will publish early in October, | Finden's Tableaux"; and four other announcements. Imprint of Bradbury and Evans as Part 16.

ADVERTISEMENTS (FRONT)

"October 2, 1837. | The Pickwick Advertiser. No. XVIII. | [The impression of the Advertising Sheet is limited to 20,000,—but the circulation | of the Work being 29,000, that number of Bills is required.]" 16 pp. unnumbered.

p. (1) "On the 2nd of October, 1837, will be published . . . | Pictorial Edition of the Book of | Common Prayer."

p. (2) "London, Sep. 30, 1837. | Messrs. Fisher and Co. | will publish the following Works . . ." Thirteen titles are detailed.

p. (3) "In October will be published, | Jennings' | Landscape Annual for 1838."

p. (4) ($\frac{1}{2}$ col.) "Uniform with Rogers' 'Poems' and 'Italy.' | . . . | The Poetical Works of | Thomas Campbell"; with Nine other announcements of Publishers and Booksellers.

p. (5) "On the Second of October, | . . . | Sketches in London." Published by Wm. S. Orr and Co.

p. (6) "Portraits of Celebrated Thorough-Bred Stallions"; and below, in half measure : Six further announcements.

p. (7) "New Works nearly ready. | In One Volume . . . | The Juvenile Budget"; and Five other titles. Chapman and Hall.

p. (8) ($\frac{1}{2}$ col.) "The Corn Trade"; and Eight other announcements.

p. (9) "The Universal Life Assurance Society"; "Hunting or Riding"; and "Wood and Barrett" with illustration of Self-acting Oven and Kitchen Range.

p. (10) ($\frac{1}{2}$ col.) "To Pedestrians, Sportsmen, &c."; "Dr. John Armstrong's Liver Pills"; and Six other announcements.

p. (11) ($\frac{1}{2}$ col.) "In Chancery"; and Six other announcements; the last with illustration of Cruet Stand.

p. (12) "Pittis & Co.'s. | Isle of Wight Arenean Soap"; "Labern's Botanic Cream"; "Laming's Tasteless . . . Salts"; "J. C. & C. Penn, Boot and Shoe Manufacturers"; with view of premises.

p. (13) "French Wool Mattresses" ; "British Consul's Office" ; with illustration ; "Adam's Improved Spectacles," with cut of spectacles ; and "List of Articles" (Mechi).

p. (14) "Influence. | . . . | Gowland's Lotion" ; and "Crosby-Hall Wine Establishment."

p. (15) ($\frac{1}{2}$ col.) "To Architects, Surveyors, | and Artists Generally" ; "To Landed Proprietors" ; and "Comfort to the Feet" ; and below, in full measure : "Reform your Tailors' Bills ! !"

p. (16) "Rowland's | Kalydor" and "Rowland's | Odonto."

ADVERTISEMENTS (BACK)

(1) "To the Nobility, Families, Keepers of Hotels, Schools, and all Large | Consumers of Tea. | The | New Tea Establishment, | 37, and 38, Gracechurch Street (near London Bridge), | Opened on the 2nd September, 1837." Follows an address beginning : "In opening the above extensive premises for the Sale of Tea . . ." ; and lower on page is price list of "Green Tea" in twelve lines.

One leaf, verso blank. (Lashmar & Bellingham.)

This publicity must not be confused with that of Ridgway, Sidney & Co.'s in Part 17, as many made-up copies have been seen with the two transposed. Here also are two issues, the notable difference being the list of prices, where in one it is set in *small type*, whilst the other is in *black-faced*.

(2) "The History of the French Revolution, | will be published September 30, 1837." (By M. A. Thiers). Below is an almost full-paged engraving of figures and incidents relative to the Work. At foot : "Richard Bentley, New Burlington Street. Verso contains the textual matter. 2 pp. unnumbered.

(3) "Simpson's Herbal Pills | The Best & Cheapest For | Coughs, Asthmas & Consumptions" ; the whole in a panelled block. In the first line below this, the word "Simpson's" appears in heavy caps. 2 pp. unnumbered, printed both sides in blue.

Four different printings of this leaflet were in use, the word "Simpson's" in two patterns of type, one heavy solid-faced, and the other a heavy decorative one. Apart from many other points of difference, the clues below are sufficient to indicate the four variants.

(1)"Simpson's" solid faced. In the fourth paragraph printed in small type, the fourth line ends : 'at all in.''

(2)   „   solid faced. Fourth line ends : "at all in a.''

(3)   „   solid faced. Fourth line ends : "at all in a recum-''

(4)   „   heavy decorative. Fourth line ends : "at all in a recumbent.''

(4) "Works | published by | J. J. Dubochet and Co.'' Announces Ten publications, each numbered I.-X. (pp. 1–4) : "Works | published by | Joseph Thomas''; twenty-four books listed, each numbered I.-XXIV. (pp. 5–8). In all, 8 pp. unnumbered. Imprint on last page : "Willoughby & Co., Printers, 109 Goswell Street, London.''

Although the above consists of two entirely separate announcements by different Publishers, yet the whole is an 8-paged sheet printed and issued as such by the printers, Willoughby & Co., and it is accordingly treated here as one inset of 8 pages.

PLATES (Two)

(No. 38) "Mr. Bob Sawyer's mode of travelling" ; signed "Phiz del'' ; no page number (p. 533).

First plate : There is no bundle on Irishman's stick. Signature very small to left of centre.

Second plate : Bundle appears on stick. Signature in centre of plate.

(No. 39) "The Rival Editors" ; signed "Phiz del'' ; no page number (p. 553).

First plate : Side of dresser has no toasting fork and jug. Signature very small to left of centre.

Second plate : Dresser has toasting fork and jug. Signature in centre of plate.

ADDRESS, BY THE PUBLISHERS

"186, Strand, | September 29, 1837 | Completion | of | The Pickwick Papers." Nine lines ; followed by eight lines, "New Work by 'Boz.' '' Verso : "Sketches by 'Boz' | | Complete in One Volume, Uniform with The Pickwick Papers." 2 pp. unnumbered.

CHARLES DICKENS.

Text, with Heading
"Chapter XLIX." pp. 531-562. (P P. Q Q. in sixteens).

Text Measurements
Extreme depth of pages :—

p. 549	=	178 mm.
p. 559	=	175 ,,
pp. 531, 547, 550, 551	=	174½ ,,
p. 555	=	173¾ ,,
pp. 532–534, 537–539, 542–544, 548, 552–554, 556–558, 560, 561	=	171¼ ,,
pp. 535, 536, 540, 541, 555, 556	=	168¼ ,,
p. 562	=	133 ,,

Parts 19 and 20.

Front Wrapper (Outside)
Same as No. XVI. except "Nos. XIX–XX. Price 2s." ; together with the omission of the bracket before "Price" and the two around imprint at foot.

Front Wrapper (Inside)
"Just Published, | . . . | Seymour's Popular Sketches." Also announcement of Two prints : "The Dying Fox-Hunter" and "The Roadsters."

Back Wrapper (Inside)
"Books published by Wm. S. Orr and Co., London, | and W. & R. Chambers, Edinburgh. | Publishing Monthly, . . . | Magazine of Domestic Economy." Below : "Natural History of Cage Birds" and "Hand-Books for the People."

Back Wrapper (Outside)
"T. Cox Savory, | Working Silversmith, Goldsmith, and Watchmaker, | 47, Cornhill, London." With two illustrations of Cruet Frames. Imprint of Bradbury and Evans, as Parts 16 and 18.

Advertisements (Front)
"The Pickwick Advertiser. | Nos. XIX. and XX." 24 pp. unnumbered.

THE PICKWICK PAPERS.

p. (1) "12, King William Street, Strand, Nov. 1, 1837. | James Bohn's Publications." Six titles.

p. (2) "An important addition to the Pickwick Papers ! | Just published, . . . | Parts I. to VI. | of | Samuel Weller's | Illustrations | to | The Pickwick Club."

p. (3) "Smirke's Illustrated Edition . . . | The History of . . . | Don Quixote de la Mancha" (Nattali).

p. (4) "Now ready . . . | The Third Volume | of | Wilson's Tales of the Border, | and of Scotland."

p. (5) "Now ready, | by Whittaker and Co., . . . | . . . | The Book of Gems : 1838." Also, "Parbury's Oriental Herald & Colonial Inteligencer" and "Bett's School Atlas."

p. (6) "Books for Presents, | Just published by Charles Tilt, Fleet Street. | Flora's Gems" ; and Seven other titles.

p. (7) "The Comic Annual for 1388" (sic). This is a letter from, and signed by, the Editor, Thomas Hood ; dated, Oct. 10th, 1837 : and occupying one half-page. Below, in half column measure, are announced Five other publications by A. H. Baily and Co.

p. (8) "Early in 1838 will commence . . . | . . . | The Tales | of A Thousand and One Nights ;"

p. (9) "Ackermann's Annuals for 1838" ; half-page. Lower half ; Charles Tilt's announcements of : "The Oriental Annual" ; "Finden's Tableaux" ; and "The Authors of England."

p. (10) ($\frac{1}{2}$ col.) "Just published, Gratis, | Bull's New System" ; with Nine other advertisements, the last one being : "Juvenile and Prize Books."

p. (11) "Just published, | by C. Penny & Son. . . | . . . | Pocket-Book Almanacks for 1838." Seven varieties are specified, together with, "The Domestic Account-Book."

p. (12) ($\frac{1}{2}$ col.) "This day is published, . . . | The Commodore and his Daughter"; with Nine additional announcements, ending with : "The Anatomical Remembrancer."

p. (13) "Completion of Alfred Crowquill's Illustrations | to the Pickwick Papers." Also : "Hodgson's British and Foreign Library" ; "Her Majesty's Stag-Hounds" ; "C. Tilt's Almanacks for 1838" ; "The Artist" ; and "To the Troubled in Shaving."

p. (14) "New Works | published by Chapman and Hall, 136, Strand. | . . . | The Juvenile Budget" ; and Five other titles.

p. (15) "Fourth Edition. | In One Volume . . . | Sketches of Young Ladies" ; followed by "Chess for Beginners" and "The Library of Fiction" (Chapman and Hall).

p. (16) "Publishing once a fortnight . . . | Webster's | Acting National Drama." Also, "The Bridal" and "Rory O'More."

p. (17) "Popular Juvenile Books," the page identical with Part 13, page 9 ; Part 14, page 2 ; and Part 17, page 1.

p. (18) "75, St. Paul's Church Yard. | Neat and Elegant Writing" ; "Hammond's Authorised Office for Advertisements" ; "Picture Frames, Window Cornices" ; "Adam's Improved Spectacles," with illustration of spectacles.

p. (19) ($\frac{1}{2}$ col.) "Fine Wines" ; "The Corn Trade" ; and Eight additional announcements.

p. (20) ($\frac{1}{2}$ col.) "Her Majesty Victoria | the First" ; (*sic*). "Aulmac's Tarnish Liquid" ; and Seven other advertisements.

p. (21) "Laming's Tasteless . . . Salts" ; "British Consul's Office," with illustration ; and in half measure, Five other advertisements.

p. (22) "Inquiry. | . . . | Gowland's Lotion" ; "Lithography" in panel, with woodcut ; and "Wood and Barrett," with illustration of Oven and Kitchen Range.

p. (23) "Labern's Botanic Cream" ; "List of Articles" (Mechi) ; and "Reform your Tailors' Bills ! !"

p. (24) "Autumn." (Rowland's Kalydor and Rowland's Macassar Oil.)

In page 7 will be noted the misprinted Year "1388" for "1838." Copies with the error are by no means common, and those containing it can be hall-marked as the earlier printing.

Advertisements (Back)

(1) Lashmar & Bellingham's New Tea Warehouse, one leaf differing from Part 18, the opening lines of Address beginning : "We stated on opening this Establishment on the 2nd September, the peculiar circumstances of the Tea Market . . ." ; and 14 lines of Green Teas are scheduled. Other slight alterations can be noticed.

There are three issues of this leaflet :—

(1) "The | New Tea Warehouse" ; with list of prices in small type.

(2) "The | New Tea Warehouse" ; with list of prices in black-faced type.

(3) "The New Tea Warehouse" all in one line, and prices in small type.

(2) Simpson's Herbal Pills. 2 pp. Identical in format and text with Part 18, in the Four Issues, but all printed in black instead of blue.

(3) "Neill on Diseases of the Eye"; with woodcut of eye at head of page. 2 pp. unnumbered. Imprint at foot of page (2): "Mitchell, Heaton, & Mitchell, Printers, Liverpool."

Four printings of this have been noted, each differing in the arrangement of type in nine lines; six on page (1) and three on page (2). The fifth line, "Diseases of the Eye" is set-up in two ways; one with solid-faced caps., and the other with open-letter caps.

This is the second instance throughout the run of "Pickwick" of an inset advertisement bearing the imprint of a Provincial printer.

(4) "Mechi's Catalogue"; 18 pp. of Text, bound in coloured paper wrappers. Details as given in Part 12 apply to this.

PLATES (FOUR)

(No. 40) "Mary and the fat boy"; signed "Phiz del"; no page number (p. 579).

Three plates were etched for this subject, and are fully detailed in the introduction on page 21.

(No. 41) "Mr. Weller and his friends drinking to Mr. Pell"; signed "Phiz del"; no page number (p. 590).

Three plates were etched for this subject, and are fully detailed in the introduction on page 22.

(No. 42) Frontispiece; signed "Phiz fecit" in lower centre, divided by the Tupman tablet.

First plate: The stool has four stripes, and signature "Phiz fecit" is divided left and right by the middle shield at foot.

Second plate: The stool has six stripes. Signature is undivided on left of shield.

(No. 43) Vignette Title; signatures vary.

First plate: The Inn sign reads: "Tony Veller," signed "Phiz fecit."

Second plate: The Inn sign reads: "Tony Weller," signed "Phiz fect."

ADDRESS, BY THE PUBLISHER
"186, Strand, | October 30, 1837. | The Pickwick Papers"
of 15 lines ; followed by : New Work by "Boz" of
7 lines. Verso : "Sketches by 'Boz' " ; identical with
verso of Address in Part 18, except, instead of "On
November 1st will be published," is substituted : "This
day (November 1st) is published." 2 pp. unnumbered.

TEXT, WITH HEADING
"Chapter LII." pp. 563–609, p. (610) blank. (R R.
T T. in sixteens). Imprint at foot of p. 609 : "London :
| Bradbury and Evans, Printers, | Whitefriars."

PRELIMINARY LEAVES
Half-title : "The | Posthumous Papers | of | The Pickwick
Club." Verso blank. (I. II.)

Title-page : dated 1837 ; verso with imprint as p. 609.
(III. IV.) See Illustration.

Dedication : To Sergeant Talfourd, dated September 27,
1837. 2 pp. (V). VI.

Preface : 3 pp. and blank. (VII). VIII. IX. (X).

Contents : 4 pp. (XI). XII. XIII. XIV.

Directions to the Binder ; verso, Errata of 6 lines. 2 pp.
(XV). (XVI).

TEXT MEASUREMENTS
Extreme depth of pages :—

p. 595	=	$176\frac{1}{4}$ mm.
pp. 563, 581	=	$174\frac{1}{2}$,,
pp. 593, 594, 596, 597, 599–607	=	173 ,,
pp. 564, 565, 567, 568, 570, 571, 573–579, 582, 583, 585, 586, 589, 590, 608	=	$171\frac{1}{4}$,,
p. 609	=	$169\frac{3}{4}$,,
pp. 566, 569, 580, 587, 588, 591, 592, 598	=	$168\frac{1}{4}$,,
p. 584	=	$161\frac{3}{4}$,,
p. 572	=	154 ,,

The Front Wrapper to the 8vo. edition of "Sketches by Boz" as published in 20 monthly parts, 1837-9. The various loose papers and articles were first published in newspapers and magazines, and also in book form, between December, 1833 and December, 1836.

SKETCHES BY BOZ

ILLUSTRATIVE OF

EVERY-DAY LIFE AND EVERY-DAY PEOPLE.

WITH FORTY ILLUSTRATIONS

BY

GEORGE CRUIKSHANK.

NEW EDITION, COMPLETE.

LONDON:
CHAPMAN AND HALL, 186, STRAND.
1839.

Sketches by " Boz "

in

20 Monthly Parts

November, 1837, to June, 1839.

THE issue of the Sketches as a periodical work, is by no means their first appearance in print, and it is only the essential chronological arrangement of this bibliography, which prevents them taking pride of place as the opening chapter; as in fact, the greater proportion had been printed and partly published, before a word of "Pickwick" was penned.

The majority were originally written for, and published by, six daily journals and magazines of the day; while a few were included for the first time, when the sketches as a whole were issued in book form. Altogether 59 distinct and separate papers come under review when considering their first appearance in the cold light of print; although in their latest phase, when combined in the octavo edition, they were published as 56 sketches or articles. In the earliest printed form, the sketches appeared as here summarised :

Key.		*Loose Papers.*		*Sketches.*
M.M.	"THE MONTHLY MAGAZINE, or BRITISH REGISTER OF POLITICS, LITERATURE, ART, SCIENCE AND THE BELLES LETTRES." New Series. 1833-35	9	or	7
M.C.	"THE MORNING CHRONICLE." 1834-36 ..	8	or	8
E.C.	"THE EVENING CHRONICLE." 1835-36 ..	20	or	19
B.L.	"BELL'S LIFE IN LONDON AND SPORTING CHRONICLE." 1835-36	12	or	12

CHARLES DICKENS.

Key.		Loose Papers.		Sketches.
C.C.	"THE CARLTON CHRONICLE OF POLITICS, LITERATURE, SCIENCE AND ART." 1836 ..	1	or	1
L.F.	"THE LIBRARY OF FICTION, OR FAMILY STORY-TELLER." 1836	2	or	2
	Sketches, First Series, Vol. 1. 1836	2	or	2
	" " " Vol. 2. 1836	3	or	3
	" Second Series. 1837	2	or	2
		59		56

The first story from the pen of Charles Dickens, to receive the full glare and glamour of publicity, was entitled "A Dinner at Poplar Walk," and appeared in *The Monthly Magazine* for December, 1833. It was not reprinted until three years later, when after considerable alteration, it was included in the published volume of the Second Series, under the new title of "Mr. Minns and his Cousin." After this initial effort in literature, Dickens continued his contributions to the magazines and journals, almost without cessation in a monthly sequence ; and by the time that Part I of Pickwick Papers was launched, he had written and published 51 separate articles, of which 46 had appeared in five out of six of the above-mentioned journals. The final sketch to be published, which with others, was specially written, and formed one of the collected papers in the Second Series of Sketches by "Boz," was "The Drunkard's Death."

A complete list has been compiled, and is now presented, giving in order of publication, full descriptions of all the 59 separate sketches, with the titles under which they were originally printed ; and subsequent reprints with altered titles—if any—previous to their final assembly in the octavo edition in monthly parts, 1837-1839. That no previous publishing history of these extremely important early efforts of Dickens had any claim to reliability, is proved by the discovery that four of the sketches had first appeared in *The Morning Chronicle*, September to October, 1834 ; these

had been attributed by previous writers, as original contributions to the Second Series in book form, published
December, 1836.   A still later examination of the files has
been undertaken by the present writers, with the results now
placed on record.   By a cross-check with the "Contents"
of the octavo edition, detailed in the collation proper, the
complete sequence of events leading to final publication in
a collected form, can thus be obtained.

(1) Dec., 1833.
> A Dinner at Poplar Walk.   Unsigned.   M.M.   Vol.
> XVI. pp. 617-624.
>> Reprinted as "Mr. Minns and his Cousin" (with many
>> alterations) in Second Series, Dec., 1836 ; pp. 257-282.

(2) Jan., 1834.
> Mrs. Joseph Porter, "over the way."   Unsigned.
> M.M.   Vol. XVII. pp. 11-18.
>> Reprinted as "Mrs. Joseph Porter" in First Series, Vol. 2,
>> Feb., 1836 ; pp. 253-272.

(3) Feb., 1834.
> Horatio Sparkins.   Unsigned.   M.M.   Vol. XVII.
> pp. 151-162.
>> Reprinted in First Series, Vol. 2, Feb., 1836 ; pp. 110-141.

(4) April, 1834.
> The Bloomsbury Christening.   Unsigned.   M.M.
> Vol. XVII. pp. 375-386.
>> Reprinted in First Series, Vol. 1, Feb., 1836 ; pp. 242-275.

(5) May, 1834.
> The Boarding House.   Unsigned.   M.M.   Vol.
> XVII. pp. 481-493.
>> Reprinted in First Series, Vol. 1, Feb., 1836 ; pp. 147-180.

(6) Aug., 1834.
> The Boarding House, No. II.   Signed "Boz."   M.M.
> Vol. XVIII. pp. 177-192.
>> Reprinted in First Series, Vol. 1, Feb., 1836 ; pp. 181-223.
>> This was the earliest paper signed "Boz."

(7) Sep. 26, 1834.

> Street Sketches.—No. I. | OMNIBUSES. Signed "Boz." M.C. Issue No. 20,306 ; nearly full column.

> Reprinted in First Series, Vol. 2, Feb., 1836 ; pp. 244-252.

(8) Oct., 1834.

> The Steam Excursion. Signed "Boz." M.M. Vol. XVIII. pp. 360-376.

> Reprinted (a passage omitted) in First Series, Vol. 2, Feb., 1836 ; pp. 273-318.

(9) Oct. 10, 1834.

> Street Sketches. — No. II. | SHOPS AND THEIR TENANTS. Signed "Boz." M.C. Issue No. 20,318 ; nearly full column.

> Reprinted in First Series, Vol. 1, Feb., 1836 ; pp. 88-96.

(10) Oct. 23, 1834.

> Street Sketches.—No. III. | THE OLD BAILEY. Signed "Boz." M.C. Issue No. 20,329 ; full column.

> Reprinted (with a few words changed in last paragraph) as "Criminal Courts" in Second Series, Dec., 1836 ; pp. 51-62.

(11) Nov. 5, 1834.

> Street Sketches.—No. IV. | SHABBY - GENTEEL PEOPLE. Signed "Boz." M.C. Issue No. 20,340 ; nearly full column.

> Reprinted in First Series, Vol. 2, Feb., 1836 ; pp. 101-109.

(12) Jan., 1835.

> Passage in the Life of Mr. Watkins Tottle. Chapter the First. Signed "Boz." M.M. Vol. XIX. pp. 15-24.

> Reprinted in First Series, Vol. 2, Feb., 1836 ; pp. 1-29.

(13) Jan. 31, 1835.

> Sketches of London.—No. I. | . . . | HACKNEY-COACH STANDS. Signed "Boz." E.C. Issue No. 1; nearly full column.

> Reprinted (with first nine words omitted) in First Series, Vol. 1, Feb., 1836 ; pp. 224-232.

(14) Feb., 1835.

> Passage in the Life of Mr. Watkins Tottle. Chapter the Second. Signed "Boz." M.M. Vol. XIX. pp. 121-137.

> Reprinted in First Series, Vol. 2, Feb., 1836 ; pp. 30-76.

(15) Feb. 7, 1835.

> Sketches of London.—No. II. | . . . | GIN SHOPS. Signed "Boz." E.C. Issue No. 4 ; little more than full column.

> Reprinted in First Series, Vol. 1, Feb., 1836 ; pp. 276-287.

(16) Feb. 19, 1835.

> Sketches of London.—No. III. | . . . | EARLY COACHES. Signed "Boz." E.C. Issue No. 9 ; one and one-eighth columns.

> Reprinted in First Series, Vol. 2, Feb., 1836 ; pp. 171-181.

(17) Feb. 28, 1835.

> Sketches of London.—No. IV. | . . . | THE PARISH. Signed "Boz." E.C. Issue No. 13 ; little over full column.

> Reprinted (with few words changed in first paragraph, and last paragraph omitted) as "The Beadle—The Parish Engine —The Schoolmaster" in First Series, Vol. 1, Feb., 1836 ; pp. 1-11.

(18) Mch. 7, 1835.

> Sketches of London.—No. V. | . . . | THE HOUSE. Signed "Boz." E.C. Issue No. 16 ; one and a quarter columns.

> The last paragraph reads : *"There are a few more portraits— some in the body of the house—others in one of the galleries—which*

we should like to lay before our readers. We have exhausted our space, and must therefore reserve them for our next sketch, which will be entitled "Bellamy's."

Reprinted (the above paragraph omitted) in conjunction with "Bellamy's" as "A Parliamentary Sketch—with a few Portraits" in Second Series, Dec., 1836 ; pp. 227-255. This sketch (The House) ends at top of page 242.

(19) Mch. 17, 1835.

Sketches of London.—No. VI. | . . . | LONDON RECREATIONS. Signed "Boz." E.C. Issue No. 20 ; one and one-eighth columns.

At the end of the article, a footnote reads : *"On consideration, we postpone for a week or two the sketch as announced in our last. We have various reasons for doing so, among which the inevitable sameness of the subject is not the least."*

Reprinted (footnote omitted) in First Series, Vol. 1, Feb., 1836 ; pp. 136-146.

(20) Apl. 7, 1835.

Sketches of London.—No. VII. | . . . | PUBLIC DINNERS. Signed "Boz." E.C. Issue No. 29 ; one and one-third columns.

A footnote appears, which reads : *"The sketch entitled ' Bellamy's,' which we announced as a continuation of ' The House,' shall form the next number of our series."*

Reprinted (footnote omitted) in First Series, Vol. 1, Feb., 1836 ; pp. 288-299.

(21) Apl. 11, 1835.

Sketches of London.—No. VIII. | . . . | BELLAMY'S. Signed "Boz." E.C. Issue No. 31 ; one and a quarter columns.

Reprinted (with few words changed at beginning, and last paragraph entirely omitted) in conjunction with "The House" ; as "A Parliamentary Sketch—with a few Portraits" in Second Series, Dec., 1836 ; pp. 227-255. This sketch (Bellamy's) begins at near the top of page 242.

(22) Apl. 16, 1835.

Sketches of London.—No. IX. | . . . | GREENWICH FAIR. Signed "Boz." E.C. Issue No. 33 ; one and three-quarter columns.

Last paragraph reads : *"Our present sketch has encroached considerably on a second column. Fortunately, however, for our readers, we have even now omitted many points we had originally intended to notice. As we propose continuing our series until it reaches something under its two hundredth number, however, we shall watch an opportunity of including them under some other head."*

Reprinted (the above paragraph omitted) in First Series, Vol. 1, Feb., 1836 ; pp. 314-330.

(23) Apl. 23, 1835.

Sketches of London.—No. X. | . . . | THOUGHTS ABOUT PEOPLE. Signed "Boz." E.C. Issue No. 36 ; slightly over full column.

Reprinted in First Series, Vol. 1, Feb., 1836 ; pp. 97-106.

(24) May 9, 1835.

Sketches of London.—No. XI. | . . . | ASTLEY'S. Signed "Boz." E.C. Issue No. 43 ; nearly one and a half columns.

Reprinted in First Series, Vol. 1, Feb., 1836 ; pp. 300-313.

(25) May 19, 1835.

Sketches of London.—No. XII. | . . . | OUR PARISH. Signed "Boz." E.C. Issue No. 47 ; about one and a quarter columns.

Reprinted (opening and last paragraphs omitted) as "The Curate—The Old Lady—The Captain" in First Series, Vol. 1, Feb., 1836 ; pp. 12-23.

(26) June 6, 1835.

Sketches of London.—No. XIII. | . . . | THE RIVER. Signed "Boz." E.C. Issue No. 55 ; one and one-third columns.

Reprinted in First Series, Vol. 2, Feb., 1836 ; pp. 182-195.

(27) June 18, 1835.

Sketches of London.—No. XIV. | . . . | OUR PARISH. Signed "Boz." E.C. Issue No. 60 ; one and one-eighth columns.

Last paragraph reads : *"As we dare not occupy any greater space at this busy period, we have only to add that we must defer any further account of the four Miss Willises until another opportunity ; that we propose in future, publishing a parochial sketch alternately with one coming more immediately under our first heading ; and*

that from this time forward we shall make no further apology for an
abrupt conclusion to an article under the title of ' Our Parish,' than
is contained in the words, ' To be continued.' "

Reprinted (the above paragraph omitted) as "The Four
Sisters" in First Series, Vol. 1, Feb., 1836 ; pp. 24-33.

(28) June 30, 1835.

Sketches of London.—No. XV. | . . . | THE PAWN-
BROKER'S SHOP. Signed "Boz." E.C. Issue
No. 65 ; slightly over one and a half columns.

Reprinted in First Series, Vol. 2, Feb., 1836 ; pp. 142-157.

(29) July 14, 1835.

Sketches of London.—No. XVI. | . . . | OUR
PARISH. Signed "Boz." E.C. Issue No. 71 ; one
and one-third columns.

Reprinted as "The Election for Beadle" in First Series,
Vol. 1, Feb., 1836 ; pp. 34-47.

(30) July 21, 1835.

Sketches of London.—No. XVII. | . . . | THE
STREETS—MORNING. Signed "Boz." E.C.
Issue No. 74 ; one and one-eighth columns.

Reprinted as "The Streets by Morning" in Second Series,
Dec., 1836 ; pp. 3-16.

(31) July 28, 1835.

Sketches of London.—No. XVIII. | . . . | OUR
PARISH. Signed "Boz." E.C. Issue No. 77 ;
nearly two columns.

A sub-heading "Mr. Bung's Narrative" appears lower down
the first column.

Reprinted as "The Broker's Man" in First Series, Vol. 1,
Feb., 1836 ; pp. 48-66.

(32) Aug. 11, 1835.

Sketches of London.—No. XIX. | . . . | PRIVATE
THEATRES. Signed "Boz." E.C. Issue No. 83 ;
one and one-third columns.

Reprinted in First Series, Vol. 2, Feb., 1836 ; pp. 196-208.

(33) Aug. 20, 1835.

Sketches of London.—No. XX. | . . . | OUR PARISH.

Signed "Boz." E.C. Issue No. 87 ; one and one-eighth columns.

Although this sketch ends with the words "To be continued" it was the last of the parochial papers, and the final contribution to *The Evening Chronicle* until Sep. 26, 1836.

Reprinted as "The Ladies Societies" in First Series, Vol. 1, Feb., 1836 ; pp. 67-78.

(34) Sep. 27, 1835.

Scenes and Characters.—No. I. | SEVEN DIALS. Signed "Tibbs." B.L. ; nearly full column.

Reprinted in Second Series, Dec., 1836 ; pp. 145-156.

(35) Oct. 4, 1835.

Scenes and Characters.—No. II. | MISS EVANS AND "THE EAGLE." Signed "Tibbs." B.L. ; nearly full column.

Reprinted in First Series, Vol. 1, Feb., 1836 ; pp. 79-87.

(36) Oct. 11, 1835.

Scenes and Characters.—No. III. | THE DANCING ACADEMY. Signed "Tibbs." B.L. ; one and one-fifth columns.

Reprinted in First Series, Vol. 2, Feb., 1836 ; pp. 158-170.

(37) Oct. 18, 1835.

Scenes and Characters.—No. IV. | MAKING A NIGHT OF IT. Signed "Tibbs." B.L. ; slightly over full column.

Reprinted in Second Series, Dec., 1836 ; pp. 35-48.

(38) Oct. 25, 1835.

Scenes and Characters.—No. V. | LOVE AND OYSTERS. Signed "Tibbs." B.L. ; one and one-eighth columns.

Reprinted as "Misplaced Attachment of Mr. John Dounce" in Second Series, Dec., 1836 ; pp. 193-208.

(39) Nov. 1, 1835.

Scenes and Characters.—No. VI. | SOME ACCOUNT OF AN OMNIBUS CAD. Signed "Tibbs." B.L. ; nine-tenths of column.

Reprinted in part in *The Carlton Chronicle*, Sep. 17, 1836. This was a flagrant piracy ; written in the first person, and omitting nearly one-half of the original text.

Reprinted (with added matter, omissions and variations) as "The Last Cab-Driver, and the First Omnibus Cad," in Second Series, Dec., 1836 ; pp. 285-308.

(40) Nov. 22, 1835.

Scenes and Characters.—No. VII. | THE VOCAL DRESS-MAKER. Signed "Tibbs." B.L. ; one and one-seventh columns.

Reprinted as "The Mistaken Milliner—A Tale of Ambition," in Second Series, Dec., 1836 ; pp. 159-174.

(41) Nov. 29, 1835.

Scenes and Characters.—No. VIII. | THE PRISONERS' VAN. Signed "Tibbs." B.L. ; nearly full column.

Reprinted (with the omission of two long opening paragraphs—nearly half the article) in First Series, Vol. 1, Feb., 1836 ; pp. 331-337.

(42) Dec. 13, 1835.

Scenes and Characters.—No. IX. | THE PARLOUR. Signed "Tibbs." B.L. ; nearly full column.

Reprinted in *The Observer*, Dec. 14, 1835.

Reprinted (with the omission of 19 lines in opening paragraph) as "The Parlour Orator" in Second Series, Dec., 1836 ; pp. 311-323.

(43) Dec. 27, 1835.

Scenes and Characters. — No. X. | CHRISTMAS FESTIVITIES. Signed "Tibbs." B.L. ; full column.

Reprinted (with slight variation at end) in *The Observer*, Dec. 28, 1835.

Reprinted again (with another minute alteration at end) in *The Observer*, Jan. 3, 1836.

Reprinted (with the omission of the 7-line last paragraph) as "A Christmas Dinner" in First Series, Vol. 1, Feb., 1836 ; pp. 338-348.

(44) Jan. 3, 1836.

Scenes and Characters.—No. XI. | THE NEW YEAR. Signed "Tibbs." B.L. ; full column.

Reprinted in *The Observer*, Jan. 4, 1836.

Reprinted in Second Series, Dec., 1836 ; pp. 79-92.

(45) Jan. 17, 1836.
> Scenes and Characters.—No. XII. | THE STREETS AT NIGHT. Signed "Tibbs." B.L. ; full column.
>> Reprinted as "The Streets by Night" in Second Series, Dec., 1836 ; pp. 19-32.
>> Dickens wrote no further papers for Bell's Life in London, but two weeks later (Jan. 31) appeared "Scenes and Characters in London—The Auction-Room," a full column, by an anonymous contributor, evidently intended to supplement the previous series. It was, however, the one and only effort.

(46) Feby., 1836.
> A Visit to Newgate. First published in First Series, Vol. 1 ; pp. 107-135.

(47) Feby., 1836.
> Brokers' and Marine-Store Shops. First published in First Series, Vol. 1 ; pp. 233-241.

(48) Feby., 1836.
> The Black Veil. First published in First Series, Vol. 2 ; pp. 77-100.

(49) Feby., 1836.
> The Great Winglebury Duel. First published in First Series, Vol. 2 ; pp. 209-243.

(50) Feby., 1836.
> Sentiment. First published in First Series, Vol. 2 ; pp. 319-342.

(51) Apl., 1836.
> The Tuggs's at Ramsgate. Signed "Boz." L.F. Part 1 ; pp. 1-18.

(52) June, 1836.
> A Little Talk about Spring, and the Sweeps. Signed "Boz." L.F. Part 3 ; pp. 113-119.
>> Reprinted as "The First of May" in Second Series, Dec., 1836 ; pp. 327-346.

(53) Aug. 6, 1836.
> The Hospital Patient. Signed "Boz." C.C.
>> Written in the first person.
>> Reprinted (in the third person) in Second Series, Dec., 1836 ; pp. 133–142.

(54) Sep. 24, 1836.

> Sketches by "Boz." New Series. No. I. | MEDITA-
> TIONS IN MONMOUTH-STREET. Signed "Boz."
> M.C. Issue No. 20,875; one and one-third
> columns.
>
> Reprinted in *The Evening Chronicle*, Sep. 26, 1836.
> Reprinted in Second Series, Dec., 1836; pp. 95-112.

(55) Oct. 4, 1836.

> Sketches by "Boz."—No. II. | (New Series) | SCOT-
> LAND-YARD. Signed "Boz." M.C. Issue No.
> 20,883; one and one-tenth columns.
>
> Reprinted in *The Evening Chronicle*, Oct. 5, 1836.
> Reprinted in *The Carlton Chronicle*, Oct. 8, 1836.
> Unauthorised, omitting a portion of text at the com-
> mencement.
> Reprinted in *Bell's Life in London*, Oct. 9, 1836.
> Unauthorised.
> Reprinted in Second Series, Dec., 1836; pp. 65-76. A
> considerable portion at the beginning of the article was
> omitted when published officially in book form.

(56) Oct. 11, 1836.

> Sketches by "Boz."—No. III. | (New Series) |
> DOCTORS' COMMONS. Signed "Boz." M.C. Issue
> No. 20,889; one and one-tenth columns.
>
> Reprinted in *The Evening Chronicle*, Oct. 12, 1836.
> Reprinted in part in *The Carlton Chronicle*, Oct. 15, 1836.
> Unauthorised, consisting only of one-third of the original
> article.
> Reprinted in *Bell's Life in London*, Oct. 16, 1836.
> Also unauthorised, although acknowledgment was made
> to *The Morning Chronicle*.
> Reprinted in Second Series, Dec., 1836; pp. 177-190.

(57) Oct. 26, 1836.

> Sketches by "Boz."—No. IV. | (New Series) |
> VAUXHALL-GARDENS BY DAY. Signed "Boz."
> M.C. Issue No. 20,902; one and a quarter
> columns.

102

Reprinted in *The Evening Chronicle*, Oct. 26, 1836.
Reprinted in *Bell's Life in London*, Oct. 30, 1836.
  Unauthorised.
Reprinted in Second Series, Dec., 1836 ; pp. 211–224.

(58) Dec., 1836.
      Our Next-Door Neighbours.   First published in
      Second Series ; pp. 115-131.

(59) Dec., 1836.
      The Drunkard's Death.   First published in Second
      Series ; pp. 349-377.

The purchase of the copyright by John Macrone, led to the collection of all the separate articles, which, with a few deletions and minor alterations of text, as well as a change in some few titles, were published for the first time in book form, as a First Series in two volumes, February, 1836 ; and a Second Series in one volume in December of the same year ; although the latter volume was dated 1837. The work ran through several editions, until an arrangement was made for the purchase outright of Macrone's copyright. An immediate re-issue in the then popular monthly numbers was immediately decided upon, and it was published as such by Chapman & Hall.

Coincident with the final monthly number of "Pickwick" (November, 1837), the first part of "Sketches by Boz" was issued ; bound in a pink paper wrapper with a design on the front by George Cruikshank ; and each succeeding month appeared regularly, until its completion with Part 20 in June, 1839. The issue price as usual was one shilling per number. There was no double number, with which to wind up the issue, although it was necessary to enlarge the two last parts to take in the allotted amount of letterpress.

The "make-up" of "Sketches by Boz" as a periodical work, bears no relation to that of its immediate predecessor, or indeed to that of any other work which followed. It was a bold experiment, but a badly designed structure. Being a re-issue of a previously published series of articles, it had but little originality of subject matter ; the familiar "green leaves," known even then in almost every household, were discarded, and substituted by an experimental pink cover. The text was very much curtailed, consisting usually of only 24 pp. to each number, instead of the average 32 pp. as in "Pickwick." Its reception by advertisers is apparent by the paucity of advertisement material, and the minimum of trade insets which found a place within the covers.

TEXT.

Very few points of a distinctive character are to be detected with facility, as between the issue in monthly parts and the reprinted volume edition. On completion of the periodical run, remainders were collected and bound up in cloth ; these represent the first edition in book form. The standing type, however, was stereotyped, and used for reprinting further issues of the 1839 octavo volume. It is between this later volume and the original parts that great differences in page measurements may be discerned, thus enabling us to determine the earliest printing when compared with the later impressions. This is a particularly important point, and must be seriously regarded, because copies have been seen containing late issue text, stitched in between the wrappers of an early issue.

Typographically the production in the monthly parts was quite good, but it is curious to find such a lack of uniformity in the fount of type used for the pagination. The figure "7" is frequently out of all character with the combining page numbers, and they appear to have been composed with an entire indifference to good appearance of the printed page. All pages are numbered, except page (3) and the four extra half-titles. It should be mentioned here, although again noted in the collation, that no indication of priority in issue is conveyed by the lack of spacing between the words "reeled before," which appear in the last page of text—526. It is a fault common to many reprints of the book in volume form, and is accounted for by the text being stereotyped before any correction was made.

Unlike any other of the periodical works, the text was run on from month to month, regardless of where a break occurred, so that in no instance does a monthly number open up with a new chapter heading.

PLATES.

A total of forty plates were drawn and etched by George Cruikshank for this octavo edition, of which twenty-seven are the original designs as they appeared in the First and Second Series of the Sketches published in volume form, 1836-7 ; these, however, were enlarged in size to match an additional thirteen etchings. Each plate bears the artist's signature, and all carry inscriptions. No imprints appear on the plates up to and including Part 5 (plates 9 and 10), but commencing with Part 6 (plates 11 and 12), the following line is added : "London : Chapman & Hall, 186, Strand." In later states of the plates, this imprint does not appear.

The original twenty-seven designs are :

First Series, Vol. 1.	1836	...	8	plates, enlarged.	
,, ,, Vol. 2	,,	...	8	,,	,,
Second Series, First Edition, 1837			9	,,	,,
,, ,, Second Edition, ,,			2	,,	,,
			27		

For the Second Series, First Edition, ten plates were originally etched, but one, "The Free and Easy," was not reproduced for this octavo edition.

The thirteen specially designed and etched plates prepared for this issue in monthly parts, are those numbered in the collation : 2, 3, 4, 13, 15, 17, 25, 27, 30, 33, 34, 35 and 38.

Attention has been drawn elsewhere in this bibliography, to the necessity for etching two subjects on one steel. For the ten plates comprised in the first edition of the Second Series, eight were etched in fours on two steels, and two on one steel; thus only three steels were required instead of five, if they had been printed in pairs by the usual method. The "twin" steel was made up of the engraved title (Balloon scene) and "Seven Dials."

WRAPPERS.

Whatever the "Sketches" may have lacked in its appeal to the reading public, an entirely different story can be written from the point of view of the collector. Although the text, plates, and advertisement insets, present little or no difficulty in assembly, yet it is a nightmare to anyone setting out to achieve the goal of perfection in a completed set of the original twenty parts. The main obstacle to be surmounted is the one of wrappers. In themselves, these pink covers are extremely flimsy, and by no means of a fast dye, and normal wear and tear has been sufficient to put out of existence, the majority of the original numbers complete with wrappers ; while very few of the survivors are in good enough condition to meet the requirements of discriminating collectors. Briefly, it may be said, and without exception for any other work dealt with in this volume, that the wrappers alone make the book.

Particular care is essential in checking up the printed advertisements on the inner-side of front covers, so as to verify the genuineness of the "Part No." on outside of the wrapper. Many copies of individual parts may be seen, where the "Part No." has been tampered with ; sometimes with the definite motive to deceive, but more often has been openly altered with the pen, as an admission that the correct wrapper was not obtainable. The "pointers" given in the collation are sufficiently detailed to authenticate any particular wrapper.

In the Dexter collection is a proof impression on India paper, of the earliest printed front wrapper to "Sketches by Boz." It was originally designed by George Cruikshank for John Macrone, who had plans for a monthly issue in parts previous to the purchase of the copyright by Dickens and his publishers. It varies in every detail from the published wrapper issued eventually by Chapman & Hall, and which was engraved by J. Jackson, who also engraved the cover to "Pickwick Papers." The wood block was cut by, and is signed, "L. Schönberg, 108, Hatton Garden," and is without any "Part No." or "Price."

ADVERTISEMENTS.

The principle of an official advertising sheet was adopted, and duly appeared in the two initial numbers. Part 3 contained four pages of the publications of Chapman & Hall, but no further insets of this character were included in any of the remaining numbers; presumably, this early demise is accounted for by the comparatively low circulation figures. Insets of individual trading firms appear at the end of Parts 3 and 9.

The modest extent to which advantage was taken of the advertising facilities, is in marked contrast to all the other monthly works of Charles Dickens, excepting only "Oliver Twist"; the publishing history of which runs almost parallel with that of the "Sketches." The financial aspect in the publication of these two works would seem to point the moral—"once a tale is told, don't re-tell it."

PART 1.

FRONT WRAPPER (OUTSIDE)
"No. I. Price 1s. | Sketches | by | B-O-Z | Illustrated | by | George Cruikshank | London | Chapman & Hall | 186 Strand | 1837." Also as part of the cover design are three panels with matter reading—"Bung for Beadle"; "Vote for Spruggins and Ten small Children"; "Signor Billsmithis Dancing Academy."
In lower left corner is signature of artist "G.Ck." and in opposite corner "J. Jackson Sc."

CHARLES DICKENS.

Front Wrapper (Inside)
"An important addition to the Pickwick Papers. | Just published, price One Shilling each, Parts I. to VI. of | Weller's Illustrations | to | The Pickwick Club."

Back Wrapper (Inside)
"T. Cox Savory" with illustrations of two clocks, half-page. Below : "Fourth Edition | . . . | Sketches of Young Ladies."

Back Wrapper (Outside)
"Now ready, | . . . | The Third Volume of | Wilson's Tales of the Borders | and of Scotland." Full page.

Advertisements (Front)
"No. I. Advertiser. Nov. 1, 1837." 8 pp. unnumbered.

p. (1) "The Pickwick Papers Complete." Full page.
p. (2) "Popular Juvenile Books," Seven titles in half-column measure, and below, Two in full measure.
p. (3) "Splendidly Illustrated Edition of Fairy Tales . . . | The Child's Fairy Library," in full measure, with Ten other works in half-measure.
p. (4) "Books Published by Wm. S. Orr and Co., London." Announcing "Magazine of Domestic Economy" ; "Natural History of Cage Birds," and "Hand-Books for the People."
p. (5) "To be continued monthly, price one shilling, | Sketches in London." (W. S. Orr & Co.)
p. (6) "The Comic Annual for 1838" ; half-page in full measure, and Five other works in half-measure.
p. (7) "Laming's Tasteless . . . Salts" ; "Comic Songs" ; "The Useful and the Useless" ; "To the Troubled in Shaving" ; and "E. P. Doudney & Son."
p. (8) "Atmospheric Influence on the Skin. | Autumn." (A. Rowland & Son.) Full page.

Plates (Two)

(No. 1) "The Election for Beadle." (Frontispiece).

(No. 2) "The Parish Engine." (to face p. 3).

Text, with Heading
"Sketches by Boz. | Our Parish. | Chapter I." pp. (3)-24 ; preceded by sub-title (pp. 1-2) "Seven Sketches | from | Our Parish" ; verso blank.

p. 18 : The figure "8" in pagination is set lower than first figure.

TEXT MEASUREMENTS

Extreme depth of odd-numbered pages :—

p. 3	=	154 mm.	p. 5	=	175 mm.
pp. 19, 21, 23	=	174 „	p. 9	=	175½ „
pp. 7, 11, 13, 15	=	174½ „	p. 17	=	179 „

CONTENTS

(No. 17) "The Beadle—The Parish Engine—The School-master." pp. 3-8.

(No. 25) "The Curate—The Old Lady—The Half-Pay Captain." pp. 9-14.

The words "Half-Pay" are here included in the title for the first time.

(No. 27) "The Four Sisters." pp. 15-20.

(No. 29) "The Election for Beadle" (continued to Part 2). pp. 21-24.

PART 2.

FRONT WRAPPER (OUTSIDE)

Same as No. I. except "No. II."

FRONT WRAPPER (INSIDE)

"Tilt's | Miniature Classical Library." Dated in lower left corner, "Dec. 1, 1837."

BACK WRAPPER (INSIDE)

"New Works." Chapman & Hall's announcements of Five works, the first being "The Juvenile Budget."

BACK WRAPPER (OUTSIDE)

"Cox Savory, Goldsmith, &c., 47, Cornhill, London," with cuts of seven Gold Chains.

ADVERTISEMENTS (FRONT)

"No. II. Advertiser. December 1, 1837." 8 pp. unnumbered.

p. (1) Fisher, Son and Co. announcements of Six books, the first : "The Himalaya Tourist."

p. (2) "Old Mother Hubbard," published by W. P. Grant, Cambridge ; lower half of page ; publications by J. J. Dubochet & Co.

p. (3) "Crosby-Hall Wine Establishment" and E. P. Doudney & Son.

p. (4) Wm. S. Orr and Co., exactly as Part 1, page 4.

p. (5) "On the 15th December . . . | The British Cyclopædia." (W. S. Orr & Co.)

p. (6) "Popular Juvenile Books." Seven titles in half-column measure, and Three below in full measure.

p. (7) "Address" by the Publishers, dated November 30, 1837. "Some Complaints have reached the Publishers of this Work, that, although each Number contains a smaller quantity of matter than the Pickwick Papers, it is charged at the same price. The price of the three volumes, which are embodied in this edition, is One Pound Sixteen Shillings ; and the whole of their contents, with the addition of many expensive Illustrations, are now publishing in Twenty Numbers, for One Pound." Continues by saying, that the Publishers having paid a very large sum for the copyright, it must be apparent to anyone who considers the subject, that the quantity of matter cannot be increased.

p. (8) "The Pickwick Papers Complete," and "Sketches of Young Ladies." Fifth Edition.

PLATES (TWO)

(No. 3) "The Broker's Man." (to face p. 29).

(No. 4) "Our Next-door Neighbours." (to face p. 45).

The two plates are stitched in between pp. 6 and 7 of the "Advertiser."

TEXT MEASUREMENTS

Extreme depth of odd-numbered pages :—

pp. 27, 29	= 174 mm.	p. 45	= 176 mm.
p. 31	= 174½ „	p. 25	= 179 „
pp. 37, 41, 43, 47	= 175 „	pp. 33, 35	= 179¾ „
p. 39	= 175½ „		

CONTENTS

(No. 29) "The Election for Beadle" (concluded). pp. 25-28.

(No. 31) "The Broker's Man." pp. 29-38.

(No. 33) "The Ladies' Societies." pp. 39-44.

(No. 58) "Our Next-Door Neighbours" (continued to Part 3). pp. 45-48.

SKETCHES BY "BOZ."

PART 3.

FRONT WRAPPER (OUTSIDE)
Same as No. I. except "No. III."

FRONT WRAPPER (INSIDE)
Advertisements of E. Grattan; John Limbaird; P. D.
Hardy; Madame Tussaud; and Crosby-Hall Wine
Establishment.

BACK WRAPPER (INSIDE)
"The New Year." (Rowlands). Full page.

BACK WRAPPER (OUTSIDE)
"T. Cox Savory." With cuts of Two Cruet Stands. Full
page.

ADVERTISEMENTS (FRONT)
Chapman and Hall's announcements, 4 pp. unnumbered.

p. (1) "Sketches of Young Gentlemen" and "Sketches of Young
Ladies." Dated January 1, 1838.

p. (2) "No. III. of Sketches by 'Boz'" and "Webster's Acting
National Drama."

p. (3) Ten titles, the first, "Morals from the Churchyard" and last,
"A Garland of Love."

p. (4) "Popular Juvenile Books." Nine titles in half measure, and
Two in full measure.

ADVERTISEMENTS (BACK)
(1) Announcements by George Virtue, 8 pp. unnumbered,
printed on green tinted paper.

p. (1) "The Waldenses." Imprint at foot: "Johnston, Printer,
Lovell's Court, St. Paul's."

p. (2) "Doddridge's Family Expositor." Imprint as above.

p. (3) "Campbell's Scenic Annual for 1838."

p. (4) "The History and Topography of Holland and Belgium."
Imprint as above.

p. (5) "Switzerland."

p. (6) "The English Counties Delineated."

p. (7) "The Life and Times of Whitefield." Imprint as above.

p. (8) "Caledonia Illustrata." Imprint as above.

(2) Mechi's Catalogue. 18 pp., together with coloured wrappers ; the front printed in green and blue, the back in green only. Otherwise the same as Part 12 of "Pickwick Papers" ($4\frac{5}{8}'' \times 3\frac{1}{4}''$).

PLATES (Two)
(No. 5) "The Streets—Morning." (to face p. 56).
(No. 6) "Scotland Yard." (to face p. 72).

TEXT
pp. 49-72. An unnumbered leaf (pp. 53-54) carries the sub-title "Scenes." Verso blank.

Page 50 : The figure "0" in page number "50" is set higher than "5."

TEXT MEASUREMENTS
Extreme depth of odd-numbered pages :—

p. 71	=	67 mm.	p. 67	=	$175\frac{1}{4}$ mm.
p. 63	=	$169\frac{1}{2}$,,	p. 61	=	176 ,,
pp. 57, 59	=	170 ,,	pp. 51, 55, 65	=	179 ,,
pp. 49, 69	=	174 ,,			

CONTENTS
(No. 58) "Our Next-Door Neighbours" (concluded). pp. 49-52.

(No. 30) "The Streets—Morning." pp. 55-60.

This title agrees with that given to the sketch when originally published. When reprinted in the "Second Series," it read: "The Streets by Morning."

(No. 45) "The Streets.—Night." pp. 61-66.

When originally published the title was "The Streets at Night." As reprinted in the "Second Series," it read: "The Streets by Night."

(No. 9) "Shops and their Tenants." pp. 67-71.

(No. 55) "Scotland-Yard" (continued to Part 4). p. 72.

PART 4.

FRONT WRAPPER (OUTSIDE)
Same as No. I. except "No. IV."

SKETCHES BY "BOZ."

FRONT WRAPPER (INSIDE)
"Hood's Own"; "The Adventures of Gil Blas"; "Her Majesty Victoria the First"; and "Webster's Acting National Drama."

BACK WRAPPER (INSIDE)
"Sketches of Young Gentlemen"; "Sketches of Young Ladies," Sixth Edition; both in full measure. Followed by Five titles in half measure, "Morals from the Church-yard"; "Edward, the Crusader's Son"; "The Juvenile Budget"; "A Visit to the British Museum"; and "Chess for Beginners." At foot in full measure, "The Pickwick Papers Complete."

BACK WRAPPER (OUTSIDE)
"T. Cox Savory." With wood-cuts of Six Clocks. Full page.

PLATES (TWO)
(No. 7) "Seven Dials." (to face p. 77).
(No. 8) "Monmouth Street." (to face p. 82).

TEXT
pp. 73-96.
Page 83. Both figures of pagination are set level, and are printed in bold black type, but in later issues the "3" is slightly raised, and the impression is weakly.

TEXT MEASUREMENTS
Extreme depth of odd-numbered pages :—

p. 93	=	58 mm.	p. 91	=	176 mm.
p. 79	=	170 „	p. 73	=	178 „
pp. 75, 77	=	174 „	p. 83	=	179 „
pp. 85, 87, 95	=	175 „	p. 81	=	180 „
p. 89	=	175½ „			

CONTENTS
(No. 55) "Scotland-Yard" (concluded). pp. 73-76.
(No. 34) "Seven Dials." pp. 77-81.
(No. 54) "Meditations in Monmouth-Street." pp. 82-88.

(No. 13) "Hackney-Coach Stands." pp. 89-93.

(No. 56) "Doctors' Commons" (continued to Part 5). pp. 94-96.

PART 5.

FRONT WRAPPER (OUTSIDE)
Same as No. I. except "No. V."

FRONT WRAPPER (INSIDE)
"Travelling and Hunting Maps" and "Webster's Acting National Drama."

BACK WRAPPER (INSIDE)
Same as "No. IV."

BACK WRAPPER (OUTSIDE)
"T. Cox Savory." With price list in half measure. Full page.

ANNOUNCEMENT
A four-paged inset, the first three occupied by a "Proclamation," written by Dickens respecting the piracies and imitations of his works, and having special reference to "Nicholas Nickleby," then about to be published. The last page advertises No. V. of "Sketches by Boz" and "The Pickwick Papers Complete."

PLATES (TWO)
(No. 9) "Hackney Coach Stands." (to face p. 89).
(No. 10) "London Recreations." (to face p. 100).

TEXT MEASUREMENTS
Extreme depth of odd-numbered pages :—

p. 106	= 31 mm.	p. 111	= 175½ mm.
p. 119	= 111 „	p. 99	= 178 „
pp. 115, 117	= 174 „	pp. 97, 113	= 179 „
pp. 101, 103, 107, 109	= 175 „		

CONTENTS
(No. 56) "Doctors' Commons" (concluded). pp. 97-99.
(No. 19) "London Recreations." pp. 100-105.
(No. 26) "The River." pp. 106-112.

(No. 24) "Astley's."   pp. 113-119.
(No. 22) "Greenwich Fair" (continued to Part 6).   p. 120.

PART 6.

FRONT WRAPPER (OUTSIDE)
Same as No. I. except "No. VI."

FRONT WRAPPER (INSIDE)
"New Work by ' Boz ' " announcing the publication of the
first number of "Nicholas Nickleby." Below : "Webster's
Acting National Drama," detailing a list of 40 plays.

BACK WRAPPER (INSIDE)
"Sketches of Young Gentlemen," Third Edition ;   the
remainder of page same as Parts 4 and 5.

BACK WRAPPER (OUTSIDE)
"T. Cox Savory Working Silversmith, 47, Cornhill,
London."   With cuts of Dish Covers, Tea Service, and
Wall Clock.   Full page.

PLATES (TWO)
(No. 11) "Greenwich Fair."   (to face p. 120).
(No. 12) "Vauxhall Gardens by Day."   (to face p. 130).

TEXT MEASUREMENTS
Extreme depth of odd-numbered pages :—

p. 135	=	76 mm.	p. 139	=	$173\frac{1}{2}$ mm.
p. 141	=	79 „	p. 121	=	177 „
pp. 123, 125, 127,			p. 131	=	$177\frac{1}{2}$ „
133, 137, 143	=	173 „	p. 129	=	178 „

CONTENTS
(No. 22) "Greenwich Fair" (concluded).   pp. 121-128.
(No. 32) "Private Theatres."   pp. 129-135.
(No. 57) "Vauxhall Gardens by Day."   pp. 136-141.
(No. 16) "Early Coaches" (continued to Part 7).
pp. 142-144.
This sketch is erroneously indexed in "Contents" list as commencing
on page 141, instead of page 142.

CHARLES DICKENS.

Part 7.

Front Wrapper (Outside)
Same as No. I. except "No. VII."

Front Wrapper (Inside)
Similar to No. VI. Webster's List of Plays number 42.

Back Wrapper (Inside)
"Sketches of Young Gentlemen," Fourth Edition; "Sketches of Young Ladies," Seventh Edition; both in full measure. Followed by Five titles in half measure: "Regal Records"; "Morals from the Churchyard"; "The Juvenile Budget"; "A Visit to the British Museum"; and "Chess for Beginners." At foot, in full measure, "The Pickwick Papers Complete."

Back Wrapper (Outside)
"Popular Juvenile Books." Seven titles in half measure: "Remember"; "The Juvenile Pianist"; "Poetry for Children"; "The Two Cousins"; "Caroline"; "The Spoiled Child Reclaimed"; "Rose and Anne"; followed by "New Scenes for Youth" and "Edward, the Crusader's Son," in full measure.

Plates (Two)
(No. 13) "Early Coaches." (to face p. 142).
(No. 14) "The Last Cabdriver." (to face p. 153).

Text Measurements
Extreme depth of odd-numbered pages :—

p. 147	= 80 mm.	pp. 163, 165, 167	=	175 mm.
p. 159	= 169½ „	p. 145	=	178½ „
pp. 149, 151	= 174 „	pp. 153, 155	=	179 „
pp. 157, 161	= 174½ „			

Contents
(No. 16) "Early Coaches" (concluded). pp. 145-147.
(No. 7) "Omnibuses." pp. 148-152.
(No. 39) "The Last Cab-Driver, and the First Omnibus Cad." pp. 153-162.

(Nos. 18 & 21) "A Parliamentary Sketch" (continued to Part 8). pp. 163-168.

PART 8.

FRONT WRAPPER (OUTSIDE)
Same as No. I. except "No. VIII."

FRONT WRAPPER (INSIDE)
"Sketches of Young Gentlemen," Fourth Edition; "Sketches of Young Ladies," Seventh Edition, etc. Identical with Part 7 inside back wrapper.

BACK WRAPPER (INSIDE)
"C. & A. Oldridge's | Balm of Columbia." Full page.

BACK WRAPPER (OUTSIDE)
"The Stanhope Lens" (with illustration of a Flea magnified). Below : "T. Cox Savory" and cut of Clock.

PLATES (TWO)
(No. 15) "Public Dinners." (to face p. 175).
(No. 16) "The First of May." (to face p. 181).

TEXT MEASUREMENTS
Extreme depth of odd-numbered pages :—

pp. 173, 177, 179, 183, 185, 187	= 174 mm.
pp. 175	= $174\frac{1}{2}$,,
pp. 181, 189, 191	= 175 ,,
p. 169	= 178 ,,
p. 171	= $178\frac{1}{2}$,,

CONTENTS
(Nos. 18 & 21) "A Parliamentary Sketch" (concluded). pp. 169-174.
(No. 20) "Public Dinners." pp. 175-180.
(No. 52) "The First of May." pp. 181-188.
(No. 47) "Brokers' and Marine-Store Shops" (continued to Part 9). pp. 189-192.

PART 9.

FRONT WRAPPER (OUTSIDE)
Same as No. I. except "No. IX."

CHARLES DICKENS.

FRONT WRAPPER (INSIDE)
Same as No. VIII.

BACK WRAPPER (INSIDE)
Same as No. VIII.

BACK WRAPPER (OUTSIDE)
"Travelling and Hunting Maps" ; "Crosse & Blackwell" ; and "T. Cox Savory," the latter with illustration of Clock.

ADVERTISEMENTS (BACK)
Francis West, 4 pp. unnumbered.
  p. (1) Text of 39 lines, no heading.
  p. (2) "A View in Fleet Street, Nov. 9, 1837," with large woodcut of premises.
  p. (3) "Important | to all who require | Spectacles."
  p. (4) "To the Public. | F. West, | Optician."

PLATES (TWO)
(No. 17) "The Gin Shop." (to face p. 194).
(No. 18) "The Pawnbroker's Shop." (to face p. 200).

TEXT MEASUREMENTS
Extreme depth of odd-numbered pages :—

p. 199	= 80 mm.	pp. 195, 197	= 174 mm.
p. 207	= 85 „	pp. 209, 211, 213, 215	= 175 „
p. 193	= 98 „	pp. 201, 203	= 179 „
p. 205	= 170 „		

CONTENTS
(No. 47) "Brokers' and Marine-Store Shops" (concluded). p. 193.
(No. 15) "Gin-Shops." pp. 194-199.
(No. 28) "The Pawnbroker's Shop." pp. 200-207.
(No. 10) "Criminal Courts." pp. 208-212.
(No. 46) "A Visit to Newgate" (continued to Part 10). pp. 213-216.

This sketch is erroneously indexed in "Contents" list as commencing on page 218, instead of page 213.

SKETCHES BY "BOZ."

PART 10.

FRONT WRAPPER (OUTSIDE)
Same as No. I. except "No. X."

FRONT WRAPPER (INSIDE)
Same as Nos. VIII. and IX.

BACK WRAPPER (INSIDE)
"Popular Juvenile Books." Same as Part 7 outside back
wrapper.

BACK WRAPPER (OUTSIDE)
"New Work by ' Boz ' | Nicholas Nickleby" ; "Maps of
the English Counties" ; and "T. Cox Savory."

PLATES (TWO)
(No. 19) "Private Theatres." (to face p. 129).
(No. 20) "Thoughts about People." (to face p. 229).

TEXT
pp. 217-240. An unnumbered leaf (pp. 227-228) carries
the sub-title "Characters." Verso blank.

TEXT MEASUREMENTS
Extreme depth of odd-numbered pages :—

pp. 217, 231, 235, 237	= 174 mm.
p. 229	= 174½ ,,
p. 239	= 175 ,,
pp. 219, 221, 225	= 178 ,,
pp. 223, 233	= 178½ ,,

CONTENTS
(No. 46) "A Visit to Newgate" (concluded). pp. 217-226.
(No. 23) "Thoughts about People." pp. 229-233.
(No. 43) "A Christmas Dinner." pp. 234-238.
(No. 44) "The New Year" (continued to Part 11).
pp. 239-240.

PART 11.

FRONT WRAPPER (OUTSIDE)
Same as No. I. except "No. XI."

FRONT WRAPPER (INSIDE)
Same as Nos. VIII., IX., and X.

BACK WRAPPER (INSIDE)
Same as No. X.

BACK WRAPPER (OUTSIDE)
"Why ? and Because." F. West ; "Maps of the English Counties" ; and "T. Cox Savory" with cut of Clock.

PLATES (Two)
(No. 21) "Jemima Evans." (to face p. 245).
(No. 22) "A Pickpocket in Custody." (to face p. 255).

TEXT MEASUREMENTS
Extreme depth of odd-numbered pages :—

p. 259	=	$26\frac{1}{4}$ mm.	p. 263	=	$174\frac{1}{2}$ mm.
p. 249	=	$97\frac{1}{2}$,,	pp. 245, 257	=	175 ,,
p. 247	=	169 ,,	p. 241	=	178 ,,
p. 261	=	170 ,,	p. 251	=	$178\frac{1}{2}$,,
p. 243	=	173 ,,	p. 253	=	179 ,,
p. 255	=	174 ,,			

CONTENTS
(No. 44) "The New Year" (concluded). pp. 241-244.
(No. 35) "Miss Evans and the Eagle." pp. 245-249.
(No. 42) "The Parlour Orator." pp. 250-254.
(No. 53) "The Hospital Patient." pp. 255-259.
(No. 38) "Misplaced Attachment of Mr. John Dounce" (continued to Part 12). pp. 260-264.

PART 12.

FRONT WRAPPER (OUTSIDE)
Same as No. I. except "No. XII."

FRONT WRAPPER (INSIDE)
Same as Nos. VIII., IX., X., and XI.

BACK WRAPPER (INSIDE)
Same as Nos. X. and XI.

BACK WRAPPER (OUTSIDE)
"West's Newly-Invented Seed Glass" ; "T. Cox Savory" ; and "Maps of the English Counties."

CHARLES DICKENS.

TEXT MEASUREMENTS
Extreme depth of odd-numbered pages :—

p. 357	= 161½ mm.	p. 347	= 174½ mm.
p. 353	= 169½ ,,	pp. 349, 351	= 175 ,,
pp. 341, 343	= 173½ ,,	pp. 337, 345	= 178 ,,
pp. 339, 355, 359	= 174 ,,		

CONTENTS

(No. 1) "Mr. Minns and his Cousin" (concluded). pp. 337-345.

(No. 50) "Sentiment." pp. 346-357.

(No. 51) "The Tuggs's at Ramsgate" (continued to Part 16). pp. 358-360.

PART 16.

FRONT WRAPPER (OUTSIDE)
Same as No. I. except "No. XVI."

FRONT WRAPPER (INSIDE)
Same as No. XIV.

BACK WRAPPER (INSIDE)
"T. Cox Savory, Watchmaker, 47, Cornhill, London."

BACK WRAPPER (OUTSIDE)
"Preparing for Publication."

PLATES (Two)

(No. 31) "Horatio Sparkins." (to face p. 379).

(No. 32) "The Winglebury Duel." (to face p. 431).

TEXT MEASUREMENTS
Extreme depth of odd-numbered pages :—

p. 373	= 170 mm.	p. 379	= 175½ mm.
p. 371	= 171 ,,	p. 375	= 176 ,,
pp. 369, 381	= 174 ,,	p. 363	= 179½ ,,
p. 365	= 174½ ,,	pp. 361, 377	= 180 ,,
p. 367	= 175 ,,	p. 383	= 180½ ,,

CONTENTS

(No. 51) "The Tuggs's at Ramsgate" (concluded). pp. 361-378.

PLATES (TWO)

(No. 27) "The Boarding House | Chap. 2nd." (to face p. 314).

(No. 28) "Mr. Minns and his Cousins." (to face p. 335).

TEXT MEASUREMENTS

Extreme depth of odd-numbered pages :—

pp. 317, 321, 327, 331, 333	=	174 mm.
pp. 319, 323, 325	=	174½ „
p. 335	=	175½ „
pp. 313, 315	=	178½ „
p. 329	=	179 „

CONTENTS

(No. 5) "The Boarding-House." Chapter the First (concluded). p. 313.

(No. 6) "The Boarding-House." Chapter the Second. pp. 314-334.

(No. 1) "Mr. Minns and his Cousin" (continued to Part 15). pp. 335-336.

PART 15.

FRONT WRAPPER (OUTSIDE)

Same as No. I. except "No. XV."

FRONT WRAPPER (INSIDE)

Same as No. XIV.

BACK WRAPPER (INSIDE)

"T. Cox Savory," with cut of Clock ; "What is the Stanhope Lens ? " and "The Pickwick Papers Complete."

BACK WRAPPER (OUTSIDE)

"New Year's Address." (A. Rowland & Son). Full page.

PLATES (TWO)

(No. 29) "Sentiment." (to face p. 346).

(No. 30) "The Tuggs at Ramsgate." (to face p. 358).

CHARLES DICKENS.

TEXT

pp. 289-312. An unnumbered leaf (pp. 295-296), carries the sub-title, "Tales." Verso blank.

TEXT MEASUREMENTS

Extreme depth of odd-numbered pages :—

p. 291	= 107 mm.	p. 311	=	$175\frac{1}{2}$ mm.
p. 309	= 174 ,,	pp. 289, 293	=	179 ,,
pp. 303, 305	= $174\frac{1}{2}$,,	p. 287	=	180 ,,
pp. 299, 301, 307 =	175 ,,			

CONTENTS

(No. 37) "Making a Night of it" (concluded). pp. 289-291.

(No. 41) "The Prisoners' Van." pp. 292-294.

(No. 5) "The Boarding-House." Chapter the First (continued to Part 14). pp. 297-312.

PART 14.

FRONT WRAPPER (OUTSIDE)

Same as No. I. except "No. XIV."

FRONT WRAPPER (INSIDE)

"Sketches of Young Gentlemen," Fourth Edition; "Sketches of Young Ladies," Seventh Edition; both in full measure. Below, in half measure, Four titles: "A Visit to the British Museum"; "Morals from the Churchyard"; "The Juvenile Budget"; "Chess for Beginners."

BACK WRAPPER (INSIDE)

"Popular Juvenile Books." Nine titles in half measure: "Tom Thumb the Great"; "Remember"; "The Juvenile Pianist"; "Poetry for Children"; "The Two Cousins"; "New Scenes for Youth"; "Caroline"; "The Spoiled Child Reclaimed"; "Rose and Anne." Below, in full measure, "Edward, the Crusader's Son."

BACK WRAPPER (OUTSIDE)

"What is the Stanhope Lens?" (F. West); "T. Cox Savory" with woodcut of Clock.

PLATES (TWO)
    (No. 23) "Mr. John Dounce."   (to face p. 260).
    (No. 24) "The Dancing Academy."   (to face p. 274).

TEXT MEASUREMENTS
    Extreme depth of odd-numbered pages :—

p. 285	=	27 mm.
p. 273	=	$35\frac{1}{2}$,,
pp. 269, 271, 275, 277, 279, 283	=	174 ,,
p. 287	=	$174\frac{1}{2}$,,
pp. 265, 267	=	178 ,,
p. 281	=	179 ,,

CONTENTS
    (No. 38) "Misplaced Attachment of Mr. John Dounce" (concluded).   pp. 265-266.
    (No. 40) "The Mistaken Milliner. A Tale of Ambition." pp. 267-273.
    (No. 36) "The Dancing Academy."   pp. 274-280.
    (No. 11) "Shabby-Genteel People."   pp. 281-285.
    (No. 37) "Making a Night of it" (continued to Part 13). pp. 286-288.

PART 13.

FRONT WRAPPER (OUTSIDE)
    Same as No. I. except "No. XIII."

FRONT WRAPPER (INSIDE)
    Same as Nos. VIII., IX., X., XI., and XII.

BACK WRAPPER (INSIDE)
    "Popular Juvenile Books," with Seven titles in half measure. Below : "T. Cox Savory," with cut of Candlestick.

BACK WRAPPER (OUTSIDE)
    "Britannia Life Assurance Company."   Full page.

PLATES (TWO)
    (No. 25) "Making a Night of it."   (to face p. 286).
    (No. 26) "The Boarding House."   (to face p. 297).

CHARLES DICKENS.

Text
 pp. 489-526, with blank leaf, pp. (527-528). Imprint at foot of p. 526 : "Whiting, Beaufort House, Strand."

> Page 515 should be numbered in top-centre. In later issues the pagination was omitted.

> Page 526. In sixth line up, the words "reeled before" are run together. This, however, is not a point of early issue, as the typographical error persisted through many printings, even to the volume edition often seen without imprint on page 526.

Preliminary Leaves
 Half-title : "Sketches by Boz." Verso blank (I., II.).

 Title-page : dated 1839. Verso, with imprint as on p. 526 (III., IV.). See illustration.

 "Advertisement." Seven lines, dated : "London, May 15, 1839." Verso blank (V., VI.).

 Contents. 2 pp. (VII., VIII.).

Text Measurements
 Extreme depth of following pages :—

p. 497	= 94 mm.
p. 526 (to the words : "The End.")	= 132 „
p. 523	= 169½ „
pp. 493, 499	= 170½ „
pp. 501, 513, 525, 526	= 174 „
pp. 509, 511	= 174½ „
pp. 489, 495, 515, 517, 519	= 175 „
p. 503	= 175½ „
p. 521	= 178 „
pp. 491, 505, 507	= 179 „

Contents
 (Nos. 12 & 14) "Passage in the Life of Mr. Watkins Tottle" (concluded). pp. 489-497.

 (No. 4) "The Bloomsbury Christening." pp. 498-514.
> This sketch is erroneously indexed in "Contents" list as commencing on page 497.

 (No. 59) "The Drunkard's Death." pp. 515-526.

Reclaimed"; "Rose and Anne." Below, in full measure, "Nursery Government."

PLATES (TWO)

(No. 37) "The Lock-up House." (to face p. 479).

(No. 38) "Mr. Watkins Tottle and Miss Lillerton." (to face p. 491).

TEXT MEASUREMENTS

Extreme depth of odd-numbered pages :—

p. 459	$= 44\frac{1}{2}$ mm.	pp. 447, 453	$= 174\frac{1}{2}$ mm.
pp. 435, 451, 481	$= 169\frac{1}{2}$,,	p. 463	$= 175$,,
pp. 461, 485	$= 170$,,	p. 473	$= 177\frac{1}{2}$,,
pp. 471, 487	$= 173\frac{1}{2}$,,	p. 443	$= 178$,,
pp. 437, 439, 445, 449,		pp. 433, 441	$= 178\frac{1}{2}$,,
455, 465, 467, 469,		pp. 457, 475	$= 179$,,
477, 479, 483	$= 174$,,		

CONTENTS

(No. 49) "The Great Winglebury Duel" (concluded). pp. 433-448.

(No. 2) "Mrs. Joseph Porter." pp. 449-459.

(Nos. 12 & 14) "Passage in the Life of Mr. Watkins Tottle" (continued to Part 20). pp. 460-488.

PART 20.

FRONT WRAPPER (OUTSIDE)

Same as No. I. except "No. XX."

FRONT WRAPPER (INSIDE)

Same as Nos. XVIII. and XIX., except no date is mentioned.

BACK WRAPPER (INSIDE)

"The Pickwick Papers Complete"; "Sketches of Young Ladies," Eighth Edition; and "Sketches of Young Gentlemen," Fifth Edition.

BACK WRAPPER (OUTSIDE)

Same as No. XIX.

PLATES (TWO)

(No. 39) "Bloomsbury Christening." (to face p. 498).

(No. 40) Engraved title-page (undated).

127

CHARLES DICKENS.

FRONT WRAPPER (INSIDE)
Similar to Part 17, except the last work reads : "On the 30th of April."

BACK WRAPPER (INSIDE)
"Proclamation ! ! ! " (F. West) ; and "The Pickwick Papers Complete."

BACK WRAPPER (OUTSIDE)
"A Certain Cure for Corns and Bunions." (Allingham).

PLATES (TWO)
(No. 35) "Mrs. Joseph Porter." (to face p. 449).
(No. 36) "Watkins Tottle." (to face p. 471).

TEXT MEASUREMENTS
Extreme depth of odd-numbered pages :—

p. 413	= 169½ mm.	pp. 419, 431	= 175 mm.
p. 417	= 170 „	p. 411	= 178 „
pp. 421, 423, 429	= 174 „	pp. 409, 415	= 178½ „
p. 427	= 174½ „	p. 425	= 179 „

CONTENTS
(No. 8) "The Steam Excursion" (concluded). pp. 409-430.
(No. 49) "The Great Winglebury Duel" (continued to Part 19). pp. 431-432.

PART 19.

FRONT WRAPPER (OUTSIDE)
Same as No. I. except "No. XIX."

FRONT WRAPPER (INSIDE)
Same as No. XVIII.

BACK WRAPPER (INSIDE)
Same as No. XVIII.

BACK WRAPPER (OUTSIDE)
"Popular Juvenile Books." Nine titles in half measure : "Tom Thumb" ; "Remember" ; "The Juvenile Pianist"; "Poetry for Children" ; "New Scenes for Youth" ; "The Two Cousins" ; "Caroline" ; "The Spoiled Child

126

(No. 3) "Horatio Sparkins" (continued to Part 17). pp. 379-384.

This sketch is erroneously indexed in "Contents" list, as commencing on p. 378, instead of p. 379.

PART 17.

FRONT WRAPPER (OUTSIDE)
Same as No. I. except "No. XVII."

FRONT WRAPPER (INSIDE)
"Preparing for Publication." Three works are announced : "Songs and Ballads" ; "A Paper—of Tobacco" ; "On the 31st of March . . . | Phiz's Fancies."

BACK WRAPPER (INSIDE)
"T. Cox Savory" ; "Proclamation" (F. West) ; "The Pickwick Papers Complete."

BACK WRAPPER (OUTSIDE)
"The Toilet. | Rowland's Macassar Oil." Full page.

PLATES (TWO)
(No. 33) "Steam Excursions | Pl. 1." (to face p. 408).
(No. 34) "Steam Excursions | Pl. 2." (to face p. 429).

TEXT MEASUREMENTS
Extreme depth of odd-numbered pages :—

p. 395	$= 26\frac{1}{2}$ mm.	pp. 387, 389, 399, 403 $= 175$ mm.
p. 407	$= 80\frac{1}{2}$,,	p. 391 $= 176$,,
pp. 393, 397, 405 $= 174$,,		p. 385 $= 179$,,
p. 401	$= 174\frac{1}{2}$,,	

CONTENTS
(No. 3) "Horatio Sparkins" (concluded). pp. 385-395.
(No. 48) "The Black Veil." pp. 396-407.
(No. 8) "The Steam Excursion" (continued to Part 18). p. 408.

PART 18.

FRONT WRAPPER (OUTSIDE)
Same as No. I. except "No. XVIII."

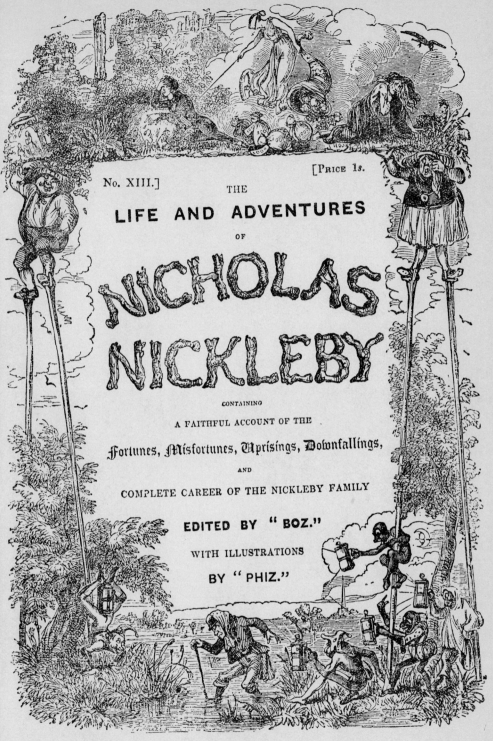

[No. XIII.]

[PRICE 1s.

THE

LIFE AND ADVENTURES

OF

NICHOLAS NICKLEBY

CONTAINING

A FAITHFUL ACCOUNT OF THE

Fortunes, Misfortunes, Uprisings, Downfallings,

AND

COMPLETE CAREER OF THE NICKLEBY FAMILY

EDITED BY "BOZ."

WITH ILLUSTRATIONS

BY "PHIZ."

LONDON   CHAPMAN AND HALL, 186, STRAND

Bradbury and Evans,]   [Printers, Whitefriars, London.

The Front Wrapper to the original edition of "Nicholas Nickleby,"
as published in 19/20 monthly parts, 1838-1839.

THE

LIFE AND ADVENTURES

OF

NICHOLAS NICKLEBY.

BY CHARLES DICKENS.

WITH ILLUSTRATIONS BY PHIZ

LONDON:
CHAPMAN AND HALL, 186, STRAND.

MDCCCXXXIX.

Nicholas Nickleby

in

19/20 Monthly Parts
April, 1838, to October, 1839.

ORIGINALLY issued in twenty numbers, bound in nineteen, price one shilling, except the last two (19 and 20), which were issued as a double number at two shillings. The wrappers of green, had a design on the front by Hablot K. Browne (Phiz). Five months had elapsed since the completion of "Pickwick," and Part 5 of "Sketches by Boz" was in circulation, when the first part of "Nickleby" was issued on April 2nd, 1838; and continued without interruption to its conclusion with Part 19/20 in October, 1839. To the collector, the book has many interesting appeals, as notwithstanding the large circulation in the early days, and which was maintained throughout the run, it cannot be regarded as the easiest of tasks to obtain first grade copies. Those which have appeared of late in the sale rooms are in anything but fine condition, and seldom in such completeness as would conform to the known requirements which are here collated; so that the offer of a "pedigree" copy would probably find many willing buyers.

TEXT.

There are two distinguishing features only, which point out early printing from later issues. These occur in Parts 4 and 5, and are duly recorded in the collations of these numbers.

PLATES.

The series of forty plates contained in the work, were designed and etched by Phiz. Following on the experience gained in the publication of "Pickwick," and in anticipation of a monthly circulation reaching 40,000 to 50,000 copies, the Author and Publishers decided to continue the system of duplicate etchings for each subject. When, however, the circulation began to show definite signs of still further expansion, and owing to the fact that Dickens was never beforehand with his manuscript, it became necessary, beginning with Part 2, to have the plates etched in triplicate, and, in several cases after Part 6, in quadruplicate.

There can be no question whatsoever as to priority of these duplicates, for they were, by reason of dire necessity, executed in rapid succession, and all of them were published simultaneously in the initial issue of the parts. Neither are there any outstanding variations of a major character in the "state" of impressions from the individual "steels." The variations, if any, are limited to those falling in the minor class.

It is possible, however, with many of the duplicated plates, to give the order in which the artist executed them, because he etched on the steels a distinguishing numeral, e.g., 1, 2, 3, 4, and in a few instances, I, II, III, IIII. These numerals or characters may be found on most of the plates appearing in Parts 6, 7, 8, 9, 10, 11, 12, 13, 15, and 17; and as a rule they are placed in the lower right corner; sometimes in the opposite corner, but in Plate 31, they are to be seen on the front of the mantelshelf.

A long-cherished delusion can be dissipated, when Plate 29 in Part 15 comes up for consideration. This plate, with the long inscription: "Nicholas makes his first visit to the lodgings of Mr. Bray," has always been given a preference in issue over the one carrying the shorter title—"Nicholas makes his first visit to Mr. Bray." Bearing in mind the statement made in the second paragraph of these notes on the plates, no exception is permissible or called for in regard to this designed subject; both the "long" and "short" titles are of equal merit and contemporaneous. In Part 14, a notice appeared to the effect that Phiz, owing to indisposition, was unable to supply the two plates for that number, but that they would appear in the succeeding issue. Four drawings, therefore, were required for the next number, and of these drawings, we know that fourteen steels were supplied— three each for Part 14, and four each for Part 15. With perhaps not more than twenty-eight days at his disposal, in which to supply this monumental number of etchings, the artist must have found himself in the embarrassing position of having to produce one steel every forty-eight hours, and it requires little imagination to conceive the inevitable rush which resulted, in an endeavour to complete the contract. Can it be wondered at, that some slight error crept in—that three of the four etchings of this same subject are seen with a different inscription to the one on the remaining steel? If we appreciate the fact that the inscription is the last operation effected, after final proofs are pulled, then we easily and quickly arrive at the answer to the question.

It is quite well known that Phiz kept his own private press, and that he always pulled his own proofs. They were fully completed and approved, sometimes before he knew what title the Author had in mind for the subject of the illustration. Accepting this fact, it follows that Phiz, after approval of his final proofs, proceeded to etch the inscriptions on the steels, without regard to the order in which they were executed, and evidently supplied the incorrect "long title" on three of them (A, C, D), before discovering his mistake. To remedy the error, he etched the correct "short title" on the remaining plate, which plate bears the figure "2" in the lower left corner, and is designated "B" in the collation.

Several collectors have pointed out that the "short title" is much more uncommon in the parts, than the "long" one. Such is the case; but this only goes further to support the contention as to non-priority of the duplicated plates. The simple explanation is—the three "long title" plates were in operation simultaneously with the one carrying the "short title"; in other words, in the proportion of three to one.

The four plates to Parts 1 and 2, were issued *with* and *without* the imprint of Chapman and Hall, but this duplication is not taken into account in the total arrived at, as plates without imprints did not appear in the earliest issues of the monthly parts, and may, therefore, be termed "second states."

The portrait for Part 19/20 must have the publishers' imprint; without such imprint it is a "second state," and does not appear in the monthly parts.

In view of the non-priority of any one etching over another of the same subject, no object is served by detailing the numerous differences—the simplest of all being the constantly changing signature of "Phiz." Suffice it to say, they exist in the variants as here scheduled :—

Part	Plates						Total
1	1	and	2	2	etchings of each		4
2	3	,,	4	3	,,	,,	6
3	5	,,	6	3	,,	,,	6
4	7	,,	8	2	,,	,,	4
5	9	,,	10	3	,,	,,	6
6	11	,,	12	3	,,	,,	6
7	13	,,	14	4	,,	,,	8
8	15	,,	16	3	,,	,,	6
9	17	,,	18	4	,,	,,	8
10	19	,,	20	3	,,	,,	6
11	21	,,	22	3	,,	,,	6
12	23	,,	24	4	,,	,,	8
13	25	,,	26	4	,,	,,	8
15	27	,,	28	3	,,	,,	6
,,	29	,,	30	4	,,	,,	8
16	31	,,	32	4	,,	,,	8
17	33	,,	34	4	,,	,,	8
18	35	,,	36	3	,,	,,	6
19/20	37,	38,	39	3	,,	,,	9
,,	40			2	,,	,,	2
							129

NICHOLAS NICKLEBY.

WRAPPERS.

Apart from the essential change of "Part No." only one variation occurs in the type matter of front cover, where in Part 10, the imprint of Bradbury and Evans is added. In Part 11, a curious and unexplainable transposition of the advertisements printed on the inside of covers, is duly noted in the collation.

ADVERTISEMENTS (FRONT).

"The Nickleby Advertiser" is found in the front of each number, varying from 8 to 32 pages. The total number of pages in the series is 296, and is second only in volume to "Our Mutual Friend." No slips or other publicity matter are called for, except the publishers' announcement in Part 14. A small slip is noted in Part 11, but this can be regarded as non-essential to the collation.

ADVERTISEMENTS (BACK).

Traders' insets appear in all, except Parts 5 and 6. Some of them are scarce, such as "Amesbury's Supports" in Part 3, and particularly "Hill's Wafers" in Part 19/20. Where the latter is found, it should have affixed, five differently coloured specimen wafers, but it is unusual to see it in a complete state; more often than not, the wafers are lacking. The leaf: "Uniform Penny Postage" for Part 13, is not uncommon; although, judging by descriptions in some sale catalogues, they might lead to a conclusion of uniqueness. Of sixty copies examined, no less than forty-five contained the leaf. It is interesting to note the first appearance, in these periodical works, of that consistent advertiser in other periodicals of the day—"Norton's Camomile Pills." He is but a fleeting visitor to Part 12, for he is seen no more in this series of works, until the opening number of "Bleak House," in March, 1852: a lapse of thirteen years.

CHARLES DICKENS.

PART 1.

FRONT WRAPPER (OUTSIDE)

"No. I.] [Price 1s. | The | Life and Adventures | of | Nicholas | Nickleby | containing | a faithful account of the | Fortunes, Misfortunes, Uprisings, Down-fallings, | and | Complete Career of the Nickleby Family. | Edited by 'Boz.' | With Illustrations | by 'Phiz.' | London : Chapman and Hall, 186, Strand."

The words "Nicholas Nickleby" are embodied in, and form part of, the cover design ; all other lettering is type-set.

FRONT WRAPPER (INSIDE)

"Gentlemen's Watches. | ... | A. B. Savory & Sons."

BACK WRAPPER (INSIDE)

"Ackermann & Co." ; with woodcut of Royal Arms.

BACK WRAPPER (OUTSIDE)

"James Bohn, | 12, King William Street, Strand."

ADVERTISEMENTS (FRONT)

"The Nickleby Advertiser." 16 pp. unnumbered.

    p. (1) "No. I.—April 2, 1838."
    p. (2) "Illustrated Edition of Froissart."
    p. (3) "New and Popular Works published by | Robert Tyas, No. 50, Cheapside."
    p. (4) "Simplicity of Living."
    p. (5) "E. Grattan's List of New Publications."
    p. (6) ($\frac{1}{2}$ col.) "This day ... | Hints for the Table."
    p. (7) "Finden's Royal Gallery of British Art."
    p. (8) ($\frac{1}{2}$ col.) "Dr. Mantell's Lectures."
    p. (9) ($\frac{1}{2}$ col.) "Literature & Music Combined."
    p. (10) "Gibbon in Monthly Volumes."
    p. (11) "Lithography." (S. Straker).
    p. (12) ($\frac{1}{2}$ col.) "Chapman's Improved Gloves."
    p. (13) "Corporation of the London Assurance."
    p. (14) "The Vernal Season." (Gowland's Lotion).
    p. (15) "Mr. Robert Best Ede."
    p. (16) "Family Endowment Society."

ADVERTISEMENTS (BACK)

Francis West, Optician. 4 pp. unnumbered.

A 4-paged inset ; the outer pages blank. Page (2) has large wood-cut of "A View in Fleet Street, Nov. 9, 1837." Page (3) with text, headed : "Important | to all who require | Spectacles."

136

NICHOLAS NICKLEBY.

PLATES (TWO)
(No. 1) "Mr. Ralph Nickleby's first visit to his poor relations." (p. 13).
(No. 2) "The Yorkshire Schoolmaster at 'The Saracen's Head.'" (p. 25).
Both plates must have the publishers' imprint.

TEXT, WITH HEADING
"Life and Adventures | of | Nicholas Nickleby, | Chapter I." pp. (1)–32.

PART 2.

FRONT WRAPPER (OUTSIDE)
Same as No. I. except "No. II."

FRONT WRAPPER (INSIDE)
"Prices of the Gray's Inn Wine Establishment." (Geo. Henekey and Compy.).

BACK WRAPPER (INSIDE)
"This day is published . . . | The Cultivation of the Dahlia. | By J. Paxton."

BACK WRAPPER (OUTSIDE)
Top of page: "The Premature Marriage"; below: "Reform Your Tailors' Bills !" (E. P. Doudney and Son).

ADVERTISEMENTS (FRONT)
"The Nickleby Advertiser." 16 pp. unnumbered.
p. (1) "No. II.—May 1, 1838."
p. (2) ($\frac{1}{2}$ col.) "Popular Songs."
p. (3) ($\frac{1}{4}$ col.) "Designed for the use of all Classes."
p. (4) "New Works | published by Chapman and Hall."
p. (5) "Elegant Present."
p. (6) "Splendid New Edition of Plays !"
p. (7) "Chess."
p. (8) "One volume . . . | A Garland of Love."
p. (9) "Sketches by 'Boz.'"
p. (10) "Price One Shilling, | A few Words on a few Wines."
p. (11) "Popular Juvenile Books."
p. (12) "Summer Tours."
p. (13) ($\frac{1}{2}$ col.) "Chapman's Improved Gloves."

p. (14) ($\frac{1}{2}$ col.) "Distortion of the Spine."
p. (15) "Heal and Son's French Mattresses."
p. (16) "Plate.—A. B. Savory and Sons."

ADVERTISEMENTS (BACK)
Mechi's Catalogue. 18 pp. with wrappers. Same as in Part 12 of "Pickwick."

PLATES (TWO)
(No. 3) "Nicholas starts for Yorkshire." (p. 38).
(No. 4) "The Five Sisters of York." (p. 45).
Both plates must have the publishers' imprint.

TEXT, WITH HEADING
"Chapter V." pp. 33–64.

PART 3.

FRONT WRAPPER (OUTSIDE)
Same as No. I. except "No. III."

FRONT WRAPPER (INSIDE)
"British College of Health." Last word of page: "Demerara."

BACK WRAPPER (INSIDE)
"New Works on the Fine Arts published by F. G. Moon."

BACK WRAPPER (OUTSIDE)
Same as No. II. except first words are "Just published."

ADVERTISEMENTS (FRONT)
"The Nickleby Advertiser." 16 pp. unnumbered.

    p. (1) "No. III.—June 1, 1838."
    p. (2) "On the 30th of June will be published . . . | Illustrations to Nicholas Nickleby."
    p. (3) ($\frac{1}{2}$ col.) "Canada."
    p. (4) ($\frac{1}{2}$ col.) "The Fine Arts."
    p. (5) "Nattali's Catalogue of Second-hand Books."
    p. (6) Same as Part 2, page 4.
    p. (7) Same as Part 2, page 5.
    p. (8) Same as Part 2, page 11.
    p. (9) "New Continental Guides."
    p. (10) "National Cognac Brandy Distillery | Company."
    p. (11) "Important to Gentlemen going abroad. | R. Kipling."

p. (12) "Pure Dublin Stout."
p. (13) (½ col.) "Laming's Effervescing Cheltenham Salts."
p. (14) "Ceremonials." (Gowland's Lotion).
p. (15) (½ col.) "To Epicures."
p. (16) "Beaufoy and Co., South Lambeth, London." With two woodcuts.

(To follow plates) :—"To Reading Clubs and Families, | in Town and Country." (Churton's Library). 2 pp. unnumbered.

ADVERTISEMENTS (BACK)

(1) Rippon and Burton; dated on first page "May 1st, 1838." Imprint of J. Bradley on last page. 4 pp. numbered (1)–4. Yellow paper.

(2) "National Loan Fund | Life Assurance Society." 16 pp. each numbered, except (1, 2) and (16). Imprint of A. H. Baily & Co. on last page, with date, 1838.

(3) Joseph Amesbury's Patent Supports. Large folding sheet (about 22″ × 8⅞″) printed both sides, with 15 numbered woodcuts and letterpress. Divided into 8 pp. numbered 1–8.

PLATES (Two)

(No. 5) "The internal economy of Dotheboys Hall." (p. 68).

(No. 6) "Kate Nickleby sitting to Miss La Creevy." (p. 89).

TEXT, WITH HEADING
"Chapter VIII." pp. 65–96.

PART 4.

FRONT WRAPPER (OUTSIDE)
Same as No. I. except "No. IV."

FRONT WRAPPER (INSIDE)
"Just Published, | . . . | Finden's Royal Gallery of British Art."

BACK WRAPPER (INSIDE)
"British College of Health."

CHARLES DICKENS.

BACK WRAPPER (OUTSIDE)
"Reform Your Tailors' Bills !" At foot of page : "The Premature Marriage."

ADVERTISEMENTS (FRONT)
"The Nickleby Advertiser." 8 pp. unnumbered.

    p. (1) "No. IV.—July 2, 1838."
    p. (2) "This day is published, | Chalon's Portrait of the Queen."
    p. (3) ($\frac{1}{2}$ col.) "Price 2s. . . . | American Broad Grins."
    p. (4) "China and Ironstone Dinner Services."
    p. (5) ($\frac{1}{4}$ col.) "Ringworm effectually cured."
    p. (6) "Tender Feet."
    p. (7) ($\frac{1}{4}$ col.) "Glass Shades."
    p. (8) "Plate.—A. B. Savory and Sons."

ADVERTISEMENTS (BACK)
(1) "Gravesend | Star Steam Packets" ; dated June 13th, 1838. One leaf, verso blank.
(2) "Poor Man's Pill" ; in a surround of portraits and a view of the Royal College of Surgeons. Verso, with view of Apothecaries' Hall. 2 pp. unnumbered.

PLATES (TWO)
(No. 7) "Newman Noggs leaves the ladies in the empty house." (p. 100).
(No. 8) "Nicholas astonishes Mr. Squeers and family." (p. 116).

TEXT, WITH HEADING
"Chapter XI." pp. 97–128.

    The first issue of text to this part, has the misprint "visiter" for "sister" in page 123, line 17.

PART 5.

FRONT WRAPPER (OUTSIDE)
Same as No. I. except "No. V."

FRONT WRAPPER (INSIDE)
"British College of Health." Last words : "page 587."

BACK WRAPPER (INSIDE)
"Steam Navigation up the Rhine."

BACK WRAPPER (OUTSIDE)
"Valuable Books." (James Bohn).

ADVERTISEMENTS (FRONT)
"The Nickleby Advertiser." 8 pp. unnumbered.

    p. (1) "No. V.—August 1, 1838."
    p. (2) ($\frac{1}{2}$ col.) "Second thousand. | Dr. Mantell's New Work."
    p. (3) ($\frac{1}{2}$ col.) "Sir George Stephen's New Work."
    p. (4) "The British Museum."
    p. (5) ($\frac{1}{2}$ col.) "To Flute Players."
    p. (6) "Gowland's Lotion."
    p. (7) "Laming's Effervescing Cheltenham Salts."
    p. (8) "Beaufoy's | instant Cure for the Tooth-ache."

PLATES (TWO)
(No. 9) "Nicholas engaged as Tutor in a private family." (p. 153).
(No. 10) "Madame Mantalini introduces Kate to Miss Knag." (p. 157).

TEXT, WITH HEADING
"Chapter XV." pp. 129–160.

    Page 160, line 6 up, should read "latter" in first issue of text. This was later corrected to "letter."

PART 6.

FRONT WRAPPER (OUTSIDE)
Same as No. I. except "No. VI."

FRONT WRAPPER (INSIDE)
"British College of Health." Last words : "The Hygeist."

BACK WRAPPER (INSIDE)
"New and Popular Works published by | Robert Tyas . . ."

BACK WRAPPER (OUTSIDE)
Same as Part 4.

ADVERTISEMENTS (FRONT)
"The Nickleby Advertiser." 8 pp. unnumbered.

    p. (1) "No. VI.—September 1, 1838."
    p. (2) "Road Books for Great Britain | and Ireland."
    p. (3) "New and cheaper Edition . . . | Kindness in Women."

p. (4) (½ col.) "Eugene Aram—Second Edition."
p. (5) "Laming's Effervescing Cheltenham Salts."
p. (6) "Labern's Botanic Cream."
p. (7) (½ col.) "Partridge Shooting."
p. (8) "A. B. Savory and Sons, Goldsmiths."

PLATES (TWO)

(No. 11) "Miss Nickleby introduced to her Uncle's friends." (p. 175).

(No. 12) "Mr. Ralph Nickleby's 'honest' composure." (p. 188).

TEXT, WITH HEADING
"Chapter XVIII." pp. 161–192.

PART 7.

FRONT WRAPPER (OUTSIDE)
Same as No. I. except "No. VII."

FRONT WRAPPER (INSIDE)
"British College of Health." Last line : "Town, Demerara."

BACK WRAPPER (INSIDE)
"Chubb's New Patent Detector Lock."

BACK WRAPPER (OUTSIDE)
Same as Nos. IV. and VI.

ADVERTISEMENTS (FRONT)
"The Nickleby Advertiser." 8 pp. unnumbered.

p. (1) "No. VII.—October 1, 1838."
p. (2) (½ col.) "Sir George Stephen's | New Work."
p. (3) "A splendid Book for Presentation."
p. (4) "British and Colonial | Trust and Assurance Company."
p. (5) (½ col.) "Compound Microscopes."
p. (6) "Gowland's Lotion."
p. (7) (½ col.) "Ornamental Hair."
p. (8) "The following | Splendid Annuals for 1839."

ADVERTISEMENTS (BACK)

(1) "Immense Saving in the purchase of Tea." (Sidney and Co.). One leaf, verso blank.

An alternative to this inset appears in the Dexter copy, the headline reading : "Immense Fall in Tea ! ! !"

(2) "On the First of November will be published | No. I. | . . . | Heads of the People." (Robert Tyas). With woodcut. 2 pp. numbered on second page. Yellow tinted paper.

PLATES (TWO)

(No. 13) "The Professional Gentlemen at Madame Mantalini's." (p. 196).

(No. 14) "The Country Manager rehearses a Combat." (p. 209).

TEXT, WITH HEADING

"Chapter XXI." pp. 193–224.

PART 8.

FRONT WRAPPER (OUTSIDE)

Same as No. I. except "No. VIII."

FRONT WRAPPER (INSIDE)

"British College of Health." Last words : "Agent for India."

BACK WRAPPER (INSIDE)

"Just published, | Jenning's Landscape Annual."

BACK WRAPPER (OUTSIDE)

Same as Nos. IV. VI. and VII.

ADVERTISEMENTS (FRONT)

"The Nickleby Advertiser." 16 pp. unnumbered.

    p. (1) "No. VIII.—November 1, 1838."

    p. (2) "In One Volume . . . | Caunter's & Daniell's Oriental Annual."

    p. (3) ($\frac{1}{2}$ col.) "Works recently published." (W. S. Orr & Co.).

    p. (4) "Ladies and Gentlemen's Pocket-Books . . ."

    p. (5) (Continuation of above).

    p. (6) "Hume & Smollett's England."

    p. (7) "The following New Works are published by | S. & J. Fuller . . ."

    p. (8) "New Annual for 1839."

    p. (9) ($\frac{1}{2}$ col.) "Just published, | Ackermann's Annuals."

    p. (10) "Oliver Twist."

    p. (11) ($\frac{1}{2}$ col.) "The Double Patent Pen."

p. (12) "Heal and Son's French Mattresses."
p. (13) (½ col.) "Hosiery."
p. (14) "Falcon Glass Works."
p. (15) "Labern's Botanic Cream."
p. (16)   Same as Part 5, page 8.

ADVERTISEMENTS (BACK)

(1) "This day is published . . . | No. 1 ; | . . . | Heads of the People." (Robert Tyas). With woodcut. 2 pp. numbered on second page. Buff paper.

(2) "Works published by William Smith." 4 pp. unnumbered. Cream paper.

(3) Mechi's Catalogue. 18 pp. of Text as Part 2. Outside front wrapper is printed with view of shop front ; other three sides blank. Outer sides of wrapper printed in yellow and black.

PLATES (TWO)

(No. 15) "The great bespeak for Miss Snevellicci." (p. 237).

(No. 16) "Nicholas instructs Smike in the Art of Acting." (p. 248).

> F. W. Pailthorpe is responsible for the statement that Plate 15 was etched five times. It is recorded in the Dexter library, although no actual specimens of the two additional plates have been traced.
>
> Of the three steels to Plate 16, two read as the above inscription, and agree with the line in list of illustrations ; they are numbered "1" and "2" in lower right of the etching. The third steel, which is numbered "3," omits the word "in."

TEXT, WITH HEADING
"Chapter XXIV." pp. 225–256.

PART 9.

FRONT WRAPPER (OUTSIDE)
Same as No. I. except "No. IX."

FRONT WRAPPER (INSIDE)
"British College of Health." Last line begins: "Mr. Thomas Gardner."

NICHOLAS NICKLEBY.

BACK WRAPPER (INSIDE)

"To Medicine Venders generally, | . . . | Sharp's Royal British Cerates and | Liniment."

BACK WRAPPER (OUTSIDE)

"On the 1st of January, 1839 | . . . | Gilbert's | New Map of England and Wales."

ADVERTISEMENTS (FRONT)

"The Nickleby Advertiser." 24 pp. unnumbered.

- p. (1) "No. IX.—December 1, 1838."
- p. (2) "Just published by Fisher, Son & Co."
- p. (3) "On the 1st of November . . . | The Pictorial Edition of Shakspere." (*sic*).
- p. (4) ($\frac{1}{2}$ col.) "To be had of all Booksellers."
- p. (5) "The Queen !—The Council !—The Coronation !"
- p. (6) "Under the superintendence of Mr. Charles Heath."
- p. (7) "Messrs. Hodgson and Graves, . . ."
- p. (8) ($\frac{1}{2}$ col.) "Just published . . . | Aristotelis Ethica . . ."
- p. (9) ($\frac{1}{4}$ col.) "The Drawing-Room | Almanack."
- p. (10) ($\frac{1}{4}$ col.) "Just published . . . | Men of Character."
- p. (11) "New Works | published by Chapman and Hall."
- pp. (12 and 13) Continuation of above. Same heading.
- p. (14) ($\frac{1}{2}$ col.) "J. Tyzack begs to inform his numerous | Friends."
- p. (15) ($\frac{1}{4}$ col.) "To Pedestrians, Sportsmen, &c."
- p. (16) "Mechi."
- p. (17) "Popular Juvenile Books."
- p. (18) Same heading as p. 6.
- p. (19) "Beds, Feathers, Bedticks, and Mattresses."
- p. (20) "C. Verrey."
- p. (21) "China Tea Company."
- p. (22) Same as Part 8, page 14.
- p. (23) "Harrison's Family Medicines."
- p. (24) "Britannia Life Assurance Company."

ADVERTISEMENTS (BACK)

(1) "Works of Art, | published by | Ackermann & Co., London." 8 pp. numbered (1)–8.

(2) "To Families, Schools, &c. | Prices of | Genuine Drugs & Medicines | sold by | J. Griffiths." 4 pp. numbered (1)–4.

CHARLES DICKENS.

PLATES (Two)
(No. 17) "Affectionate behaviour of Messrs. Pyke & Pluck."
(p. 261).
(No. 18) "Nicholas hints at the probability of his leaving
the Company." (p. 288).

TEXT, WITH HEADING
"Chapter XXVII." pp. 257–288.

PART 10.

FRONT WRAPPER (OUTSIDE)
Same as No. I. except "No. X." and with an additional
imprint at foot : "Bradbury and Evans,]. . .[Printers,
Whitefriars, London."

FRONT WRAPPER (INSIDE)
"British College of Health." Last words : "the double 'r.'"

BACK WRAPPER (INSIDE)
"Britannia Life Assurance Company."

BACK WRAPPER (OUTSIDE)
"Valuable Works."

ADVERTISEMENTS (FRONT)
"The Nickleby Advertiser." 16 pp. unnumbered.
p. (1) "No. X.—January 1, 1839."
p. (2) "Interesting Works for Young People."
p. (3) "Preparing for Publication."
p. (4) "Finden's Royal Gallery of British Art."
p. (5) ($\frac{1}{2}$ col.) "New Works just published by J. Rickerby."
p. (6) ($\frac{1}{2}$ col.) "To the Learned . . ."
p. (7) ($\frac{1}{2}$ col.) "Instructive and Amusing Presents for Youth."
p. (8) "New Series of Churton's Portrait . . . Gallery."
p. (9) ($\frac{1}{2}$ col.) "Gentlemen's Dress Coats."
p. (10) "Mechi." Same as Part 9, page 16.
p. (11) ($\frac{1}{2}$ col.) "Berdoe's New Waterproof | Clothing."
p. (12) "To the Heads of Public and Private Schools."
p. (13) Same as Part 8, page 14.
p. (14) "Gowland's Lotion."
p. (15) "Beds, Feathers, and Mattresses."
p. (16) Same as Part 5, page 8. (Beaufoy's).

NICHOLAS NICKLEBY.

ADVERTISEMENTS (BACK)

(1) Rippon and Burton ; dated on first page, "January 1st, 1839." Imprint of J. Bradley on last page. 4 pp. numbered (1)–4. Yellow paper.

(2) "Steel Pens. | Joseph Gillott." With cut of Royal Arms. One leaf, verso blank. Blue, Green, or Pink paper.

PLATES (TWO)

(No. 19) "Theatrical emotion of Mr. Vincent Crummles." (p. 300).

(No. 20) "Nicholas attracted by the mention of his Sister's name in the Coffee Room." (p. 310).

TEXT, WITH HEADING
"Chapter XXX." pp. 289–320.

PART 11.

FRONT WRAPPER (OUTSIDE)
Same as No. X. except "No. XI."

FRONT WRAPPER (INSIDE)
"British College of Health." Last word : "circulation."

BACK WRAPPER (INSIDE)
"Catalogue of Operas, | published by | J. J. Ewer & Co."

BACK WRAPPER (OUTSIDE)
"Just published, . . . | Illustrations to Nicholas Nickleby."

An examination of 45 copies of this part, has disclosed a most curious transposition of the two printed advertisements upon the inside of wrappers. Three of these copies differed ; having "Catalogue of Operas" within the front, and "British College of Health" within the back wrapper.

ADVERTISEMENTS (FRONT)
"The Nickleby Advertiser." 16 pp. unnumbered.

p. (1) "No. XI.—February 1, 1839."
p. (2) (½ col.) Mr. Colburn's New Publications.
p. (3) "Important to Ladies, Milliners, & Dress-makers."
p. (4) (½ col.) "Now ready . . . | The Lady and the Saints."
p. (5) "This day . . . | History of Napoleon" :

p. (6) "Hodgson's British & Foreign Library."
p. (7) "Society of Guardians."
p. (8) (½ col.) "For softening the Skin . . ."
p. (9) Falcon Glass Works. Same as Part 8, page 14.
p. (10) "British and Colonial | Trust and Assurance Company."
p. (11) (½ col.) "British Waterproofing | Company."
p. (12) "Mechi." Same as Part 9, page 16.
p. (13) "Important to Gentlemen."
p. (14) "C. Verrey."
p. (15) "Upholder by appointment | Thomas Fox."
p. (16) "Fables." (Charles Tilt).

> In many copies seen, there is to be found pasted within the front wrapper, a small yellow slip (4½″ × 3″), issued by Charles Tilt, Fleet Street. On one side it is headed, "New books for Children. | Tales of Shipwrecks & Disasters at Sea," and on verso, "Unique Present,—"

ADVERTISEMENTS (BACK)

"Ackermann & Co., 96, Strand, London. | To all Protestants." 8 pp. numbered 1–8. Printed in blue.

PLATES (TWO)

(No. 21) "Mr. and Mrs. Mantalini in Ralph Nickleby's Office." (p. 322).

(No. 22) "Emotion of Mr. Kenwigs, on hearing the family news from Nicholas." (p. 351).

TEXT, WITH HEADING

"Chapter XXXIV." pp. 321–352.

PART 12.

FRONT WRAPPER (OUTSIDE)

Same as No. X. except "No. XII."

FRONT WRAPPER (INSIDE)

"New Works just published . . ." (Darton and Clark).
Below : "Reform Your Tailors' Bills !"

BACK WRAPPER (INSIDE)

"Mr. Moon, her Majesty's Publisher . . . | The Waterloo Banquet."

BACK WRAPPER (OUTSIDE)

"Britannia Life Assurance Company."

NICHOLAS NICKLEBY.

ADVERTISEMENTS (FRONT)

"The Nickleby Advertiser." 16 pp. unnumbered.

p. (1) "No. XII.—March 1, 1839."
p. (2) ($\frac{1}{2}$ col.) "Just published by Dean & Munday."
p. (3) "186, Strand, March 1, | New Works."
p. (4) ($\frac{1}{2}$ col.) "To Parents, Tutors, & Others."
p. (5) "Just published, . . . | The Handbook of Domestic Cookery."
p. (6) "In oblong Quarto, . . . | Phiz's Fancies."
p. (7) ($\frac{1}{2}$ col.) "To Pedestrians, Sportsmen, &c."
p. (8) "Falcon Glass Works." Same as Part 8, page 14.
p. (9) "Chubb's | New Patent Locks, Fire-proof Safes."
p. (10) "Mechi." Different to Part XI.
p. (11) "Wholesale and for Exportation." (Joseph Gillott).
p. (12) ($\frac{1}{2}$ col.) "Gentlemen's Dress Coats."
p. (13) "Best Hats. Lowest Prices."
p. (14) "Upholstery | Warehouse."
p. (15) "Comfort for Tender Feet, &c."
p. (16) "Beaufoy's." Same as Part 5, page 8.

ADVERTISEMENTS (BACK)

(1) "Norton's | Camomile Pills." This line preceded at head of first page by 17 lines, in small italic type. Dated on third page : "Beccles 1st. Sept ; 1833." 4 pp. unnumbered.

(2) "New and Popular Works published by R. Tyas. | . . . | The History of | Napoleon." On third page : "No. I. | of | Shakspere" (*sic*). 4 pp. unnumbered. Yellow tinted paper.

PLATES (TWO)

(No. 23) "Mr. Linkinwater intimates his approval of Nicholas." (p. 356).

Of the four steels to Plate 23, three read as the above inscription. The fourth steel, which is signed on the floor boards to left of centre, omits " Mr." and agrees with list of illustrations.

(No. 24) "A sudden recognition, unexpected on both sides." (p. 373).

TEXT, WITH HEADING

"Chapter XXXVII." pp. 353–384.

CHARLES DICKENS.

PART 13.

FRONT WRAPPER (OUTSIDE)
Same as No. X. except "No. XIII."

FRONT WRAPPER (INSIDE)
"National Loan Fund."

BACK WRAPPER (INSIDE)
Same as No. XII. Inside Front Wrapper.

BACK WRAPPER (OUTSIDE)
Same as No. XII.

ADVERTISEMENTS (FRONT)
"The Nickleby Advertiser." 16 pp. unnumbered.
- p. (1) "No. XIII.—April 1, 1839."
- p. (2) "Splendidly and copiously illustrated work."
- p. (3) "Maxwell's Life of Wellington."
- p. (4) ($\frac{1}{2}$ col.) "Bees."
- p. (5) "Illustrations to Nicholas Nickleby."
- p. (6) "This day is published. | .. | Finden's Female Portraits .."
- p. (7) ($\frac{1}{2}$ col.) "Portable Fountains."
- p. (8) "Heal & Son's French Mattresses."
- p. (9) "Falcon Glass Works." Same as Part 8, page 14.
- p. (10) ($\frac{1}{2}$ col.) "British Waterproofing."
- p. (11) "Wholesale and for Exportation."
- p. (12) "New National Newspaper."
- p. (13) "Mechi." Same as Part 12, page 10.
- p. (14) "Before you purchase | Spectacles."
- p. (15) "Atmospheric Influence upon the Skin. | Spring."
- p. (16) "Upholder by appointment | Thomas Fox."

ADVERTISEMENTS (BACK)

(1) "Important, Valuable, and Cheap | Maps, | ... | published by | Grattan and Gilbert. 8 pp. numbered (1)–8.

(2) "New Weekly Journal, | The | Social Gazette :" 8 pp. all numbered, except 1, 3 and 8.

(3) "Queen Victoria | and the Uniform Penny Postage." 2 pp. unnumbered. All in half-measure.

PLATES (TWO)
(No. 25) "Nicholas recognizes the Young Lady unknown."
(p. 390).
(No. 26) "The Gentleman next door declares his passion
for Mrs. Nickleby." (p. 404).

TEXT, WITH HEADING
"Chapter XL." pp. 385–416.

PART 14.

FRONT WRAPPER (OUTSIDE)
Same as No. X. except "No. XIV."

FRONT WRAPPER (INSIDE)
Same as No. XIII.

BACK WRAPPER (INSIDE)
"Parris's Grand Authentic Coronation Picture."

BACK WRAPPER (OUTSIDE)
"Thos. Harris & Son, | Opticians to the Royal Family."
(The whole within single-rule border).

ADVERTISEMENTS (FRONT)
"The Nickleby Advertiser." 16 pp. unnumbered.
p. (1) "No. XIV.—May 1, 1839."
p. (2) "Merimee on Oil Painting, by Taylor."
p. (3) "Valentine Vox : by Sherry !"
p. (4) "In medium 8vo . . . | Smith's Standard Library."
p. (5) "New Edition . . . | Lady Lytton Bulwer's Novel."
p. (6) ($\frac{1}{2}$ col.) "Just published . . . | The Ladies' Flower Garden."
p. (7) ($\frac{1}{2}$ col.) "On the 1st of May . . . | Pickwick Abroad."
p. (8) "Published this day . . . | Three Expeditions . . ."
p. (9) "Furnishing Ironmongery Warehouse."
p. (10) "Easy Shoes."
p. (11) "Mechi." Same as Part 12, page 10.
p. (12) ($\frac{1}{2}$ col.) "To Anglers—Golden Perch."
p. (13) "T. Cox Savory."
p. (14) "The Seasons." (Gowland's Lotion).

p. (15) "British Empire Life Assurance Company."
p. (16) "New Works just published . . ." (Darton and Clark).
Same as Part 12 Inside Front Wrapper.

(To follow "Advertiser") Single leaf, printed on both sides. Verso reads: "NOTICE. | The Publishers regret to state, that in conse- | quence of the sudden indisposition of the Artist, | the Plates which should have accompanied this | Number are unavoidably postponed till next | Month, when Four will be given. | 186, Strand, | April 30, 1839." Below: five lines, announcing that the publication of "Phiz's Fancies" and "A Paper | of Tobacco," is postponed. Reverse of leaf has Chapman and Hall's announcements.

ADVERTISEMENTS (BACK)
(1) "Established 1795. | S. Alderman," with woodcut of premises. A view of other premises on back page. 4 pp. unnumbered. On either white, blue, pink, yellow, or yellow-tinted paper.
(2) "Kirby, Beard, & Kirby's." One leaf, verso blank. Printed in red on yellow paper.

PLATES
(None issued with this part.)

TEXT, WITH HEADING
"Chapter XLIII." pp. 417–448.

PART 15.

FRONT WRAPPER (OUTSIDE)
Same as No. X. except "No. XV."

FRONT WRAPPER (INSIDE)
"Parris's New Portrait of Her Majesty."

BACK WRAPPER (INSIDE)
"The | Magazine of Domestic Economy."

BACK WRAPPER (OUTSIDE)
Same as No. XIV.

NICHOLAS NICKLEBY.

ADVERTISEMENTS (FRONT)

"The Nickleby Advertiser." 16 pp. unnumbered.

p. (1) "No. XV.—June 1, 1839."
p. (2) "Finden's Royal Gallery of British Art."
p. (3) (½ col.) "Now ready . . . | Festus. A Poem."
p. (4) "This day is published . . . | Heads from Nicholas Nickleby."
p. (5) (½ col.) "New and interesting | Juvenile Books."
p. (6) "Now ready. | . . . | Sketches by 'Boz.' "
p. (7) (½ col.) "Smith's Standard Library."
p. (8) "Mechi." Same as Part 12, page 10.
p. (9) (½ col.) "Hosiery."
p. (10) (½ col.) "Patent Portable Water Closets."
p. (11) "Cheap, Plain, and Ornamental | Picture-Frames."
p. (12) "Charles Viner."
p. (13) "China, Glass, Earthenware, Lamps, Trays, &c."
p. (14) (½ col.) "A. J. Hemming, 341, Strand."
p. (15) "Most Important Information." With three woodcuts.
p. (16) Same as Part 14.

ADVERTISEMENTS (BACK)

"Mr. Adolphus's | History of England." 2 pp. un-numbered.

PLATES (FOUR)

(No. 27) "Mr. Mantalini poisons himself for the seventh time." (p. 435).

(No. 28) "Mr. Snawley enlarges on parental instinct." (p. 444).

(No. 29) "Nicholas makes his first visit to the lodgings of Mr. Bray." (p. 457).

(No. 30) "The Consultation." (p. 462).

Plate 29. Impressions from the four "steels" etched by "Phiz" for this plate, are distinguishable by the following :—

First : Long title as given above. Signature in caps. ; a dot precedes letter "P," and another dot appears between last two letters. This etching is not numbered.

Second : With short title—"Nicholas makes his first visit to Mr. Bray," as given in list of illustrations. Signature in caps. ; no dots. Figure "2" is seen faintly in lower left corner.

Third : Long title. Signature in script. Character "III" is etched below footstool on right.

Fourth : Long title. Signature in script, and touches shading of floor. Character "IIII" is etched below footstool on right.

TEXT, WITH HEADING
"Chapter XLVI." pp. 449–480.

PART 16.

FRONT WRAPPER (OUTSIDE)
Same as No. X. except "No. XVI."

FRONT WRAPPER (INSIDE)
"Mechi." Same as No. XII., page 10, of "Nickleby Advertiser."

BACK WRAPPER (INSIDE)
Same as No. XII. Inside Front Wrapper.

BACK WRAPPER (OUTSIDE)
"Thos. Harris & Son" (no rule around subject matter).

ADVERTISEMENTS (FRONT)
"The Nickleby Advertiser." 16 pp. unnumbered.

p. (1) "No. XVI.—July 1, 1839."
p. (2) "Just published, | 'The Army and Navy.' "
p. (3) "Edward Lacey."
p. (4) "Simplicity of Living."
p. (5) ($\frac{1}{2}$ col.) "The Mirror of Literature."
p. (6) "Maxwell's Life of Wellington."
p. (7) "Finden's Royal Gallery of British Art."
p. (8) "Midsummer Presents . . . | New Juvenile Books."
p. (9) "Ackermann's Photogenic Drawing-Box."
p. (10) "The China Tea Company."
p. (11) ($\frac{1}{2}$ col.) "Patent Fire-Proof Safes."
p. (12) "Important Case. | Mr. James Morison."
p. (13) ($\frac{1}{2}$ col.) "Carpet & Floor-Cloth | Manufacturers."
p. (14) "Perfection of the Toilet."

p. (15) "Beaufoy and Co. ; South Lambeth, London."
p. (16) "True Economy | ... | Thomas Fox."
> A slip, "Mary Ashby," is often called for in American sale catalogues, but this is a non-essential item. It is an after-insertion by the publishers, or a bookseller.

ADVERTISEMENTS (BACK)

(1) "Published by Darton and Clark." 8 pp. unnumbered. Each page headed as this, with woodcut on pp. 2, 3, and 4. Imprint of D. A. Doudney on first and last pages.

(2) "The Dublin Discussion.—Church Edition." 4 pp. numbered (1)-4. Imprint on pp. 1 and 4 : "Clarke, Printers, Silver Street, Falcon Square, London."

(3) "The | Medical Casket." 16 pp. numbered (1, 2)-16. Except the first page, all printed in half measure. Imprint on p. 16 : "W. Tyler, Printer, Bolt-court, London."

PLATES (TWO)

(No. 31) "Mysterious appearance of the Gentleman in the small clothes." (p. 487).

(No. 32) "The last brawl between Sir Mulbery and his pupil." (p. 500).

TEXT, WITH HEADING
"Chapter XLIX." pp. 481–512.

PART 17.

FRONT WRAPPER (OUTSIDE)
Same as No. X. except "No. XVII."

FRONT WRAPPER (INSIDE)
"Mechi." Same as No. XVI.

BACK WRAPPER (INSIDE)
"Dr. Perrengton's | Tonic Aperient Liqueur." Last words : "Boston, U.S."

BACK WRAPPER (OUTSIDE)
Same as No. XII. Inside Front Wrapper.

ADVERTISEMENTS (FRONT)
"The Nickleby Advertiser." 16 pp. unnumbered.

p. (1) "No. XVII.—August 1, 1839."
p. (2) "Just published . . . | A Third Preface . . ."
p. (3) "Just published . . . | . . . | Robert Morrison."
p. (4) ($\frac{1}{2}$ col.) "Popular Science."
p. (5) "Now ready | 'The Army and Navy.' "
p. (6) ($\frac{1}{2}$ col.) "The Golden Perch."
p. (7) "Cheap, Plain, and Ornamental | Picture-Frames."
p. (8) "Most Important Information." With three woodcuts.
p. (9) ($\frac{1}{2}$ col.) "No. 28, Bishopsgate Street."
p. (10) "The China Tea Company."
p. (11) ($\frac{1}{2}$ col.) "A certain Cure for Corns | and Bunions."
p. (12) "Wood and Barrett." With cut of kitchen range.
p. (13) "Comfort for Tender Feet, &c."
p. (14) "Thos. Harris & Son." Same as Part 16, Outside Back Wrapper.
p. (15) (To follow plates) : "186, Strand. | August, 1839. | New Work by 'Boz.' "
p. (16) Now ready, | . . . | A Paper—of Tobacco."

ADVERTISEMENTS (BACK)
"Tyas's Illustrated Classics. | . . . | Robinson | Crusoe" ; verso, with specimen illustration. 2 pp. unnumbered.

PLATES (TWO)
(No. 33) "Great excitement of Miss Kenwigs at the hair dressers shop." (p. 518).

(No. 34) "Nicholas congratulates Arthur Gride on his Wedding Morning." (p. 543).

TEXT, WITH HEADING
"Chapter LII." pp. 513–544.

PART 18.

FRONT WRAPPER (OUTSIDE)
Same as No. X. except "No. XVIII."

FRONT WRAPPER (INSIDE)
"Mechi." Same as No. XVI.

NICHOLAS NICKLEBY.

BACK WRAPPER (INSIDE)
"Dr. Perrengton's | Tonic Aperient Liqueur." Last words : "United States of America."

BACK WRAPPER (OUTSIDE)
Same as No. XII. Inside Front Wrapper.

ADVERTISEMENTS (FRONT)
"The Nickleby Advertiser." 16 pp. unnumbered.
  p. (1) "No. XVIII.—September 1, 1839."
  p. (2) "In 18 mo . . . | Outlines of English History."
  p. (3) "Works published by W. S. Orr and Co."
  p. (4) "On the first of every month . . . | Charley Chalk."
  p. (5) "G. Alexander Macfarren's | . . . | Devil's Opera."
  p. (6) (½ col.) "To articled Clerks."
  p. (7) "Now publishing . . . | . . . | Illustrated Fables."
  p. (8) "Mosley's Metallic Pens."
  p. (9) (½ col.) "To Anglers—Golden Perch."
  p. (10) "Important Case." (Morison).
  p. (11) (¼ col.) "The New Light Field Hat."
  p. (12) "Gowland's Lotion."
  p. (13) "Cheap, Plain, and Ornamental | Picture-Frames."
  p. (14) "Beaufoy." Same as Part 16, page 15.
  p. (15) (To follow plates) : Similar to Part 17.
  p. (16) (To follow plates) : "Shortly will be published, | . . . | The Hand-book of Swindling."

ADVERTISEMENTS (BACK)
  (1) "The Chunk Patent Stove" (Rippon and Burton), dated at foot of first page, August, 1839. 4 pp. numbered (1)–4. Yellow paper.
  (2) "The Saint Ann's Society Schools." 2 pp. unnumbered.
  (3) "Illustrated | Beauties of the Ballet." 2 pp. unnumbered. Lilac paper.

PLATES (TWO)
  (No. 35) "Mr. Squeers and Mrs. Sliderskew unconscious of Visitors." (p. 571).
  (No. 36) "The recognition." (p. 574).

TEXT, WITH HEADING
"Chapter LV." pp. 545–576.

CHARLES DICKENS.

PARTS 19 AND 20.

FRONT WRAPPER (OUTSIDE)
Same as No. X. except "Nos. XIX. & XX. Price 2s."

FRONT WRAPPER (INSIDE)
"Mechi." Same as No. XVI.

BACK WRAPPER (INSIDE)
"The Library of Medicine."

BACK WRAPPER (OUTSIDE)
Same as No. XII. Inside Front Wrapper.

ADVERTISEMENTS (FRONT)
"The Nickleby Advertiser." 32 pp. unnumbered.

    p. (1) "Nos. XIX. & XX.—October 1, 1839."
    p. (2) "On the 1st of November . . . | The Rector's Progress."
    p. (3) ($\frac{1}{2}$ col.) "Published Gratis . . . | Bull's New System."
    p. (4) "Edward Lacey."
    p. (5) "On Monday, December 2 . . . | Poor Jack."
    p. (6) "Interesting Works for Young Persons."
    p. (7) ($\frac{1}{2}$ col.) "Annuals for 1840."
    p. (8) "New Works by Ackermann & Co."
    p. (9) "On November 1st . . . | Pocket-Books with Almanacks."
    p. (10) "In one vol. . . . | A Visit to the British Museum."
    p. (11) "Popular Juvenile Books."
    p. (12) "In one volume . . . | The Pickwick Papers."
    p. (13) "Just published . . . | The Elements of Algebra."
    p. (14) ($\frac{1}{2}$ col.) "Fifth Edition, greatly enlarged."
    p. (15) ($\frac{1}{2}$ col.) "Carpet and Floor-Cloth | Manufacturers."
    p. (16) ($\frac{1}{2}$ col.) "The Golden Perch."
    p. (17) "Good Tea."
    p. (18) "An extraordinary Case of Cure."
    p. (19) "J. & E. Atkinson."
    p. (20) "White's | Essence of Eglantine."
    p. (21) "Cheap, Plain, and Ornamental | Picture-Frames."
    p. (22) "T. Cox Savory."
    p. (23) ($\frac{1}{4}$ col.) "Thos. Harris & Son's."
    p. (24) "Come | and | See ! ! !" Woodcuts of two eyes.
    p. (25) "Important to Invalids and Others."
    p. (26) "Falcon Glass Works."

p. (27) "Kirby, Beard & Kirby's."
p. (28) "Beaufoy and Co."
To follow plates, and conjugating with above :—
p. (29) "Portrait of Mr. Dickens" (facing portrait).
p. (30) "The Hand-book of Swindling," etc.
p. (31) "New Work by 'Boz.' " Dated September 30, 1839.
p. (32) "Nicholas Nickleby." Dated as above.

ADVERTISEMENTS (BACK)

(1) "Tyas's | Popular Publications." Dated : "50, Cheapside, Oct. 1." 12 pp. unnumbered, together with a specimen illustration on plate paper from Valentine Vox, to face page (6).

(2) "New and Splendid Edition . . . | Part I. | of | Gulliver's Travels." 2 pp. unnumbered. Woodcut on each page.

(3) Slip :—"De Foe's Novels," etc. 4 pp. numbered (1)–4. ($6\frac{3}{4}'' \times 4\frac{1}{4}''$).

(4) "Hill's Seal Wafers" ; with five specimen coloured wafers attached. One leaf, verso blank.

PLATES (FOUR)

(No. 37) "The breaking up at Dotheboys Hall." (p. 615).
(No. 38) "Reduced circumstances of Mr. Mantalini." (p. 617).
(No. 39) "The children at their cousin's grave." (p. 624).
(No. 40) Portrait of Charles Dickens, with imprint of Chapman & Hall, dated Oct. 1, 1839.

TEXT, WITH HEADING

"Chapter LIX." pp. 577–624. Imprint at foot of p. 624 : "London | Bradbury and Evans, Printers, Whitefriars."

PRELIMINARY LEAVES

Half-title : "Life and Adventures | of | Nicholas Nickleby." Verso blank. (I. II.).

CHARLES DICKENS.

Title-page : dated 1839. Verso, with imprint as p. 624. (III. IV.). See Illustration.

Dedication : "To | W. C. Macready, Esq." Verso blank. (V. VI.).

Preface : 4 pp. (VII.) VIII. IX. X.

Contents : 4 pp. (XI.) XII. XIII. XIV.

List of Plates : 2 pp. (XV.) XVI.

MASTER HUMPHREY'S CLOCK.

BY CHARLES DICKENS.

WITH ILLUSTRATIONS

BY

GEORGE CATTERMOLE AND HABLOT BROWNE.

VOL. I.

LONDON:

CHAPMAN AND HALL, 186, STRAND.

MDCCCXL.

Master Humphrey's Clock

in

20 Monthly Parts

April, 1840, to November, 1841.

THE earliest form of publication of this work, was in weekly numbers, commencing with No. 1 on April 4th, 1840, at the price of threepence per copy. It was issued as a folded sheet of sixteen pages, uncut and unopened : of which twelve were numbered pages of letterpress —the other four pages (two leaves) forming the outer wrapper. Every fourth or fifth week the text portion of the weekly numbers was collected, and made up into a single part, each being bound in green paper wrappers, and these constitute the monthly parts now under review. When wrappered, the edges were lightly trimmed at the foot, so that they always appear shorter than the original weekly numbers. Upon completion of the issue in these two periodical forms, the whole was bound in three volumes, cloth. Altogether there are four distinct issues of the first printing, as follows :—

(1) Weekly numbers, untrimmed and unopened. $10\frac{1}{2}'' \times 7''$.

(2) Monthly parts, bound from the weekly Nos. and trimmed. $10\frac{3}{8}'' \times 7''$.

(3) Three-Vols. Yellow end-papers, trimmed edges. $10\frac{1}{8}'' \times 6\frac{3}{4}''$.

(4) Three-Vols. Marbled end-papers, and marbled edges. $10'' \times 6\frac{5}{8}''$.

CHARLES DICKENS.

Eight of the monthly parts consist of five-weekly numbers each, priced at 1s. 3d. ; whilst each of the remaining twelve parts consist of four-weekly numbers, priced at 1s. each.

WRAPPERS.

The design for the front cover was made by George Cattermole, and engraved on wood by E. Landells. The inner-sides and outer-side of back cover are as usual printed with advertisements. On the front is a line giving the dates of issue, or serial numbers of the particular weekly issues which make up the monthly part. This line varies in the manner of describing the monthly contents, thus :—

> Parts 1, 2, 6, 7, give dates of first and last weekly number and the year ; e.g. : "Part 1. April 4 to 25, 1840."
>
> Parts 3, 4, 5, give month of issue, and first and last weekly number ; e.g. : "Part 3. June.—Nos. 9 to 13."
>
> Part 8 to end, gives month and year of issue, together with first and last weekly number ; e.g. : "November 1840. Nos. 31 to 35."

ADVERTISEMENTS.

No official advertising sheet forms a part of this monthly periodical issue. Only twenty-one insets appear throughout the twenty numbers, and none of them present much difficulty in assembling, with the possible exception of the 8 pp. announcements of George Virtue in Part 20.

ILLUSTRATIONS.

For the first time, a departure is made from the use of etchings on steel ; all the illustrations are engraved on wood, and with the exception of the three Frontispieces (engraved by Landells) they appear within the body of the text. The design of the Frontispiece to Vol. 1, is by George Cattermole, and those for Vols. 2 and 3 by Hablot K. Browne. Altogether there are 198 distinct drawings (not 194) as detailed below, and of these, 25 are Initial letters and 170 woodcut designs

within text. The latter are engraved by E. Landells (86);
C. Gray (74); S. Williams (5); and Vasey (5).

Frontispieces to Vols. 1, 2, 3	3
Woodcuts in text	170
Initial letters, beginning Chapters . . .	25
	198

The Illustrations are distributed as follows :—

Extraneous Clock.	Frontispieces . .	3	
,, ,,	Woodcuts . . .	19	
,, ,,	Initials	6	
			28
Old Curiosity Shop.	Woodcuts . . .	75	
,, ,, ,,	Initials . . .	8	
			83
Barnaby Rudge.	Woodcuts . . .	76	
,, ,,	Initials	11	
			87
			198

The Artists' work is apportioned :—

H. K. Browne: 2 Frontispieces, 130 Woodcuts, 25 Initials . . . . =	157
George Cattermole : 38 Woodcuts, 1 Frontispiece . . . . =	39
S. Williams: 1 Woodcut (Part 1, No. 4, Page 46) . . . . =	1
Daniel Maclise: 1 Woodcut (Part 8, No. 35, Page 108) . . . . . . =	1
	198

PART 1.

FRONT WRAPPER (OUTSIDE)
   "Part 1. Price 1s. | Master | Humphrey's | Clock | by
   'Boz' | April 4 to 25, 1840. | With Illustrations | by |
   G. Cattermole and H. K. Browne. | Bradbury and
   Evans, Printers, Whitefriars. | London : Chapman and

Hall, 186, Strand"; followed by a list, in 7 lines, of 32 agents, with names and addresses.

The title is engraved as part of the cover design, all other lettering being type-set.

FRONT WRAPPER (INSIDE)

"Thos. Harris & Son, | Opticians to the Royal Family, | opposite the entrance to | The British Museum, London." With view of Museum entrance.

BACK WRAPPER (INSIDE)

"In 1 vol, . . . | China and its resources." (Gilbert and Grattan). Page headed : "Advertisements."

BACK WRAPPER (OUTSIDE)

"Mechi (embodied in view of premises) | Leadenhall Street, London. | Mechi's Address | to | His Customers and the Public." Dated, March 31, 1840, and signed "J. J. Mechi."

ADVERTISEMENTS (BACK)

(1) "Rippon & Burton's General Ironmongery Catalogue. | . . . | The Chunk Stove." Dated, March 1st, 1840. Imprint on p. 4 : "J. Bradley, Printers, 78, Great Titchfield-street, London." 4 pp. 8vo, numbered (1)–4. Yellow paper.

(2) "Beart's Patent Pneumatic | Coffee Filter." With cut of Royal Arms at head of page. One leaf, 4to. Verso blank. Yellow paper.

(3) "Tyas's Popular Illustrated Publications. | This day is published, Part XIII., Price Ninepence, of | Tyas's Illustrated Shakspere" : verso, announcing No. VI. of the Second Series of "Heads of the People" : 2 pp. 4to, unnumbered. Imprint in left bottom corner of both pages : "Vizetelly & Co., 135 Fleet Street."

TEXT, WITH HEADING

"Master Humphrey's Clock." pp. (1)–48, all numbered, except 1, 25 and 37. Comprising 4 Weekly numbers,

1, 2, 3 and 4. Ten woodcut illustrations in Text, at pp. (1), 6, 12, 13, 17, 24, (25), 36, (37), 46. Four woodcut Initial letters in pp. 1, 13, 25, 37.

The opening chapter of "The Old Curiosity Shop" begins at page (37).

PART 2.

FRONT WRAPPER (OUTSIDE)
Same as Part 1, except "Part 2. | May 2 to 23." List of agents at foot is increased to 8 lines, with 36 names and addresses.

FRONT WRAPPER (INSIDE)
Same as Part 1.

BACK WRAPPER (INSIDE)
"America Illustrated . . . | American Scenery ; or Land, Lake, and River Illustrations of | Transatlantic Nature." Page headed : "Advertisements."

BACK WRAPPER (OUTSIDE)
Same as Part 1.

TEXT, WITH HEADING
"Master Humphrey's Visitor." pp. (49)–96, all numbered except 49 and 73. Comprising 4 Weekly numbers, 5, 6, 7 and 8. Ten woodcut illustrations in Text, at pp. (49), 56, 60, 66, 70, (73), 79, 82, 94, 96. Two woodcut Initial letters in pp. 49, 73.

The extraneous matter of "Master Humphrey" occupies pp. 49–79, introducing Pickwick in p. 50, and Sam Weller with "Tony" in p. 52. "The Old Curiosity Shop" recommences in p. 80.

PART 3.

FRONT WRAPPER (OUTSIDE)
Same as Part 1, except "Part 3. Price 1s. 3d. | June.— Nos. 9 to 13." List of agents at foot in 8 lines, with 38 names and addresses.

FRONT WRAPPER (INSIDE)
Same as Part 1.

BACK WRAPPER (INSIDE)

"Mr. Moon . . . 20, Threadneedle Street, | London, has the honour to announce the following | Important National Engraving. | The Waterloo Banquet." Page headed : "Advertisements."

BACK WRAPPER (OUTSIDE)

Same as Part 1.

TEXT, WITH HEADING

"Mr. Weller's Watch." pp. (97)–156, all numbered except (97), (133) and (145). Comprising 5 Weekly numbers, 9, 10, 11, 12 and 13. Ten woodcut illustrations in Text, at pp. (97), 107, 109, 117, 125, 129, (133), 142, 146, 156. Two woodcut Initial letters in pp. 97, 109.

"Mr. Weller's Watch" fills pp. (97)–103. "The Old Curiosity Shop" is resumed, pp. 104–128. "Master Humphrey" intervenes in pp. 128–132, and the serial is again taken up, and continues uninterrupted to the end of the story in Part 11, page 223.

PART 4.

FRONT WRAPPER (OUTSIDE)

Same as Part 1, except "Part 4. | July.—Nos. 14 to 17." List of agents as Part 3.

FRONT WRAPPER (INSIDE)

Same as Part 1.

BACK WRAPPER (INSIDE)

"H. Walker's Needles." The page partly in half measure. Page headed : "Advertisements."

BACK WRAPPER (OUTSIDE)

Same as Part 1.

ADVERTISEMENTS (BACK)

"Magazine of Domestic Economy"; being the heading to first 7 pages, all printed in three-column measure. Page (8): "Bechstein's Cage-Birds." 8 pp. 8vo, all numbered except first and last.

Text, with Heading
"The Old Curiosity Shop. | Chapter the Thirteenth."
pp. 157-204, all numbered except p. 193. Comprising
4 Weekly numbers, 14, 15, 16 and 17. Eight woodcut
illustrations in Text, at pp. 158, 168, 172, 177, 185, 188,
193, 198. One woodcut Initial letter in page 193.

PART 5.

Front Wrapper (Outside)
Same as Part 1, except "Part 5. | August.—Nos. 18 to 21."
List of agents as Part 3.

Front Wrapper (Inside)
Same as Part 1.

Back Wrapper (Inside)
"Gowland's Lotion." Page headed : "Advertisements."

Back Wrapper (Outside)
Same as Part 1.

Advertisements (Back)
"Beart's." One leaf, 4to. Same as Part 1.

Text, with Heading
"The Old Curiosity Shop. | Chapter the Twenty-first."
pp. 205–252, all numbered. Comprising 4 Weekly
numbers, 18, 19, 20 and 21. Eight woodcut illustrations
in Text, at pp. 211, 216, 218, 226, 231, 237, 246, 251.

PART 6.

Front Wrapper (Outside)
Same as Part 1, except "Part 6. Price 1s. 3d. | Augt. 30 to
Sept. 26, 1840." List of agents at foot in 8 lines, with
40 names and addresses.

Front Wrapper (Inside)
Same as Part 1.

Back Wrapper (Inside)
"Master Humphrey's Clock. | Early in October will be
published (with the Volume), . . . | Hands to Hum-
phrey's Clock." Page headed : "Advertisements."

BACK WRAPPER (OUTSIDE)

Same as Part 1.

ADVERTISEMENTS (BACK)

Robert Tyas. 4 pp. 4to, unnumbered, and one specimen plate.

p. (1) "New and enlarged edition, | . . . | On the First of November will appear Part I. of, | The Sentiment of Flowers."

p. (2) "See Specimen on opposite page. | Now publishing in Monthly Parts . . . | . . . | Illustrations | of | Master Humphrey's | Clock. | By T. Sibson."

p. (3) "Important and Valuable Works."

p. (4) "Popular Treatises on Law."

The specimen plate which is placed between the two leaves, varies in the subject illustrated.

TEXT, WITH HEADING

"The Old Curiosity Shop. | Chapter the Twenty-ninth." pp. (253)–306, all numbered except p. 253. Comprising 5 Weekly numbers, 22, 23, 24, 25 and 26. Ten woodcut illustrations in Text, at pp. (253), 260, 270, 276, 280, 288, 293, 300, 304, 306. One woodcut Initial letter in page 253.

PRELIMINARY LEAVES

Frontispiece. Recto blank. (I. II).

Title-page. Vol. I. Dated 1840. Verso, with imprint: "London : | Bradbury and Evans, Printers, Whitefriars." (III. IV).

"Preface." Dated on p. IV. : "Devonshire Terrace, York Gate, | September 1840." 2 pp. numbered (III). IV. Should be : (V). VI.

Dedication : "To | Samuel Rogers, Esquire." Verso, blank. (VII. VIII).

The usual conjugation of Weekly No. 26 is as follows :—

Front Wrapper	with	Dedication leaf.
Frontispiece	,,	Title-page.
Preface (III). IV.	,,	Pages 305–6.
Pages 301–2	,,	Pages 303–4.

In the possession of a Liverpool collector is a copy in the following unusual conjugation :—

Front Wrapper	*with*	Dedication leaf.
Frontispiece	„	Pages 305–6.
Title-page	„	Preface.
Pages 301–2	„	Pages 303–4.

PART 7.

FRONT WRAPPER (OUTSIDE)

Same as Part 1, except "Part 7. | Oct. 3 to Oct. 24, 1840." List of agents as Part 6.

FRONT WRAPPER (INSIDE)

"New and enlarged edition, | . . . | The Sentiment of Flowers." Page headed : "Advertisements."

BACK WRAPPER (INSIDE)

"A Clock is no use without hands ! ! Then, buy | the | Hands to Humphrey's Clock." Page headed : "Advertisements."

BACK WRAPPER (OUTSIDE)

Same as Part 1.

ADVERTISEMENTS (BACK)

(1) Grattan and Gilbert. 16 pp. Sm. 8vo, numbered (1, 2)–16.

p. (1) "Important, Valuable, and Cheap | Maps."
pp. (2), 3, 4. "Ordnance County Maps."
p. 5. "Gilbert's Map of the World."
pp. 6, 7. "Gilbert's | Illustrated Map of the World."
pp. 8, 9. "Gilbert's | Modern Atlas of the Earth."
p. 11. "Gilbert's | New Map of Europe."
p. 13. "Kelvey's Royal Genealogical Chart."
p. 15. "The | Surveyor, Engineer, & Architect."

(2) "Annuals, &c. for 1841. | . . . | Published and sold by | Fisher, Son, & Co. Newgate St. London." Imprint on last page : "Fisher, Son, & Co., Printers." 4 pp. 8vo, numbered (1)–4.

TEXT, WITH HEADING

"The Old Curiosity Shop. | Chapter the Thirty-eighth." pp. (1)–48, all numbered except page (1). Comprising

Four Weekly numbers, 27, 28, 29 and 30. Eight woodcut illustrations in Text, at pp. (1), 11, 15, 24, 27, 34, 41, 45. One woodcut Initial letter in page 1.

PART 8.

FRONT WRAPPER (OUTSIDE)

Same as Part 1, except "Part 8. Price 1s. 3d. | November, 1840.—Nos. 31 to 35." List of agents at foot is increased to 9 lines, with 41 names and addresses. Five words in last line.

FRONT WRAPPER (INSIDE)

Same as Part 1.

BACK WRAPPER (INSIDE)

"Published by A. H. Baily & Co. . . . | The Duke of Wellington . . . | by W. H. Maxwell." Page headed : "Advertisements."

BACK WRAPPER (OUTSIDE)

"Mechi (embodied in view of premises) | Leadenhall Street, London. | Mechi's Bagatelle Tables." With illustration of Bagatelle Table. At foot, a three-column price list, headed : "List of Articles."

ADVERTISEMENTS (FRONT)

Henry Washbourne's List of Publications. 8 pp. 8vo, numbered (1)–8.

pp. (1)-4. "Works of Henry Fielding."

pp. 5-8. "The following Works have been recently | published by | Henry Washbourne." Imprint on p. 8 :—"London : Printed by William Clowes and Sons, Stamford Street."

ADVERTISEMENTS (BACK)

(1) "Rippon & Burton's General Ironmongery Catalogue, | . . . | The Vesta Stove." Dated, Nov. 1st, 1840. pp. 2–4, exactly as Part 1. 4 pp. 8vo, numbered (1)–4. Yellow paper.

(2) "Great National Undertaking. | . . . | The | National Advertiser." Verso, with imprint : "Printed by Barnett Blake, 3 Crane-court, Fleet-street."

TEXT, WITH HEADING
"The Old Curiosity Shop. | Chapter the Forty-sixth."
pp. (49)–108, all numbered except page (49). Comprising 5 Weekly numbers, 31, 32, 33, 34 and 35.
Ten woodcut illustrations in Text, at pp. (49), 55, 61,
70, 79, 82, 86, 95, 103, 108. One woodcut Initial
letter at page 49.

PART 9.

FRONT WRAPPER (OUTSIDE)
Same as Part 1, except "Part 9. | December, 1840.—Nos. 36
to 39. List of agents as Part 8.

FRONT WRAPPER (INSIDE)
"Elegant Books of Plates, &c., for Presents."

BACK WRAPPER (INSIDE)
"In 8vo, cloth, price 8s. | Wanderings in Germany." Page
headed : "Advertisements."

BACK WRAPPER (OUTSIDE)
"Mechi." Same as Part 8, except heading to price list at
foot, reads : "Christmas Presents and New Year's
Gifts."

TEXT, WITH HEADING
"The Old Curiosity Shop. | Chapter the Fifty-sixth."
pp. (109)-156, all numbered except page (109). Comprising 4 Weekly numbers, 36, 37, 38 and 39. Seven
woodcut illustrations in Text at pp. (109), 120, 124,
135, 142, 147, 155. One woodcut Initial letter in page
109.

PART 10.

FRONT WRAPPER (OUTSIDE)
Same as Part 1, except "Part 10. Price 1s. 3d. | January,
1841.—Nos. 40 to 44." List of agents as Part 8.

FRONT WRAPPER (INSIDE)
"Barnaby Rudge." Dated, "186, Strand, January 1841."

BACK WRAPPER (INSIDE)
Thos. Harris & Son. Same as Inside Front Wrapper of Part 1.

BACK WRAPPER (OUTSIDE)
"Mechi." With illustrations of Skate, Knife and Fork, and Bagatelle Table.

ADVERTISEMENTS (BACK)
(1) "On Saturday, March 6, 1841, will be published, | by Charles Knight and Co., | . . . | London." Imprint on p. 4 : "London : Printed by William Clowes and Sons, Stamford Street." 4 pp. 8vo, numbered (1)–4.

(2) George Virtue's Publications. 8 pp. 8vo, unnumbered.
p. (1) "List of | Popular and Standard Works."
p. (3) "Works by William Beattie, M.D."
p. (5) "The Twentieth Edition of 1000 each."
p. (7) "Works by the Rev. Robert Philip . . ."

TEXT, WITH HEADING
"The Old Curiosity Shop. | Chapter the Sixty-fourth." pp. 157–216, all numbered. Comprising 5 Weekly numbers, 40, 41, 42, 43 and 44. Ten woodcut illustrations in Text at pp. 158, 167, 172, 175, 187, 190, 196, 204, 210, 216. One woodcut Initial letter in page 157.

PART 11.

FRONT WRAPPER (OUTSIDE)
Same as Part 1, except "Part 11. | February, 1841.—Nos. 45 to 48." List of agents as Part 8.

FRONT WRAPPER (INSIDE)
Same as Part 1.

BACK WRAPPER (INSIDE)
"On the First of March will be published." James Fraser's announcements, in half column measure. Page headed : "Advertisements."

BACK WRAPPER (OUTSIDE)
"Standard Portraits | of | Her Most Gracious Majesty the Queen | and | His Royal Highness Prince Albert." Page headed : "Advertisements."

ADVERTISEMENTS (BACK)
John Cumberland & Son. 4 pp. 8vo, unnumbered.
pp. (1, 2) "National Drama. | Cumberlands | British and Minor
Theatre." Imprint at foot of p. (2).
p. (3) "Hume, Smollett, and Burke's History of England."
Also : "Berger's edition of Ireland's Life of Napoleon
Buonaparte" : Imprint at foot, and on last page.

TEXT, WITH HEADING
"The Old Curiosity Shop. | Chapter the last." pp. 217–
264, all numbered except p. (229). Comprising 4
Weekly numbers, 45, 46, 47 and 48. Eight woodcut
illustrations in Text at pp. 223, 228, (229), 233, 242,
252, 259, 260. One woodcut Initial letter in page 229.
The opening chapter of "Barnaby Rudge" begins in weekly
number 46, page (229). "Master Humphrey" re-appears in
pp. 224–228.

PART 12.

FRONT WRAPPER (OUTSIDE)
Same as Part 1, except "Part 12. | March, 1841.—Nos. 49
to 52." List of agents as Part 8.

FRONT WRAPPER (INSIDE)
Same as Part 1.

BACK WRAPPER (INSIDE)
"Master Humphrey's Clock. | Early in April will be
published . . . | The Second Volume of | Master
Humphrey's Clock." Page headed : "Advertisements."

BACK WRAPPER (OUTSIDE)
"Published by W. Brittain, 11, Paternoster Row. | The
Magazine of Science, | and School of Arts." Except
for the first line, the whole page in half measure.
Page headed : "Advertisements."

TEXT, WITH HEADING
"Chapter the Sixth." pp. (265)–306 (+3 leaves) all
numbered except page (265). Comprising 4 Weekly
numbers, 49, 50, 51 and 52. Seven woodcut illustrations in Text at pp. (265), 276, 280, 286, 291, 297,
306. One woodcut Initial letter in page 261.

Preliminary Leaves

Title-page. Vol. II. Dated 1841. Verso, with imprint as Vol. I. (I. II).

Frontispiece. Recto blank. (III. IV).

"Preface." Dated on p. VI : "Devonshire Terrace, London, | March, 1841." 2 pp. numbered (V). VI.

The conjugation of Weekly No. 52 is as follows :—

Front Wrapper	*with*	Back Wrapper.
Frontispiece	,,	Title-page.
Preface (V). VI.	,,	Pages 305-6.
Pages 301-2	,,	Pages 303-4.

PART 13.

Front Wrapper (Outside)

Same as Part 1, except "Part 13. Price 1s. 3d. | April, 1841.—Nos. 53 to 57." List of agents as Part 8, but only three words in last line.

Front Wrapper (Inside)

"Domestic Devotion." Upper portion of page in half column measure. Page headed : "Advertisements."

Back Wrapper (Inside)

"Hosiery.—Pope & Plante." Upper half of page in half column measure. Page headed : "Advertisements."

Back Wrapper (Outside)

"Webster & Son." With two woodcuts.

This page is identical with Outside Back Wrapper of the Weekly issue No. 54.

Advertisements (Back)

New Works published by Longman and Co. 4 pp. 8vo, numbered (1)–4.

p. (1) "Maunder's useful and popular Works."
p. (3) "Maunder's | Biographical Treasury."

Text, with Heading

"Barnaby Rudge. | Chapter the Thirteenth." pp. (1)–60, all numbered except page (1). Comprising 5 Weekly numbers, 53, 54, 55, 56 and 57. Nine woodcut illustrations in Text at pp. (1), 10, 14, 21, 28, 35, 45, 49, 60. One woodcut Initial letter in page 1.

PART 14.

FRONT WRAPPER (OUTSIDE)
Same as Part 1, except "Part 14. | May, 1841.—Nos. 58 to 61." List of agents as Part 13.

FRONT WRAPPER (INSIDE)
Same as Part 1.

BACK WRAPPER (INSIDE)
"West's Unique & Elegant Gold | Spectacles." Upper half of page in half column measure. Page headed : "Advertisements."

BACK WRAPPER (OUTSIDE)
"Now publishing, in Weekly Numbers . . . | The Pictorial History of France." Page headed : "Advertisements."

ADVERTISEMENTS (BACK)
(1) "Knight's | Store of Knowledge | for all Readers." 2 pp. 8vo, unnumbered.
(2) "Periodical Works | published by | Grattan & Gilbert, 51, Paternoster Row." 2 pp. 8vo, unnumbered.

TEXT, WITH HEADING
"Chapter the Twenty-third." pp. (61)–108, all numbered except page (61). Comprising 4 Weekly numbers, 58, 59, 60 and 61. Seven woodcut illustrations in Text at pp. (61), 68, 77, 80, 89, 101, 107. One woodcut Initial letter in page 61.

PART 15.

FRONT WRAPPER (OUTSIDE)
Same as Part 1, except "Part 15. | June, 1841.—Nos. 62 to 65." List of agents as Part 13.

FRONT WRAPPER (INSIDE)
"Works of Mr. Charles Dickens." Last announcement on page : "Maps of the English Counties." Page headed : "Advertisements."

BACK WRAPPER (INSIDE)
"The Visitor's Guide to the Watering Places." The page
set mainly in half column measure. Page headed:
"Advertisements."

BACK WRAPPER (OUTSIDE)
"Published by W. Brittain, 11, Paternoster Row. | . . . |
The London Saturday Journal." Page headed:
"Advertisements."

ADVERTISEMENT (BACK)
"In Weekly Numbers, and Monthly Parts, | by Charles
Knight & Co. . . . | The | Christian Traveller." 2 pp.
8vo, numbered on second page.

TEXT, WITH HEADING
"Chapter the Thirty-first." pp. (109)–156, all numbered
except pp. (109) and (121). Comprising 4 Weekly
numbers, 62, 63, 64, 65. Seven woodcut illustrations
in Text at pp. (109), 118, (121), 131, 137, 152, 156.
Two woodcut Initial letters in pp. 109, 121.

PART 16.

FRONT WRAPPER (OUTSIDE)
Same as Part 1, except "Part 16. Price 1s. 3d. | July,
1841.—Nos. 66 to 70." List of agents as Part 13.

FRONT WRAPPER (INSIDE)
Same as Part 1.

BACK WRAPPER (INSIDE)
"The Visitor's Guide to the | Watering-Places." Followed
by: "Sketches of Young Couples." Page headed:
"Advertisements."

BACK WRAPPER (OUTSIDE)
"Works published by W. Strange, 21, Paternoster Row."

TEXT, WITH HEADING
"Chapter the Thirty-ninth." pp. (157)–216, all numbered
except page (157). Comprising 5 Weekly numbers, 66,
67, 68, 69 and 70. Ten woodcut illustrations in Text

at pp. (157), 161, 175, 180, 183, 188, 195, 199, 208, 213. One woodcut Initial letter in page 157.

PART 17.

FRONT WRAPPER (OUTSIDE)
Same as Part 1, except "Part 17. | August, 1841.—Nos. 71 to 74." List of agents as Part 13.

FRONT WRAPPER (INSIDE)
"Works of Mr. Charles Dickens." Last announcement on page: "Written Caricatures." Page headed: "Advertisements."
This page is identical with Inside Front Wrappers of the Weekly issues Nos. 72, 73 and 75.

BACK WRAPPER (INSIDE)
"New Work, Edited by Boz. | The Pic Nic Papers." Page headed : "Advertisements."

BACK WRAPPER (OUTSIDE)
"Mechi." Line below view of premises : "Superb Novelties in Papier Mache Goods."

TEXT, WITH HEADING
"Chapter the Forty-ninth." pp. (217)–264, all numbered except page (217). Comprising 4 Weekly numbers, 71, 72, 73 and 74. Seven woodcut illustrations in Text at pp. (217), 236, 240, 246, 250, 254, 264. One woodcut Initial letter in page 218.

PART 18.

FRONT WRAPPER (OUTSIDE)
Same as Part 1, except "Part 18. | September, 1841.— Nos. 75 to 78." List of agents as Part 13.

FRONT WRAPPER (INSIDE)
"The Society for the Diffusion of Useful | Knowledge." Page headed : "Advertisements."

BACK WRAPPER (INSIDE)
"Works of Mr. Charles Dickens" : half page. Lower half : "Maps of the English Counties." Page headed : "Advertisements."

179

CHARLES DICKENS.

BACK WRAPPER (OUTSIDE)
"The Poet Wordsworth." At foot: "E. P. Doudney & Son," printed crosswise.

ADVERTISEMENTS (BACK)
John Bett's announcement of Maps and Atlases. 4 pp. 8vo, unnumbered. With woodcut at head of first page.

TEXT, WITH HEADING
"Chapter the Fifty-seventh." pp. (265)–312, all numbered except page (265). Comprising 4 Weekly numbers, 75, 76, 77 and 78. Seven woodcut illustrations in Text at pp. (265), 276, 279, 284, 294, 300, 309. One woodcut Initial letter in page 265.

PART 19.

FRONT WRAPPER (OUTSIDE)
Same as Part 1, except "Part 19. Price 1s. 3d. | October 1841.—Nos. 79 to 83." List of agents as Part 13.

FRONT WRAPPER (INSIDE)
"To the | Readers of 'Master Humphrey's Clock.'" An address by the Author: beginning, "Dear Friends," and signed, "It's Author." Dated, "September, 1841."
This page is identical with Inside Front Wrappers of the Weekly issues Nos. 80, 81, 82 and 84.

BACK WRAPPER (INSIDE)
"The Last Military Portrait of the Duke." Page headed: "Advertisements."

BACK WRAPPER (OUTSIDE)
"Theatre Royal, Drury Lane." Dated, "Oct. 4th, 1841." Page headed: "Advertisements."

TEXT, WITH HEADING
"Chapter the Sixty-fifth." pp. (313)–372, all numbered except page (313). Comprising 5 Weekly numbers, 79, 80, 81, 82 and 83. Nine woodcut illustrations in Text at pp. (313), 324, 331, 336, 343, 346, 355, 367, 370. One woodcut Initial letter in page 313.

MASTER HUMPHREY'S CLOCK.

PART 20.

FRONT WRAPPER (OUTSIDE)
Same as Part 1, except "Part 20. Price 1s. 3d. | November, 1841.—Nos. 84 to 88." List of agents as Part 13.

FRONT WRAPPER (INSIDE)
"Mechi." Similar to Part 17 Outside Back Wrapper.

BACK WRAPPER (INSIDE)
"Dedicated by special permission, to | His Royal Highness the Duke of Sussex. | . . . | Advice to the Bilious." Page headed : "Advertisements."

BACK WRAPPER (OUTSIDE)
"Works published by William Curry, Jun. & Co., Dublin ; | . . . | Our Mess. | by Harry Lorrequer." Page headed : "Advertisements."

This page is identical with Outside Back Wrapper of the Weekly issue No. 84.

ADVERTISEMENTS (FRONT)
Chapman & Hall's Announcements, etc. 4 pp. 4to, numbered (1), 2, 3, (4).

    p. (1) "Master Humphrey's Clock, | The Third Volume." With six additional titles.

    p. 2. "Eighth edition . . . | Sketches of Young Ladies."

    p. 3. "The Society for the Diffusion of Useful | Knowledge."

    p. (4) "To the | Readers of 'Master Humphrey's Clock.' " An address by the Author, identical with that on the Inside Front Wrapper of Part 19 ; but with the addition of a "Postscript," in which he takes farewell of his readers for twelve months, until the return from his American tour. "We part until next November." Dated, November, 1841.

ADVERTISEMENTS (BACK)
"List of | Popular and Standard Works, | published by | George Virtue, Ivy Lane, London." 8 pp. 8vo, unnumbered. Lilac paper. Pages (2)–8 are each headed : "G. Virtue's List of Popular and Standard Works." Imprint of George Virtue at foot of each page.

Text, with Heading

"Chapter the Seventy-fifth." pp. (373)–426, all numbered except page (373). Comprising 5 Weekly numbers, 84, 85, 86, 87 and 88. Eight woodcut illustrations in Text at pp. (373), 382, 391, 395, 400, 406, 415, 426. One woodcut Initial letter in page 373.

Preliminary Leaves

Frontispiece. Recto blank. (I. II).

Title-page. Vol. III. Dated 1841. Verso, with imprint as Vols. I. and II.

"Preface to Barnaby Rudge." Dated on p. VI. : "Devonshire Terrace, York Gate, | November 1841." 2 pp. numbered (V). VI.

The final Weekly number (88), Sig. OO, conjugates in this manner :—

Front Wrapper	*with*	Back Wrapper.
Frontispiece	,,	Preface.
Title-page	,,	Pages 425–6.
Pages 421–2	,,	Pages 423–4.

THE

LIFE AND ADVENTURES

OF

MARTIN CHUZZLEWIT.

———◆———

BY CHARLES DICKENS.

WITH ILLUSTRATIONS BY PHIZ.

LONDON:
CHAPMAN AND HALL, 186, STRAND.
———
MDCCCXLIV.

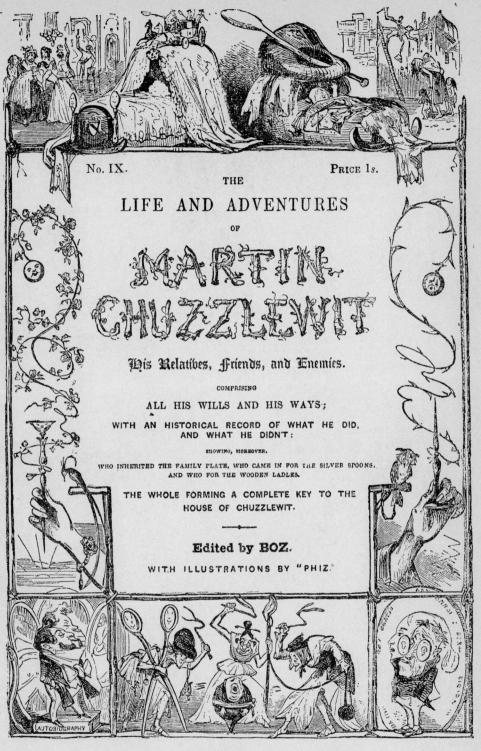

No. IX.

PRICE 1s.

THE

LIFE AND ADVENTURES

OF

MARTIN CHUZZLEWIT

His Relatives, Friends, and Enemies.

COMPRISING

ALL HIS WILLS AND HIS WAYS;

WITH AN HISTORICAL RECORD OF WHAT HE DID,
AND WHAT HE DIDN'T:

SHOWING, MOREOVER,

WHO INHERITED THE FAMILY PLATE, WHO CAME IN FOR THE SILVER SPOONS,
AND WHO FOR THE WOODEN LADLES.

THE WHOLE FORMING A COMPLETE KEY TO THE
HOUSE OF CHUZZLEWIT.

Edited by BOZ.

WITH ILLUSTRATIONS BY "PHIZ."

LONDON: CHAPMAN & HALL, 186, STRAND.

September 1843

The Front Wrapper to the original edition of "Martin Chuzzlewit,"
as published in 19/20 monthly parts, 1843-1844.

Martin Chuzzlewit

in

19/20 Monthly Parts

January, 1843, to July, 1844.

ORIGINALLY issued in twenty numbers, bound in nineteen, price one shilling, except the last two (19 and 20), which were issued as a double number at two shillings. The usual green wrappers were retained ; the design upon the front being executed by Phiz, who also etched the forty plates. The first number was published January, 1843, and arrived at completion with Part 19/20 in July, 1844, without any break in the sequence of monthly issues.

TEXT.

There are no points which distinguish early from late printings. Text measurements are of no assistance, as the printing from the very commencement was all produced by the use of stereotype plates.

WRAPPERS.

Apart from the essential changes of "Part No." and date of issue at foot, no changes of textual matter were made in the front wrapper. Both inner sides and outside of back wrapper carried full-page advertisements ; the house of "Mechi" occupying the back throughout the whole run of the work.

PLATES.

As was the case with the production of "Nickleby," the quantities required were too great for one steel to effect

185

in the allotted time of four weeks between each monthly issue. Additional steels were, therefore, provided in advance of publication, for each of the forty plates comprised in the work : some in duplicate, and others in triplicate, each differing —sometimes very considerably—in detail. This duplication was responsible for ninety separate steels, as shown in the table below ; and it must be repeated, that no priority of issue can be given to any of them, for the good and sufficient reasons already fully explained in the "Nickleby" chapter. Again, many of the plates have the artist's distinguishing figure, which denotes the order in which they were etched, but not necessarily the order in which they were printed, as all were in use at one and the same moment. These figures will be found on many plates in Parts 2, 3, 7, 10, 11, 12, 14, 18, 19/20. Here, again, the signature of Phiz always varies with the duplicate plates.

The etched title in Part 19/20 shows a reward bill affixed to the signpost, reading, in some impressions, "100£," and in others "£100." The former is generally referred to as "the transposed £," and is always quoted in catalogues as "first state" of this illustration ; for the same reason, a part in which it appears is described as "first issue." Impressions showing the "transposed £" have no more right to be termed "first state" than those from numerous other steels in "Chuzzlewit" or "Nickleby" which show variations in execution. At that time, writers often expressed themselves in this way when referring to sterling values, and it is more likely that "Phiz" made the transposition purposely than that he made an error. It is merely one of the five cases in "Chuzzlewit" of triplicated steels, one of them reading "100£," and the other two "£100." In the detailed collation, the "transposed £" is designated as the first plate, although it might reasonably be argued that there is a figure "2" in the lower right corner. It makes no difference, however, which plate was etched first ; they were contemporary, and all three of them were in use during the issue in parts. Furthermore, an examination of over eighty

186

copies of this plate has revealed (as in the case of "Nickleby," No. 29) a proportion of one-third reading "100£" compared with two-thirds reading "£100."

Following is set out a list showing the number of duplicated etchings to each monthly part :—

Part	Plates							Total
1	1	and	2	3	etchings of each			6
2	3	,,	4	3	,,	,,	,,	6
3	5	,,	6	3	,,	,,	,,	6
4	7	,,	8	2	,,	,,	,,	4
5	9	,,	10	2	,,	,,	,,	4
6	11	,,	12	2	,,	,,	,,	4
7	13	,,	14	2	,,	,,	,,	4
8	15	,,	16	2	,,	,,	,,	4
9	17	,,	18	2	,,	,,	,,	4
10	19	,,	20	2	,,	,,	,,	4
11	21	,,	22	2	,,	,,	,,	4
12	23	,,	24	2	,,	,,	,,	4
13	25	,,	26	2	,,	,,	,,	4
14	27	,,	28	3	,,	,,	,,	6
15	29	,,	30	2	,,	,,	,,	4
16	31	,,	32	2	,,	,,	,,	4
17	33	,,	34	2	,,	,,	,,	4
18	35	,,	36	2	,,	,,	,,	4
19/20	37	,,	38	2	,,	,,	,,	4
,,	39	,,	40	3	,,	,,	,,	6
								90

ADVERTISEMENTS (FRONT).

The "Chuzzlewit Advertiser" appeared regularly in each number, varying from 8 pp. to 32 pp. Each page has the headline "Advertisements," with the exception always of the first in each part, as well as the following :—

Part 1 :   pp. 5, 8, 9, 14, 17, 24.
  ,,   3 :   p. 16.
  ,,   4 :   pp. 15, 16.
  ,, 11 :   pp. 15, 16.

CHARLES DICKENS.

Part 12 :   pp. 3, 15, 16.
„   13 :   pp. 7, 15, 16.
„   14 :   pp. 4, 5, 6, 7, 15, 16.
„   16 :   pp. 7, 16.
„ 19/20 pp. 23, 24.

The pagination is completely absent in the first part, and occasionally in other parts. Whether, in these cases, the page-numbers were ever set-up, or the figures had dropped out, cannot be definitely established.

ADVERTISEMENTS (BACK).

These are noteworthy for the four small booklets of E. Moses and Son, which should appear in Parts 9, 10, 11 and 16, but very frequently are missing. They are essential to every perfect copy.

PART 1.

FRONT WRAPPER (OUTSIDE)
"No. I.   Price 1s. | The | Life and Adventures | of | Martin | Chuzzlewit | His Relatives, Friends, and Enemies. | Comprising | All his Wills and his Ways : | With an Historical Record of what he did, | and what he didnt : | showing,   moreover, | Who   inherited   the Family Plate, Who came in for the Silver Spoons, | and Who for the Wooden Ladles. | The whole forming a complete Key to the | House of Chuzzlewit. | Edited by   Boz. | With   Illustrations   by 'Phiz.' | London : Chapman & Hall, 186, Strand. | January, 1843."

FRONT WRAPPER (INSIDE)
"Thos. Harris & Son, | Opticians to the Royal Family."

BACK WRAPPER (INSIDE)
Doudney Brothers, Fashionable Tailors, etc., within the centre of a decorative floral design, embracing seven views and scenes. Signed : "J. Claringbull, del."

BACK WRAPPER (OUTSIDE)
"Mechi, | . . . | Papier Maché Goods, | . . . | New Years' Gifts." With seven illustrations.

MARTIN CHUZZLEWIT.

BACK WRAPPER (INSIDE)
Same as No. I.

BACK WRAPPER (OUTSIDE)
Same as No. I.

ADVERTISEMENTS (FRONT)
"Chuzzlewit Advertiser." 16 pp. numbered (1)–(15, 16).
- p. (1) "No. IV., April, 1843."
- p. 2. "Under the | immediate superintendence | of | the Council . . ."
- p. 3. "Prizes on View—Fine-Art Distribution."
- p. 4. "Tait's Edinburgh Magazine."
- p. 5. "In Preparation. | The Baronial Halls."
- p. 6. "Under the Superintendence of | The Society . . ."
- p. 7. "The Foreign Library."
- p. 8. "Works of Thomas Carlyle."
- p. 9. "Under the Superintendence of the Society . . ."
- p. 10. ($\frac{1}{2}$ col.) "Just Published . . . | A Glance at the Temple."
- p. 11. "How to make your own Will."
- p. 12. "Deanean Plate."
- p. 13. ($\frac{1}{2}$ col.) "Chubb's Locks."
- p. 14. "This day is published . . . | Betts's Family Atlas."
- p. (15) "The | Foreign Quarterly Review, | No. LXI."
- p. (16) "Nearly ready for Publication. | Past and Present."

ADVERTISEMENTS (BACK)
(1) "Eagle | Life Assurance Company." 2 pp. un-numbered.
(2) "Corn Laws. | Extracts | from the Works of | Col. T. Perronet Thompson." 16 pp. numbered (1)–16. All in half measure. ($8\frac{1}{8}'' \times 5\frac{1}{4}''$).

PLATES (TWO)
(No. 7) "M. Todgers and the Pecksniffs call upon Miss Pinch." (p. 103).
(No. 8) "Truth prevails and Virtue is triumphant." (p. 120).
In the List of Plates, No. 7 reads : "Mrs. Todgers."

TEXT, WITH HEADING
"Chapter IX." pp. 97–128.

193   N

CHARLES DICKENS.

PART 5.

FRONT WRAPPER (OUTSIDE)
Same as No. I. except "No. V." and at foot, "May."

FRONT WRAPPER (INSIDE)
Same as Inside Back Wrapper of No. I. (Doudney Brothers).

BACK WRAPPER (INSIDE)
"Save Your Income Tax." (Doudney and Son). Almost identical with Inside Front Wrapper of No. II.

BACK WRAPPER (OUTSIDE)
"Mechi, | No. 4, Leadenhall Street, London, | ... | Papier Maché Manufactures." Six illustrations. (The address here is all in one line).

ADVERTISEMENTS (FRONT)
"Chuzzlewit Advertiser." 12 pp. numbered (1)–12.

p. (1) "No. V., May, 1843."
p. 2. "Now Ready ... | ... | Views of the Architecture of the Heavens."
p. 3. "Preparing ... | The | Principles & the Practice of Art."
p. 4. "Douglas Jerrold's Magazine."
p. 5. "In Preparation | The Baronial Halls."
p. 6. "The Foreign Library."
p. 7. ($\frac{1}{2}$ col.) "Published this day ... | The Story-Teller."
p. 8. "Economical Radiating Stove."
p. 9. "Deanéan Plate."
p. 10. ($\frac{1}{2}$ col.) "Royal Nursery."
p. 11. ($\frac{1}{2}$ col.) "European | Life Insurance Company."
p. 12. "Price One Shilling ... | The Art-Union."

Of sixty copies examined, pages 6 and 9 were not numbered.

ADVERTISEMENTS (BACK)

(1) "Established 1820. | Rippon & Burton's." Dated at foot : "May, 1843." 4 pp. numbered (1)–4. Yellow paper.

(2) "This day is published, Part I., | . . . | The | Old Sailor's | Jolly Boat." Full-page illustration. 2 pp. unnumbered. (R. Tyas).

(3) "Prospectus | . . . | Thomas Boys." 8 pp. Same as Part 2.

194

MARTIN CHUZZLEWIT.

PLATES (TWO)
(No. 9) "Mr. Jonas Chuzzlewit entertains his cousins."
(p. 138).
(No. 10) "Mr. Pecksniff renounces the deceiver." (p. 160).
TEXT, WITH HEADING
"Chapter XI." pp. 129–160.

PART 6.

FRONT WRAPPER (OUTSIDE)
Same as No. I. except "No. VI." and at foot, "June."
FRONT WRAPPER (INSIDE)
Same as No. V. Inside Back Wrapper.
BACK WRAPPER (INSIDE)
Same as No. I.
BACK WRAPPER (OUTSIDE)
Same as No. V.
ADVERTISEMENTS (FRONT)
"Chuzzlewit Advertiser." 8 pp. numbered (1)–8.
    p. (1) "No. VI., June, 1843."
    p. 2. "The Foreign Library."
    p. 3. "In Preparation. | The Baronial Halls."
    p. 4. ($\frac{1}{2}$ col.) "To be completed . . . | China and India."
    p. 5. "To Reading and Book Societies . . ."
    p. 6. "Economical Radiating Stove . . ."
    p. 7. ($\frac{1}{2}$ col.) "Carpet and Floor-Cloth | Manufactory."
    p. 8. "The Western Life-Assurance Society."
ADVERTISEMENTS (BACK)
"The National Art-Union." 8 pp. numbered (1)–8.
Printed in blue on thin paper.
PLATES (TWO)
(No. 11) "Martin meets an acquaintance at the house of
a mutual relation." (p. 166).
(No. 12) "Mr. Tapley acts Third Party with great dis-
cretion." (p. 178).
TEXT, WITH HEADING
"Chapter XIII." pp. 161–192.

CHARLES DICKENS.

PART 7.

FRONT WRAPPER (OUTSIDE)
Same as No. I. except "No. VII." and at foot, "July."

FRONT WRAPPER (INSIDE)
"Established 1820. | Rippon and Burton's | Furnishing Ironmongery Warehouses."

BACK WRAPPER (INSIDE)
"On the 30th instant . . . | The Fourth Volume | of | Punch."

BACK WRAPPER (OUTSIDE)
Same as No. V.

ADVERTISEMENTS (FRONT)
"Chuzzlewit Advertiser." 8 pp. numbered (1)–8.

p. (1) "No. VII., July, 1843."
p. 2. "New Work by Thomas Carlyle."
p. 3. "The Illustrated edition of 'Windsor Castle.'"
p. 4. ($\frac{1}{2}$ col.) "The Zoologist."
p. 5. ($\frac{1}{2}$ col.) "Carpet and Floor-Cloth | Manufactory."
p. 6. "Economical Radiating Stove . . ."
p. 7. "Human Life." (Parr's Life Pills).
p. 8. "The Western Life-Assurance Society."

Slip : (to follow Front Wrapper). "Neatly bound in cloth . . . | Price 4s. each volume, | Scenes and Incidents of | Foreign Travel." 2 pp. unnumbered. ($6\frac{3}{4}'' \times 4''$).

Although a rare item, this slip is essential to the collation, being an original inset as stitched in by the binder. It has been noted in only six copies.

PLATES (TWO)

(No. 13) "Mr. Jefferson Brick proposes an appropriate sentiment." (p. 199).

(No. 14) "Mr. Tapley succeeds in finding a 'jolly' subject for contemplation." (p. 212).

TEXT, WITH HEADING
"Chapter XVI." pp. 193–224.

MARTIN CHUZZLEWIT.

ADVERTISEMENTS (FRONT)
"Chuzzlewit Advertiser." 32 pp. unnumbered.

p. (1) "No. I., Jan. 1843."
p. (2) (½ col.) "Second edition of 'The Traduced.'"
p. (3) "Mr. Murray | has just published . . ." (Eleven titles).
p. (4) "Now ready, | Jack Hinton, the Guardsman."
p. (5) "Publishing every Saturday . . . | Punch." Woodcut.
p. (6) "The Standard Library."
p. (7) "Recently published | by Smith, Elder and Co. . . ."
p. (8) "Nearly ready in One Volume . . . | Annual Biography."
p. (9) "Annual Biography (Continued)."
p. (10) "Works | published by W. Strange . . ."
p. (11) "Works of Thomas Carlyle."
p. (12) "The | Illustrated London News."
p. (13) "A Book for Christmas Parties."
p. (14) "Works of Mr. Charles Dickens."
p. (15) "Maps published by James Wyld."
pp. (16, 17) "Society for the Diffusion of Useful Knowledge."
pp. (18, 19) "Elegant Books of Plates, &c. for Presents."
p. (20) "Capital Book for Presents."
p. (21) (½ col.) "New Periodical."
p. (22) "To the Public."
p. (23) "The Pictorial Museum | of | Animated Nature."
p. (24) "Under the Superintendence of | The Society . . ."
p. (25) "Cheap Re-Issue of . . . Dibdin's Songs."
p. (26) (½ col.) "Family Mourning."
p. (27) "Economical Radiating Stove . . ."
p. (28) (½ col.) "J. Sparkes Hall's Patent."
p. (29) (½ col.) "Frames for Art-Union | Prints."
p. (30) "Parr's Life Pills."
p. (31) (½ col.) "Chubb's Locks . . ."
p. (32) "Save Your Income Tax." (Doudney).

(To follow plates): "The | Foreign Quarterly Review | No. LX. is Published this day." Verso: "The Foreign Library." 2 pp. unnumbered. Lilac paper.

ADVERTISEMENTS (BACK)

(1) "Gilbert's | Modern Atlas. | On January 1, 1843, was published," 4 pp. unnumbered. Page 4: printed broadside across; "Gilbert's Large Maps Reduced in Price."

(2) Slip : "Bentley's | Hand-Books | of | Science, Literature, and Art." 2 pp. unnumbered. ($7\frac{5}{8}'' \times 4\frac{3}{8}''$).

(3) "Tea. | Reduction of Six-pence per Pound." (Robt. Roberts & Company). One leaf, verso blank.

(4) Slip : "Wyld's Globes." 8 pp. numbered on pp. 3–7. With a front cover only, printed on tinted paper. ($5\frac{1}{2}'' \times 3\frac{1}{4}''$).

(5) "Extracts | from | The Britannia." 16 pp. all numbered, except 1, 2, 3, 5 and 8. pp. 3 and 4, with "Address," and p. (16) "List of Agents." pp. (5)–15, all headed with title as above.

PLATES (Two)

(No. 1) "Meekness of Mr. Pecksniff and his charming daughters." (p. 14).

(No. 2) "Martin Chuzzlewit suspects the landlady without any reason." (p. 24).

TEXT, WITH HEADING
"Life and Adventures | of | Martin Chuzzlewit. | Chapter 1" pp. (1)–32.

PART 2.

FRONT WRAPPER (OUTSIDE)
Same as No. I. except "No. II." and at foot, "February."

FRONT WRAPPER (INSIDE)
"Save Your Income Tax." (Doudney and Son). Same as p. 32 of "Advertiser" in No. I.

BACK WRAPPER (INSIDE)
Same as No. I.

BACK WRAPPER (OUTSIDE)
Same as No. I.

ADVERTISEMENTS (FRONT)
"Chuzzlewit Advertiser." 16 pp. numbered (1)–16.

 p. (1) "No. II., Feb. 1843."
 p. 2. "Foreign Library—continued."
 p. 3. ($\frac{1}{2}$ col.) "Second edition of 'The Traducer.' "
 p. 4. "Just published . . . | Annual Biography."

MARTIN CHUZZLEWIT.

p. 5. "Annual Biography (Continued)." Same as No. I., page 9.
p. 6. "London, 1843. | To Circulating Libraries . . ."
p. 7. "Publishing every Saturday . . . | Punch." No woodcut.
p. 8. "Under the Superintendence of | The Society . . ."
p. 9. "The | Foreign Quarterly Review, | No. LX . . ."
pp. 10 & 11. "Society for the Diffusion of Useful Knowledge."
p. 12. "Works of Thomas Carlyle."
p. 13. ($\frac{1}{2}$ col.) "Elegant Present."
p. 14. ($\frac{1}{2}$ col.) "The Toilet of Beauty."
p. 15. ($\frac{1}{2}$ col.) "Chubb's Locks . . ."
p. 16. "Complete French School. By Mons. Le Page."

ADVERTISEMENTS (BACK)

(1) "Prospectus | of | the important and attractive | Fine Art Distribution | . . . by | Thomas Boys." 8 pp. numbered (1)–8.

(2) "Authorities | against the Corn Laws." Page 3: "The Anti-Corn-Law League." In all, 4 pp. numbered on pp. 2 and 4.

(3) "Mary-le-Bone Iron Works." 4 pp. numbered (1)–4. White, yellow, or pink paper.

PLATES (TWO)

(No. 3) "Pleasant little family party at Mr. Pecksniff's." (p. 42).

(No. 4) "Pinch starts homeward with the new Pupil." (p. 58).

TEXT, WITH HEADING
"Chapter IV." pp. 33–64.

PART 3.

FRONT WRAPPER (OUTSIDE)
Same as No. 1. except "No. III." and at foot, "March."

FRONT WRAPPER (INSIDE)
Same as No. II.

BACK WRAPPER (INSIDE)
Same as No. I.

BACK WRAPPER (OUTSIDE)
Same as No. I.

ADVERTISEMENTS (FRONT)
"Chuzzlewit Advertiser." 16 pp. numbered (1)–(16).
    p. (1) "No. III., March, 1843."
    p. 2. "Under the Superintendence of the Society . . ."
    p. 3. "Just Published . . . | A Memoir on Ireland."
    p. 4. "Works of Mr. Charles Dickens."
    p. 5. "Books Published by William Tait."
    pp. 6 & 7. "The Foreign Library."
    pp. 8 & 9. "Works | under the Superintendence of the Society . . ."
    p. 10. ($\frac{1}{2}$ col.) "Published this day . . . | The Book of Fun."
    p. 11. "Just Published . . . | The Annual Biography."
    p. 12. "Economical Radiating Stove . . ."
    p. 13. ($\frac{1}{2}$ col.) "Chubb's Locks . . ."
    p. 14. ($\frac{1}{2}$ col.) "J. Sparkes Hall's Patent."
    p. 15. "Family Mourning." With Illustration. (W. C. Jay).
    p. 16. "Important to Ladies." (Kirby, Beard, & Co.).

ADVERTISEMENTS (BACK)
(1) "Wedgwood's Manifold Writer." 2 pp. unnumbered. Pink paper.
(2) "Dialogue | on | The Corn Laws, | between a Gentleman and a Farmer." 8 pp. numbered (1)–8. ($8\frac{1}{8}'' \times 5\frac{1}{4}''$).

PLATES (TWO)
(No. 5) "Mr. Pinch and the new pupil on a social occasion." (p. 70).
(No. 6) "Mark begins to be jolly under creditable circumstances." (p. 88).

TEXT, WITH HEADING
"Chapter VI." pp. 65–96.

PART 4.

FRONT WRAPPER (OUTSIDE)
Same as No. I. except "No. IV." and at foot, "April."

FRONT WRAPPER (INSIDE)
Same as No. II.

MARTIN CHUZZLEWIT.

BACK WRAPPER (INSIDE)
Same as No. I.

BACK WRAPPER (OUTSIDE)
Same as No. I.

ADVERTISEMENTS (FRONT)
"Chuzzlewit Advertiser." 16 pp. numbered (1)–(15, 16).

    p. (1) "No. IV., April, 1843."
    p. 2. "Under the | immediate superintendence | of | the Council . . ."
    p. 3. "Prizes on View—Fine-Art Distribution."
    p. 4. "Tait's Edinburgh Magazine."
    p. 5. "In Preparation. | The Baronial Halls."
    p. 6. "Under the Superintendence of | The Society . . ."
    p. 7. "The Foreign Library."
    p. 8. "Works of Thomas Carlyle."
    p. 9. "Under the Superintendence of the Society . . ."
    p. 10. ($\frac{1}{2}$ col.) "Just Published . . . | A Glance at the Temple."
    p. 11. "How to make your own Will."
    p. 12. "Deanean Plate."
    p. 13. ($\frac{1}{2}$ col.) "Chubb's Locks."
    p. 14. "This day is published . . . | Betts's Family Atlas."
    p. (15) "The | Foreign Quarterly Review, | No. LXI."
    p. (16) "Nearly ready for Publication. | Past and Present."

ADVERTISEMENTS (BACK)

(1) "Eagle | Life Assurance Company." 2 pp. unnumbered.

(2) "Corn Laws. | Extracts | from the Works of | Col. T. Perronet Thompson." 16 pp. numbered (1)–16. All in half measure. ($8\frac{1}{8}'' \times 5\frac{1}{4}''$).

PLATES (TWO)

(No. 7) "M. Todgers and the Pecksniffs call upon Miss Pinch." (p. 103).

(No. 8) "Truth prevails and Virtue is triumphant." (p. 120).
    In the List of Plates, No. 7 reads : "Mrs. Todgers."

TEXT, WITH HEADING
"Chapter IX." pp. 97–128.

PART 5.

FRONT WRAPPER (OUTSIDE)
Same as No. I. except "No. V." and at foot, "May."

FRONT WRAPPER (INSIDE)
Same as Inside Back Wrapper of No. I. (Doudney Brothers).

BACK WRAPPER (INSIDE)
"Save Your Income Tax." (Doudney and Son). Almost identical with Inside Front Wrapper of No. II.

BACK WRAPPER (OUTSIDE)
"Mechi, | No. 4, Leadenhall Street, London, | ... | Papier Maché Manufactures." Six illustrations. (The address here is all in one line).

ADVERTISEMENTS (FRONT)
"Chuzzlewit Advertiser." 12 pp. numbered (1)–12.

  p. (1) "No. V., May, 1843."
  p. 2. "Now Ready ... | ... | Views of the Architecture of the Heavens."
  p. 3. "Preparing ... | The | Principles & the Practice of Art."
  p. 4. "Douglas Jerrold's Magazine."
  p. 5. "In Preparation | The Baronial Halls."
  p. 6. "The Foreign Library."
  p. 7. ($\frac{1}{2}$ col.) "Published this day ... | The Story-Teller."
  p. 8. "Economical Radiating Stove."
  p. 9. "Deanéan Plate."
  p. 10. ($\frac{1}{2}$ col.) "Royal Nursery."
  p. 11. ($\frac{1}{2}$ col.) "European | Life Insurance Company."
  p. 12. "Price One Shilling ... | The Art-Union."
  Of sixty copies examined, pages 6 and 9 were not numbered.

ADVERTISEMENTS (BACK)

  (1) "Established 1820. | Rippon & Burton's." Dated at foot : "May, 1843." 4 pp. numbered (1)–4. Yellow paper.

  (2) "This day is published, Part I., | . . . | The | Old Sailor's | Jolly Boat." Full-page illustration. 2 pp. unnumbered. (R. Tyas).

  (3) "Prospectus | . . . | Thomas Boys." 8 pp. Same as Part 2.

MARTIN CHUZZLEWIT.

PLATES (TWO)
(No. 9) "Mr. Jonas Chuzzlewit entertains his cousins."
(p. 138).
(No. 10) "Mr. Pecksniff renounces the deceiver." (p. 160).

TEXT, WITH HEADING
"Chapter XI." pp. 129–160.

PART 6.

FRONT WRAPPER (OUTSIDE)
Same as No. I. except "No. VI." and at foot, "June."

FRONT WRAPPER (INSIDE)
Same as No. V. Inside Back Wrapper.

BACK WRAPPER (INSIDE)
Same as No. I.

BACK WRAPPER (OUTSIDE)
Same as No. V.

ADVERTISEMENTS (FRONT)
"Chuzzlewit Advertiser." 8 pp. numbered (1)–8.
    p. (1) "No. VI., June, 1843."
    p. 2. "The Foreign Library."
    p. 3. "In Preparation. | The Baronial Halls."
    p. 4. ($\frac{1}{2}$ col.) "To be completed . . . | China and India."
    p. 5. "To Reading and Book Societies . . ."
    p. 6. "Economical Radiating Stove . . ."
    p. 7. ($\frac{1}{2}$ col.) "Carpet and Floor-Cloth | Manufactory."
    p. 8. "The Western Life-Assurance Society."

ADVERTISEMENTS (BACK)
"The National Art-Union." 8 pp. numbered (1)–8.
Printed in blue on thin paper.

PLATES (TWO)
(No. 11) "Martin meets an acquaintance at the house of
a mutual relation." (p. 166).
(No. 12) "Mr. Tapley acts Third Party with great dis-
cretion." (p. 178).

TEXT, WITH HEADING
"Chapter XIII." pp. 161–192.

195

CHARLES DICKENS.

PART 7.

FRONT WRAPPER (OUTSIDE)
Same as No. I. except "No. VII." and at foot, "July."

FRONT WRAPPER (INSIDE)
"Established 1820. | Rippon and Burton's | Furnishing
Ironmongery Warehouses."

BACK WRAPPER (INSIDE)
"On the 30th instant . . . | The Fourth Volume | of |
Punch."

BACK WRAPPER (OUTSIDE)
Same as No. V.

ADVERTISEMENTS (FRONT)
"Chuzzlewit Advertiser." 8 pp. numbered (1)–8.

    p. (1) "No. VII., July, 1843."
    p. 2. "New Work by Thomas Carlyle."
    p. 3. "The Illustrated edition of 'Windsor Castle.' "
    p. 4. ($\frac{1}{2}$ col.) "The Zoologist."
    p. 5. ($\frac{1}{2}$ col.) "Carpet and Floor-Cloth | Manufactory."
    p. 6. "Economical Radiating Stove . . ."
    p. 7. "Human Life." (Parr's Life Pills).
    p. 8. "The Western Life-Assurance Society."

Slip : (to follow Front Wrapper). "Neatly bound in cloth
. . . | Price 4s. each volume, | Scenes and Incidents of
| Foreign Travel." 2 pp. unnumbered. ($6\frac{3}{4}'' \times 4''$).

Although a rare item, this slip is essential to the collation, being
an original inset as stitched in by the binder. It has been noted
in only six copies.

PLATES (TWO)

(No. 13) "Mr. Jefferson Brick proposes an appropriate
sentiment." (p. 199).

(No. 14) "Mr. Tapley succeeds in finding a 'jolly' subject
for contemplation." (p. 212).

TEXT, WITH HEADING
"Chapter XVI." pp. 193–224.

MARTIN CHUZZLEWIT.

PART 8.

FRONT WRAPPER (OUTSIDE)
Same as No. I. except "No. VIII." and at foot, "August."

FRONT WRAPPER (INSIDE)
"137, Fleet Street, London, 1843. | Modern and Standard Novels and Romances. | D. Dodson."

BACK WRAPPER (INSIDE)
"The Foreign Library."

BACK WRAPPER (OUTSIDE)
Same as No. V.

ADVERTISEMENTS (FRONT)
"Chuzzlewit Advertiser." 8 pp. numbered (1)–(7. 8).
    p. (1) "No. VIII., August, 1843."
    p. 2. "Under the immediate superintendence of the Council . . ."
    p. 3. "Mons. Le Page's French School."
    p. 4. (½ col.) "Meerschaum Pipes."
    p. 5. "Economical Radiating Stove . . ."
    p. 6. (½ col.) "In 8vo, price 4s., | Launcelot of the Lake."
    p. 7. (½ col.) "Carbonate of Soda."
    p. 8. "Established Sixty Years." (Schweppe).

PLATES (TWO)
(No. 15) "The dissolution of Partnership." (p. 232).
(No. 16) "Mr. Pecksniff on his Mission." (p. 235).

TEXT, WITH HEADING
"Chapter XVIII." pp. 225–256.

PART 9.

FRONT WRAPPER (OUTSIDE)
Same as No. I. except "No. IX." and at foot, "September."

FRONT WRAPPER (INSIDE)
"The Foreign Library." First work announced : "Austria. By J. G. Kohl."

BACK WRAPPER (INSIDE)
"Published Weekly . . . | . . . | The Illustrated London | News."

CHARLES DICKENS.

BACK WRAPPER (OUTSIDE)

"Mechi, | No. 4, Leadenhall Street, | London, | . . . | Papier Maché Manufactures." At each side of name and address are five short additional lines. With six illustrations.

The address here is set in two lines, in contradistinction to all preceding parts.

ADVERTISEMENTS (FRONT)

"Chuzzlewit Advertiser." 8 pp. numbered (1)–(7, 8).

p. (1) "No. IX., September, 1843."
p. 2. "Bell's | Weekly Messenger."
p. 3. "Horticulture." (Continuation of page 2).
p. 4. "London Congregational Board."
p. 5. "Economical Radiating Stove . . ."
p. 6. "The Perfect Substitute for Silver." (Rippon and Burton).

(To follow plates) : "On the First of October will be Published . . . | The first number | of | The Baronial Halls." 2 pp. numbered (1), 2 ; conjugating with pp. (1) and 2 of "Advertiser."

ADVERTISEMENTS (BACK)

"The | Eighth Wonder | of the World." A booklet issued by E. Moses & Son, consisting of 32 pp. bound in pink wrappers, with title as above printed on front and back. ($4\frac{5}{8}'' \times 3\frac{5}{8}''$).

PLATES (TWO)

(No. 17) "The thriving City of Eden as it appeared on paper." (p. 268).

(No. 18) "The thriving City of Eden as it appeared in fact." (p. 288).

TEXT, WITH HEADING

"Chapter XXI." pp. 257–288.

PART 10.

FRONT WRAPPER (OUTSIDE)

Same as No. I. except "No. X." and at foot, "October."

MARTIN CHUZZLEWIT.

Front Wrapper (Inside)
"The Foreign Library." Same as No. IX.

Back Wrapper (Inside)
"The Illustrated London News." Same as No. IX.

Back Wrapper (Outside)
"Mechi." Same as No. IX., with an additional line in heavy-faced type immediately above the six illustrations : "Superior Table Cutlery & Sheffield Plate."

Advertisements (Front)
"Chuzzlewit Advertiser." 8 pp. numbered (1)–8.

p. (1) "No. X., October, 1843."
p. 2. "Books published by William Tait."
p. 3. "Economical Radiating Stove . . ."
p. 4. "Genuine Havannah Cigars."
p. 5. ($\frac{1}{2}$ col.) "Carpet and Floor-Cloth | Manufactory."
p. 6. "The Perfect Substitute for Silver."
p. 7. "This day, October 1st, is Published . . . | The first number | of | The Baronial Halls."
p. 8. "The | Foreign Quarterly Review, | No. LXIII . . ."

Advertisements (Back)

(1) "C. Ralph & Co. | Ironmongers" ; with view of premises below. Illustration of Phœnix Stove on page (4). Imprint on last page : "Jones & Causton, Printers, 47, Eastcheap, London." 4 pp. unnumbered. Blue paper.

(2) "The | 'Pride of London,' | a Poem." A booklet issued by E. Moses & Son, consisting of 32 pp. mainly set to verse, bound in pink wrappers, with title as above printed on front and back. ($4\frac{5}{8}'' \times 3\frac{5}{8}''$).

Plates (Two)

(No. 19) "Balm for the wounded orphan." (p. 296).

(No. 20) "Mrs. Gamp has her eye on the future." (p. 320).

Text, with Heading
"Chapter XXIV." pp. 289–320.

CHARLES DICKENS.

PART 11.

FRONT WRAPPER (OUTSIDE)
 Same as No. I. except "No. XI." and at foot, "November."

FRONT WRAPPER (INSIDE)
 "The Only Safe and Healthy Stoves." Woodcut. (Rippon
 and Burton).

BACK WRAPPER (INSIDE)
 "The Illustrated | London News." With view of the
 Thames and St. Paul's.

BACK WRAPPER (OUTSIDE)
 Same as No. X.

ADVERTISEMENTS (FRONT)
 "Chuzzlewit Advertiser." 16 pp. numbered (1)–(15, 16).
  p. (1) "No. XI., November, 1843."
  p. 2. "New Works Just Published | by Chapman and Hall."
  p. 3. "In One Volume . . . | Past and Present. | By Thomas
    Carlyle."
  p. 4. "Books published by W. Tait, Edinburgh."
  p. 5. "Almanacks and Pocket-Books."
  pp. 6 & 7. "The Foreign Library."
  pp. 8 & 9. "Under the Superintendence of the Society . . ."
  p. 10. ($\frac{1}{2}$ col.) "Carpet and Floor-Cloth | Manufactory."
  p. 11. "Economical Radiating Stove . . ."
  p. 12. ($\frac{1}{2}$ col.) "H. Walker's Needles."
  p. 13. ($\frac{1}{2}$ col.) "Works | published by W. Brittain . . ."
  p. 14. "Removed from 163, Strand." (Robins's).
  p. (15) "Completion of the Maps."
  p. (16) "To be continued . . . | The Baronial Halls."

ADVERTISEMENTS (BACK)
 "The | 'Pride of London,' | a Poem." 32 pp. and wrappers.
 Same as in Part 10.

PLATES (TWO)
 (No. 21) "The Board." (p. 327).
 (No. 22) "Easy Shaving." (p. 346).

TEXT, WITH HEADING
 "Chapter XXVII." pp. 321–352.

MARTIN CHUZZLEWIT.

PART 12.

FRONT WRAPPER (OUTSIDE)
Same as No. I. except "No. XII." and at foot, "December."

FRONT WRAPPER (INSIDE)
"The Foreign Library." First work announced : "Ireland. By J. G. Kohl."

BACK WRAPPER (INSIDE)
Same as No. XI.

BACK WRAPPER (OUTSIDE)
Same as No. X.

ADVERTISEMENTS (FRONT)
"Chuzzlewit Advertiser." 16 pp. numbered (1)-(15, 16), except p. 3.

p. (1) "No. XII., December, 1843."
p. 2. "Completion of the Maps."
p. 3. Full-page Illustration of "Saint James's" Tower.
p. 4. "Published by W. Tait, Edinburgh."
p. 5. "Notice ! | . . . | Mr. Ainsworth's 'Windsor Castle.' "
p. 6. "Amusement for Winter Parties."
p. 7. "New Works Just Published." (Chapman and Hall).
p. 8. "Present-Books for the Season."
p. 9. "Economical Radiating Stove . . ."
p. 10. "Writing, Book-Keeping, &c."
p. 11. ($\frac{1}{2}$ col.) "Cut Glass, China, Earthen- | ware . . ."
p. 12. ($\frac{1}{2}$ col.) "Mr. Punch is always Publishing . . ."
p. 13. ($\frac{1}{2}$ col.) "Illustrated by 'Phiz.' | The Commissioner."
p. 14. "An entire new series of seventy-two Puzzles."

(To follow plates) : "New Christmas Book by Mr. Dickens." Verso, "Just published . . . | The second number of | The Baronial Halls." 2 pp. unnumbered ; conjugating with pp. (1) and 2 of "Advertiser."

ADVERTISEMENTS (BACK)

(1) "C. Ralph & Co." 4 pp. Same as Part 10, but pink paper.

(2) "The Winter Season." (E. Moses & Son). 4 pp. numbered (1)–4.

201

(3) "Part I., Published November 1, 1843. | Sylvester Sound | the | Somnambulist." Full page illustration. 2 pp. unnumbered. Salmon coloured paper.

(4) "The League Fund. | (£100,000.)" 2 pp., second page numbered.

PLATES (TWO)

(No. 23) "Mr. Moddle is both particular and peculiar in his attentions." (p. 384).

(No. 24) "Mr. Pecksniff discharges a duty which he owes to Society." (p. 387).

Plate No. 24 should obviously face page 376, not 387.

TEXT, WITH HEADING
"Chapter XXX." pp. 353–384.

PART 13.

FRONT WRAPPER (OUTSIDE)
Same as No. I. except "No. XIII." and at foot, "January 1844."

FRONT WRAPPER (INSIDE)
Rippon and Burton, same as No. XI.

BACK WRAPPER (INSIDE)
Same as No. XI.

BACK WRAPPER (OUTSIDE)
"Mechi." Almost identical with No. I., except there appears the five additional lines each side of name and address as in No. IX. Seven illustrations.

ADVERTISEMENTS (FRONT)
"Chuzzlewit Advertiser." 16 pp. numbered (1)–(15, 16), except p. 7.
p. (1) "No. XIII., January, 1844."
p. 2. "Just Published . . . | Payne's Universum."
p. 3. "The | Foreign Quarterly Review, | No. LXIV. . . ."

p. 4. "Published by W. Tait, Edinburgh." Different to Part 12.
p. 5. "Completion of the Maps."
p. 6. "Whittaker's | Popular Library of Modern . . . | Authors."
p. 7. "Publishing every alternate month." (Baronial Halls).
p. 8. ($\frac{1}{2}$ col.) "A Book for the Holidays."
p. 9. ($\frac{1}{2}$ col.) "Twenty Years Loss of | Hair . . ."
p. 10. "Economical Radiating Stove . . ."
p. 11. ($\frac{1}{2}$ col.) "Cut Glass, China, Earthen- | ware . . ."
p. 12. "Writing, Book-Keeping, &c."
p. 13. ($\frac{1}{2}$ col.) "To Flute Players."
p. 14. "Palmer and Co.'s Patent | . . . | Candle Lamps."
(To follow plates) : "New Christmas Book by Mr. Dickens." Verso blank. 2 pp. unnumbered ; conjugating with pp. (1) and 2 of "Advertiser."

ADVERTISEMENTS (BACK)

(1) "The New Year." (E. Moses and Son). 4 pp. numbered (1)–4.

(2) "New Weekly Newspaper. | . . . | Municipal & Poor Law Gazette." 2 pp., second page numbered.

(3) "Punch's Christmas Piece !" 2 pp. unnumbered.

(4) "Hood's Magazine." 2 pp., second page numbered.

(5) "Eagle | Life Assurance Company." 2 pp. Same as Part 4.

(6) "English Grammar | and | Key." 2 pp., second page numbered.

(7) "For Schools and Families. | . . . | Foster's Post-Copy-Books." 4 pp. numbered (1), 2, 3, (4).

PLATES (TWO)

(No. 25) "Mr. Tapley is recognised by some fellow citizens of Eden." (p. 386).

(No. 26) "Martin is much gratified by an imposing ceremony." (p. 415).

TEXT, WITH HEADING
"Chapter XXXIII." pp. 385–416.

CHARLES DICKENS.

PART 14.

FRONT WRAPPER (OUTSIDE)
Same as No. I. except "No. XIV." and at foot, "February 1844."

FRONT WRAPPER (INSIDE)
"Britannia Life Assurance Company."

BACK WRAPPER (INSIDE)
"From the New York Herald, | . . . | Parr's Life Pills."

BACK WRAPPER (OUTSIDE)
Same as No. XIII.

ADVERTISEMENTS (FRONT)
"Chuzzlewit Advertiser." 16 pp. numbered (1)–(15, 16).
> p. (1) "No. XIV., February, 1844."
> p. 2. "New Works Just Published." (Chapman and Hall).
> p. 3. "Interesting Works." (Smith, Elder, and Co.).
> pp. 4–7. "Under the Superintendence of the Society for the Diffusion of Useful Knowledge."
> p. 8. "An entire new series of seventy-two Puzzles."
> p. 9. ($\frac{1}{2}$ col.) "Now ready . . . | Whimsicalities."
> p. 10. "Payne's Universum ; or, Pictorial World."
> p. 11. "Economical Radiating Stove . . ."
> p. 12. ($\frac{1}{2}$ col.) "Chubb's New Patent De- | tector Locks . . ."
> p. 13. "Bett's Patent Brandy."
> p. 14. "The New Light. | . . . | The Patent Camphine Lamp."
> (To follow plates) : "Third Edition. | . . . | A Christmas Carol."
> > Verso blank. 2 pp. unnumbered ; conjugating with pp. (1) and 2 of "Advertiser."

Slip : (to follow "Advertiser"). "Baronial Halls" with six lines of text, and dated, 31st January, 1844. Verso blank. ($3'' \times 5\frac{1}{4}''$).

ADVERTISEMENTS (BACK)
"A Brief Glance | at the | Origin, Improvement, & Perfection | of Clothing." (E. Moses & Son). 4 pp. numbered (1)–4.

PLATES (TWO)
(No. 27) "Mr. Pinch departs to seek his fortune." (p. 419).

(No. 28) "Mr. Nadgett breathes, as usual, an atmosphere of mystery." (p. 448).

TEXT, WITH HEADING
"Chapter XXXVI." pp. 417–448.

PART 15.

FRONT WRAPPER (OUTSIDE)
Same as No. I. except "No. XV." and at foot, "March 1844."

FRONT WRAPPER (INSIDE)
"The New Light. | Great Novelty ! | The Patent Camphine Lamp." (Rippon and Burton). Same text as Page 14, in No. XIV. of "Chuzzlewit Advertiser." Last words on page : "Oxford-street, London."

BACK WRAPPER (INSIDE)
Same as No. XIV.

BACK WRAPPER (OUTSIDE)
Same as No. XIII.

ADVERTISEMENTS (FRONT)
"Chuzzlewit Advertiser." 16 pp. numbered (1)–16, except pp. 3 and 10.

p. (1) "No. XV., March, 1844."
pp. 2 & 3. "The Library of Travel." (Chapman & Hall).
p. 4. "This day is published, | The Heretic."
p. 5. "This day, March 1, is published . . . | The Baronial Halls."
p. 6. ($\frac{1}{2}$ col.) "Just published . . . | Mrs. Opie's Works."
p. 7. "Fifth Edition. | . . . | A Christmas Carol."
p. 8. "The Foreign Library."
p. 9. "On the 5th of March . . . | A New | Spirit of the Age."
p. 10. "Completion of the Maps."
p. 11. ($\frac{1}{2}$ col.) "Ease and Comfort in Shaving."
pp. 12 & 13. "Betts and Co.'s Circular."
p. 14. "Economical Radiating Stove . . ."
p. 15. "Parasols." (W. & J. Sangster). With woodcuts.
p. 16. "The | Panklibanon Iron Works."

ADVERTISEMENTS (BACK)

(1) "The Spring." (E. Moses and Son). 4 pp. numbered (1)–4.

(2) "West Strand, | March, 1844. | Collections in Popular Literature, | publishing by | John W. Parker . . ." 8 pp. numbered (1)–8.

(3) "C. Ralph & Co." 4 pp. Same as Part 10, but pink paper.

PLATES (TWO)

(No. 29) "Mr. Pinch and Ruth unconscious of a visitor." (p. 452).

(No. 30) "Mysterious Installation of Mr. Pinch." (p. 460).

TEXT, WITH HEADING
"Chapter XXXIX." pp. 449–480.

PART 16.

FRONT WRAPPER (OUTSIDE)
Same as No. 1. except "No. XVI." and at foot, "April 1844."

FRONT WRAPPER (INSIDE)
"F. G. Moon's Publications."

BACK WRAPPER (INSIDE)
" 'La Sylphide' Parasol." (W. & J. Sangster).

BACK WRAPPER (OUTSIDE)
Same as No. XIII.

ADVERTISEMENTS (FRONT)
"Chuzzlewit Advertiser." 16 pp. numbered (1) – 16, except p. 7.

    p. (1) "No. XVI., April, 1844."
    p. 2. "Library of Travel." Continued from page (1).
    p. 3. "The | Foreign Quarterly Review, | No. LXV."
    p. 4. "The Foreign Library."

p. 5. "Shortly will be published, | . . . | The Mysteries of Paris."
p. 6. "New Publications." (Chapman and Hall).
p. 7. "Completion of the Maps."
p. 8. ($\frac{1}{2}$ col.) "In one volume . . . | Chess for Beginners."
p. 9. "Publishing every alternate month, | The Baronial Halls."
p. 10. "The 'Medical Times,' the leading Medical Journal."
p. 11. "Economical Radiating Stove . . ."
p. 12. ($\frac{1}{2}$ col.) "Comfort in a Night-Cap ! "
p. 13. "New Travelling Atlas."
p. 14. "City Steam Press, Long Lane, London."
p. 15. "The Patent Brandy."
p. 16. "The | Panklibanon Iron Works."

ADVERTISEMENT (BACK)

"The | Temple of Fashion." A booklet issued by E. Moses & Son, consisting of 32 pp. bound in wrappers of blue or yellow ; with title as above, printed on front and back. ($4\frac{5}{8}'' \times 3\frac{5}{8}''$).

PLATES (TWO)

(No. 31) "Mr. Jonas exhibits his presence of mind." (p. 485).

(No. 32) "Mr. Pecksniff announces himself as the shield of Virtue." (p. 497).

TEXT, WITH HEADING

"Chapter XLII." pp. 481–512.

PART 17.

FRONT WRAPPER (OUTSIDE)

Same as No. I. except "No. XVII." and at foot, "May 1844."

FRONT WRAPPER (INSIDE)

"The New Light. | Great Novelty ! | The Patent Camphine Lamp." (Rippon and Burton). Different text to No. XV. Last line on page : "Established 1820."

BACK WRAPPER (INSIDE)

Same as No. XVI.

CHARLES DICKENS.

BACK WRAPPER (OUTSIDE)
"Mechi, | No. 4, Leadenhall Street, | London, | ... | Papier Maché Goods, | . . . | Presentation." With seven illustrations.

> Identical with No. XIII. except the word "Presentation" appears in place of "New Years' Gifts."

ADVERTISEMENTS (FRONT)
"Chuzzlewit Advertiser." 16 pp. numbered (1)–16.

> p. (1) "No. XVII., May, 1844."
> pp. 2 & 3. "The Library of Travel." Similar to Part 15.
> p. 4. "This day is published, . . . | The Baronial Halls."
> Above is cut of Royal Arms, and 4 lines of Subscribers.
> p. 5. "Completion of the Maps."
> p. 6. "An entire new series of seventy-two Puzzles."
> p. 7. "Just Published, | ... | The Book of Symbols."
> p. 8. "The Prince of Wales' Library."
> p. 9. ($\frac{1}{2}$ col.) "Hood's Magazine for May."
> p. 10. "Worsdell's Pills, by John Kaye."
> p. 11. ($\frac{1}{2}$ col.) "Castor Oil."
> p. 12. "Ease in Walking and | Comfort to the Feet."
> p. 13. "The Patent Brandy."
> p. 14. "Economical Radiating Stove . . ."
> p. 15. "City Steam Press, Long Lane, London."
> p. 16. "In the course of May . . . | The Mysteries of Paris."

ADVERTISEMENTS (BACK)
(1) "Public Opinion." (E. Moses and Son). 4 pp. numbered (1)–4.

(2) "C. Ralph & Co."; above: a view of premises. 4 pp. unnumbered. White paper.

> Different from Parts 10, 12, 15, having no illustration of Phœnix Stove on page (4).

PLATES (TWO)
(No. 33) "Mr. Moddle is led to the contemplation of his destiny." (p. 521).

(No. 34) "Mrs. Gamp makes tea." (p. 528).

TEXT, WITH HEADING
"Chapter XLV." pp. 513–544.

MARTIN CHUZZLEWIT.

PART 18.

FRONT WRAPPER (OUTSIDE)
Same as No. I. except "No. XVIII." and at foot, "June 1844."

FRONT WRAPPER (INSIDE)
Similar to No. XVII, but with a paragraph headed: "Shower Baths," not appearing in that number.

BACK WRAPPER (INSIDE)
"The | Illuminated Magazine" ; last word of text : "day."

BACK WRAPPER (OUTSIDE)
Same as No. XVII.

ADVERTISEMENTS (FRONT)
"Chuzzlewit Advertiser." 20 pp. numbered (1)–20.

    p. (1) "No. XVIII., June, 1844."
    p. 2. "The only English Edition authorised by M. Eugène Sue."
    p. 3. "Completion of the Maps."
    p. 4. "Under the Superintendence of the Society . . ."
    p. 5. "Dr. Furnivall on Consumption and Scrofula."
    p. 6. "Published by W. Tait, Edinburgh."
    p. 7. "The Library of Travel. | Part the Second."
    p. 8. Same as Part 17, page 4.
    p. 9. "The Foreign Library." (Part Fifteen).
    p. 10. "New Travelling Atlas."
    p. 11. "New Works, Just Published." (Chapman and Hall).
    p. 12. "Sander & Co."
    p. 13. "Writing, Book-Keeping, &c."
    p. 14. "Economical Radiating Stove . . ."
    p. 15. "Worsdell's Pills, by John Kaye."
    p. 16. ($\frac{1}{2}$ col.) "New Guide to Paris."
    p. 17. ($\frac{1}{2}$ col.) "Castor Oil."
    p. 18. ($\frac{1}{2}$ col.) "Just published . . . | The Illustrated Oxford | Bible."
    p. 19. "Necessary Precaution."
    p. 20. " 'La Sylphide' Parasol." With four woodcuts.

ADVERTISEMENTS (BACK)
"London and Paris : | The Two Great Rivals." (E. Moses and Son). 4 pp. numbered (1)–4.

PLATES (TWO)

(No. 35) "Mrs. Gamp propoges a toast." (p. 563).

(No. 36) "Mr. Pinch is amazed by an unexpected apparition." (p. 576).

TEXT, WITH HEADING

"Chapter XLVIII." pp. 545–576.

PARTS 19 AND 20.

FRONT WRAPPER (OUTSIDE)

Same as No. I. except "Nos. XIX. & XX. Price 2s.";
and at foot, "July 1844."

FRONT WRAPPER (INSIDE)

"Reform Your Tailors' Bills." (Doudney).

BACK WRAPPER (INSIDE)

"The | Illuminated Magazine." Same as No. XVIII.

BACK WRAPPER (OUTSIDE)

Same as Nos. XVII. & XVIII.

> The first issue of Back Wrapper, both inside and outside, is identical with Part 18. Before many copies had been printed, two additional lines were inserted at the foot of inside back, reading: "A few copies in splendid binding, adapted to the drawing-room table, or forming an elegant souvenir."

ADVERTISEMENTS (FRONT)

"Chuzzlewit Advertiser." 24 pp. numbered (1)–(23, 24).

p. (1) "Nos. XIX. & XX., July, 1844."
p. 2. "Completion of the Maps." Same as Part 18, page 3.
p. 3. "The | Foreign Quarterly Review, | No. LXVI."
p. 4. "The Library of Travel. | Part the Third."
p. 5. "On the 1st of July . . . | The New Quarterly Review."
p. 6. "New Works, Just Published." Same as Part 18, page 11.
p. 7. ($\frac{1}{2}$ col.) "Fisher, Son, & Co.'s Works."
p. 8. ($\frac{1}{2}$ col.) "Continental Tourists."
p. 9. Similar to Part 17, page 4, except "Part the Fifth."
p. 10. "New Travelling Atlas." Same as Part 18, page 10.
p. 11. "The Foreign Library." (Part Seventeen).
p. 12. "An entire new series of seventy-two puzzles."
p. 13. ($\frac{1}{2}$ col.) "Scottish Institution."
p. 14. "Dakin and Company."

MARTIN CHUZZLEWIT.

p. 15.   Continuation of page 14.
p. 16.   "Worsdell's Pills, by John Kaye."
p. 17.   (½ col.) "Comfort in a Night-Cap !"
p. 18.   (⅓ col.) "Castor Oil."
p. 19.   "Necessary Precaution."
p. 20.   "The Patentee of Robins' Royal Filter."
p. 21.   "Oldridge's Balm of Columbia."
p. 22.   "Manufacturers by Appointment." (W. & J. Sangster).
(To follow plates) : "In October, | England in the Reign of | Henry the Eighth" ; verso : "July 1, 1844. | Martin Chuzzlewit." 2 pp. unnumbered ; conjugating with pp. 17 and 18 of "Advertiser."

ADVERTISEMENTS (BACK)

(1) "Improvements." (E. Moses and Son). 4 pp. numbered (1)–4.

(2) "The Rising Wonder !" (F. Browne's Hair Cutting Saloon). 16 pp. on thin paper ; numbered (1)–16, except page 6.

PLATES (FOUR)

(No. 37) "Warm reception of Mr. Pecksniff by his venerable friend." (p. 599).

(No. 38) "The Nuptials of Miss Pecksniff receive a temporary check." (p. 622).

(No. 39) Frontispiece.

(No. 40) Vignette Title ; dated 1844.

Plate 40, Engraved title. Impressions from the three "steels" etched by Phiz for this plate, may be distinguished by the following :—

First : Signed "Phiz fecit." With reversed "100£" on signpost. Seven studs in lid of Pinch's trunk.

Second : Signed "Phiz." Signpost with "£100" ; the first figure "1" is blurred. Six studs in lid of trunk.

Third : Signed "Phiz." Signpost with "£100" ; the first figure is sharply defined. Five studs in lid of trunk.

TEXT, WITH HEADING

"Chapter LI." pp. 577–624. Imprint at foot of p. 624 : "London : | Bradbury and Evans, Printers, Whitefriars."

CHARLES DICKENS.

> The errata leaf is more often in evidence with 14 lines of corrections, although the actual details coincide. The 13-line setting is the earlier issue,—in this original set-up, it was rather crudely balanced, and was consequently reset to 14 lines.

THE

ADVENTURES

OF

OLIVER TWIST;

OR,

The Parish Boy's Progress.

BY

CHARLES DICKENS.

————•————

WITH TWENTY-FOUR ILLUSTRATIONS ON STEEL, BY
GEORGE CRUIKSHANK.

A NEW EDITION, REVISED AND CORRECTED.

LONDON:
PUBLISHED FOR THE AUTHOR,
BY BRADBURY & EVANS, WHITEFRIARS.
MDCCCXLVI.

Oliver Twist

in

10 Monthly Parts
January to October, 1846.

THE publication in ten monthly parts, commenced with the turn of the year, January, 1846, and arrived at completion in October, 1846. In like manner to "Sketches by Boz," the parts issue of the present work, followed on previous publications; firstly as a serial in "Bentley's Miscellany," from February, 1837 (except June, 1837) to March, 1839. Before the close of the serial, it came out in three-volume form; the first edition dated 1838, the second 1839, and the third 1841; whilst between these extreme dates are four other issues with varying title-pages.

Complete sets of the ten parts can, without exaggeration, be described as of the utmost rarity, whether in fine, moderate, or poor condition, and only exceeded by the "high-spots" of "Pickwick" and the "Sketches." As recently as 1931, it would have been an impossibility to purchase any kind of conditioned copy in the London book-market; for the simple reason that none were on offer or could be offered. The very scarcity alone, of the book in parts, gives added zest to the tracking down of copies, but many would-be owners are doomed to disappointment in their efforts to effect a capture, in face of the very limited supply available.

TEXT.

The general appearance of the typography in this octavo edition, is by no means pleasing—it stands out in sharp

215

contrast to any other of the periodical issues printed by Bradbury & Evans. The spacing between lines is closer than usual, and there is a lack of uniformity in the page depth-measurements. Particularly insignificant are the figures used in the pagination, which seem entirely foreign to such a work, and in effect spoil the whole appearance of the page. No textual differences arise to separate early and late impressions.

PLATES.

The twenty-four plates by George Cruikshank are those originally designed for "Bentley's Miscellany" and also used in the three-volume edition. For this issue in parts they were re-touched, re-bitten, and further added to, but this was not done by Cruikshank, but by an etcher named Findlay, who at that time etched many plates as frontispieces to plays. The imprint of Bentley, which appeared on the plates in the "Miscellany" and volume edition, was erased. The plates were not however enlarged, as has been stated by one or two writers. Page-number references as given in the collation are those quoted in "List of Illustrations," and have no relation whatsoever to their position in the sequence of parts.

When first issued in "Bentley's Miscellany," on November 1, 1838, plate No. 19 of Part 9, with the name "Bolter," was etched to read : "Dolter." The error passed unnoticed in the early copies, but was corrected during the publication in that issue of the magazine, and also before its use in the three-volume edition. The alteration in the plate when examined, is quite easily detectable.

WRAPPERS.

The usual green coloured wrapper was adopted, although Part 1 has been seen (though rarely) with blue. George Cruikshank designed and etched the front wrapper drawing, depicting eleven scenes and incidents of the story. The design is generally acknowledged as a clever effort, and certainly compares more than favourably with other cover designs by Seymour, "Phiz" or the later artists. The back

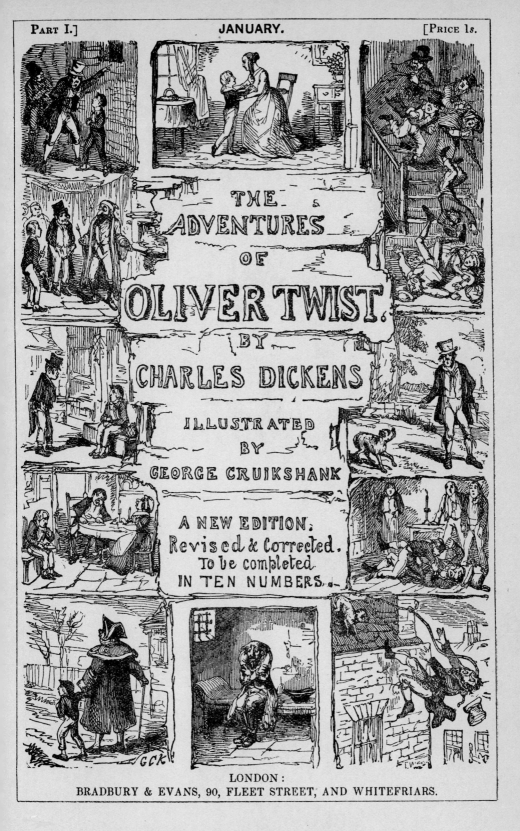

The rare Front Wrapper to the new edition of "Oliver Twist,"
as published in 10 monthly parts, 1846. The story first appeared
as a serial in *Bentley's Miscellany*, 1837-1839.

wrappers require careful checking, as copies of some of the parts are in circulation with backs from quite a different periodical, viz: "Comic History of England," which was publishing during a part of the period concurrent with "Oliver Twist"; some of these backs having a great similarity to each other, both in colour and texture of paper and in some cases the advertisements printed on them.

ADVERTISEMENTS.

Very little inset material was included with the parts— actually only three lay claim to any at all, viz: 1, 2 and 10. The "Oliver Twist Advertiser" appears only in the first two numbers, each consisting of eight pages; and very unusually is placed at the end, as opposed to the orthodox method of insertion at the front. Part 10 carries the solus "trade" inset, being a single leaf, printed on yellow paper, and stitched within the front wrapper.

PART 1.

FRONT WRAPPER (OUTSIDE)
"Part I.] January. [Price 1s. | The | Adventures | of | Oliver Twist | by | Charles Dickens. | Illustrated | by | George Cruikshank | A new edition. | Revised & corrected. | To be completed | In Ten Numbers. | London: | Bradbury & Evans, 90, Fleet Street, and Whitefriars." Artist's initials in lower left corner.

The first and last two lines are set up in type, the other text being engraved and forming part of the cover design. A series of eleven scenes are depicted, all arising from incidents in the story.

FRONT WRAPPER (INSIDE)
"New Edition of Dr. Lindley's School Botany"; "The Vegetable Kingdom"; "Works by Mr. Douglas Jerrold."

BACK WRAPPER (INSIDE)
"Mr. Dickens's Works," announcing issue of Part I. of "Oliver Twist." Also, "The Cricket on the Hearth"; "A Christmas Carol" and "The Chimes."

BACK WRAPPER (OUTSIDE)

"New Morning Paper. | To commence at the Opening of Parliament. | The Daily News." Full page. Imprint at foot : "Bradbury and Evans, Printers, Whitefriars."

ADVERTISEMENTS (BACK)

"Oliver Twist Advertiser." 8 pp. unnumbered.

p. (1) "January, 1846. | Oliver Twist Advertiser. No. I."

p. (2) "Works published by Mr. Dickens." Seven titles.

p. (3) (½ col.) "Bechstein's Cage Birds" and other works published by W. S. Orr & Co.

p. (4) "Works published by William Smith," below in half measure, a list of twenty-five works.

p. (5) "Smith's Standard Library," below in half measure, a numbered list of ninety-two works.

p. (6) "Mrs. Caudle's Curtain Lectures" ; "The Almanack of the Month" ; and "The Comic Blackstone" ; all published at the "Punch" office. "Stooping of the Shoulders" with two woodcuts, and "Of Importance to everybody reading unbound Publications."

p. (7) "Established [in Wells Street] 1820," followed by illustration of premises, and below this, "The perfect substitute for Silver." (Rippon & Burton). Full page.

p. (8) "The Chronicles of Clovernook" and "Our Own Times" published by Bradbury & Evans. "Dr. Locock's Pulmonic Wafers" ; and "Acceptable Presents" (Rowlands).

Page 7 is identical in text and arrangement, with the outside back wrapper of Part 2.

PLATES (TWO)

(No. 1) "Oliver asking for more." (p. 9).

(No. 2) "Oliver escapes being bound apprentice to the Sweep." (p. 16).

TEXT, WITH HEADING

"Oliver Twist. | Chapter I." pp. (1)–32.

PART 2.

FRONT WRAPPER (OUTSIDE)

Same as Part I. except "Part II. February."

FRONT WRAPPER (INSIDE)

Same as Part I.

OLIVER TWIST.

PART 5.

FRONT WRAPPER (OUTSIDE)
Same as Part I. except "Part V. May."

FRONT WRAPPER (INSIDE)
"New Works by Mr. Dickens." Announcements of early
publication of "Pictures from Italy" and "A New English
Story" (Dombey). Below: "Rowlands Macassar Oil."

BACK WRAPPER (INSIDE)
"The Chronicles of Clovernook"; "Dr. Locock's Pulmonic Wafers"; "Holloway's" and "Keating's."

BACK WRAPPER (OUTSIDE)
Same as Part 4.

PLATES (TWO)
(No. 9) "Master Bates explains a professional tech-
nicality." (p. 100).
(No. 10) "The Burglary." (p. 123).

TEXT, WITH HEADING
"Chapter XXIV." pp. (129)–160.

PART 6.

FRONT WRAPPER (OUTSIDE)
Same as Part I. except "Part VI. June."

FRONT WRAPPER (INSIDE)
"On and after this Day, the First of June, | The Daily
News, | London Morning Newspaper, | at | Twopence
Halfpenny." Full page.

BACK WRAPPER (INSIDE)
"Comic History of England," and "An infallible Hair
Dye" (Rowlands).

BACK WRAPPER (OUTSIDE)
"Established [in Wells Street] A.D. 1820." (Illustration of
premises). "Shower Baths.—Novel Show," followed
by nine lines in small type. Full page.

PLATES (TWO)
(No. 12) "Mr. Claypole as he appeared when his master
was out." (p. 150).

(No. 13) "Oliver Twist at Mrs. Maylie's door." (p. 156).

TEXT, WITH HEADING
"Chapter XXX." pp. 161–162.

PART 7.

FRONT WRAPPER (OUTSIDE)
Same as Part I. except "Part VII. July."

FRONT WRAPPER (INSIDE)
"On Saturday, July the 18th, | . . . | Douglas Jerrold's Weekly | Newspaper"; followed by : "From the First of June, | The Daily News, | London Morning Newspaper, | at | Twopence Halfpenny."

BACK WRAPPER (INSIDE)
"Comic History of England. | On the First of July, 1846, will be published | . . . | The First Part | of the | Comic History of England"; followed by : "Ladies." (Rowlands). Half page to each.

BACK WRAPPER (OUTSIDE)
"Established [in Wells Street] A.D. 1820." (Illustration of premises). "Shower Baths, with Curtains, 9s. each"; followed by nine lines in small type. Full page.

PLATES (Two)
(No. 14) "Oliver waited on by the Bow Street Runners." (p. 171).
(No. 15) "Monks and the Jew." (p. 192).

TEXT, WITH HEADING
"Chapter XXXV." pp. 193-224.

PART 8.

FRONT WRAPPER (OUTSIDE)
Same as Part I. except "Part VIII. August."

FRONT WRAPPER (INSIDE)
"New Work by Mr. Dickens." An announcement of "A New English Story" is now in preparation (Dombey). Below : "Just published . . . | Pictures from Italy."

222

BACK WRAPPER (INSIDE)
  "Works by Mr. Dickens" ; "Heal & Sons' List of Bedding";
    "Holloway's Pills" ; and "Purity of Complexion."

BACK WRAPPER (OUTSIDE)
  Same as Part 7.

PLATES (TWO)
  (No. 17) "The evidence destroyed." (p. 213).
  (No. 22) "The Last Chance." (p. 292).

TEXT, WITH HEADING
  "Chapter XL." pp. 225–256.

PART 9.

FRONT WRAPPER (OUTSIDE)
  Same as Part I. except "Part IX. September."

FRONT WRAPPER (INSIDE)
  "New Work in Monthly Parts, | By Mr. Charles Dickens.
    | On the First of October will be published . . . | The
    First Number | of | Dombey & Son." Full page.

BACK WRAPPER (INSIDE)
  "Heal & Sons' List of Bedding" ; "Holloway's Ointment" ;
    "Stooping of the Shoulders" ; and, "Purity of Com-
    plexion." (Rowlands).

BACK WRAPPER (OUTSIDE)
  Identically the same text and format as Part 4, but the
    paragraph headed "Fenders, Stoves, and Fire-Irons"
    has four words in small type instead of caps. Full page.

PLATES (THREE)
  (No. 18) "Mr. Fagin and his pupil recovering Nancy."
    (p. 216).
  (No. 19) "The Jew and Morris Bolter begin to understand
    each other." (p. 241).
  (No. 20) "The Meeting." (p. 261).

TEXT, WITH HEADING
  "Chapter XLV." pp. 257–288.

CHARLES DICKENS.

PART 10.

FRONT WRAPPER (OUTSIDE)
Same as Part I. except "Part X.   October."

FRONT WRAPPER (INSIDE)
Same as Part 9 except the words "will be published" are omitted in the third line.

BACK WRAPPER (INSIDE)
Same as Part 9 except the Rowland's advertisement is headed, "An infallible Hair Dye."

BACK WRAPPER (OUTSIDE)
"Established [in Wells Street] A.D. 1820."   (Illustration of premises).   "Light.—Camphine, Candles."   Full page.

ADVERTISEMENT (FRONT)
"New Weekly Periodical of Original Music. | The Music Book."   One leaf, verso blank.   Yellow paper.

PLATES (THREE)
(No. 21) "Sikes attempting to destroy his dog."   (p. 277).
(No. 23) "Fagin in the condemned cell."   (p. 304).
(No. 24) "Rose Maylie and Oliver."   (p. 310).
> Plate No. 24.   Rose Maylie's dress and bonnet are *black*, as opposed to *white* when issued in "Bentley's Miscellany" and the three-volume editions.

TEXT
(Continuation of Chapter LX.)   pp. 289–(312).   In centre of p. (312) imprint : "London : | Bradbury and Evans, Printers, Whitefriars."

PRELIMINARY LEAVES
Half-title : "The | Adventures | of | Oliver Twist."   Verso blank.   (I. II.).

Title-page : Dated 1846.   Verso with imprint as p. (312).   (III. IV.).   See Illustration.

Contents and List of Illustrations :   4 pp. (V.), VI., VII., (VIII.).

The Author's Preface to The Third Edition : 4 pp., dated April, 1841.   (IX.), X., XI., XII.

224

BACK WRAPPER (INSIDE)

"Silver Superseded, | . . . | Albata Plate" ; "The Earl of Aldborough & Holloway's | Pills" ; "Dr. Locock's Pulmonic Wafers."

BACK WRAPPER (OUTSIDE)

"Established [in Wells Street] 1820." (Illustration of premises). "The perfect substitute for Silver," followed by six lines in small type. (Rippon & Burton). Full page.

ADVERTISEMENTS (BACK)

"Oliver Twist Advertiser." 8 pp. unnumbered.

- p. (1) "February, 1846. | Oliver Twist Advertiser. No. II."
- p. (2) Same as Part I.
- p. (3) Same as Part I.
- p. (4) Same as Part I.
- p. (5) Same as Part I.
- p. (6) "Mrs. Caudle's Curtain Lectures" ; "The Almanack of the Month" ; "The Comic Blackstone" ; "The Chronicles of Clovernook" ; "Our Own Times."
- p. (7) Same as inside back wrapper to Part I. except announces "Part II." of "Oliver Twist."
- p. (8) "Smith's Souvenir Classics" ; "Keating's Cough Lozenges" ; "Of importance to everybody reading unbound Publications" ; "Tea Trays, Tea Urns," etc.

PLATES (THREE)

(No. 3) "Oliver plucks up a spirit." (p. 31).

(No. 11) "Mr. Bumble and Mrs. Corney taking tea." (p. 126).

(No. 16) "Mr. Bumble degraded in the eyes of the Paupers." (p. 204).

TEXT, WITH HEADING

"Chapter VII." pp. 33–64.

PART 3.

FRONT WRAPPER (OUTSIDE)

Same as Part I. except "Part III. March."

FRONT WRAPPER (INSIDE)

"Douglas Jerrold's | Shilling Magazine" ; and "Rowland's Macassar Oil."

BACK WRAPPER (INSIDE)

"Dr. Locock's Pulmonic Wafers" ; "The Earl of Aldborough & Holloway's | Pills" ; "Keating's Cough Lozenges" ; "Of importance to everybody reading unbound Periodicals."

BACK WRAPPER (OUTSIDE)

Same as Part 2.

PLATES (THREE)

(No. 4) "Oliver introduced to the respectable Old Gentleman." (p. 43).

(No. 5) "Oliver amazed at the Dodger's mode of 'going to work.' " (p. 50).

(No. 8) "Oliver's reception by Fagin and the boys." (p. 85).

TEXT, WITH HEADING

"Chapter XIII." pp. 65–96.

PART 4.

FRONT WRAPPER (OUTSIDE)

Same as Part I. except "Part IV. April."

FRONT WRAPPER (INSIDE)

"Douglas Jerrold's Shilling Magazine" ; "The Chronicles of Clovernook" ; "To Ladies." (Rowlands).

BACK WRAPPER (INSIDE)

"Our Own Times" ; "Dr. Locock's Pulmonic Wafers" ; "The Earl of Aldborough & Holloway's | Pills" ; "Keating's Cough Lozenges."

BACK WRAPPER (OUTSIDE)

"Established [in Wells Street] A.D. 1820." (Illustration of premises). "The perfect substitute for Silver," followed by five lines in small type. Full page.

PLATES (TWO)

(No. 6) "Oliver recovering from the fever." (p. 61).

(No. 7) "Oliver claimed by his affectionate friends." (p. 82).

TEXT, WITH HEADING

"Chapter XVIII." pp. 97–128.

Nº VI.   MARCH.   PRICE 1s.

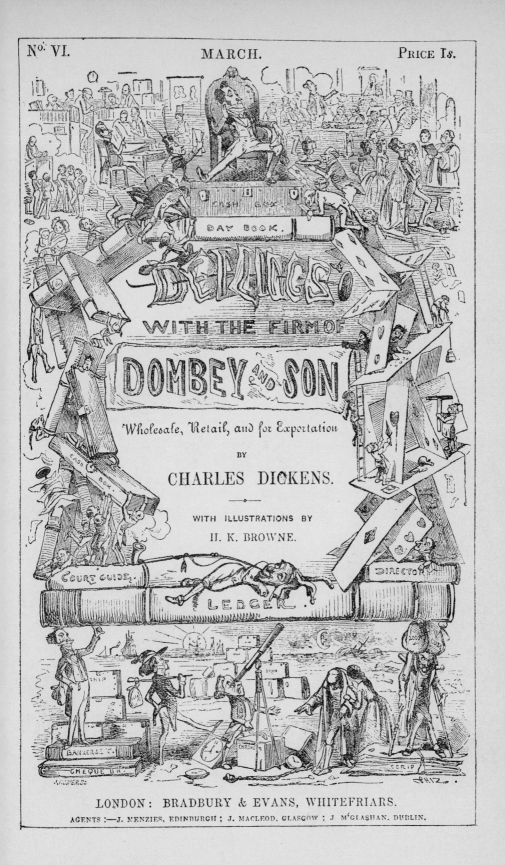

DEALINGS

WITH THE FIRM OF

DOMBEY AND SON

Wholesale, Retail, and for Exportation

BY

CHARLES DICKENS.

WITH ILLUSTRATIONS BY

H. K. BROWNE.

LONDON: BRADBURY & EVANS, WHITEFRIARS.

AGENTS:—J. MENZIES, EDINBURGH; J. MACLEOD, GLASGOW; J. M'GLASHAN, DUBLIN.

The Front Wrapper to the original edition of "Dombey and Son,"
as published in 19/20 monthly parts, 1846-1848.

DOMBEY AND SON.

BY

CHARLES DICKENS.

WITH ILLUSTRATIONS BY H. K. BROWNE.

LONDON:

BRADBURY AND EVANS, 11, BOUVERIE STREET.
1848.

Dombey and Son

in

19/20 Monthly Parts
October, 1846, to April, 1848.

ORIGINALLY issued in twenty numbers, bound in nineteen, price one shilling monthly, except the last two (19 and 20) which were issued as a double number at two shillings. The design for the green wrappers is by Hablot K. Browne ("Phiz"), who also etched the forty plates. The first number appeared in October, 1846, and the final one in April, 1848.

TEXT.

Two typographical errors, which have a bearing on priority of issue, occur in Parts 11 and 14. The use of word "Delight" for "Joy" in Part 9 was never corrected during the issue in parts, and is not referred to in the "errata."

PLATES.

Two sets of plates for each of the forty designs were etched by "Phiz." Even so, it was found impossible to print a sufficient number of the etchings to supply the demand, and lithographic transfers were therefore made from the steels. Every copy of "Dombey and Son" that was issued in the parts, contained a certain number of these lithographic illustrations, and every complete set of the parts varies as to quantity. From an examination of 1486 plates, the writer has been able to discover their appearance in eight numbers, viz.: 3, 6, 8, 10, 11, 14, 16, 17; but this record is not necessarily complete—more than likely every plate was reproduced by the "litho" process.

227

CHARLES DICKENS.

Although this is the first work in which any quantity of lithographs are present, they were not unknown even before this, because there are specimens in the Dexter collection of two plates to Part 15 of "Pickwick Papers," and whilst it is certain they had no place in the early parts issue, it is equally certain they were published for the volume edition of no later date than 1838.

It is not suggested that copies containing lithographs are of later printing or later issue than those with etchings—they were all in use at the same time—but sets of parts in which etchings have been substituted for lithographs, would naturally be more desirable than sets in which the two processes are mixed.

Attention is drawn to Plate No. 35 in Part 18—"On the dark Road"—which is the first published example of what later became known as "Dark Plates." The subject is fully dealt with in the introduction to "Bleak House," in which book a more general use was made of the process.

In all the previous works which have passed under review, the illustrations were etched vertically on the steels, but, commencing with "Dombey," a departure from this custom was made in Plate No. 20—"Coming home from Church"— by etching the subject horizontally. Once started, the fashion continued, and oblong, or horizontally etched plates are to be found in this, and the later works, as follows :

Dombey and Son	-	-	-	-	5 Plates.
David Copperfield	-	-	-	-	21 ,,
Bleak House	-	-	-	-	19 ,,
Little Dorrit	-	-	-	-	27 ,,
Tale of Two Cities	-	-	-	-	14 ,,

The oversight by the artist when designing the vignette, in placing the hook on the left arm of Captain Cuttle, instead of on the right, is duly noted in the collation of Part 19/20.

WRAPPERS.

Apart from the essential change of "Part No." and month of issue, no other alteration of textual matter was effected in the front covers during the periodical issue. Both the inner sides, as well as the outside of the back wrapper, carried the usual trade advertisements. Clues to those of the back cover are noted only with respect to the outer-side, where E. Moses and Son vary their matter each issue, and the "pointer" to these is sufficient to identify the correct wrapper. The insides of back cover are occupied throughout the series of parts by William S. Burton (late Rippon and Burton), General Furnishing Ironmonger; with an illustration of premises at the head of the page.

ADVERTISEMENTS.

At the front, the "Dombey Advertiser" appears in each of the nineteen parts; varying from 8 pp. to 24 pp. Each page has the headline "Advertisements," with the exception of the first in each part, and page 23 in Part 19/20; and again, excepting p. (1) of each part, all are numbered. Several inset slips are to be found within the front portion of certain numbers; they are stitched in with other material, and should be present in Parts 2, 3, 5, 6, 7, 13, 15, 16, 17, 18, 19/20.

PART 1.

FRONT WRAPPER (OUTSIDE)
"No. I. October. Price 1s. | Dealings | with the Firm of | Dombey and Son | Wholesale, Retail, and for Exportation | by | Charles Dickens. | With Illustrations by | H. K. Browne. | London : Bradbury & Evans, Whitefriars. | Agents:—J. Menzies, Edinburgh; J. Macleod, Glasgow ; J. M'Glashan, Dublin."
The above text of cover is partly type-set and partly engraved and embodied in the cover design. Other wording is present, but has no reference to the general title.

FRONT WRAPPER (INSIDE)
"Thos. Harris & Son's | Crystal Spectacles." With two woodcuts.

BACK WRAPPER (OUTSIDE)
"To the Many." (E. Moses & Son).

CHARLES DICKENS.

ADVERTISEMENTS (FRONT)
"Dombey & Son Advertiser." 16 pp. numbered (1)–16.

  p. (1) "No. I.—October, 1846."
  p. 2. "Published Monthly . . . | The Dublin University Magazine."
  p. 3. "Cheap Edition of Popular Works."
  p. 4. "By the Author of ' Harry Lorrequer.' "
  p. 5. "Chapman and Hall's Series."
  p. 6. "Mr. Colburn's New Publications."
  p. 7. "Books published by | John W. Parker, London."
  p. 8. "On the First of November . . . | Punch's Pocket Book."
  p. 9. "Works by Mr. Dickens."
  p. 10. "Smith, Elder, & Co.'s New Publications."
  p. 11. "Douglas Jerrold's | Weekly Newspaper."
  p. 12. ($\frac{1}{2}$ col.) "In the Press, | Corner's History of Rome."
  p. 13. "Maugham's Patented Carrara Water."
  p. 14. ($\frac{1}{2}$ col.) "Shooting Season, 1846."
  p. 15. ($\frac{1}{2}$ col.) "No Brewing Utensils re- | quired."
  p. 16. "The Gentleman's real Head of Hair."

ADVERTISEMENTS (BACK)

(1) "New Weekly Periodical of Original Music. | The Music Book." 1 leaf, verso blank. Yellow paper.

(2) "Will be published on November the First | . . . | Rowland Bradshaw." 1 leaf, verso blank. Green paper.

(3) "Just Published . . . Gilbert's College Atlas." 8 pp. unnumbered.

  p. (3) "The Importance of an Atlas of the World."
  pp. (4 & 5) "Gilbert's . . . | Pronouncing Dictionary."
  p. (7) "Gilbert's | Modern Atlas of the World."

PLATES (TWO)

  (No. 1) "Miss Tox introduces ' the Party.' " (p. 10).
  (No. 2) "The Dombey Family." (p. 22).

TEXT, WITH HEADING
"Dombey and Son. | Chapter I." pp. (1)–32.

PART 2.

FRONT WRAPPER (OUTSIDE)
Same as No. I. except "No. II. November."

DOMBEY AND SON.

FRONT WRAPPER (INSIDE)
Same as No. I.

BACK WRAPPER (OUTSIDE)
"The Clothing Establishment, | of | E. Moses and Son."

ADVERTISEMENTS (FRONT)
"Dombey & Son Advertiser." 16 pp. numbered (1)–16.

    p. (1) "No. II.—November, 1846."
    p. 2. "Chapman and Hall's | Announcement . . ."
    p. 3. "Now ready . . . | January Eve."
    p. 4. "Important Books on Commerce."
    p. 5. "This day is published . . . | Comic History of England."
   pp. 6 & 7. "Edward Moxon's Publications."
    p. 8. "Works by Mr. Dickens."
    p. 9. "Bohn's Standard Library."
    p. 10. ($\frac{1}{2}$ col.) "Mr. Colburn's | New Publications."
    p. 11. "Bechstein's Cage Birds."
    p. 12. "Lett's Diaries for 1847."
    p. 13. ($\frac{1}{2}$ col.) "The Proof of the Tea is in | the Drinking."
    p. 14. ($\frac{1}{2}$ col.) "F. & C. Osler's | Glass Chandeliers."
    p. 15. "Umbrellas. | W. & J. Sangster."
    p. 16. Same as Part 1.
  Slip : (to face p. 1 of "Advertiser"). "In December will be published, | ... | A New Christmas Tale, | by Charles Dickens." Pink paper. ($5\frac{9}{16}'' \times 3\frac{1}{16}''$).

ADVERTISEMENTS (BACK)

(1) "Now Published, November the First, | ... | Rowland Bradshaw." Verso : "Raby Rattler." 2 pp. unnumbered. Green paper.

(2) Slip :—"Published Weekly | Punch ! " Verso : "Punch's Pocket-Book," etc. 2 pp. unnumbered. ($7\frac{5}{8}'' \times 4\frac{3}{8}''$).

(3) "New Weekly Periodical of Original Music. | The Music Book." 2 pp. unnumbered; printed in blue and red.

(4) "Bentick & Pelham's" with cut of Royal Arms. Verso : "British | Hong-Kong Tea Company." 2 pp. unnumbered.

(5) "The Best Family Medicine extant | is Worsdell's | Vegetable Restorative Pills." 2 pp., second page numbered (2).

Nos. 4 and 5 above form a 4-page inset.

231

CHARLES DICKENS.

PLATES (TWO)
(No. 3) "The Christening Party." (p. 40).
(No. 4) "Polly rescues the Charitable Grinder." (p. 50).

TEXT, WITH HEADING
"Chapter V.   pp. 33-64.

PART 3.

FRONT WRAPPER (OUTSIDE)
Same as No. I. except "No. III.   December."

FRONT WRAPPER (INSIDE)
"Feather Beds | Purified by Steam ! | Heal and Son."
This advertisement continues throughout the series.

BACK WRAPPER (OUTSIDE)
" ' E. Moses & Son's ' Lines to 'A Bull.' "

ADVERTISEMENTS (FRONT)
(Preceding "Advertiser").   4 pp. unnumbered.
p. (1) "New Work by Michael Angelo Titmarsh. | . . . | No. I. of | Vanity Fair :" verso blank.
p. (3) "Christmas Present. | . . . | George Cruikshank's | Table-Book."
p. (4) "Vanity Fair" ; "Works by Douglas Jerrold" ; "Works by Gilbert à Beckett."

"Dombey & Son Advertiser."   16 pp. numbered (1)–16.
p. (1) "No. III.—December, 1846."
p.   2. "Books for Presents and Prizes."
p.   3. "Otto Speckter's Christmas Story."
p.   4. "Published Monthly . . . | The Home and Colonial Library."
p.   5. "Bechstein's Cage Birds."
p.   6. "New Edition of Dr. Lindley's Vegetable Kingdom."
p.   7. "As a Christmas Present."
p.   8. ($\frac{1}{2}$ col.) "Ease and Comfort in | Shaving."
p.   9. "E. M. Clarke."   With woodcut.
p. 10. "Umbrellas. | W. & J. Sangster."
p. 11. ($\frac{1}{2}$ col.) "Edmiston & Son."
p. 12. "Cocoa-Nut Fibre Warehouse."
p. 13. ($\frac{1}{2}$ col.) "Amusement for Christmas ! "
p. 14. "Honnor's newly-invented ' Passe-Partout.' "

p. 15. "Under Royal Patronage."

p. 16. Same as Parts 1 & 2.

Slip : (to precede text). "Mr. Dickens's Christmas Book. | . . . | The | Battle of Life." Verso : "Mr. Dickens's New Monthly Work." (5⅝" × 4⅜").

ADVERTISEMENTS (BACK)

(1) "Chapman and Hall's New Publications." 8 pp. numbered (1)–(8). Dated on page 1 ; "186, Strand, | December 1, 1846." Printed on white or light-brown paper.

(2) Slip :—"Punch." Same as in Part 1.

(3) "The Atlas." 2 pp. unnumbered.

(4) "Richards's | Universal | Daily Remembrancer." 4 pp. numbered. (1)–4. Printed on white paper, in either black or red ink.

PLATES (Two)

(No. 5) "Paul and Mrs. Pipchin." (p. 75).

(No. 6) "Captain Cuttle consoles his Friend." (p. 87).

TEXT, WITH HEADING

"Chapter VIII." pp. 65–96.

PART 4.

FRONT WRAPPER (OUTSIDE)

Same as No. I. except "No. IV. January."

FRONT WRAPPER (INSIDE)

Same as No. III.

BACK WRAPPER (OUTSIDE)

"The Feet, the Legs, the Waist, the Back, and the Head." (E. Moses and Son).

ADVERTISEMENTS (FRONT)

"Dombey & Son Advertiser." 16 pp. numbered (1)–16.

p. (1) "No. IV.—January, 1847."

p. 2. "Christmas Present. | . . . | George Cruikshank's | Table-Book."

p. 3. "Notice | . . . | The Nelson Letters and Dispatches."

p. 4. (½ col.) "Elegant and useful Christmas Present."

CHARLES DICKENS.

p. 5. "Works by Douglas Jerrold."
p. 6. "Varty's Series of Dissected Maps."
p. 7. "New and Important Work on Natural History."
p. 8. "By Mr. Michael Angelo Titmarsh."
p. 9. "New Work by Michael Angelo Titmarsh." (Vanity Fair).
p. 10. "Price Threepence. | The Daily News."
p. 11. "New edition of Dr. Lindley's Vegetable Kingdom."
p. 12. "Perfect Freedom from Coughs in Ten minutes."
p. 13. "To the Tea-Drinkers . . ." (Dakin & Co.).
p. 14. (½ col.) "Ease and Comfort in | Shaving."
p. 15. "City of London Life Assurance Society."
p. 16. "The Gentleman's Real Head of Hair." Same as Parts 1, 2 & 3, with extra line at foot of page; "W. C. Jay & Co."

ADVERTISEMENTS (BACK)

(1) "Lett's Diaries." A 4-fold sheet, giving the size, price, and description of the various editions of Lett's Diary. With a number of specimen leaves.

(2) "Chambers' Edinburgh Journal." 2 pp., second page numbered; "Works | published by Wm. S. Orr and Co.," 6 pp. numbered (3)–8. In all, 8 pp.

(3) "Prospectus | of | Jullien's Album for 1847." 4 pp. unnumbered; printed on varying tints of paper, with gilt edges.

(4) "Eagle | Life Assurance Company." 2 pp. unnumbered.

(5) Slip:—"The Man in the Moon." Verso blank. (4½" × 5¾").

(6) "Published every Saturday . . . | The Lady's Newspaper." Verso : "Wives of England." Printed in red. 2 pp. unnumbered.

(7) "Cheap and Elegant | Christmas-Book." 2 pp. unnumbered.

PLATES (TWO)

(No. 7) "Doctor Blimber's Young Gentlemen as they appeared when enjoying themselves." (p. 113).
(No. 8) "Paul's Exercises." (p. 117).

TEXT, WITH HEADING
"Chapter XI." pp. 97-128.

234

DOMBEY AND SON.

PART 5.

FRONT WRAPPER (OUTSIDE)
Same as No. I. except "No. V. February."

FRONT WRAPPER (INSIDE)
Same as Nos. III. and IV. except first two lines are in
larger type.

BACK WRAPPER (OUTSIDE)
"Furs ! Furs ! ! Furs ! ! !" (E. Moses and Son).

ADVERTISEMENTS (FRONT)
"Dombey & Son Advertiser." 12 pp. numbered (1)–12.

p. (1) "No. V.—February, 1847."
p. 2. "Announcement | of the re-publication . . ."
p. 3. "New Monthly Work,"
p. 4. ($\frac{1}{2}$ col.) "Just published by | R. Yorke, Clarke, and Co."
p. 5. "The Illustrated | London | News."
p. 6. "The Battle of Life."
p. 7. "Now publishing . . . | Italy : Classical, Historical . . ."
p. 8. "Sovereign Life Assurance Company."
p. 9. ($\frac{1}{2}$ col.) "Smith's Gold Reviver."
p. 10. "Under the Patronage of Royalty . . ." (Keating).
p. 11. Dakin and Co. Same as Part 4, page 13.
p. 12. Same as Part 4, page 16.

ERRATA SLIP (preceding plates) 12 lines. ($5\frac{1}{2}'' \times 3''$).

ADVERTISEMENTS (BACK)
"Catalogue of Books | published by | Charles Cox, |
12, King William Street, Strand." 8 pp. numbered (1)–8.
Dated on p. (1) "February 1, 1847."

PLATES (TWO)
(No. 9) "Paul goes home for the holidays." (p. 145).
(No. 10) "Profound cogitation of Captain Cuttle." (p. 151).

TEXT, WITH HEADING
"Chapter XIV." pp. 129–160.

PART 6.

FRONT WRAPPER (OUTSIDE)
Same as No. I. except "No. VI. March."

CHARLES DICKENS.

FRONT WRAPPER (INSIDE)
Same as No. V.

BACK WRAPPER (OUTSIDE)
"Public Applause." (E. Moses and Son).

ADVERTISEMENTS (FRONT)
Slip :—"Cheap Edition of the Works of | Mr. Charles
Dickens. | On Saturday, the 27th of March, will
commence." 4 pp. numbered on pp. 2 and 3. Page
(4) is a specimen of page 20 of "The Pickwick Papers,"
in half-column measure. (7⅝" × 5").
"Dombey & Son Advertiser." 12 pp. numbered (1)–12.
p. (1) "No. VI.—March, 1847."
p. 2. "Sharpe's Corresponding Maps—continued."
p. 3. "Heath's Illustrated New Testament."
p. 4. "Mr. Disraeli's New Work."
p. 5. "Works by Mr. Dickens. | The Battle of Life."
p. 6. (½ col.) "A New Novel for One Shilling."
p. 7. "The New Treatise on Cookery—French and English."
p. 8. (½ col.) "Meerschaum Pipes."
p. 9. "Sovereign Life Assurance Company."
p. 10. "Number One, Saint Paul's Churchyard." Last words—
"Agents wanted." (Dakin).
p. 11. "Clarke's Patent Mortar Lamps and Lamp Mortars."
p. 12. Same as Part 5.

ADVERTISEMENTS (BACK)
(1) "Valuable | Educational Works, | published by |
Hamilton & Co. ; and Simpkin & Co. ; London."
Imprint of Publishers at foot of each page. 8 pp.
unnumbered. White, pink, or brick-red paper.
(2) "Portrait of a Horse." With illustration. (Morison).
1 leaf, verso blank. Yellow, green, pink, or light-
green paper.
(3) "Introduction to Zoology | for the use of Schools, | by
Robert Patterson." Illustrations on each page. 4 pp.
numbered (1)–4.

PLATES (TWO)
(No. 11) "Poor Paul's Friend." (p. 179).

DOMBEY AND SON.

(No. 12) "The Wooden Midshipman on the look out."
(p. 185).
Text, with Heading
"Chapter XVII. pp. 161–192.

PART 7.

Front Wrapper (Outside)
Same as No. I. except "No. VII. April."
Front Wrapper (Inside)
Same as No. V.
Back Wrapper (Outside)
"Lord Chesterfield's Advice to his Son." (E. Moses & Son).
Advertisements (Front)
Slip :—Very similar to Part 6 ; the third line on first page
reading : "Now publishing." 4 pp. (7⅝"×5").
"Dombey & Son Advertiser." 16 pp. numbered (1)–16.

p. (1) "No. VII.—April, 1847."
p. 2. "In Two Volumes . . . | The Works of Walter Savage
Landor."
p. 3. "On the 27th of every Month . . . | Wyld's Popular |
| Atlas . . ."
p. 4. "Works by Professor Lindley."
p. 5. "This day is published . . . | Baronial & Ecclesiastical
Antiquities of Scotland."
p. 6. "New Work by Michael Angelo Titmarsh."
p. 7. (½ col.) "The Cabinet Edition."
p. 8. "This day is published . . . | The first volume | of the
Music Book."
p. 9. "Works by Mr. Dickens."
p. 10. "Complete in One Volume . . . | The Fortunes of Torloch
O'Brien."
p. 11. "British College of Health."
p. 12. "To Smokers."
p. 13. (½ col.) "Meerschaum Pipes."
p. 14. "Sovereign Life Assurance Company."
p. 15. Dakin and Compy. Similar to Part 6, page 10.
p. 16. Same as Part 6, page 12.
Advertisements (Back)
"Heath's Illustrated New Testament." 2 pp. ; and "Sharpe's
Corresponding Maps." 2 pp. In all, 4 pp. unnumbered.

237

CHARLES DICKENS.

PLATES (TWO)

(No. 13) "Major Bagstock is delighted to have that opportunity." (p. 204).

(No. 14) "Mr. Toots becomes particular—Diogenes also." (p. 223).

TEXT, WITH HEADING
"Chapter XX." pp. 193–224.

PART 8.

FRONT WRAPPER (OUTSIDE)
Same as No. I. except "No. VIII. May."

FRONT WRAPPER (INSIDE)
Same as No. V.

BACK WRAPPER (OUTSIDE)
"A Gentleman." (E. Moses and Son).

ADVERTISEMENTS (FRONT)
"Dombey & Son Advertiser." 12 pp. numbered (1)–12.

    p. (1) "No. VIII.—May, 1847."
    p. 2. "New Work by Grace Aguilar."
    p. 3. "A New Novel for One Shilling."
    p. 4. "Douglas Jerrold's Weekly | Newspaper."
    p. 5. "On the 1st of May . . . | Vanity Fair."
    p. 6. ($\frac{1}{2}$ col.) "Berdoe's Light Over- | coat . . ."
    p. 7. "Clarke's Patent Mortar Lamps & Lamp Mortars."
    p. 8. Dakin and Compy. Same as Part 7, page 15.
    p. 9. "Parasols." With woodcuts. (Sangsters).
    p. 10. "British College of Health."
    p. 11. Continuation of p. 10. Two woodcuts of Silver-plate.
    p. 12. Same as Part 6.

PLATES (TWO)

(No. 15) "Solemn reference is made to Mr. Bunsby." (p. 238).

(No. 16) "Mr. Carker introduces himself to Florence & the Skettles family." (p. 249).

TEXT, WITH HEADING
"Chapter XXIII." pp. 225–256.

DOMBEY AND SON.

PART 9.

FRONT WRAPPER (OUTSIDE)
  Same as No. I. except "No. IX.   June."

FRONT WRAPPER (INSIDE)
  Same as No. V.

BACK WRAPPER (OUTSIDE)
  "My Choice." (E. Moses and Son).

ADVERTISEMENTS (FRONT)
  "Dombey & Son Advertiser."   8 pp. numbered (1)–8.
    p. (1) "No. IX.—June, 1847."
    p. 2. "Just published . . . | On the Foot of the Horse."
    p. 3. "Mr. Leigh Hunt's New Work."
    p. 4. (½ col.) "Mr. Colburn's | New Publications."
    p. 5. "Stooping of the Shoulders . . ."   Two woodcuts.
    p. 6. "Clarke's Patent Mortar Lamps & Lamp Mortars."
    p. 7. "British College of Health."
    p. 8. Same as Part 8, page 12.

ADVERTISEMENTS (BACK)
  (1) "Just Published . . . | Gilbert's | . . . | Dictionary | of
      | The English Language."   8 pp. unnumbered.
    p. (3) "Just Published . . . | Gilbert's College Atlas."
    p. (4) "Gilbert's | Modern Atlas of the World."
    p. (5) "Importance of an Atlas of the World."
    p. (7) "Outlines of English History," etc.
    An alternative inset appears in many copies, this being a 16mo. in
    size (6¼" × 4"), 8 pp., and the arrangement of the text follows very
    closely the 8vo. inset of Part 1.
  (2) Slip :—"To be completed in Six Monthly Parts . . . |
      The | Disgrace to the Family."   Printed one side only.
      (7⅛" × 4⅛").
  (3) "Dakin & Compy. | Tea Merchants."   With large
      woodcut.   Verso : "Dakin & Compy's Price Current."
      2 pp. unnumbered ; printed in blue.

PLATES (TWO)
  (No. 17) "Joe B is sly Sir, devilish sly."   (p. 267).
  (No. 18) "Mr. Dombey introduces his daughter Florence."
      (p. 288).

CHARLES DICKENS.

TEXT, WITH HEADING
"Chapter XXVI."   pp. 257–288.

> In page 284 appear two errors which were not included in the errata.   The word "Delight" is twice mentioned instead of "Joy."

PART 10.

FRONT WRAPPER (OUTSIDE)
Same as No. I. except "No. X.   July."

FRONT WRAPPER (INSIDE)
Same as No. V.

BACK WRAPPER (OUTSIDE)
" 'The Top of the Tree.' "   (E. Moses and Son).

ADVERTISEMENTS (FRONT)
"Dombey & Son Advertiser."   8 pp. numbered (1)–8.

> p. (1) "No. X.—July, 1847."
> p. 2. "On the 1st of August . . . | The Drawing-Room Magazine."
> p. 3. "£25 | Prize for Knitting."
> p. 4. "Night Lights."
> p. 5. "Sovereign Life Assurance Company."
> p. 6. (½ col.) "Fine Flowing Ringlets."
> p. 7. "Number One, St. Paul's Churchyard."   Last word on page: "London."   (Dakin and Compy.).
> p. 8. "The Gentleman's Real Head of Hair . . ."   At foot of page: "Doudney & Son."

ADVERTISEMENTS (BACK)
(1) Slip :—"Letts, Son, & Steer."   Verso: "Maps, Guides, Charts, &c."   2 pp. unnumbered.   Pink paper. $(7\frac{5}{8}'' \times 5\frac{1}{4}'')$.

(2) Gilbert's Dictionary, etc.   8 pp.   Same as Part 9.

PLATES (TWO)
(No. 19) "The eyes of Mrs. Chick are opened to Lucretia Tox."   (p. 294).

(No. 20) "Coming home from Church."   (p. 316).

TEXT, WITH HEADING
"Chapter XXIX."   pp. 289–320.

DOMBEY AND SON.

PART 11.

FRONT WRAPPER (OUTSIDE)
Same as No. I. except "No. XI. August."

FRONT WRAPPER (INSIDE)
Same as No. V.

BACK WRAPPER (OUTSIDE)
"To the London Stone."   (E. Moses and Son).

ADVERTISEMENTS (FRONT)
"Dombey & Son Advertiser."   8 pp. numbered (1)–8.

    p. (1) "No. XI.—August, 1847."
    p. 2. "Mons. Lepage's L'Echo de Paris."
    p. 3. ($\frac{1}{2}$ col.) "Edmiston & Son."
    p. 4. ($\frac{1}{2}$ col.) "Elegant Fans."
    p. 5. Dakin and Compy.   Same as Part 10, page 7.
    p. 6. "Sovereign Life Assurance Company."
    p. 7. "Letter Copying Machines."
    p. 8. "Coffee as in France."   With woodcut.

ADVERTISEMENTS (BACK)
Slip :—Letts, Son, & Steer.   Same as in Part 10.   2 pp.

PLATES (TWO)
(No. 21) "A Visitor of distinction."   (p. 325).
(No. 22) "The rejected alms."   (p. 352).

TEXT, WITH HEADING
"Chapter XXXII."   pp. 321–352.

> The last line on page 324 contains an error, "Capatin" for "Captain."   The error is a point of earliest issue ; the correction being made very early.

PART 12.

FRONT WRAPPER (OUTSIDE)
Same as No. I. except "No. XII. September."

FRONT WRAPPER (INSIDE)
Same as No. V.

BACK WRAPPER (OUTSIDE)
"Remember September."   (E. Moses and Son).

CHARLES DICKENS.

ADVERTISEMENTS (FRONT)
"Dombey & Son Advertiser."   8 pp. numbered (1)–8.
 p. (1) "No. XII.—September, 1847."
 p. 2. "Cheap Edition of the Novels and Tales of | Sir Edward Bulwer Lytton, Bart."
 p. 3. "Letter Copying Machines."
 p. 4. (½ col.) "Meerschaum Pipes."
 p. 5. Dakin and Compy. Same as Part 11.
 p. 6. "Sovereign Life Assurance Company." Second advertisement : "C. Watson's Solid Albata Plate."
 p. 7. "The Gentleman's Real Head of Hair."
 p. 8. "Coffee as in France." Slightly different to Part 11.

ADVERTISEMENTS (BACK)
" 'Question ! Question ! Question ! ' " (Kaye's Worsdell's Pills). Imprint on last page : "Printed at Richard Barrett's Steam Press, 13, Mark Lane." 4 pp. numbered (1)–4.

PLATES (TWO)
(No. 23) "Mrs. Dombey at Home." (p. 366).
(No. 24) "Miss Tox pays a visit to the Toodle Family."

TEXT, WITH HEADING
"Chapter XXXV. pp. 353–384.

PART 13.

FRONT WRAPPER (OUTSIDE)
Same as No. I. except "No. XIII. October."

FRONT WRAPPER (INSIDE)
Same as No. V.

BACK WRAPPER (OUTSIDE)
" ' N.B.' " (E. Moses and Son).

ADVERTISEMENTS (FRONT)
Slip :—"Cheap Edition of the Novels and Tales of | Sir Edward Bulwer Lytton, Bart. | On the 30th of October, | Messrs. Chapman & Hall will issue." 4 pp. numbered on pp. 2 and 3. Page (4) is a specimen of page 4 of "Rienzi, the last of the Tribunes," in half-column measure. ($7\frac{5}{8}'' \times 5''$).

DOMBEY AND SON.

"Dombey & Son Advertiser."   12 pp. numbered (1)–12.

    p. (1) "No. XIII.—October, 1847."
    p. 2. Same heading as Part 12.
    p. 3. "Works by Mr. Dickens."   Same as Part 7, page 9.
    p. 4. "New Work by the Author of | ' The Greatest Plague of Life.' "
    p. 5. "Just Published . . . | Bits of Books."
    p. 6. ($\frac{1}{2}$ col.) "The Parlour Library."
    p. 7. ($\frac{1}{4}$ col.) "Jones's £4 4s. 0d. Silver . . . | Watches."
    p. 8. "Sovereign Life Assurance Company."
    p. 9. Same heading as Part 12, page 7.
    p. 10. "King's | Respiratory | Lozenges."
    p. 11. Dakin and Compy.   Same as Part 12, page 5.
    p. 12. "Coffee as in France."   Same as Part 12, page 8.

The date "October, 1847" at head of first page, is more generally to be seen in a broken state, e.g., "Octo   18 47," and in fewer cases "Octo er 1847."   It is reasonable to assume the unbroken state would be the earlier printing.

PLATES (TWO)

(No. 25) "The Midshipman is boarded by the enemy." (p. 394).

(No. 26) "A chance Meeting."   (p. 408).

TEXT, WITH HEADING

"Chapter XXXIX."   pp. 385–416.

PART 14.

FRONT WRAPPER (OUTSIDE)

Same as No. I. except "No. XIV.   November."

FRONT WRAPPER (INSIDE)

Same as No. V.

BACK WRAPPER (OUTSIDE)

"New Publications."   (E. Moses and Son).

ADVERTISEMENTS (FRONT)

"Dombey & Son Advertiser."   12 pp. numbered (1)–12.

    p. (1) "No. XIV.—November, 1847."
    p. 2. "Works by Mr. Dickens."   Same as Part 7, page 9.
    p. 3. "Cheap Edition . . .of | Sir Edward Bulwer Lytton, Bart."
    p. 4. "This day is published . . . | Punch's Pocket Book."
    p. 5. ($\frac{1}{2}$ col.) "To Lady Knitters who read Dombey."

p. 6. (½ col.) "Superior Winter Over- | coats."
p. 7. "For Exportation.—Night Lights."
p. 8. Same heading as Part 12, page 7.
p. 9. "Sovereign Life Assurance Company."
p. 10. "King's | Respiratory | Lozenges." Different to Part 13.
p. 11. Dakin and Compy. Text begins :—"The very best Teas that the Chinese have shipped to England."
p. 12. "Coffee as in France." Same as Part 12, page 8.

PLATES (TWO)

(No. 27) "Mr. Dombey and his ' confidential agent.' " (p. 424).

(No. 28) "Florence parts from a very old friend." (p. 439).

TEXT, WITH HEADING

"Chapter XLII." pp. 417–448.

In earlier copies the page-number "431" is omitted.

Page 426, line 9, the first word "if" is omitted in earliest issue.

PART 15.

FRONT WRAPPER (OUTSIDE)
Same as No. I. except "No. XV. December."

FRONT WRAPPER (INSIDE)
Same as No. V.

BACK WRAPPER (OUTSIDE)
"December." (E. Moses and Son).

ADVERTISEMENTS (FRONT)
"Dombey & Son Advertiser." 12 pp. numbered (1)–12.

p. (1) "No. XV. — December 1847." (no comma after "December").
p. 2. "Punch's Almanack for 1848."
p. 3. "Chapman & Hall's New Publications."
p. 4. "Leigh Hunt's Christmas Book."
p. 5. "Picture Catalogues of Summerby's Art-Manufac | tures."
p. 6. "New London Daily Paper . . . | London Telegraph."
p. 7. (½ col.) "Mechi's Preparations."
p. 8. (½ col.) "Removal.—Mrs. Mellish."
p. 9. Same heading as Part 12, page 7.
p. 10. "Sovereign Life Assurance Company."

DOMBEY AND SON.

p. 11. Dakin and Compy. Same as Part 14.

p. 12. "Coffee as in France." Same as Part 12, page 8.

Slip : (to follow plates). "Notice." An announcement of six lines by the Publishers, that "no Christmas Book by Mr. Dickens will be published this year." Dated : 1st December, 1847. $(3'' \times 5\frac{9}{16}'')$.

ADVERTISEMENTS (BACK)

(1) Slip :—"New Story by Douglas Jerrold. | . . . | Twiddlethumb Town." Verso blank. $(4\frac{1}{2}'' \times 5\frac{1}{2}'')$.

(2) Letts, Son & Steer. 8 pp. numbered on pp. 2, 5, 6, 8 ; together with about 18 specimens of Diary leaves, dated between 1840 and 1848.

p. (1) Dated at foot, "November 1847."

p. (3) "Index to the Ordnance map of England."

p. 5. "Contents of Letts's Diaries."

p. (7) "Account Books."

The quantity of Diary leaf specimens varies in many copies.

PLATES (TWO)

(No. 29) "Abstraction & Recognition." (p. 450).

(No. 30) "Florence & Edith on the Staircase." (p. 469).

TEXT, WITH HEADING

"Chapter XLVI." pp. 449–480.

PART 16.

FRONT WRAPPER (OUTSIDE)

Same as No. I. except "No. XVI. January."

FRONT WRAPPER (INSIDE)

Same as No. V.

BACK WRAPPER (OUTSIDE)

"The New Year. | 1848." (E. Moses and Son).

ADVERTISEMENTS (FRONT)

"Dombey & Son Advertiser." 16 pp. numbered (1)–16.

p. (1) "No. XVI.—January 1848." (no comma after "January").

p. 2. "Books Published by | William Blackwood & Sons."

p. 3. "Works by W. M. Thackeray."

p. 4. London Telegraph. Same as Part 15, page 6.

p. 5. Same heading as Part 15.

p. 6. ($\frac{1}{2}$ col.) "To Seminaries and Private Families."

p. 7. ($\frac{1}{2}$ col.) "Meerschaum Pipes."

p. 8. "Sovereign Life Assurance Company."
p. 9. "Nunn's made Mustard."
p. 10. "Extract from ' The Patent Journal.' "   (William Dakin).
p. 11. "Coffee as in France."   Same as Part 12, page 8.
p. 12. "Wonder of the Season ! ! ! | Punch's Almanack."
p. 13. "Works by Gilbert A. à Beckett."
p. 14. "Works by Douglas Jerrold."
p. 15. "Works by Mr. Thackeray."
p. 16. "Works by Mr. Dickens."

Slip : (to follow plates). "Punch's Almanack." 8 lines, and at foot : "Punch Office, 85, Fleet Street." Verso blank. ($3\frac{3}{4}'' \times 5\frac{1}{4}''$).

ADVERTISEMENTS (BACK)

"John Kendrick, | Bookseller, | 4, Charlotte Row, Mansion House, London. | Libraries or Small Parcels of Books purchased." 4 pp. unnumbered. ($8\frac{3}{8}'' \times 4\frac{7}{8}''$).

This inset is different from that in Parts 19/20, having here a four-line heading, as opposed to three lines.

PLATES (TWO)

(No. 31) "The Shadow in the little parlor." (p. 491).

(No. 32) "Mr. Dombey and the World." (p. 508).

TEXT, WITH HEADING

"Chapter XLIX." pp. 481–512.

PART 17.

FRONT WRAPPER (OUTSIDE)

Same as No. I. except "No. XVII. February."

FRONT WRAPPER (INSIDE)

Same as No. V.

BACK WRAPPER (OUTSIDE)

"The Rival Mart." (E. Moses and Son).

ADVERTISEMENTS (FRONT)

"Dombey & Son Advertiser." 8 pp. numbered (1)–8.

p. (1) "No. XVII.—February 1848."(no comma after"February").
p. 2. "Just Published . . . | The Book of Snobs."
p. 3. ($\frac{1}{2}$ col.) "13, Great Marlborough Street."
p. 4. ($\frac{1}{2}$ col.) "Chubb's Locks and Fire- | proof Safes."
p. 5. ($\frac{1}{2}$ col.) "Jones's £4 4s. 0d. Silver . . . | Watches."
p. 6. "The Standard of Cognac."

p. 7. "Sovereign Life Assurance Company."
p. 8. William Dakin. Same as Part 16, page 10.
Slip : (to follow plates). "Early in March, with Illustrations, | The Life and Adventures of Oliver Goldsmith" (by John Forster). Verso blank. (3″×5½″).

ADVERTISEMENTS (BACK)

(1) Slip :—"Catalogue of Works published by C. Cox, 12, King William Street, Strand." First page announces, "A monthly re-issue, in Complete Works, of Knight's Shilling Volumes." 12 pp., numbered (1, 2)–12. (6″×3⅞″).

(2) Slip :—Mechi's Catalogue, consisting of 24 pp. all numbered except pp. 1, 2 and 22, and bound in wrappers of varied tinted paper. The wrappers are printed on all four sides with shop front on page 1, and woodcuts on pp. 2, 3 and 4. (4⅝″×3¼″).

(3) "The Eagle and Protector | Life Assurance Company." 2 pp. unnumbered.
Note the altered title as compared with the inset in Part 4.

(4) "Waterlow & Sons." 8 pp. numbered (1, 2)–8.
p. (2) "Patent Letter Copying Machines," with two woodcuts.
p. 3. "Writing Papers."
p. 4. "Improved Patent Account Books."
p. 5. (½ col.) "Extra superfine | Drawing Papers."
p. 6. (½ col.) "Drawing Pencils."
p. 7. (½ col.) 14 Illustrations of office utensils.

PLATES (TWO)
(No. 33) "Secret intelligence." (p. 516).
(No. 34) "Mr. Carker in his hour of triumph." (p. 539).

TEXT, WITH HEADING
"Chapter LII." pp. 513-544.

PART 18.

FRONT WRAPPER (OUTSIDE)
Same as No. I. except "No. XVIII. March."

FRONT WRAPPER (INSIDE)
Same as No. V.

BACK WRAPPER (OUTSIDE)
"The Spring Season."   (E. Moses and Son).

ADVERTISEMENTS (FRONT)
"Dombey & Son Advertiser."   12 pp. numbered (1)–12.
   p. (1) "No. XVIII.—March 1848." (no comma after "March").
   p. 2. "In Two handsome Volumes . . . | The Works | of |
        Walter Savage Landor."
   p. 3. "Early in March . . . | The Life and Adventures of Oliver
        Goldsmith."
   p. 4. "Uniform with Mr. Murray's Edition of Lord Byron's
        Works."
   p. 5. "On March 31st . . . | Gavarni in London ! "
   p. 6. "This day is Published . . . | Vanity Fair."
   p. 7. ($\frac{1}{2}$ col.) "Mr. Colburn's New Publi- | tions." (*sic*).
   p. 8. ($\frac{1}{2}$ col.) "Jones's £4 4s. 0d. Silver . . . | Watches."
   p. 9. "Send Eight Postage Stamps."   (Watson's Albata Plate).
   p. 10. "Deformities of the Chest | and Spine."   Two woodcuts.
   p. 11. "Pelican Life Insurance Office."
   p. 12.   William Dakin.   Same as Part 16, page 10, with one extra
        line in last paragraph.
   Slip : (to follow plates).   "Stitched in a neat Wrapper, price One
   Shilling the Set | . . . | The Four Portraits | of | Edith, Alice,
   Florence, & Little Paul."   Verso blank.   ($2\frac{7}{8}'' \times 5\frac{1}{2}''$).

ADVERTISEMENTS (BACK)
"Dr. Radcliffe's Alleviators." 2 pp. unnumbered ($8\frac{1}{4}'' \times 4\frac{7}{8}''$).

PLATES (TWO)
(No. 35) "On the dark Road."   (p. 547).
(No. 36) "An Arrival."   (p. 565).

TEXT, WITH HEADING
"Chapter LV."   pp. 545–576.

PARTS 19 AND 20.

FRONT WRAPPER (OUTSIDE)
Same as No. I. except "Nos. XIX. & XX. April.   Price 2s."

FRONT WRAPPER (INSIDE)
Same as No. V.

BACK WRAPPER (OUTSIDE)
"The Last Advertisement."   (E. Moses and Son).

DOMBEY AND SON.

ADVERTISEMENTS (FRONT)

"Dombey & Son Advertiser." 24 pp. numbered (1)–24, except p. 23.

- p. (1) "Nos. XIX. & XX.—April, 1848."
- p. 2. "New Works Just Published | by Mr. Murray."
- p. 3. "New Works | Nearly Ready for Publication." (Longman).
- p. 4. "New Work by the Authors of | 'The Greatest Plague of Life.'"
- p. 5. "New Books by Popular Authors." (Smith, Elder & Co.).
- p. 6. "Notice to Advertisers." (Daily News).
- p. 7. "This day . . . | The Dublin University Magazine."
- p. 8. "Price Fourpence . . . | The Athenæum."
- p. 9. "Emilia Wyndham for One Shilling."
- p. 10. "National Provident Institution."
- p. 11. "Botánical Works by Professor Lindley."
- p. 12. "New Life of Goldsmith." With portrait.
- p. 13. "Monthly Work by Mr. Thackeray." (Vanity Fair).
- p. 14. "Now ready, in Two Volumes . . . | The Comic History of England."
- p. 15. "Douglas Jerrold's | Magazine."
- p. 16. "Published Weekly . . . | Punch."
- p. 17. ($\frac{1}{2}$ col.) "Beautiful Women."
- p. 18. "Sovereign Life Assurance Company."
- p. 19. William Dakin. Similar to Part 18, page 12.
- p. 20. Same as Part 18, page 10.
- p. 21. "The Gentleman's Real Head of Hair."
- p. 22. ($\frac{1}{2}$ col.) "Jones's £4 4s. 0d. Silver . . . | Watches."
- p.(23) "Five Special Appointments." (Doudney).
- p. 24. "Parasols. | W. & J. Sangster." Four woodcuts.

Slip : (to follow plates). "New Life of Goldsmith." (By John Forster). Verso blank. ($4\frac{1}{2}'' \times 5\frac{5}{8}''$).

ADVERTISEMENTS (BACK)

(1) "Waterlow & Sons." 8 pp. Identical with Part 17.

(2) "Important Educational Works, | published by Jarrold and Sons . . ." 8 pp. unnumbered.

(3) "Dr. Locock's | Lotion," within decorative border on first page. Pages (2)–(8) are Testimonials, etc., of Coffee. Issued by Lea & Perrins, Worcester. 8 pp. unnumbered.

(4) "Liverpool, (See Within.)" Robt. Roberts & Compy., Liverpool. 4 pp. unnumbered. Blue tinted paper.

(5) "John Kendrick, | Bookseller, | 4, Charlotte Row, Mansion House, London." 4 pp. unnumbered.

Differs with the inset in Part 16. This has a three-line heading, and is the full size of the periodical.

(6) Chapman & Hall's List of New Works. 8 pp. numbered (1)–8.

p. (1) Dated : "186, Strand, London, April, 1848."
p. 3. "Beautiful Gift-Books."
p. 5. "Volume First of | the | Romance of the Peerage."
p. 7. "The | Baronial Halls and Picturesque | Edifices of England."

PLATES (FOUR)

(No. 37) "Let him remember it in that room, years to come." (p. 595).

(No. 38) "Another Wedding." (p. 607).

(No. 39) Frontispiece.

(No. 40) Vignette Title ; dated 1848.

The scene depicted on the vignette title, discloses an oversight on the part of the Artist, who has placed the hook on the left arm of Captain Cuttle.

TEXT, WITH HEADING

"Chapter LVIII." pp. 577-624. Imprint at foot of p. 624 : "London: | Bradbury and Evans, Printers, Whitefriars."

PRELIMINARY LEAVES

"Errata" (of Two lines). Verso blank. (I., II.).

Half-title : "Dombey and Son." Verso blank. (III., IV.).

Title-page : dated 1848. Verso, with imprint as p. 624. (V., VI.). See Illustration.

Dedication to, "The Marchioness of Normandy." Verso blank. (VII., VIII.).

"Preface." Dated : "Devonshire Terrace, | Twenty-Fourth March, 1848." Verso blank. (IX., X.).

"Contents." 4 pp. (XI.), XII., XIII., XIV.

"List of Plates." 2 pp. (XV.), XVI.

The two-line "Errata" should be given preference over another consisting of eight lines—the latter must obviously be of a later issue.

THE PERSONAL HISTORY

OF

DAVID COPPERFIELD.

BY CHARLES DICKENS.

WITH ILLUSTRATIONS BY H. K. BROWNE.

LONDON:

BRADBURY & EVANS, 11, BOUVERIE STREET.

1850

David Copperfield

in

19/20 Monthly Parts

May, 1849, to November, 1850.

ORIGINALLY issued in twenty numbers bound in nine-teen monthly parts, price one shilling per number, except the last two (19 and 20) which were issued as a double number at two shillings.   The design for the green wrappers and the forty plates were again executed by "Phiz." Publication began in May, 1849, and continued uninterruptedly to completion in November, 1850.

PLATES.

The forty designs were etched in duplicate, and, though the steels are not numbered, the plates are distinguishable by the changing signature of "Phiz," as well as by other slight variations.   The demand for the first part was not so great as "Dombey," but the circulation increased as the book pro-gressed ; and as Dickens was well in advance with his MS. there was no necessity for lithographic transfers, the two sets of steels being sufficient to cope with the situation.   When printed, the duplicate plates were again distributed indiscrimi-nately, so that no two sets are alike, and several copies of the nineteen parts would be required to complete a collection of the eighty plates.

As in the case of "Dombey and Son," an attempt is to be seen in the production of a "dark" plate.   This is No. 31 in Part 16, "The River," and is the second published example of the process ; afterwards so successfully featured in many of the etchings of the two following works.   The subject is commented upon at some length in the introduction to "Bleak House."

WRAPPERS.

No change is effected in textual matter throughout the run, except "Part No." and month of issue. Trade advertisements occupy both the inner sides as well as the outside of back wrapper. The clues to the back wrapper are noted only in respect to the inner side, where E. Moses and Son vary the "make-up" with each issue, and the pointer to these is sufficient to identify the correct wrapper. Outside of back covers to every number has the varying announcement of H. J. & D. Nicoll. Reprints of "Copperfield" were issued in wrappers without any advertisements; these are useless in a set of first issue parts. Similar wrappers are seen also in great numbers in "Dombey" and "Bleak House."

ADVERTISEMENTS (FRONT).

The "Copperfield Advertiser" appears in each of the nineteen parts, although there is a notable decline in the popularity of this advertising medium; a scant four pages in many numbers following on an initial burst of 32 pages. Each page has headline "Advertisements," with the exception of the first in each part, and:—Part 1, p. 32; Part 2, p. 12; Part 14, p. 8; Part 19, pp. 8 & 9. In addition to the "Advertiser," thirteen other insets are called for—essential to a complete copy.

ADVERTISEMENTS (BACK).

The number of insets is fewer than in any other set of nineteen parts. A particularly scarce one is "Lett's Diaries" in Part 8, which should contain a folded sheet and several specimen diary leaves, but is more often than not a missing quantity.

PART 1.

FRONT WRAPPER (OUTSIDE)
"No. I. May. Price 1s. | The | Personal History, Adventures, | Experience, & Observation | of | David |

DAVID COPPERFIELD.

Copperfield | The Younger | of Blunderstone Rookery. | (Which He never meant to be Published on any Account.) | By Charles Dickens. | With Illustrations by H. K. Browne. | London : Bradbury & Evans, Whitefriars. | Agents : — J. Menzies, Edinburgh ; T. Murray, Glasgow ; J. M'Glashan, Dublin."

FRONT WRAPPER (INSIDE)

"Heal & Son's | Bedding Manufactory." With three lines in small type below this heading.

BACK WRAPPER (INSIDE)

"Analysis of the name of Moses & Son." (E. Moses & Son).

ADVERTISEMENTS (FRONT)

"Copperfield Advertiser." 32 pp. numbered (1)–(32).

    p. (1) "No. I.—May, 1849."
    p. 2. "John Kendrick, | Bookseller."
    p. 3. "Mr. Bentley's New Publications, | now ready."
    p. 4. "Books for the Young." (Grant and Griffith).
    p. 5. "New Works of Interest." (Smith, Elder, & Co.).
    p. 6. "Botanic Garden and Fruitist." In oval frame.
    p. 7. "Mr. Colburn's Select Publications."
    p. 8. "Bohn's Standard Library."
    p. 9. "New Edition of Mrs. Loudon's Companion . . ."
    p. 10. "Works by Mr. Charles Dickens."
    p. 11. "New Classical Dictionaries."
    p. 12. "English Poetry Books."
    p. 13. "New Books and New Editions." (Wm. S. Orr & Co.).
    p. 14. "Early in May . . . | The Enchanted Doll."
    p. 15. "Botanical Works by Professor Lindley."
    p. 16. "Works by W. M. Thackeray."
    p. 17. "This day . . . | The New Volume . . . | Barnaby Rudge."
    p. 18. "Published Weekly . . . | Punch."
    p. 19. "Published on the 1st of each Month, | The Parlour Library."
    p. 20. "In One Large Volume . . . | Oliver Goldsmith."
    p. 21. "On the First of every Month . . . | Frank Fairlegh."
    p. 22. "Standard Works now Publishing, | by J. & F. Tallis."
    p. 23. "Price Fourpence . . . | The Athenæum."
    p. 24. "Nissen and Parker."
    p. 25. "National Provident Institution."
    p. 26. "Number One, St. Paul's Churchyard, London." (Dakin).
    p. 27. ($\frac{1}{2}$ col.) "Pelican Life Assurance | Office."

p. 28. "Just Published . . . | Homœopathy in acute Diseases."
p. 29. "British College of Health."
p. 30. "Under Royal Patronage. | Dr. Locock's . . . Wafers."
p. 31. "Mechi."
p.(32) "Five Special Appointments."   (Doudney's).

ADVERTISEMENTS (BACK)

(1) "Now Publishing, in Monthly Numbers . . . | The | Journal of Design."   2 pp. unnumbered.

(2) "The Theory of Musical Composition | Completely Developed."   2 pp. unnumbered.

PLATES (TWO)

(No. 1) "Our Pew at Church."   (p. 11).

(No. 2) "I am hospitably received by Mr. Peggotty." (p. 23).

TEXT, WITH HEADING

"The | Personal   History   and   Experience | of | David Copperfield the Younger. | Chapter I."   pp. (1)–32.

PART 2.

FRONT WRAPPER (OUTSIDE)
Same as No. I. except "No. II.   June."

FRONT WRAPPER (INSIDE)
Same as No. I.   (Heal & Sons).

BACK WRAPPER (INSIDE)
"Opinions of the Press | of | Moses and Son's Attire."

ADVERTISEMENTS (FRONT)
"Copperfield Advertiser."   12 pp. numbered (1)–(12).

p. (1) "No. II.—June, 1849."
p. 2. "Mr. Colburn's New Publications."
p. 3. "This day is Published . . . | The Enchanted Doll."
p. 4. "Works by Mr. Charles Dickens."
p. 5. "Now ready . . . | London Catalogue of Books."
p. 6. ($\frac{1}{2}$ col.) "New and Important Work | on Blight."
p. 7. "Children's Frocks, Coats, & Pelisses."
p. 8. "No more Pills nor any other Medicine."
p. 9. "Under Royal Patronage. | Dr. Locock's . . . Wafers."
p. 10. "Use | Kirby, Beard & Co.'s | . . . Needles."
p. 11. "Alpaca Umbrellas."
p.(12) "Five Special Appointments."   Same as Part 1, page 32.

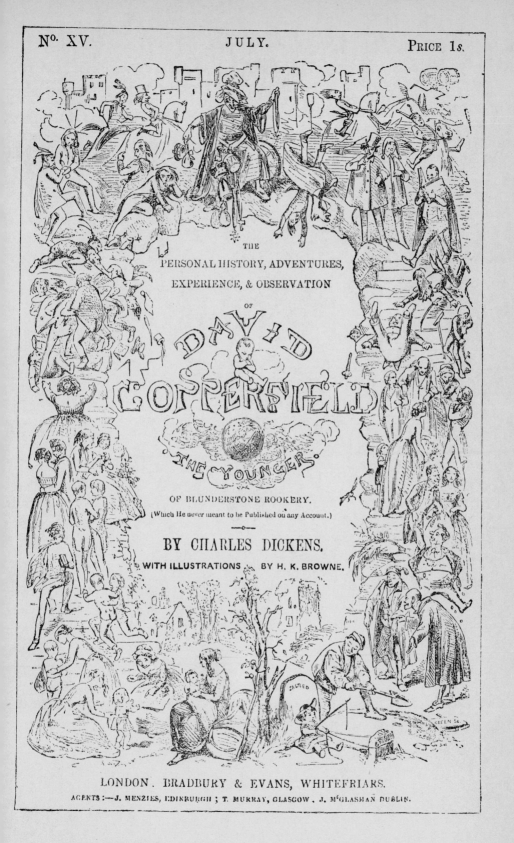

Nº. XV.   JULY.   PRICE 1s.

THE

PERSONAL HISTORY, ADVENTURES,

EXPERIENCE, & OBSERVATION

OF

DAVID COPPERFIELD

THE YOUNGER

OF BLUNDERSTONE ROOKERY.

(Which He never meant to be Published on any Account.)

BY CHARLES DICKENS.

WITH ILLUSTRATIONS BY H. K. BROWNE.

LONDON. BRADBURY & EVANS, WHITEFRIARS.
AGENTS:—J. MENZIES, EDINBURGH; T. MURRAY, GLASGOW. J. M'GLASHAN DUBLIN.

The Front Wrapper to the original edition of "David Copperfield,"
as published in 19/20 monthly parts, 1849-1850.

DAVID COPPERFIELD.

ADVERTISEMENTS (BACK)

"Completion | of | Knight's Shilling Volumes | for all Readers, | published by | C. Cox, 12, King William Street, Strand." This list fills pages 1–10; and pp. 11–12 announce "Knight's Pictorial Works." In all, 12 pp. numbered (1)–12.

PLATES (TWO)

(No. 3) "The friendly Waiter and I." (p. 49).
(No. 4) "My musical breakfast." (p. 55).

TEXT, WITH HEADING

"Chapter IV." pp. 33–64.

PART 3.

FRONT WRAPPER (OUTSIDE)

Same as No. I. except "No. III. July."

FRONT WRAPPER (INSIDE)

Same as No. I. (Heal & Sons).

BACK WRAPPER (INSIDE)

"To Old Neptune." (E. Moses & Son).

ADVERTISEMENTS (FRONT)

"Copperfield Advertiser." 12 pp. numbered (1)–12.

    p. (1) "No. III.—July, 1849."
    p. 2. "Now Publishing, in Monthly Numbers . . . | Pendennis."
    p. 3. "Works by Mr. Charles Dickens."
    p. 4. "Published Weekly . . . | Punch."
    p. 5. "This day is Published . . . | The Enchanted Doll."
    p. 6. "British College of Health, New Road, London."
    p. 7. "Children's Frocks . . ." Same as Part 2.
    p. 8. "Number One, St. Paul's Churchyard, London."
    p. 9. "Warren's Sketches of Character."
    p. 10. "Under Royal Patronage. | Dr. Locock's . . . Wafers."
    p. 11. "Alpaca Umbrellas." Below :—"S. Straker's."
    p. 12. "No more Pills nor any other Medicine."

ADVERTISEMENTS (BACK)

"By Her Majesty's Royal Letters Patent. | The Patent | Cork Floating Mattress & Boat Cushion." 4 pp. numbered (1)–4.

PLATES (TWO)
  (No. 5) "Steerforth and Mr. Mell." (p. 70).
  (No. 6) "Changes at Home." (p. 79).
TEXT, WITH HEADING
  "Chapter VII." pp. 65–96.

PART 4.

FRONT WRAPPER (OUTSIDE)
  Same as No. I. except "No. IV. August."
FRONT WRAPPER (INSIDE)
  "Heal & Son's." Third line from bottom contains only
  three words :—"to their Factory."
BACK WRAPPER (INSIDE)
  "The Vaunting Marts of Rivalry." (E. Moses & Son).
ADVERTISEMENTS (FRONT)
  "Copperfield Advertiser." 8 pp. numbered (1) – 8.
  (see below).
    p. (1) "No. IV.—August, 1849."
    p. 2. "In the Press . . . | The Solitary, and other Poems."
    p. 3. "In One Large Volume . . . | Oliver Goldsmith."
    p. 4. "Copy Your Letters."
    p. (5) "Under Royal Patronage. | Dr. Locock's . . . Wafers."
    p. 6. "Treloar's Cocoa-Nut Fibre Warehouse."
    p. 7. "Alpaca Umbrellas." Below :—"Warren's Sketches of
      Character."
    p. 8. "No more Pills nor any other Medicine."
PLATES (TWO)
  (No. 7) "Mrs. Gummidge casts a damp on our departure."
    (p. 105).
  (No. 8) "My magnificent order at the public-house. (p. 117).
TEXT, WITH HEADING
  "Chapter X." pp. 97-128.

PART 5.

FRONT WRAPPER (OUTSIDE)
  Same as No. I. except "No. V. September."
FRONT WRAPPER (INSIDE)
  Same as No. IV. (Heal & Sons).

DAVID COPPERFIELD.

BACK WRAPPER (INSIDE)
"My Sea-Side Trip."

ADVERTISEMENTS (FRONT)
"Copperfield Advertiser." 4 pp. numbered (1)–4.
- p. (1) "No. V.—September, 1849."
- p. 2. "New Works | for Book-Clubs . . ."
- p. 3. (½ col.) "To secure Household Linen . . ."
- p. 4. "Alpaca Umbrellas."

PLATES (TWO)
(No. 9) "I make myself known to my Aunt." (p. 137).
(No. 10) "The momentous interview." (p. 149).

TEXT, WITH HEADING
"Chapter XIII." pp. 129–160.

PART 6.

FRONT WRAPPER (OUTSIDE)
Same as No. I. except "No. VI. October."

FRONT WRAPPER (INSIDE)
"Heal & Son's." A list of prices appears below "Bed Feathers."

BACK WRAPPER (INSIDE)
"Twenty Years Ago." (E. Moses & Son).

ADVERTISEMENTS (FRONT)
"Copperfield Advertiser." 8 pp. numbered (1)–8.
- p. (1) "No. VI.—October, 1849."
- p. 2. "Just published . . . | A Short Inquiry . . ."
- p. 3. "Smith, Elder & Co.'s | New Publications."
- p. 4. "Now Ready . . . | Mrs. Trollope's New Novel."
- p. 5. "Early in October . . . | The Caxtons :"
- p. 6. (½ col.) "Easiest and quickest method of | acquiring French."
- p. 7. "The Gentleman's Real Head of Hair."
- p. 8. "Alpaca Umbrellas."

ADVERTISEMENTS (BACK)
Waterlow & Sons. 8 pp. numbered (1)–8. At head of first page, a view of premises ; and at foot a 6-line

paragraph, last line reading : "their immediate super-intendence." Pages 2, 4 have running headline : "Water-low & Sons, Wholesale and Export" ; pp. 3, 5 : "Stationers and Account Book Manufacturers" ; p. 6 : "Waterlow & Sons, Wholesale and Retail" ; p. 7 : "Manufacturing Stationers."

p. 2. "Writing Papers" ; "Envelopes" ; "Improved Adhesive Envelopes."
p. 3. "Whatman's Drawing Paper."
p. 4. "Improved Patent Account Books."
p. 5. "Pure Cumberland Lead Pencils" ; "Metallic Pens."
p. 6. ($\frac{1}{2}$ col.) "Surveyor's Measuring Books," etc. ; "Sundries"; "Postage Scales and Balances."
p. 7. Woodcuts of 13 office appliances.
p. 8. "Patent Letter Copying Machines," with three woodcuts.

PLATES (TWO)
(No. 11) "I return to the Doctor's after the party." (p. 175).
(No. 12) "Somebody turns up." (p. 182).

TEXT, WITH HEADING
"Chapter XVI." pp. 161–192.

PART 7.

FRONT WRAPPER (OUTSIDE)
Same as No. I. except "No. VII. November."

FRONT WRAPPER (INSIDE)
Same as No. VI. (Heal & Sons).

BACK WRAPPER (INSIDE)
"The Whale in the Thames." (E. Moses & Son).

ADVERTISEMENTS (FRONT)
"Copperfield Advertiser." 8 pp. numbered (1)–8.

p. (1) "No. VII.—November, 1849."
p. 2. "Notice. | . . . | The | Ladder of Gold."
p. 3. "Early in November, | Luke Limner's New Work."
p. 4. "Now ready . . . | The Enchanted Doll."
p. 5. "Warren's Sketches of Character."
p. 6. "The Gentleman's Real Head of Hair."

260

p. 7. "No more Pills nor any other Drugs."

p. 8. "Alpaca Umbrellas."

Slip : (to follow plates). "This day is published, . . . | **Punch's** | Pocket-Book | for 1850. Printed in blue ; verso : four **lines,** printed in red along the page. ($6\frac{3}{4}'' \times 4\frac{1}{4}''$).

ADVERTISEMENTS (BACK)

"Chapman and Hall's | Announcement of | New Books and New Editions | now ready and in preparation." Dated at top of page 1 : "186, Strand, November 1st, 1849." 8 pp. numbered (1)–8.

Each of the eight pages is bordered by panel ruling, within **which** are printed quotations of eminent literary characters.

PLATES (TWO)

(No. 13) "My first fall in life." (p. 201).

(No. 14) "We arrive unexpectedly at Mr. Peggotty's fireside." (p. 220).

TEXT, WITH HEADING

"Chapter XIX." pp. 193-224.

PART 8.

FRONT WRAPPER (OUTSIDE)

Same as No. I. except "No. VIII. December."

FRONT WRAPPER (INSIDE)

Same as No. VI. (Heal & Sons).

BACK WRAPPER (INSIDE)

"The Proper Field for ' Copperfield.' " (E. Moses & Son).

ADVERTISEMENTS (FRONT)

"Copperfield Advertiser." 12 pp. numbered (1)–12.

p. (1) "No. VIII.—December, 1849."

p. 2. "Cheap Re-issue of | Mr. Ainsworth's Works."

p. 3. "Forster's Lile of Goldsmith." (*sic*).

p. 4. "Mr. M. A. Titmarsh's | . . . | Rebecca and Rowena."

p. 5. "Illustrated Works for Christmas Presents."

p. 6. "Now ready . . . | Medical & Œconomical Botany."

p. 7. "Works by Mr. Charles Dickens."

p. 8. "Just Published . . . | Ruins of Many Lands."

p. 9. ($\frac{1}{2}$ col.) "For Purifying the Blood . . ."

p. 10. "The Gentleman's Real Head of Hair."
p. 11. "Alpaca Umbrellas" and "Dr. Locock's . . . Wafers."
p. 12. "No more Pills nor any other Medicine."
As a point of first issue, page 3 should have the mis-spelt word "Lile" for "Life."

"New Weekly Illustrated Periodical for | Ladies. | On Saturday, December 29, will be published . . . | The Ladies' Companion." Verso : "Early in December . . . | Manners and Customs of Ye Englyshe | in 1849. | By Richard Doyle." 2 pp. unnumbered. Green paper.

ADVERTISEMENTS (BACK)
"Lett's Diaries for 1850." A sheet, folded in five, with specimen leaves of diaries, dated from 1846 to 1849. These specimens are a varying quantity, but generally number eight pieces.

PLATES (TWO)
(No. 15) "I make the acquaintance of Miss Mowcher." (p. 233).
(No. 16) "Martha." (p. 238).

TEXT, WITH HEADING
"Chapter XXII." pp. 225–256.

PART 9.

FRONT WRAPPER (OUTSIDE)
Same as No. I. except "No. IX. January."

FRONT WRAPPER (INSIDE)
"The Greatest Luxury | for the Bed-Room is | The Eider-Down Quilt." (Heal and Son).

BACK WRAPPER (INSIDE)
"January." (E. Moses & Son).

ADVERTISEMENTS (FRONT)
"Copperfield Advertiser." 12 pp. numbered (1)–12.
p. (1) "No. IX.—January, 1850."
p. 2. "Mr. Dickens' Christmas Books."
p. 3. "Now ready . . . Punch's Almanack for 1850."
p. 4. "Illustrated Works for Christmas Presents."
p. 5. "Dedicated by Command . . . | The Art-Journal;"

p. 6. "New Monthly Work, by Mrs. Ellis ;"
p. 7. "On the 3rd January . . . | The Domestic Economist."
p. 8. "Will be published . . . | Wanderings of a Pilgrim."
p. 9. "Waterlow and Sons."
p. 10. "Warren's Sketches of Character."
p. 11. ($\frac{1}{2}$ col.) "For purifying the Blood . . ."
p. 12. "Alpaca Umbrellas" and "Dr. Locock's . . . Wafers."

Slip : (to follow plates). "New Weekly Miscellany | of General Literature, | Conducted by Charles Dickens." Dated in top right corner, December 27, 1849. Verso, blank. Light-green paper. ($4\frac{3}{8}'' \times 5\frac{1}{2}''$).

ADVERTISEMENTS (BACK)

(1) "Works | published by A. Hall, Virtue & Co. | 25, Paternoster Row, London." 20 pp. unnumbered, but carrying three signatures, A., A.2, A.5. Imprint of Publishers at foot of each page, except p. (19).

(2) "Now ready, | Part I. | . . . | Leila ; | or | The Siege of Granada." Verso : "Books Published or Sold by J. & D. A. Darling," the first : "The Art of Etching." 2 pp. unnumbered. Printed both sides in red.

PLATES (TWO)

(No. 17) "Uriah persists in hovering near us at the dinner party." (p. 262).

(No. 18) "I fall into captivity." (p. 274).

TEXT, WITH HEADING
"Chapter XXV." pp. 257-288.

PART 10.

FRONT WRAPPER (OUTSIDE)
Same as No. I. except "No. X. February."

FRONT WRAPPER (INSIDE)
"Heal & Sons'." With $4\frac{1}{2}$ lines in small type below.

BACK WRAPPER (INSIDE)
"The Winter of 1814."

ADVERTISEMENTS (FRONT)
"Copperfield Advertiser." 12 pp. numbered (1)–12.
p. (1) "No. X.—February, 1850."
p. 2. "Mr. Colburn's New Novels."

p. 3. "11, Bouverie Street. | . . . | A New Weekly Miscellany."
p. 4. "New Periodical." (Gardeners' Magazine of Botany).
p. 5. "This day . . . | The Ladies' Companion."
p. 6. "Illustrated Works for Presents."
p. 7. "Works by Mr. Charles Dickens."
p. 8. "Published every Saturday . . . | Punch ;"
p. 9. "Adventures of a Medical Student."
p. 10. "Alpaca Umbrellas."
p. 11. "Warren's Sketches of Character."
p. 12. "Number One, Saint Paul's Church Yard."

ADVERTISEMENTS (BACK)
Waterlow & Sons. 8 pp. Same as Part 6.

PLATES (TWO)
(No. 19) "We are disturbed in our cookery." (p. 292).
(No. 20) "I find Mr. Barkis, ' going out with the tide.' "
(p. 313).

TEXT, WITH HEADING
"Chapter XXVIII." pp. 289–320.

PART 11.

FRONT WRAPPER (OUTSIDE)
Same as No. I. except "No. XI. March."

FRONT WRAPPER (INSIDE)
"Five Special Appointments." (Doudneys).

BACK WRAPPER (INSIDE)
"A Sketch for the Spring." (E. Moses & Son).

ADVERTISEMENTS (FRONT)
"Copperfield Advertiser." 8 pp. numbered (1)–8.
p. (1) "No. XI.—March, 1850."
p. 2. "Smith, Elder, & Co.'s New Publications."
p. 3. "Works by Mr. Charles Dickens."
p. 4. "Mr. Colburn's New Publications."
p. 5. "Warren's Sketches of Character."
p. 6. ($\frac{1}{2}$ col.) "Balsam Copaiba . . ."
p. 7. "Under Royal Patronage. | Dr. Locock's . . . Wafers."
p. 8. "Parasols," "Ross & Sons" and "Kirby, Beard & Co."
Slip : (to follow plates). "Familiar in their Mouths as Household Words. | On Saturday, March 30, will be published . . . | No. I. of | Household Words." 1 leaf. Verso blank. White paper. ($6\frac{7}{8}'' \times 4\frac{1}{2}''$).

DAVID COPPERFIELD.

PLATES (TWO)
(No. 21) "Mr. Peggotty and Mrs. Steerforth." (p. 330).
(No. 22) "My Aunt astonishes me." (p. 350).

TEXT, WITH HEADING
"Chapter XXXII." pp. 321–352.

PART 12.

FRONT WRAPPER (OUTSIDE)
Same as No. I. except "No. XII. April."

FRONT WRAPPER (INSIDE)
Same as No. X. (Heal & Sons).

BACK WRAPPER (INSIDE)
"On an old Picture." (E. Moses & Son).

ADVERTISEMENTS (FRONT)
"Copperfield Advertiser." 8 pp. numbered (1)–8.
  p. (1) "No. XII.—April, 1850."
  p. 2. "Second Edition . . . | Ruins of Many Lands."
  p. 3. "Notice ! | Mr. Eliot Warburton's New Romance."
  p. 4. "The only rational Remedy | is | Parr's Life Pills."
  p. 5. "Hydropathic Establishment." View of premises.
  p. 6. "Children's Frocks, Coats, and Pelisses."
  p. 7. "Parasols."
  p. 8. "Five Special Appointments."
Slip : (to follow plates). "Familiar in their Mouths as Household Words."
  Dated, "March 30, 1850." Verso blank. Green paper. ($4\frac{1}{2}'' \times 5\frac{1}{2}''$).

ADVERTISEMENTS (BACK)
(1) "Cheap Edition | of the | Works of Mr. Charles
  Dickens." 2 pp., numbered on second page.
  Contains the "Preface to the Cheap Edition of Oliver Twist."
  Dated, March, 1850.
(2) "The Working Man's Library," etc. 8 pp. unnumbered ; comprising John Cassell's publications (5 pp.),
  and John Kaye's Worsdell's Pills (3 pp.).
  p. (1) First line as above.
  p. (2) "The Literature of Working Men."
  p. (3) "Almanacks for 1850."
  pp. (4, 5) "The Working Man's Friend." Both pages wholly
    taken up with "Opinions of the Public Press."
  p. (6) "The Triumphs of Medicine." (Kaye).

p. (7) "Complication of Disorders." (Kaye).

p. (8) "Rheumatism, Gout," etc. (Kaye).

(2A) This is an alternative to above (No. 2), being a 4-paged inset, instead of 8 pp. It omits the three pages of Kaye's matter, and also "Almanacks," page 3.

(3) "Exhibition | of | Industry of all Nations," 8 pp. numbered (1)–(8).

(4) Slip :—"Visit to the Exhibition of Ancient and Mediæval Art." Verso : "Part III. of the Ladies' Companion." ($4\frac{3}{8}'' \times 5\frac{1}{2}''$).

PLATES (TWO)

(No. 23) "Mr. Wickfield and his partner wait upon my Aunt." (p. 364).

(No. 24) "Mr. Micawber delivers some valedictory remarks." (p. 378).

TEXT, WITH HEADING

"Chapter XXXV." pp. 353–384.

PART 13.

FRONT WRAPPER (OUTSIDE)

Same as No. I. except "No. XIII. May."

FRONT WRAPPER (INSIDE)

Same as No. XI. (Doudneys).

BACK WRAPPER (INSIDE)

" ' So-So.' "

ADVERTISEMENTS (FRONT)

"Copperfield Advertiser." 8 pp. numbered (1)–(8).

    p. (1) "No. XIII.—May, 1850."

    p. 2. "A Bit of My Mind. | See Punch."

    p. 3. ($\frac{1}{2}$ col.) "A certain and speedy Cure . . ."

    p. 4. "Price One Florin each." (Milton's Hair Lubricant).

    p. 5. "Under Royal Patronage | Dr. Locock's . . . Wafers."

    p. 6. "Parasols."

    p. 7. "Warren's Sketches of Character."

    p. (8) "Number One Saint Paul's Church-Yard." With view of St. Paul's Cathedral at head of page.

Slip : (to follow plates). "To be Published Monthly . . . | The Household Narrative | of | Current Events." 2 pp., numbered on second page. Green paper. ($7\frac{1}{2}'' \times 5''$).

DAVID COPPERFIELD.

ADVERTISEMENTS (BACK)
Slip :—"New Illustrated Weekly Periodical for | Ladies. | Published every Thursday . . . | The | Ladies' Companion." 2 pp., numbered on second page. Light-green paper. (6″×3¾″).

PLATES (TWO)
(No. 25) "Traddles makes a figure in parliament and I report him." (p. 386).
(No. 26) "The Wanderer." (p. 412).

TEXT, WITH HEADING
"Chapter XXXVIII." pp. 385–416.

PART 14.

FRONT WRAPPER (OUTSIDE)
Same as No. I. except "No. XIV. June."

FRONT WRAPPER (INSIDE)
Same as No. X.

BACK WRAPPER (INSIDE)
"The Powdered-Headed Gentleman." (E. Moses & Son).

ADVERTISEMENTS (FRONT)
"Copperfield Advertiser." 8 pp. numbered (1)–(8).
 p. (1) "No. XIV.—June, 1850."
 p. 2. "New Books of Travel."
 p. 3. "Published on the First of June."
 p. 4. "Waterlow's Patent Copying Presses."
 p. 5. (½ col.) "Hobson's Choice—' That or None.' "
 p. 6. "Invalids Remember This ! " (Parr's Life Pills).
 p. 7. "Parasols."
 p. (8) "Reform Your Tailor's Bills."
Slip : (to follow plates). Advertising "Household Words" and "The Household Narrative," with footnote on last page : "The Number for May will be | published on the 1st of June." 4 pp. numbered (1), 2, (3), 4. Green paper. (6¾″×4½″).

PLATES (TWO)
(No. 27) "Traddles and I, in conference with the Misses Spenlow." (p. 420).
(No. 28) "I am Married." (p. 447).

TEXT, WITH HEADING
"Chapter XLI." pp. 417–448.

PART 15.

FRONT WRAPPER (OUTSIDE)
Same as No. I. except "No. XV. July."

FRONT WRAPPER (INSIDE)
"Hydropathic Establishment." With view of the Hydro
at Sudbrook Park, near Richmond.

BACK WRAPPER (INSIDE)
"The Dog-Days." (E. Moses & Son).

ADVERTISEMENTS (FRONT)
"Copperfield Advertiser." 4 pp. numbered (1)–4.
  p. (1) "No. XV.—July, 1850."
  p. 2. (½ col.) "Mr. Colburn's | New Publications."
  p. 3. "Kirby, Beard, & Co."
  p. 4. "Alpaca Umbrellas."

"Household Words." Details firstly, "Contents of Part
III." followed by Part II. and Part I. 2 pp. 8vo.,
numbered on second page. Pink or green paper.

ADVERTISEMENTS (BACK)
  (1) "Illustrated Weekly Journal for Ladies. | Published
      Weekly . . . | The | Ladies' Companion." Verso :
      "Now ready | . . . | Manners and Customs of Ye
      Englyshe | in 1849. | By Richard Doyle." 2 pp. un-
      numbered. Pink, green, or light-blue paper.
  (2) "Penny Maps. | On the 1st of August will be Published
      . . . | A New Series of Maps." 1 leaf, verso blank.
  (3) "The most remarkable publication of the day. | The
      Working Man's Friend." Page 3 : "Almanacks for
      1850." 4 pp., numbered on second page only.

PLATES (TWO)
  (No. 29) "Our Housekeeping." (p. 454).
  (No. 30) "Mr. Dick fulfils my Aunt's prediction." (p. 465).

TEXT, WITH HEADING
"Chapter XLIV." pp. 449–480.

DAVID COPPERFIELD.

PART 16.

FRONT WRAPPER (OUTSIDE)
Same as No. I. except "No. XVI. August."

FRONT WRAPPER (INSIDE)
"Heal & Son's | List of Bedding." (9 lines in all).

BACK WRAPPER (INSIDE)
"A Taking Establishment." (E. Moses & Son).

ADVERTISEMENTS (FRONT)
"Copperfield Advertiser." 4 pp. numbered (1)–4.
p. (1) "No. XVI.—August, 1850."
p. 2. ($\frac{1}{2}$ col.) "New Monthly Work by Dr. Lindley."
p. 3. ($\frac{1}{2}$ col.) "The Author of ' Emilia Wyndham.' "
p. 4. "Kirby, Beard, & Co."

Slip : (to precede "Advertiser"). "Now on Sale . . . | Punch's Holidays." Verso blank. Pale-yellow paper. ($5\frac{5}{8}''\times4\frac{1}{2}''$).

Slip : (to follow plates). "Household Words." Similar to Part 14, but gives Contents of Part IV., and is smaller in size. 4 pp. numbered on last page only. Green paper. ($6''\times3\frac{3}{4}''$).

PLATES (TWO)
(No. 31) "The River." (p. 482).
(No. 32) "Mr. Peggotty's dream comes true." (p. 512).

TEXT, WITH HEADING
"Chapter XLVII." pp. 481-512.

PART 17.

FRONT WRAPPER (OUTSIDE)
Same as No. I. except "No. XVII. September."

FRONT WRAPPER (INSIDE)
"The Great Remedy for all Diseases . . . | Parr's Life Pills." Woodcut of Thomas Parr's birthplace.

BACK WRAPPER (INSIDE)
"The Lady and the Peacock." (E. Moses & Son).

ADVERTISEMENTS (FRONT)
"Copperfield Advertiser." 4 pp. numbered (1)–4.
p. (1) "No. XVII.—September, 1850."
p. 2. "Illustrated Weekly Periodical for Ladies."
p. 3. "Hair an Ornament." (Milton's Lubricant).
p. 4. "Warren's Sketches of Character."

ADVERTISEMENTS (BACK)
"By Royal Letters Patent | . . . | Waterlow's | Patent
Portable | Copying Apparatus." Verso : "Waterlow's
| Patent | Autographic Press." 2 pp. unnumbered.
Yellow, blue, or pink paper.

PLATES (TWO)
(No. 33) "Restoration of mutual confidence between Mr.
and Mrs. Micawber." (p. 539).
(No. 34) "My child-wife's old companion." (p. 544).

TEXT, WITH HEADING
"Chapter LI." pp. 513–544.

PART 18.

FRONT WRAPPER (OUTSIDE)
Same as No. I. except "No. XVIII. October."

FRONT WRAPPER (INSIDE)
"The Blood." (Parr's Life Pills).

BACK WRAPPER (INSIDE)
"Daniel Lambert's Suit." (E. Moses & Son).

ADVERTISEMENTS (FRONT)
"Copperfield Advertiser." 8 pp. numbered (1)–8.
  p. (1) "No. XVIII.—October, 1850."
  p. 2. "Illustrated Weekly Periodical for Ladies."
  p. 3. "Warren's Sketches of Character."
  p. 4. "Milton's | Hair | Lubricant."
  p. 5. "Comfort in a Storm ! "
  p. 6. "Perfect Health is invariably restored."
  p. 7. "Children's Frocks, Coats, & Pelisses."
  p. 8. "Purity of Flavour . . ." (Dakin & Compy.).
"This day is published . . . | The First Volume | of |
Household Words." With "Contents" in 3-column
measure. 2 pp. unnumbered. Green paper.

ADVERTISEMENTS (BACK)
(1) Waterlow & Sons. 8 pp. Same as Part 6.
  An alternative to above, consists of 2 pages only. "By Royal
  Letters Patent. | . . . | Waterlow's | Patent Portable | Copying
  Apparatus." Verso : "Waterlow's | Patent | Autographic Press."
  Unnumbered. Salmon coloured paper.

(2) "Now Publishing, Weekly . . . | Eliza Cook's Journal."
1 leaf, verso blank. Yellow, pink, or green paper.

PLATES (TWO)
(No. 35) "I am the bearer of evil tidings." (p. 566).
(No. 36) "The Emigrants." (p. 575).

TEXT, WITH HEADING
"Chapter LIV." pp. 545–576.

PARTS 19 AND 20.

FRONT WRAPPER (OUTSIDE)
Same as No. I. except "Nos. XIX. & XX. November.
Price 2s."

FRONT WRAPPER (INSIDE)
Same as No. XVI. (Heal & Sons).

BACK WRAPPER (INSIDE)
"To the Statue on Bloomsbury Church." (E. Moses
& Son).

ADVERTISEMENTS (FRONT)
"Copperfield Advertiser." 16 pp., all numbered except
(1), (8, 9).
  p. (1) "Nos. XIX. & XX.—November, 1850."
  p. 2. "Publishing Weekly . . . | The Ladies' Companion."
  p. 3. "New Works | published by | Chapman and Hall. . . ."
  p. 4. "The Completion of the Cheap Edition of the Works of
    | Mr. Charles Dickens."
  p. 5. "Knight's Pictorial Shakspere :"
  p. 6. "Works on Gardening and Botany."
  p. 7. "Completion of David Copperfield."
  pp. (8, 9) "Contents of Volume the First of Household Words."
  p. 10. ($\frac{1}{2}$ col.) "To be had . . . | Popular New Novels."
  p. 11. "Under Royal Patronage | Dr. Locock's . . . Wafers."
  p. 12. "Comfort in a Storm !"
  p. 13. "Alpaca Umbrellas."
  p. 14. "Button's Amunorigon, or Medicated Shield."
  p. 15. "Any One who will call on or send to Dakin . . ."
  p. 16. "Reform Your Tailor's Bills."
Slip : (to follow "Advertiser"). "Punch's | Pocket-Book | for 1851."
  Similar to Part 7. 2 pp.
Slip : (to follow plates). "The Writings | of | Douglas Jerrold." 1 leaf,
  verso blank. Green paper. ($7'' \times 4\frac{3}{4}''$).

271

CHARLES DICKENS.

ADVERTISEMENTS (BACK)

(1) "Cundall and Addey's | List of | Illustrated Publications." 8 pp. numbered (1)–8. Imprint at foot of last page: "London: G. Barclay, Castle St., Leicester Sq."

(2) "New Work . . . | Lewis Arundel." Verso: "Critical Notices | of | Frank Fairlegh." 2 pp. unnumbered.

(3) "The cheapest maps . . . | Philip's Series | of | Large Sixpenny Maps." Verso: "A New Series of Penny Maps." 2 pp. unnumbered.

(4) "Waterlow & Sons," with view of premises above. 8 pp. numbered (1)–8. Pages 2–7 have the heading: "Waterlow & Sons, | Wholesale and Retail Manufacturing Stationers, | Printers, Lithographers & Engravers." Page (8): "By Royal Letters Patent. | Waterlow's | Patent | Autographic Press."
Alternatively, same as Parts 6, 10, 18.

PLATES (FOUR)

(No. 37) "I am shewn two interesting penitents." (p. 605).
The "List of Plates" has "shown" for "shewn."

(No. 38) "A Stranger calls to see me." (p. 615).

(No. 39) "Frontispiece."

(No. 40) Vignette Title. Dated 1850.

TEXT, WITH HEADING

"Chapter LVIII." pp. 577–624. Imprint at foot of p. 624: "London: | Bradbury and Evans, Printers, Whitefriars."

PRELIMINARY LEAVES

Half-title: "David Copperfield." Verso, blank. (I., II.).

Title-page: dated 1850. Verso, with imprint as page 624. (III., IV.). See Illustration.

Dedication: "To | The Hon. Mr. and Mrs. Richard Watson, | of | Rockingham, Northamptonshire." Verso, blank. (V., VI.).

"Preface." Dated, "London, | October, 1850." 2 pp. numbered (VII.), VIII.

"Contents." 4 pp. numbered (IX.), X., XI., XII.

"List of Plates." 2 pp. numbered (XIII.), XIV.

"Errata" of 6 lines; verso, blank. (XV., XVI.).

272

BLEAK HOUSE.

BY

CHARLES DICKENS.

WITH ILLUSTRATIONS BY H. K. BROWNE.

LONDON:
BRADBURY AND EVANS, 11, BOUVERIE STREET.
1853.

Bleak House

in

19/20 Monthly Parts

March, 1852, to September, 1853.

ORIGINALLY issued in twenty numbers, bound in nineteen monthly parts, price one shilling per number, except the last two (19 and 20) which formed a double-number at two shillings. Each part was bound in blue paper wrappers, the front bearing the wording as given in the collation following; printed partly in type, and partly as embodied in the design by "Phiz."

WRAPPERS.

Apart from the essential change in "Part No." and month of issue, only one variation occurs in the type-setting on front cover, where in Part 5 and all succeeding numbers, the footnote is altered to refer to the Author's rights of translation. The inside front covers are occupied with full-page advertisements of two firms : Edmiston & Son, and William S. Burton. The first four numbers have the announcements of Edmiston, and commencing in Part 5, Burton appears alternately with Edmiston. Inside of back wrappers is utilized by E. Moses and Son for the entire series ; the heading and "address" to their public changing with each monthly issue. Heal and Son's bedsteads appear throughout upon the outside back wrappers, but are not detailed in the collation, as "E. Moses and Son" is sufficiently distinctive to identify the correctness or otherwise.

CHARLES DICKENS.

PLATES.

These consist of forty designs etched by "Phiz." Of this number, ten are known as "The Dark Plates" and two distinct etchings of each were executed by the Artist, making a total of 50 steels for the book. Many, if not all, of the other thirty designs were also reproduced by lithographic transfers from the steels, and are to be found mixed indiscriminately with etchings. An examination of 1000 odd parts has revealed the presence of "lithos" in Parts 4, 6, 9, 10, 11 and 13, but the probabilities are that all of the thirty designs were reproduced by this process. The ten "Dark Plates" are :—

Part 12.	No. 24.	The Ghost's Walk.
„ 13.	„ 26.	Sunset in the long Drawing Room.
„ 14.	„ 28.	Tom all alone's.
„ 15.	„ 29.	A new meaning in the Roman.
„ 16.	„ 32.	Shadow.
„ 17.	„ 34.	The lonely figure.
„ 18.	„ 35.	The Night.
„ 18.	„ 36.	The Morning.
„ 19/20	„ 38.	The Mausoleum at Chesney Wold.
„ „	„ 39.	Frontispiece.

The first dark plate to be published, marking a departure from the ordinary method of etching, was Dombey No. 35, and the second was Copperfield No. 31. They were followed by the above-mentioned ten in "Bleak House," and subsequently by eight more in "Little Dorrit."

These dark etchings were the result of "machine-tinting" the steels, which gave an effect equivalent to that of "mezzo-tinting." The steel was first closely ruled with fine lines, and the design was then etched over the ruling, After that, by a further process of "stopping-out" and "burnishing," the effect of light and shadow was heightened.

In the case of "Bleak House," as with previous books, there was no priority in issue of the ten duplicated plates, but there is a distinguishing clue which applies in nearly every case. Most of the "first" plates have a somewhat flat appearance, whereas, in the "second" plates, which must have received more "work," the chiaroscuro is intensified.

This contrast is especially noticeable in plates 32, 34, 35, 36. In that connection, J. F. Dexter says : "The electro-typing of steel plates which had just been invented, was probably not a perfected process at that time, for they failed to reproduce clearly the delicate machine-tint lines in the backgrounds." Nevertheless, some fine effects were obtained, comparing favourably with the companion plate etched in the usual method.

Dombey No. 35 is an exceptionally striking plate ; the effect of light and shade being most marked. It was probably "pulled" by hand rather than by mechanical means.

Copperfield No. 31 was a continuation of the experiment, but can hardly be considered an improvement in the process.

It is not generally known that "Phiz" had been experimenting with the machine-tint idea long before Dombey, for there is, in the Dexter collection, a proof of Nickleby plate No. 39, showing the ruled steel with the machine-tint effect. This proof, which must have been hand-pulled, is infinitely more brilliant than any of the "Bleak House" and "Little Dorrit" plates. The only one in those books which approaches it in brilliancy, is "Damocles" ("Little Dorrit" No. 39). J. F. Dexter says : "I bought this proof at the sale of A. Welby Pugin, the architect ; it had been given to him by ' Phiz ' himself, together with many other proofs which are in my possession."

The accident to plate No. 17 is explained in the detailed collation.

ADVERTISEMENTS (FRONT).

These in the main consist of the "Bleak House Advertiser," and appear in each part ; varying from 8 pages up to 24 pages. Every page throughout the series—with the exception of page 1—is headed "Advertisements" and foliated. In all numbers except Parts 1, 10 and 11, was inserted a slip ($4\frac{1}{2}'' \times 5\frac{1}{2}''$) announcing the publication in weekly numbers of "Household Words" ; and the publication at the end of every month of "The Household Narrative of Current Events." There were six distinct issues, and they varied from time to time as to the number of volumes then in issue of "Household Words"; either four, five, six or seven. Many misplacements of these slips have been noted in parts to which they are foreign, and the following compilation is necessary in checking copies for the slip which is applicable to any particular part. A distinguishing "issue number" is given to each variant, and this number only is quoted in the collation. Two colours of paper were employed: light-green and dark-green, but they were apparently not used indiscriminately, except in Part 5, where certainly both colours are to be found.

Issue No. 1.	Part	2.	"Four vols."	Light-green.
,, ,,	,,	3.	,,	,,
,, ,,	,,	4.	,,	,,
,, ,,	,,	5.	,,	,,
,, ,,	,,	6.	,,	,,
,, No. 2.	,,	7.	"Four vols."	Dark-green.
,, No. 3.	,,	8.	"Five vols."	Dark-green.
,, ,,	,,	9.	,,	,,
,, ,,	,,	12.	,,	,,
,, No. 4.	,,	13.	"Six vols."	Dark-green.
,, ,,	,,	14.	,,	,,
,, ,,	,,	15.	,,	,,
,, No. 5.	,,	16.	"Six vols."	Light-green.
,, ,,	,,	17.	,,	,,
,, ,,	,,	18.	,,	,,
,, No. 6.	,,	19.	"Seven vols."	Light-green.

ADVERTISEMENTS (BACK).

A total of 82 individual trade insets are bound in at the end, a number only exceeded by "Our Mutual Friend." Without exception they are present in every part, and as detailed in the collation are essential to a complete and perfect copy. A rather scarce item (often wanting) is "The Village Pastor," which should appear in Part 15. This small booklet was

either of a limited issue at time of publication, or was extracted
to make use of the subscription form which appears on inside
of back wrapper.

PART 1.

FRONT WRAPPER (OUTSIDE)

"No. I. March.   Price 1s. | Bleak House | by | Charles
Dickens. | With Illustrations by H. K. Browne. |
London : Bradbury & Evans, Bouverie Street. | Agents :
J. Menzies, Edinburgh ; Murray and Son, Glasgow ;
J. M'Glashan, Dublin. | Notice is hereby given that
the Author of ' Bleak House ' reserves to | himself the
right of publishing a Translation in France."

The title alone, "Bleak House," is embodied in the cover design,
all other lettering is type-set.

FRONT WRAPPER (INSIDE)

Edmiston & Son.   Second line from bottom, reads :—
"Agents Appointed."

BACK WRAPPER (INSIDE)

"Anti-Bleak House."   (E. Moses & Son).

ADVERTISEMENTS (FRONT)

"Bleak House Advertiser."   24 pp. numbered (1)–24.

p. (1) "No. I.—March, 1852."
p. 2. "New and Popular Books for the Young." (Grant and
         Griffith).
p. 3. "Groombridge and Sons' New Works."
p. 4. "Mr. Murray's List."
p. 5. "In Preparation. | The Autobiography of William Jerdan."
p. 6. "New and Popular Books." (Taylor, Walton & Co.).
p. 7. "Smith, Elder & Co.'s New Publications."
p. 8. "The Traveller's Library." (Longman, Brown).
p. 9. "In Weekly Numbers . . . | Household Words."
p. 10. "Colburn & Co.'s New Publications."
p. 11. "Valuable and Interesting Works." (Colburn).
p. 12. ($\frac{1}{2}$ col.) "On 31st March, | . . . | The Life of Lord
         Jeffrey."
p. 13. "Important Announcement."
p. 14. "American and Continental Literary Agency."
p. 15. "Newspaper for the Farming and Gardening Interest."
p. 16. "The Publishers of ' The Parlour Library.' "

279

p. 17. "Crown 8vo . . . | The French in England."
p. 18. "The Human Hair." (Rowland).
p. 19. "Prize Medal." (Watherston & Brogden).
p. 20. (¼ col.) "Thos. Harris & Son's." Woodcut of Spectacles.
p. 21. "The Hair." (Milton's Hair Lubricant).
p. 22. "Messrs. J. Holmes & Co." With cut of Royal Arms.
p. 23. "The London General Mourning Warehouse." (W. C. Jay).
p. 24. "Poulson & Compy." With view of premises.

ADVERTISEMENTS (BACK)

(1) W. Mott. 2 pp. unnumbered. Pink paper.

p. (1) "12, Cheapside, City." With illustrations of a 4-piece Tea Service, and one Spoon.
p. (2) "Manufactory, 36, Cheapside, London." With two views of face and back of a watch.

(2) Norton's Camomile Pills. 4 pp. numbered (1), 2, 3, (4).

p. 2. First word in first column . . . "stomach"
     Last ,, ,, second ,, . . . "their"
p. 3. Last ,, ,, first ,, . . . "promptly"
     First ,, ,, second ,, . . . "assist"

(3) Waterlow & Sons. 4 pp. unnumbered.

p. (1) (View of premises) "Waterlow & Sons, | Manufacturing Stationers."
p. (2) "Bankers' Cheques."
p. (3) "By Royal Letters Patent. | . . . | Waterlow's | Patent Autographic Press."
p. (4) Headline : "Waterlow and Sons, Wholesale, Retail, and Export Stationers." Followed by :—"Patent Letter Copying Presses," with cuts of Four Presses.

Three variants of Waterlow's inset have been traced in copies of this number, in each instance with 8 pages, as against 4 pages noted in the above collation.

Variant A. This has the letter "B" in right top corner of front page. Otherwise the collation is exactly as that appearing in "David Copperfield," Part 19/20.

Variant B. The same as preceding, with the exceptions that the letter "B" does not appear, whilst the view of premises and the text on front page are different. Pages 2 to 8 are identical.

Variant C. This has the letter "S" in right top corner of front page. All other pages are differently arranged. Pages 2 to 8 are numbered.

p. 2. "Whatman's Drawing Paper."
p. 4. "Writing Papers."

p. 5. "Envelopes."
p. 6. "Sundries."
p. 7. "Patent Letter Copying Presses."
p. 8. "Lithography."

PLATES (TWO)

(No. 1) "The little old Lady."   (p. 23).

(No. 2) "Miss Jellyby."   (p. 31).

TEXT, WITH HEADING

"Bleak House. | Chapter I. | In Chancery."   pp. (1)–32.

PART 2.

FRONT WRAPPER (OUTSIDE)

Same as No. I. except "No. II.   April."

FRONT WRAPPER (INSIDE)

Edmiston & Son.   At foot of page is a list of nine agents, including "Radcliffe & Corley, Liverpool."

BACK WRAPPER (INSIDE)

"April Showers."   (E. Moses & Son).

ADVERTISEMENTS (FRONT)

"Bleak House Advertiser."   16 pp. numbered (1)–16.

p. (1) "No. II.—April, 1852."
p. 2. "Messrs. Blackwood & Sons' | Publications."
p. 3. "On April 30th will be published . . . | The Charm :"
p. 4. ($\frac{1}{2}$ col.) "Sam Slick's New Comic Work."
p. 5. "Works on Gardening and Botany."
p. 6. "New Works and New Editions."
p. 7. "New Works."   (Bradbury and Evans).
p. 8. "Just Published . . . | The Life . . . | of | Lord Jeffrey."
p. 9. ($\frac{1}{2}$ col.) "Now ready . . . | The Half-Century."
p. 10. "Fifth Division of Profits."   (Clerical Medical).
p. 11. "Queenwood College . . . Hants."
p. 12. ($\frac{1}{2}$ col.) "The Ten Guinea Harmo- | nium."
p. 13. "Prize Medal."   (Watherston & Brogden).
p. 14. "Spencer's Pulmonic Elixir."
p. 15. ($\frac{1}{2}$ col.) "Thos. Harris & Sons."
p. 16. "Poulson & Compy."

(To follow "Advertiser"). "New Weekly Publication. | On Saturday, May 1st, 1852 . . . | People's Illustrated Journal." 2 pp. numbered on second page.

Slip : (to follow plates). "Household Words."   Issue No. 1.

CHARLES DICKENS.

ADVERTISEMENTS (BACK)

(1) David Bogue's Publications.   8 pp. numbered (1)–(8).
    p. (1) "Webster's Quarto Dictionary Unabridged."
    pp. 2, 3, 4.   Continuation of page (1).
    pp. 5, 6, 7. "Published by David Bogue, Fleet Street."
    p. 8. "Practical Works on Drawing and Painting."

(2) Adam and Charles Black, Edinburgh. 8 pp. unnumbered.
    p. (1) "Just Published, | . . . | The Life of Lord Jeffrey."
    pp. (2 & 3) "Prospectus | of | The Library Edition | of the | Waverley Novels."
    pp. (5 & 6) "A New Edition of the | Encyclopædia Britannica."
    p. (7) "Black's General Atlas of the World." Twelve titles in all.

(3) Waterlow & Sons. 4 pp. Same as Part 1.

(4) Slip :—"Notice of Removal." (Ford's Eureka Shirts). Verso blank. Yellow paper. (4½″ × 5½″).

PLATES (Two)

(No. 3) "The Lord Chancellor copies from memory." (p. 41).
(No. 4) "Coavinses." (p. 52).

TEXT, WITH HEADING
"Chapter V."   pp. 33–64.

PART 3.

FRONT WRAPPER (OUTSIDE)
Same as No. I. except "No. III.   May."

FRONT WRAPPER (INSIDE)
Edmiston & Son.   List of agents increased to ten.

BACK WRAPPER (INSIDE)
"May Flowers." (E. Moses & Son).

ADVERTISEMENTS (FRONT)
"Bleak House Advertiser."   16 pp. numbered (1)–16.
    p. (1) "No. III.—May, 1852."
    p. 2. "Works on Gardening and Botany."
    p. 3. "Just Published . . . | Vol. 1 . . . | The Waverley Novels."
    p. 4. "Colburn and Co.'s New Publications."

p. 5. "New Works." Eight titles. (Bradbury and Evans).
p. 6. "Now Publishing. | New Medical Dictionary . . ."
p. 7. "Now Ready . . . | Burke's Peerage & Baronetage, for 1852."
p. 8. "Completion of Lives of the Queens."
p. 9. "The First Volume of | A Child's History of England."
p. 10. "Rowlands' Macassar Oil."
p. 11. "Children's Frocks, Coats, and Pelisses ; "
p. 12. "Milton's | Hair | Lubricant."
p. 13. "Barker & Compy."
p. 14. ($\frac{1}{2}$ col.) "Use Ludlam's Electric | Rubber."
p. 15. "May. | . . . | Parr's Life Pills."
p. 16. Same as Part 2. (Poulson).
Slip : (to follow plates). "Household Words." Issue No. 1.

ADVERTISEMENTS (BACK)

(1) Norton's Camomile Pills. 4 pp. Same as Part 1.

(2) Arthur Hall, Virtue, and Co. 4 pp. unnumbered.

> p. (1) "The Autobiography of William Jerdan."
> p. (3) "Works by the Rev. John Cumming, D.D."

(3) "New London Weekly Newspaper, Price Fourpence" ; below : a woodcut representing the "Origin of the Stocking-Loom." Verso, continuation, with imprint of Frederick Tallis. 2 pp. unnumbered.

(4) Waterlow & Sons. 4 pp. unnumbered.

> p. (1) "Waterlow's | Patent Improved Autographic Press."
> p. (2) "The | Patent Autographic Press, | (Hand Power)."
> p. (3) "Waterlow & Sons' | Patent Autographic Press."
> p. (4) "Patent Letter Copying Presses." Five woodcuts.

(5) Slip :—"Crochet Cotton | for the Million. | Marsland, Son, & Co." Verso ; a specimen design of a D'Oyley, and there are in issue four distinctly different patterns. The text printed above the design changes with each one :—

> (1) 5-line heading, with "page 285, Nov. 22nd, 1851 ;"
> (2) 5-line heading, with "page 205, 1851 ;"
> (3) 6-line heading, with "page 182, March 27th, 1852 ;"
> (4) 4-line heading (no page or date quoted).

Each slip is printed both sides in red, on white paper ($5\frac{3}{4}'' \times 4\frac{1}{2}''$).

PLATES (TWO)
(No. 5) "The visit at the Brickmaker's." (p. 75).
(No. 6) "In Re Guppy. Extraordinary proceedings." (p. 88).

TEXT, WITH HEADING
"Chapter VIII." pp. 65–96.

PART 4.

FRONT WRAPPER (OUTSIDE)
Same as No. I. except "No. IV. June."

FRONT WRAPPER (INSIDE)
Edmiston & Son. List of nine agents; the name of Radcliffe & Corley now deleted.

BACK WRAPPER (INSIDE)
"A Suit in Chancery and a Suit out of Chancery." (E. Moses & Son).

ADVERTISEMENTS (FRONT)
"Bleak House Advertiser." 12 pp. numbered (1)–12.
p. (1) "No. IV.—June, 1852."
p. 2. "New Works." (Bradbury and Evans).
p. 3. "Paxton's Flower-Garden."
p. 4. "Works by Dr. Lindley."
p. 5. "The Ladies' Companion to the Flower- | Garden."
p. 6. ($\frac{1}{2}$ col.) "The Gorget."
p. 7. "Pulvermacher's Patent Portable | . . . Chain."
p. 8. "Barker & Compy."
p. 9. "French Organdie Muslins."
p. 10. "Ladies Travelling." (Rowlands).
p. 11. "A New Stove.—Great Novelty."
p. 12. Same as Part 2, page 16. (Poulson).
Slip : (to follow "Advertiser"). "Cheap Edition | of the | Works of Mr. Charles Dickens." Verso blank. ($3\frac{3}{4}'' \times 5\frac{1}{8}''$).
Slip : (to follow plates). "Household Words." Issue No. 1.

ADVERTISEMENTS (BACK)
(1) "The | British | Journal." 1 leaf, verso blank.
(2) John Cassell's Publications. 4 pp. unnumbered.
p. (1) "Will be ready July 1, | . . . | The Illustrated Exhibitor | and | Magazine of Art."
p. (3) "John Cassell's Library, Complete."

(3) Darton's Publications. 8 pp. numbered on page 2 only. Yellow paper ($8\frac{1}{4}'' \times 5\frac{3}{8}''$).

    p. (1) "In the Press . . . | . . . | The Dial of Love."
    p. (3) "Standard Juvenile Books."
    p. (5) "Juvenile and Educational."
    p. (7) "Blair's Mother's Catechisms."

(4) Waterlow & Sons. 4 pp. Same as Part 3.

(5) Slip :—"Use | Marsland, Son, & Co.'s | Unrivalled and Registered | Griffin | Crochet Cotton." Verso ; a specimen bird designed D'Oyley, with 5 lines of text above, and 7 lines below. Printed both sides in red, on yellow paper ($5\frac{5}{8}'' \times 4\frac{1}{4}''$).

PLATES (Two)

(No. 7) "Mr. Guppy's desolation." (p. 121).

(No. 8) "The family portraits at Mr. Bayham Badger's." (p. 123).

TEXT, WITH HEADING

"Chapter XI." pp. 97-128.

PART 5.

FRONT WRAPPER (OUTSIDE)

Same as No. I. except "No. V. July," and a variation of the footnote, now reading : "The Author of this Work notifies that it is his intention to reserve the | right of translating it."

FRONT WRAPPER (INSIDE)

"The Best Show of Iron Bedsteads in the | Kingdom is William S. Burton's."

BACK WRAPPER (INSIDE)

"New Empire." (E. Moses & Son).

ADVERTISEMENTS (FRONT)

"Bleak House Advertiser." 12 pp. numbered (1)–12.

    p. (1) "No. V.—July, 1852."
    p. 2. "This day is published . . . | The British Winter Garden."
    p. 3. "New and Popular Books for the Young."
    p. 4. "For Book Clubs and Lending Libraries."
    p. 5. (printed crosswise, in 3-column measure).

CHARLES DICKENS.

p. 6. "New Sporting Publication . . . | Mr. Sponge's Sporting Tour."
p. 7. (½ col.) "Colburn & Co.'s New Publications."
p. 8. (½ col.) "Chubb's Fire-proof Safes and Locks."
p. 9. "Ladies Travelling." (Rowlands).
p. 10. "Prize Medal."
p. 11. "Barker & Compy ;" and "Children's Frocks," etc.
p. 12. Same as Part 2, page 16. (Poulson).

Slip : (to follow plates). "Household Words." Issue No. 1, or Issue No. 2.

ADVERTISEMENTS (BACK)

(1) "Allsopp's | Pale or Bitter Ale." 4 pp. numbered (1)–4.

(2) Edward Lloyd's Announcements. 8 pp. unnumbered.

p. (1) "Cheapest | Largest & Best | Family Newspaper | Lloyd's | Weekly London | Newspaper." The whole embodied in full-page woodcut.
p. (3) Full-page illustration ; entitled : "The Red-Hot Politician."
p. (5) Full-page illustration ; entitled : "The Latest Intelligence."
p. (7) "All who have Gardens should purchase | Lloyd's cheap | Treatises on Popular Flowers, &c."

(3) John Kaye's Pills. 4 pp. unnumbered.

p. (1) "To the Electors and Non-Electors | of the | United Kingdom." Dated, May, 1852.
p. (4) "John Kaye's | Infant's Restorative."

(4) Slip :—Crochet Cotton. Same as Part 4, except printed in red, on white paper.

PLATES (TWO)

(No. 9) "The Dancing School." (p. 134).
(No. 10) "Consecrated ground." (p. 160).

TEXT, WITH HEADING

"Chapter XIV." pp. 129–160.

PART 6.

FRONT WRAPPER (OUTSIDE)
Same as No. V. except "No. VI. August."

FRONT WRAPPER (INSIDE)
Edmiston & Son. Same as Part 4.

Back Wrapper (Inside)
    "A Bold Stroke." (E. Moses & Son).

Advertisements (Front)
    "Bleak House Advertiser." 8 pp. numbered (1)–8.
        p. (1) "No. VI.—August, 1852." Woodcut by "Phiz."
        p. 2. "Mr. Hogarth has the honour to announce . . ."
        p. 3. "Autobiography of William Jerdan." (15 Titles in all).
        p. 4. ($\frac{1}{2}$ col.) "The Ten Guinea Harmo- | nium . . ."
        p. 5. ($\frac{1}{2}$ col.) "Chubb's Fire-proof Safes and Locks."
        p. 6. "Prize Medal."
        p. 7. "Barker & Compy."
        p. 8. "Poulson & Compy."
  Slip : (to follow plates). "Household Words." Issue No. 1.

Advertisements (Back)
    (1) "The Oak | Mutual Life Assurance & Loan Company." A 3-folded sheet, opening out to $5\frac{3}{8}'' \times 9\frac{1}{8}''$: printed as 6 pages, unnumbered. Light-green paper.
    (2) Slip :—"New Serial by Mr. Charles Lever. | On the 31st of August will be published . . . | The Dodd Family Abroad." Verso blank. Printed on seven varying tints of paper ($4\frac{1}{2}'' \times 5\frac{1}{2}''$).
    (3) Virtue, Hall, and Virtue. 4 pp. unnumbered. Grey paper.
        p. (1) "New Works and New Editions." First title : "Lewis Arundel."
        p. (3) First title : "The Art-Journal."
    (4) W. Mott. 2 pp. Same as Part 1.
    (5) Slip :—Crochet Cotton. The same series as in Part 3, but printed in black, on white, thin paper. In addition the same series was printed on a stouter paper, of a lightish-brown tint. Again remainders of Part 5 are to be found in this number. Thus nine varieties of this slip may be seen, all applicable to Part 6.

Plates (Two)
    (No. 11) "Caddy's flowers." (p. 170).
    (No. 12) "The little church in the park." (p. 177).

Text, with Heading
    "Chapter XVII." pp. 161–192.

CHARLES DICKENS.

PART 7.

FRONT WRAPPER (OUTSIDE)
Same as No. V. except "No. VII.   September."

FRONT WRAPPER (INSIDE)
"William S. Burton's."   Below name and addresses are two short notices set in half column measure.

BACK WRAPPER (INSIDE)
"What a Stir."   (E. Moses & Son).

ADVERTISEMENTS (FRONT)
"Bleak House Advertiser."   12 pp. numbered (1)–12.

p. (1) "No. VII.—September, 1852."
p. 2. "Works by Mr. Charles Dickens."
p. 3. "Popular Serials." (Arthur Hall, Virtue and Co.).
p. 4. "New Works." (Bradbury and Evans).
p. 5. "On the 20th September . . . | Household Words."
p. 6. "To Emigrants !" With half-page illustration.
p. 7. ($\frac{1}{2}$ col.) "Chubb's Fire-proof Safes and Locks."
p. 8. "Prize Medal."
p. 9. "Children's Frocks, Coats & Pelisses."
p. 10. "All who have tried | Parr's Life Pills."
p. 11. "Barker & Compy." and "Rowlands."
p. 12. "Poulson & Compy."

Slip : (to follow plates).   "Household Words."   Issue No. 2.

ADVERTISEMENTS (BACK)

(1) Norton's Camomile Pills.   4 pp.   Same as Part 1.

(2) Slip :—"The Dodd Family Abroad" ; same as Part 6, but reads : "This day is published . . ."

(3) "Allsopp's."   4 pp.   Same as Part 5.

(4) "The | Practical Mechanic's Journal | Prospectus." 8 pp., numbered on pp. 3, 5, 6.   Woodcuts on pp. 1, 2, 8.

p. 3. "The | Practical Mechanic's Journal."
pp. (4) 5, 6. "Index to plates."
p. (8) Same as first page, but different woodcut design.

(5) "The | London Weekly Paper."   2 pp. unnumbered.

(6) W. Mott.   2 pp.   Same as Part 1.

(7) "Atlas Fire and Life Assurance Office." 2 pp., second page numbered. Brown tinted paper.

(8) Slip :—"Use | Marsland, Son, & Co.'s | . . . | Griffin | Crochet Cotton." Verso : with specimen bird design ; 4 lines of text along each side of the pattern. Printed both sides in red, on white paper. ($6\frac{3}{4}'' \times 4\frac{1}{4}''$).

With the exception of 8 additional words, the text both sides is identical with Part 4. This issue is larger in size, and the bird design is different.

PLATES (TWO)

(No. 13) "Mr. Guppy's entertainment." (p. 195).

(No. 14) "The Smallweed family." (p. 208).

TEXT, WITH HEADING

"Chapter XX." pp. 193-224.

PART 8.

FRONT WRAPPER (OUTSIDE)

Same as No. V. except "No. VIII. October."

FRONT WRAPPER (INSIDE)

Edmiston & Son. Same as Parts 4 and 6.

BACK WRAPPER (INSIDE)

"A Change." (E. Moses & Son).

ADVERTISEMENTS (FRONT)

"Bleak House Advertiser." 12 pp. numbered (1)–12.

p. (1) "No. VIII.—October, 1852."
p. 2. "Works by Mr. Charles Dickens." Same as Part 7.
p. 3. "New Edition . . . | The Women of Israel."
p. 4. "Now ready . . . | Household Words :"
p. 5. "Works on Gardening and Botany."
p. 6. ($\frac{1}{2}$ col.) "Colburn & Co.'s | New Publications."
p. 7. "Partridge and Oakey's Standard Pictorial Editions."
p. 8. "Prize Medal."
p. 9. "Children's Frocks, Coats, & Pelisses."
p. 10. "The successful results of the last Half-century."
p. 11. "Barker & Compy." Below : "Rimmel's Toilet."
p. 12. "Poulson & Compy." and "Great Exhibition."

Slip : (to follow plates). "Household Words." Issue No. 3.

ADVERTISEMENTS (BACK)

(1) "Waterlow's | Patent Improved Autographic Press," with woodcut of press at head of page. Verso: "Patent Letter Copying Presses" and cuts of four presses beneath. 2 pp. unnumbered.

(2) W. Mott. 2 pp. Same as Part 1.

(3) Slip :—Crochet Cotton. Same as Part 7 in regard to textual matter, but a different fount of type is used. Verso : with the usual specimen design, headed : "Marsland, Son, & Co.'s | Newly Registered, Variegated, and Colored | Crochet Cotton." Additional text appears at the foot of pattern. Printed both sides in blue, on white paper. ($7\frac{1}{4}'' \times 5\frac{1}{2}''$).

PLATES (TWO)

(No. 15) "A model of parental deportment." (p. 232).

(No. 16) "Mr. Chadband 'improving' a tough subject." (p. 254).

TEXT, WITH HEADING

"Chapter XXIII." pp. 225–256.

PART 9.

FRONT WRAPPER (OUTSIDE)

Same as No. V. except "No. IX. November."

FRONT WRAPPER (INSIDE)

"William S. Burton's." Below second ruling : "New and Cheerful Registered Stove."

BACK WRAPPER (INSIDE)

"Legal Expectations." (E. Moses & Son).

ADVERTISEMENTS (FRONT)

"Bleak House Advertiser." 8 pp. numbered (1)–8.

    p. (1) "No. IX.—November, 1852."
    p. 2. "Now ready . . . | How to Print, and when to Publish."
    p. 3. "On the 1st of November . . . | Hannah Bolton's First Drawing Book."
    p. 4. "Public Library, Conduit Street."
    p. 5. ($\frac{1}{2}$ col.) "Rodger's Improved Shirt."

p. 6. "Children's Frocks, Coats, & Pelisses."
p. 7. "Prize Medal."
p. 8. "Poulson & Compy." and "Great Exhibition."
Slip : (to follow plate).   Three lines, reading : "An accident having happened to the Plate, it has been necessary to cancel one of the Illustrations to the present Number.   It will be supplied in the next Monthly Part."   ($1\frac{5}{8}'' \times 5\frac{1}{2}''$).
Slip : (to follow above).   "Household Words."   Issue No. 3.

ADVERTISEMENTS (BACK)
(1) "Allsopp's | Pale or Bitter Ale."   8 pp. all numbered, except pp. 1 and 4.
    pp. (1), 2, 3. "Remarks | upon | the alleged use of Strychnine." Dated on p. 3 : May 6, 1852.
    pp. (4)–8. A long list of Testimonials.
(2) W. Mott.   2 pp.   Same as Part 1.
(3) John Cassell's Publications.   4 pp. unnumbered.
    p. (1) "Publications and Works | issued by | John Cassell."
    p. (3) "The Illustrated Magazine of Art."

PLATES (ONE)
(No. 18) "The Young Man of the name of Guppy" (p. 283).
    The explanation of the *accident* to Plate No. 17, to face page 261, "Visitors to the Shooting Gallery," is, that "Phiz" made a *mistake* by introducing Grandmother Smallweed into the etching, instead of the fair "Judy."   In consequence it was cancelled, and never published.   The Dexter collection contains a proof of this cancelled plate, which is probably unique and is here reproduced in facsimile.   When the plate, as issued in the next number, is compared with the cancelled etching it will be seen that, in addition to correcting the *mistake*, a change was made in the inscription.

TEXT, WITH HEADING
"Chapter XXVI."   pp. 257–288.

PART 10.

FRONT WRAPPER (OUTSIDE)
Same as No. V. except "No. X.   December."

FRONT WRAPPER (INSIDE)
Edmiston & Son.   Lower half of page : "The Versatio."

CHARLES DICKENS.

BACK WRAPPER (INSIDE)
"Christmas." (E. Moses & Son).

ADVERTISEMENTS (FRONT)
"Bleak House Advertiser." 16 pp. numbered (1)–16.

    p. (1) "No. X.—December, 1852."
    p. 2. "Second Edition of ' Esmond.' "
    p. 3. "New and Popular Books | for the Young."
    p. 4. "Messrs. Addey and Co."
    p. 5. Continuation of Addey's List.
    p. 6. "Sure Guide to Domestic Happiness."
    p. 7. "New Works this Season."
    p. 8. "Christmas Gifts."
    p. 9. ($\frac{1}{2}$ col.) "Colburn & Co.'s | New Publications."
    p. 10. "Punch's Almanack | for 1853 will be published . . ."
    p. 11. ($\frac{1}{2}$ col.) "Working Tailors' Joint | Stock Company."
    p. 12. "Children's Frocks, Coats, & Pelisses."
    p. 13. "Prize Medal." At foot : "Ford's Eureka Shirts."
    p. 14. "Pulvermacher's." At foot : "Keatings."
    p. 15. "Christmas." (Rowlands).
    p. 16. "Poulson & Compy."

Bradbury and Evans Announcements. 4 pp. unnumbered.

    p. (1) "This day is published . . . | The Second Volume | of
        | A Child's History of England."
    p. (3) "Miscellaneous Works."

Slip : (to follow plates). "On the 18th of December will be published
. . . | An extra Number | of | Household Words ; " Verso blank.
White paper. ($4\frac{5}{8}'' \times 5\frac{1}{2}''$).

ADVERTISEMENTS (BACK)

(1) "New and Important Works | published by George
    Cox . . ." 12 pp. all numbered, except pp. (1) and (7).
    pp. 2 & 3. "List of Maps."
    pp. 4, 5, 6. "Important Works | just published."
    pp. (7)–10. "Knight's | 160 Copyright | Shilling Volumes."
    pp. 11, 12. "Knight's Pictorial Works."

(2) W. Mott. 2 pp. Same as Part 1.

(3) Waterlow & Sons. 2 pp. Same as Part 8.

(4) "New Sporting Newspaper. | The Field." 1 leaf,
    verso blank.

(5) Slip :—Crochet Cotton. Same as Part 8.

PLATES (THREE)
  (No. 17) "Visitors at the Shooting Gallery." (p. 261).
  (No. 19) "Nurse and Patient." (p. 309).
  (No. 20) "The appointed time." (p. 320).
TEXT, WITH HEADING
  "Chapter XXX." pp. 289–320.

PART 11.

FRONT WRAPPER (OUTSIDE)
  Same as No. V. except "No. XI. January."

FRONT WRAPPER (INSIDE)
  "William S. Burton's." Below second ruling : "Lamps
  of all Sorts and Patterns."

BACK WRAPPER (INSIDE)
  "The Story of the Season." (E. Moses & Son).

ADVERTISEMENTS (FRONT)
  "Bleak House Advertiser." 16 pp. numbered (1)–16.
      p. (1) "No. XI.—January, 1853."
      p. 2. "Notice. | Re-Issue of Lives of the Queens of | England."
      p. 3. "Crown 8vo. . . . | Mr. Dickens's Christmas Books."
      p. 4. "A Christmas Tale, by Frank Fairlegh."
      p. 5. "13, Great Marlborough-Street, Jan., 1853."
      p. 6. ($\frac{1}{2}$ col.) "Grace Aguilar's Works."
      p. 7. "Works by Charles Dickens."
      p. 8. "Illustrated Works Suitable for Presents."
      p. 9. "Works in Preparation."
      p. 10. ($\frac{1}{2}$ col.) "British College of Health."
      p. 11. "The New Year."
      p. 12. "Children's Frocks, Coats, & Pelisses."
      p. 13. "Prize Medal." Same as Part 10.
      p. 14. "Pulvermacher's." At foot : "Soyer's Relish."
      p. 15. "City of Glasgow."
      p. 16. "Poulson & Compy."
  Slip : (to follow "Advertiser"). "On January 31st will be published
      . . . | Handley Cross ;" verso blank. Pink paper. ($4\frac{5}{8}'' \times 5\frac{1}{2}''$).
  Slip : (to follow plates). "Household Words" ; with the seventh
      line reading : "A Round of Stories by the Christmas Fire." Verso
      blank. Dark green paper. ($4\frac{5}{8}'' \times 5\frac{1}{2}''$).

CHARLES DICKENS.

ADVERTISEMENTS (BACK)

(1) Slip :—"New Sporting Newspaper. | ... | The Field."
Verso blank. (4⅜″ × 5½″).

(2) "New Works | Published this Season." 16 pp. un-
numbered.

The foot of each page has the imprint of the publishers : "Arthur
Hall, Virtue, & Co. ; 25, Paternoster Row."

(3) Slip :—"Kaye's Worsdell's Pills, | The best Family
Medicine." Last page : "Kaye's Infant's Restorative."
4 pp. numbered (1)–(4). (7¼″ × 4¾″).

(4) Waterlow & Sons. 2 pp. Same as Part 8.

(5) W. Mott. 2 pp. Same as Part 1.

(6) Slip :—"Use | Marsland, Son, & Co.'s | . . . | Griffin
Crochet Cotton." Verso : "On January 1st, 1853."
Printed both sides in blue, on white paper. (7¼″ × 5½″).

PLATES (Two)

(No. 21) "The old man of the name of Tulkinghorn."
(p. 331).

(No. 22) "Mr. Smallweed breaks the pipe of peace."
(p. 338).

TEXT, WITH HEADING

"Chapter XXXIII." pp. 321–352.

PART 12.

FRONT WRAPPER (OUTSIDE)
Same as Part V. except "No. XII. February."

FRONT WRAPPER (INSIDE)
Edmiston & Son. Same as Part 10.

BACK WRAPPER (INSIDE)
"A few Claims." (E. Moses & Son).

ADVERTISEMENTS (FRONT)
"Bleak House Advertiser." 16 pp. numbered (1)–16.

p. (1) "No. XII.—February, 1853."
p. 2. "Handley Cross."
p. 3. "T. Bosworth's New Publications."
pp. 4, 5, 6. "Books published by | Bradbury and Evans."

p. 7. (½ col.) "Hurst & Blackett." Address above.
p. 8. "Just published. . . . "Spirits of the Past."
p. 9. "The Registered Needle Envelope and Epitome."
p. 10. (½ col.) "Rodgers's Improved Shirt."
p. 11. "Important from Australia."
p. 12. "Children's Frocks, Coats, & Pelisses."
p. 13. "Prize Medal."
p. 14. "Pulvermacher's." Below : "Banks of Deposit," etc.
p. 15. "National Provident Institution."
p. 16. "Poulson & Compy."
Slip : (to follow plates). "Household Words." Issue No. 3.

ADVERTISEMENTS (BACK)

(1) W. Mott. 2 pp. Same as Part 1.

(2) "Established 1841. | . . . | Partridge and Cozens."
4 pp. unnumbered. Cream tinted paper.

(3) Waterlow & Sons. 2 pp. Same as Part 8.

(4) Slip :—Crochet Cotton. Similar to Part 11 ; verso
begins : "New Work ! ! ! | Just Published, Part II. of
| Marsland's Manual." Printed in black. (6½″ × 5″).

PLATES (TWO)

(No. 23) "Lady Dedlock in the Wood." (p. 357).

(No. 24) "The Ghost's Walk." (p. 361). Dark plate.
No. 24 is the first of the dark plates, and was etched in duplicate.

TEXT, WITH HEADING
"Chapter XXXVI." pp. 353–384.

PART 13.

FRONT WRAPPER (OUTSIDE)
Same as No. V. except "No. XIII. March."

FRONT WRAPPER (INSIDE)
"William S. Burton's." Below third ruling : "Cutlery,
Warranted."

BACK WRAPPER (INSIDE)
"March Gales." (E. Moses & Son).

ADVERTISEMENTS (FRONT)
"Bleak House Advertiser." 16 pp. numbered (1)–16.
p. (1) "No. XIII.—March, 1853."
p. 2. "New Sporting and Family Newspaper."

p. 3. "New Works."   (William Blackwood).
p. 4. "Knight's | Geography of the British Empire."
p. 5. "On the 7th of March . . . | Household Words."
p. 6. (½ col.) "Smith, Elder & Co.'s | New Publications."
p. 7. "Works by Charles Dickens."
p. 8. "This day is published . . . | Wellington."
p. 9. (½ col.) "Sure Guide to Domestic Happiness."
p. 10. "Now first offered . . . | Dr. Williams's Phthisan."
p. 11. "The successful results of the last Half Century."
p. 12. "Children's Frocks, Coats, & Pelisses."
p. 13. "Prize Medal."
p. 14. "British College of Health."
p. 15. "The Best is the Cheapest."   (Phillips).
p. 16. "Poulson & Compy."

Slip : (to follow "Advertiser"). "On 28th February was published . . . | Handley Cross ;" verso, blank. Pink paper. ($4\frac{5}{8}'' \times 5\frac{1}{2}''$).

Slip : (to follow plates). "Household Words." Issue No. 4.

ADVERTISEMENTS (BACK)

(1) Slip :—"Grace Aguilar's Works."   8 pp. unnumbered. ($6\frac{1}{2}'' \times 4\frac{1}{8}''$).

    pp. (1)–(7) Each headed as above.
    p. (8) "Mrs. Crosland's New Domestic Story."

(2) W. Mott. 2 pp. Same as Part 1.

(3) Waterlow & Sons. 2 pp. Same as Part 8.

PLATES (TWO)

(No. 25) "Attorney and Client, fortitude and impatience." (p. 388).

(No. 26) "Sunset in the long Drawing-room at Chesney Wold." (p. 397).   Dark plate.

    No. 26 is the second of the dark plates, and was etched in duplicate.

TEXT, WITH HEADING
"Chapter XXXIX."   pp. 385–416.

PART 14.

FRONT WRAPPER (OUTSIDE)
Same as No. V. except "No. XIV. April."

BLEAK HOUSE.

FRONT WRAPPER (INSIDE)
   Edmiston & Son. Third line from bottom reads:
   "Water Beds on Sale or Hire." No list of agents.

BACK WRAPPER (INSIDE)
   "Prologue to many Changes." (E. Moses & Son).

ADVERTISEMENTS (FRONT)
   "Bleak House Advertiser." 16 pp. numbered (1)–16.
   p. (1) "No. XIV.—April, 1853."
   p. 2. "People's Edition. | Alison's | History of Europe."
   p. 3. Continuation of page 2.
   p. 4. "Works in Preparation." (Arthur Hall, Virtue, & Co.).
   p. 5. "New Sporting Newspaper. | Enlarged to 72 Columns."
   p. 6. "T. Bosworth's New Publications."
   p. 7. "Works by Charles Dickens."
   p. 8. "The | Leader."
   p. 9. ($\frac{1}{2}$ col.) "New Publications." (Chapman & Hall).
   p. 10. "Works on Gardening and Botany."
   p. 11. ($\frac{1}{2}$ col.) "The Working Tailors' | Joint Stock Company."
   p. 12. "Children's Frocks, Coats, & Pelisses."
   p. 13. "Prize Medal."
   p. 14. "The Teeth and Breath." (Rowlands).
   p. 15. "Opera Glasses."
   p. 16. "Poulson & Compy."
   Dedicated, by Permission, to Her Majesty. | . . . | No. 1 of the
      | English Cyclopædia." 2 pp., second page numbered.
   Slip : (to follow plates). "Household Words." Issue No. 4.

ADVERTISEMENTS (BACK)

(1) Slip :—"Ali Ahmed's | Treasures of the Desert." 8 pp.
    numbered (1, 2)–8. Printed on thin paper, either light
    or dark green. ($7\frac{1}{2}'' \times 4\frac{3}{4}''$).

(2) "New Geographical and Educational Works, | pub-
    lished by W. and A. K. Johnston." 2 pp. unnumbered.
    Pink, salmon, or yellow paper.

(3) Waterlow & Sons. 2 pp. Same as Part 8.

(4) W. Mott. Differs from Part 1, in having Tea-spoon
    immediately under heading of page 1. 2 pp.

(5) Norton's Camomile Pills. 4 pp. Same as Part 1.

297

(6) Slip :—2 leaves, the outer sides only printed. Front :
"Frank Merryweather." Back : "The Two Widows."
Printed in blue, on brown paper. ($4\frac{5}{8}'' \times 5\frac{1}{2}''$).

(7) Slip :—"Use | Marsland, Son, & Co.'s | . . . | Griffin
Crochet Cotton. | New Work ! ! ! Now Ready ! |
Part 1 & 2 | . . . | Marsland's Manual." Verso, with
bird design, and line of text along top and two lines
down each side. Printed both sides in black, on white
paper. ($7\frac{1}{2}'' \times 5''$).

PLATES (TWO)
(No. 27) "Sir Leicester Dedlock." (p. 424).
(No. 28) "Tom all alone's." (p. 442). Dark plate.
No. 28 is the third of the dark plates, and was etched in duplicate.

TEXT, WITH HEADING
"Chapter XLIII." pp. 417–448.

PART 15.

FRONT WRAPPER (OUTSIDE)
Same as No. V. except "No. XV. May."

FRONT WRAPPER (INSIDE)
"William S. Burton's." Below second ruling : "Gas
Chandeliers and Brackets."

BACK WRAPPER (INSIDE)
"Spring and Summer Dress." (E. Moses & Son).

ADVERTISEMENTS (FRONT)
"Bleak House Advertiser." 12 pp. numbered (1)–12.
p. (1) "No. XV.—May, 1853."
p. 2. "Dedicated . . . | English Cyclopædia."
p. 3. " ' Le Follet ' for May."
p. 4. (½ col.) "Messrs. Hurst & Blackett."
p. 5. "New Works." The first : "Handley Cross."
p. 6. (½ col.) "Important Announcement." (Joseph Gillott).
p. 7. "The successful results of the last Half Century."
p. 8. "Ali Ahmed's Treasures of the Desert . . ."
p. 9. "Prize Medal." At foot : "Doudney's."
p. 10. "Children's Frocks," etc. At foot : "Mechi."
p. 11. "Opera Glasses." Below : "Clerical, Medical," etc.
p. 12. "Poulson & Compy."
Slip : (to follow plates). "Household Words." Issue No. 4.

ADVERTISEMENTS (BACK)

(1) Slip :—"The Village Pastor." 8 pp. each numbered at foot. Bound in cream wrappers ; front reads : "A Descriptive Sketch | by | Mrs. S. C. Hall, | of the Engraving | of the | Village Pastor." Inside of back wrapper printed with subscription form. (6¼"×4").

(2) "Partridge and Cozens." 4 pp. Same as Part 12.

(3) W. Mott. 2 pp. Same as Part 14.

(4) "Mayall's | Daguerreotype Portrait | Galleries." 4 pp. numbered on pages 2 & 3. (7½"×4⅝").

PLATES (TWO)

(No. 29) "A new meaning in the Roman." (p. 470). Dark plate.

(No. 30) "Friendly behaviour of Mr. Bucket." (p. 477).

No. 29 is the fourth of the dark plates, and was etched in duplicate.

TEXT, WITH HEADING

"Chapter XLVII." pp. 449–480.

PART 16.

FRONT WRAPPER (OUTSIDE)
Same as No. V. except "No. XVI. June."

FRONT WRAPPER (INSIDE)
Edmiston & Son. Last line : "Calcutta—Colvin & Co."

BACK WRAPPER (INSIDE)
"Description." (E. Moses & Son).

ADVERTISEMENTS (FRONT)
"Bleak House Advertiser." 12 pp. numbered (1)–12.

p. (1) "No. XVI.—June, 1853."
p. 2. (½ col.) "Notice . . . | Burke's Peerage and Baronetage . . ."
p. 3. "Smith, Elder, & Co.'s New Publications."
p. 4. "Now ready . . . | Part I. of the | English Cyclopædia."
p. 5. "Freeholds for all Classes in all Countries."
p. 6. (½ col.) "Royal Asylum of St. Ann's | Society."
p. 7. "Clerical, Medical, and General Life . . ."
p. 8. "Summer." At foot : "Cooper & Fryer."
p. 9. "Prize Medal." Same as Part 15.

p. 10. "Children's Frocks," etc. At foot : "Phillips & Company."
p. 11. "Opera Glasses." Below : "Breidenbach's."
p. 12. "Poulson & Compy."
Slip : (to follow plates). "Household Words." Issue No. 5.

ADVERTISEMENTS (BACK)

(1) Slip:—"Grace Aguilar's Works." 8 pp. Same as Part 13.
(2) Clarke, Beeton, and Co.'s Publications. 8 pp. unnumbered.

pp. (1, 2) "The | Anti-Slavery Reporter."
p. (3) "Works on American Slavery."
p. (5) "Readable Books."
p. (7) "The Penny Cyclopædia."

(3) Slip :—"Ladies ! ! Ask for | Marsland, Son, & Co.'s
| Celebrated | Crochet and Guipure Cotton." Verso :
"New Work ! ! ! | Just published | Marsland's
Manual." Printed both sides in black, on white paper.
($7\frac{1}{2}'' \times 5''$).

PLATES (TWO)

(No. 31) "Light." (p. 493).
(No. 32) "Shadow." (p. 512). Dark plate.

No. 32 is the fifth of the dark plates, and was etched in duplicate.

TEXT, WITH HEADING

"Chapter L." pp. 481–512.

PART 17.

FRONT WRAPPER (OUTSIDE)

Same as No. V. except "No. XVII. July."

FRONT WRAPPER (INSIDE)

"William S. Burton's." Below first ruling : "Baths and
Toilette Ware."

BACK WRAPPER (INSIDE)

"Table-Moving." (E. Moses & Son).

ADVERTISEMENTS (FRONT)

"Bleak House Advertiser." 12 pp. numbered (1)–12.

p. (1) "No. XVII.—July, 1853."
p. 2. "Works by Charles Dickens."

p. 3. "Publishing . . . | The | English Cyclopædia."
p. 4. (½ col.) "Hurst & Blackett."
p. 5. "New Works." The first : "Handley Cross."
p. 6. (½ col.) "The Toilet of Beauty . . ."
p. 7. Same as Part 16. (Clerical Medical).
p. 8. "Summer." At foot : "The Gentleman's Real Head of
     Hair."
p. 9. "Prize Medal." At foot : "Cooper & Fryer."
p. 10. "Children's Frocks," etc. At foot : "Breidenbach's."
p. 11. "National Provident Institution."
p. 12. "Poulson & Compy."
Slip : (to follow plates). "Household Words." Issue No. 5.

ADVERTISEMENTS (BACK)

(1) Norton's Camomile Pills. 4 pp. Same as Part 1.

(2) W. Mott. 2 pp. Same as Part 14.

(3) Slip :—"The Largest Newspaper in Europe. | . . . |
    The Field." Verso, blank. Green paper. ($7\frac{1}{2}'' \times 4\frac{7}{8}''$).

PLATES (TWO)

(No. 33) "Mrs. Bagnet returns from her expedition."
    (p. 530).

(No. 34) "The lonely figure." (p. 544). Dark plate.
    No. 34 is the sixth of the dark plates, and was etched in duplicate.

TEXT, WITH HEADING
"Chapter LIV." pp. 513–544.

PART 18.

FRONT WRAPPER (OUTSIDE)
Same as No. V. except "No. XVIII. August."

FRONT WRAPPER (INSIDE)
Edmiston & Son. Same as Part 16.

BACK WRAPPER (INSIDE)
"A Sporting Party." (E. Moses & Son).

ADVERTISEMENTS (FRONT)
"Bleak House Advertiser." 8 pp. numbered (1)–8.
    p. (1) "No. XVIII.—August, 1853."
    p. 2. "On the 30th of July . . . | The English Cyclopædia."
    p. 3. "New Works." The first : "The Vegetable Kingdom."

p. 4. (½ col.) "Chubb's Fire-proof Safes and Locks."
p. 5. "Ladies Travelling." (Rowlands).
p. 6. "Children's Frocks, Coats, & Pelisses."
p. 7. "Prize Medal."
p. 8. "For the Seaside, the Road, the Rail . . ." (Poulson).
Slip : (to follow plates). "Household Words." Issue No. 5.

ADVERTISEMENTS (BACK)

(1) Slip :—"People's Edition | of | Alison's History of Europe." Verso, blank. Light-blue paper. (4¼″ × 5⅜″).

(2) Slip :—"Treasure of the Desert." Each page headed as this. 8 pp. numbered (1)–8. Thin, white paper. (7⅛″ × 4¾″).

(3) W. Mott. 2 pp. Same as Part 14.

PLATES (TWO)

(No. 35) "The Night." (p. 547). Dark plate.
(No. 36) "The Morning." (p. 576). Dark plate.

These plates are the seventh and eighth respectively of the dark plates, and both were etched in duplicate.

TEXT, WITH HEADING
"Chapter LVII." pp. 545–576.

PARTS 19 AND 20.

FRONT WRAPPER (OUTSIDE)
Same as No. V. except "Nos. XIX. & XX. September. Price 2s."

FRONT WRAPPER (INSIDE)
"William S. Burton's." Below first ruling : "The Perfect Substitute for Silver."

BACK WRAPPER (INSIDE)
"The Closing of the Story." (E. Moses & Son).

ADVERTISEMENTS (FRONT)
"Bleak House Advertiser." 20 pp. numbered (1)–20.

p. (1) "Nos. XIX. & XX.—September, 1853."
p. 2. "Messrs. Blackwood & Son's | Recent Publications."
p. 3. "Cheap Editions." (Chapman and Hall).
p. 4. "For the use of Travellers on the Continent . . ."

BLEAK HOUSE.

p. 5. "Messrs. Southgate and Barrett."
p. 6. "Publishing in Monthly Parts . . . | Handley Cross ;"
p. 7. "Publishing . . . | The English Cyclopædia."
p. 8. "Ingram, Cooke, and Co.'s | List of New Books . . ."
p. 9. "Works on Gardening and Botany."
p. 10. "This day . . . | The Provocations of Madame Palissy."
p. 11. "The Book of the Garden."
p. 12. (½ col.) "Hubert's Roseate Powder."
p. 13. (½ col.) "Chubb's Fire-proof Safes and Locks."
p. 14. "The decline of Life."   (Parr's Life Pills).
p. 15. "Diamond Pressed Glass" with cuts of 4 decanters.
p. 16. "Children's Frocks, Coats, & Pelisses."
p. 17. "Prize Medal"; "Kirby Beard & Co."; and "Richard Ford."
p. 18. "Notice of Dividend ; | Bank of Deposit."
p. 19. "Number One, Saint Paul's Churchyard."   (Dakin).
p. 20. "Messrs. Poulson and Co.'s | . . . Pardessus."
Slip : (to precede "Advertiser"). "New Periodical Work . . . | On the 1st of October will be published . . . | No. I. of | The Newcomes." Verso, blank.   Yellow paper.   (4¼" × 5¼").
Slip : (to follow plates). "Household Words."   Issue No. 6.

ADVERTISEMENTS (BACK)

(1) Ransome's Patent Stone Filters.   16 pp. all numbered, except (1), (2) and (16).

   p. (1) "Descriptive Particulars | of | Ransome's Patent Stone Filters."   With woodcut.
   pp. (2)–15. All with running headline : "Ransome's Patent Stone Filters."   With 21 woodcuts.
   p. (16) "The Patent Iris Fountain."

(2) Slip :—"Works | of | Samuel Warren."   Verso, blank. Light-blue paper.   (4⅛" × 5½").

(3) W. Mott.   2 pp.   Same as Part 14.

(4) John Cassell's Publications.   16 pp.   unnumbered. Thin, white paper.   (8" × 5½").

   p. (1) "Illustrated and other Works | published by | John Cassell, Ludgate-Hill, | London."   With specimen engraving, almost full-page.
   pp. (2–15) All with running headline : "Works published by John Cassell, Ludgate Hill, London."
   p. (16) Same running head, and specimen engraving, full-paged.

CHARLES DICKENS.

PLATES (FOUR)

(No. 37) "Magnanimous conduct of Mr. Guppy." (p. 612).

(No. 38) "The Mausoleum at Chesney Wold." (p. 619). Dark plate.

(No. 39) "Frontispiece." Dark plate.

(No. 40) Vignette Title. Dated 1853.

> Nos. 38 and 39 are the ninth and tenth respectively of the dark plates, and both were etched in duplicate.

TEXT, WITH HEADING

"Chapter LX." pp. 577–624. Imprint at foot of p. 624 : "London : | Bradbury and Evans, Printers, White-friars."

PRELIMINARY LEAVES

Half-title : "Bleak House." Verso, blank. (I. II.).

Title-page : dated 1853. Verso, with imprint as p. 624. (III. IV.). See Illustration.

Dedication : "To my Companions | in the | Guild of Literature and Art." Verso, blank. (V. VI).

"Preface." Dated, "London, | August, 1853." 4 pp. numbered (VII.), VIII. IX. X.

"Contents." 4 pp. numbered (XI.), XII. XIII. XIV.

"List of Plates," with 5-line "Errata." 2 pp. numbered (XV.) XVI.

No. IX. AUGUST. PRICE 1s.

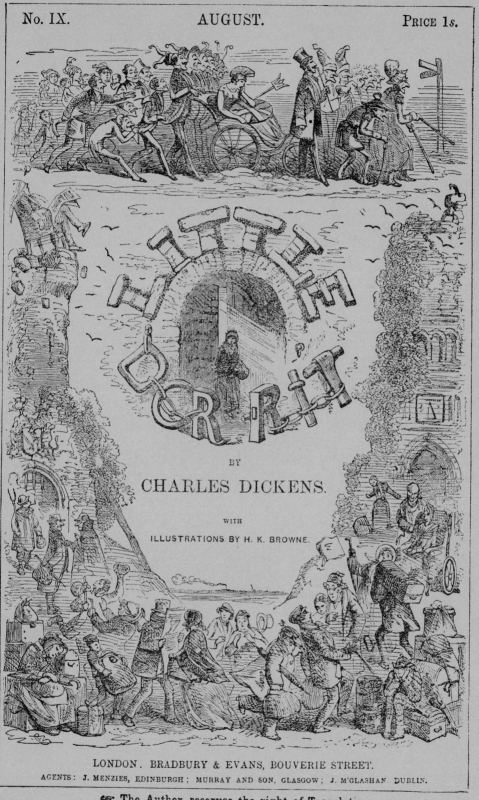

BY

CHARLES DICKENS.

WITH

ILLUSTRATIONS BY H. K. BROWNE.

LONDON. BRADBURY & EVANS, BOUVERIE STREET.
AGENTS: J. MENZIES, EDINBURGH; MURRAY AND SON, GLASGOW; J. M'GLASHAN. DUBLIN.

☞ The Author reserves the right of Translation.

The Front Wrapper to the original edition of "Little Dorrit,"
as published in 19/20 monthly parts, 1855-1857.

LITTLE DORRIT.

BY

CHARLES DICKENS.

WITH ILLUSTRATIONS BY H. K. BROWNE.

LONDON:
BRADBURY AND EVANS, 11, BOUVERIE STREET.
1857.

Little Dorrit

in

19/20 Monthly Parts

December, 1855, to June, 1857.

ORIGINALLY issued in twenty numbers, bound in nineteen monthly parts, price one shilling per number, except the last two (19 and 20) which formed a double-number, priced at two shillings. Blue paper wrappers were again employed; the design for the front being executed by Hablot K. Browne, who also etched the forty plates. Circulation figures were abnormal, equal almost to the record-breaking numbers of "Bleak House."

PLATES.

Of the forty plates which are comprised in the book, thirteen were etched vertically, and twenty-seven horizontally. They include eight "dark" plates, all of which were etched horizontally, and seven of these were duplicated, the exception being No. 37, "Damocles." The seven "dark" plates in duplicate are :

Part 1.	Plate No. 1.	The Birds in the Cage.
„ 2.	„ „ 4.	The Room with the Portrait.
„ 3.	„ „ 6.	Making off.
„ 4.	„ „ 8.	Little Dorrit's Party.
„ 5.	„ „ 10.	The Ferry.
„ 7.	„ „ 13.	Visitors at the Works.
„ 8.	„ „ 16.	Floating Away.

U 2

In addition, the two plates to Part 11 were also etched in duplicate, so that a total of forty-nine separate steels were employed in the printing of the forty illustrations.

TEXT.

Very few points of early issue can be noted, the one outstanding being that mentioned in the collation to Part 15.

ADVERTISEMENTS.

The "Little Dorrit Advertiser," as usual, appears in each part, and excepting Parts 1 and 16, is uniformly of 12 pages. Each page is headed "Advertisements," and fully paginated. Only three slip insets are essential in the front. At the back, fifty-seven individual insets and slips are required in the collation of the nineteen parts, each being represented by one or more.

FRONT WRAPPERS.

Apart from the essential change in "Part No." and month of issue, no variation of type-setting occurs on the outside front cover. The inner side is used for the advertisement of Edmiston & Son, which appeared in every part of the series, although the arrangement of the matter has six changes, details of which are noted in the collation for each individual monthly number.

BACK WRAPPERS.

These were printed with the advertisements of two tradesmen : William S. Burton, Ironmonger, occupying the outer side, and W. G. Taylor, Outfitter and Haberdasher, the inside. With most of the covers, the "make-up" at first glance appears uniform, but actually the arrangement of textual matter differs considerably. These differences are by no means easy to memorise, or to detect in a casual scrutiny, but with the assistance of the appended table, checking and collating will be greatly simplified.

LITTLE DORRIT.

		Outside (W. S. Burton).	Inside (Taylor).
Part.	Para-graph.	Heading to Paragraph.	Top-line.
1	Second	Fenders, Stoves and Fire-Irons.	Babies' White Cash-mere.
2	Second	The Perfect Substitute for Silver.	do. do.
3	Second	Hot Air, Gas, Vesta, Joyce's Stoves.	do. do.
4	Second	The Best Show of Iron Bedsteads.	Babies' Berceau-nettes.
	Third	The Perfect Substitute for Silver.	
5	Second	The Best Show of Iron Bedsteads.	do. do.
	Third	Paper Mâché and Iron Tea-Trays.	
6	Second	Bedsteads, Baths, and Lamps.	do. do.
	Third	Tea Urns, of London Make Only.	
	Fourth	Paper Mâché and Iron Tea-Trays.	
7	Second	Bedsteads, Baths, and Lamps.	do. do.
	Third	Tea Urns, of London Make Only.	
	Fourth	The Perfect Substitute for Silver.	
8	Second	Bedsteads, Bedding, and Furni-ture.	do. do.
	Third	Bath and Toilette Ware.	
9 &10	Second	The Best Show of Iron Bedsteads.	Similar to Part 4, with extra line—"Black Merino Habits for
	Third	The Perfect Substitute for Silver.	Little Girls."
11		(Entire page as Part 8).	do. do.
12		(Illustration of Fireplace).	do. do.
13	Second	Lampes à Moderateur. 4 lines only in First Paragraph.	do. do.
14	Second	Lampes à Moderateur. 6 lines in First Paragraph.	Identical Text to Part 9, but two paras. set in oblong ruled frame.
15		(Illustration of Bedstead).	do. do.
16	Second	Fenders, Stoves, and Fire-Irons.	do. do.
	Third	Dish Covers and Hot Water Dishes.	
17	Second	Fenders, Stoves and Fire-Irons.	do. do.
	Third	The Perfect Substitute for Silver.	
18	Second	Cutlery Warranted.	do. do.
19	Second	Beds, Mattresses, and Bedsteads.	do. do.

CHARLES DICKENS.

PART 1.

FRONT WRAPPER (OUTSIDE)
"No. I.   December.   Price 1s. | Little | Dorrit | by | Charles Dickens. | with | Illustrations by H. K. Browne. | London :   Bradbury & Evans, Bouverie Street. | Agents : J. Menzies, Edinburgh ; Murray and Son, Glasgow ;   J. M'Glashan, Dublin. | (Pointing hand) The Author reserves the right of Translation."

FRONT WRAPPER (INSIDE)
"For the Crimea. | (Woodcut) | Edmiston's | Crimean Outfit, | £18 18s."

ADVERTISEMENTS (FRONT)
"Little Dorrit Advertiser."   32 pp. numbered (1)–32.

    p. (1) "No. I.—December, 1855."
    p. 2. "New and Popular Gift and Prize Books."
    p. 3. "Grace Aguilar's Works."
    p. 4. "Messrs. Hurst and Blackett."
    p. 5. "New Work by the Rev. Thomas Guthrie, D.D."
    p. 6. "Household Words."
    p. 7. "Gifts for Christmas, | in Elegant Bindings."
  pp. 8, 9. "Waverley Novels."   (p. 9 is a specimen page).
    p. 10. "Price Sixpence. | ... | The Idler."
    p. 11. "Chapman & Hall's Publications."
    p. 12. "Messrs. Blackwood & Sons' | New Publications."
    p. 13. "Forthcoming Works."   (John Murray).
    p. 14. "Smith, Elder, & Co.'s | New Publications."
    p. 15. ($\frac{1}{2}$ col.) "Works by the Rev. John Cumming, D.D."
    p. 16. ($\frac{1}{2}$ col.) "New Poem . . . | The Poetry of Creation."
    p. 17. "Crystal Palace, 1855."
    p. 18. "Fireside Reading."
    p. 19. ($\frac{1}{2}$ col.) "A Gift Book for Christmas . . ."
    p. 20. "Profusely illustrated . . . | Treasures in Needlework."
    p. 21. "The Cheapest, Largest . . ." (Lloyd's Newspaper).
    p. 22. "Boosey's Musical Library."
    p. 23. "Important to Merchants. | Letter Copying Ink."
    p. 24. "Christmas Presents."   (Rowlands).
    p. 25. "Travellers' and Marine | Insurance Company."
    p. 26. "Notice of Removal. | W. Callaghan."
    p. 27. "The best Food for Children . . ."
    p. 28. "The Closing of the French Industrial Exhibition."

p. 29. "The Caspiato, or Folding Bonnet."
p. 30. (½ col.) "James Lewis's Iodine Soap."
p. 31. "Jay's Maison de Nouveautés."
p. 32. "Dr. De Jongh's | . . . Cod Liver Oil."

"List of Books | published by Bradbury and Evans."
Dated on first and last pages : December, 1855. 16 pp.
numbered (1)–16. Headline as above, runs through
pp. 2 to 15. Thin line border round each page.

ADVERTISEMENTS (BACK)

(1) "Norton's Camomile Pills." 4 pp. numbered (1), 2, 3, (4).

p. 2. First word in first column   ..   "stomach"
Last   ,,   ,, second ,,   ..   "their"
p. 3. Last   ,,   ,, first   ,,   ..   "burden"
First   ,,   ,, second ,,   ..   "thus"
p. 4. "A Clear Complexion. | Godfrey's Extract of Elder
Flowers."

(2) James Gilbert's Publications. 4 pp. unnumbered.

pp. (1, 2) "Ince's . . . | Outlines | of | English History."
p. (3)   "Ince's . . . | Outlines | of | French History."
p. (4)   "Ince's . . . | Outlines | of | General Knowledge."

(3) "The National Review." 4 pp. numbered (1)–4. Thin
paper. Imprint of William Tyler on page 4.

(4) Slip :—"Price One Shilling, Monthly. | No. 1 of | The
Train ;" verso blank. Green paper. ($4\frac{1}{2}'' \times 5\frac{1}{4}''$).

(5) Slip :—"Theatre Royal, | Covent Garden, | Winter
Season, 1855-6. Verso blank. Yellow paper. ($7\frac{1}{2}'' \times 5''$).

(6) "John Cassell's | Works and Publications, | published
by | W. Kent & Co." 16 pp., each page numbered in
outer bottom corner, 1–16. Running headline along
top of pages 2–16 : "Works published by W. Kent
& Co., Paternoster Row, London."

PLATES (TWO)

(No. 1) "The Birds in the Cage." (p. 2). Dark plate.

(No. 2) "Under the Microscope." (p. 20).

No. 1 is the first of the dark plates, and was etched in duplicate.

CHARLES DICKENS.

TEXT, WITH HEADING
  "Little Dorrit. | In Two Books. | Chapter I." pp. (1)–32.
  Page (1) is not numbered. There are only two other instances
  throughout the book with no pagination, viz.:—Part 4, page 97 ;
  Part 11, page 323.

PART 2.

FRONT WRAPPER (OUTSIDE)
  Same as No. I. except "No. II. January."

FRONT WRAPPER (INSIDE)
  "(Woodcut) | Edmiston's | Crimean Outfit, £18 18s." The
  same as Part 1, without first line.

ADVERTISEMENTS (FRONT)
  "Little Dorrit Advertiser." 12 pp. numbered (1)–12.
  p. (1) "No. 2.—January, 1856."
  p. 2. "No more Pills, nor any other Medicine."
  p. 3. "Travellers' and Marine Insurance Company."
  p. 4. "Commencement of the Third Division of the English
      Cyclopædia."
  p. 5. "Gifts for Christmas."
  p. 6. "Just published . . . | The Poetry of Creation."
  p. 7. (½ col.) "Christmas Book, by Frank Fairlegh."
  p. 8. "The best Food for Children . . ."
  p. 9. "Royal Insurance Company."
  p. 10. (¼ col.) "Piesse & Lubin." (in circular frame).
  p. 11. "Jay's Maison de Nouveautés."
  p. 12. "Dr. De Jongh's." Ninth line : "Testimonial from
      Arthur H. Hassell."

ADVERTISEMENTS (BACK)
  (1) Slip:—"On 1st of January, 1856 . . . | Popular | History
      of England :" verso, blank. Pink paper. (4½" × 5½").
  (2) Jarrold & Sons' Announcements. 8 pp. unnumbered.
      p. (1) "Elementary Works, | by William Martin."
      p. (3) "A Guide to the Knowledge of Life."
      p. (5) "Helps to Bible Students . . ."
      p. (7) "Approved Educational Works."
  (3) Slip :—"Important Commercial Works for 1856. | The
      | Desk Directory | 1856." 2 pp. Yellow, blue or
      pink paper. (6" × 5½").

312

(4) "Pictures and Statues . . . | The Art-Journal." 2 pp. unnumbered. White or pink paper.

(5) "The Eclectic Review." Dated on last page: January 21st, 1856. Page 3: "Sharpe's London Magazine." 4 pp. unnumbered. Pages 1 & 4 are printed in blue, on rice paper.

PLATES (TWO)

(No. 3) "Mr. Flintwinch mediates as a friend of the Family." (p. 37.)

(No. 4) "The Room with the Portrait." (p. 40). Dark plate.
No. 4 is the second of the dark plates, and was etched in duplicate.

TEXT, WITH HEADING
"Chapter V." pp. 33–64.

PART 3.

FRONT WRAPPER (OUTSIDE)
Same as No. I. except "No. III. February."

FRONT WRAPPER (INSIDE)
Same as No. II.

ADVERTISEMENTS (FRONT)
"Little Dorrit Advertiser." 12 pp. numbered (1)–12.

p. (1) "No. 3.—February, 1856."
p. 2. "Mr. Thackeray's Collected Works."
p. 3. "Medicine Chests."
p. 4. ($\frac{1}{2}$ col.) "The New Novels."
p. 5. "The Popular | History of England."
p. 6. "Now ready . . . | New and Choice Books." (Mudie's).
p. 7. "Metallic Pens for all Writers."
p. 8. "The best Food for Children . . ."
p. 9. "New Label." (Rowlands).
p. 10. ($\frac{1}{2}$ col.) "Notice of Dividend. | Bank of Deposit."
p. 11. "Jay's Maison de Nouveautés."
p. 12. "Dr. De Jongh's." Seventh line: "Opinion of A. B. Granville."

ADVERTISEMENTS (BACK)
Norton's Camomile Pills. 4 pp. Same as Part 1, except:

p. 3. Last word in first column . . . . "as-"
First „ „ second „ . . . . "sist"

PLATES (TWO)
  (No. 5) "Little Mother." (p. 73).
  (No. 6) "Making Off." (p. 96). Dark plate.
      No. 6 is the third of the dark plates, and was etched in duplicate.

TEXT, WITH HEADING
  "Chapter IX." pp. 65–96.

PART 4.

FRONT WRAPPER (OUTSIDE)
  Same as No. I. except "No. IV. March."

FRONT WRAPPER (INSIDE)
  Same as No. II.

ADVERTISEMENTS (FRONT)
  "Little Dorrit Advertiser." 12 pp. numbered (1)–12.
      p. (1) "No. 4.—March, 1856."
      p. 2. "Travellers' and Marine | Insurance Company."
      p. 3. "Medicine Chests."
      p. 4. "Household Words." Contents of Part 71.
      p. 5. "Now ready . . . | Popular | History of England."
      p. 6. "This day . . . | A Manual | of | British Butterflies . . ."
      p. 7. (½ col.) "New Works & New Editions."
      p. 8. "Politics, Literature, . . . | The | Leader."
      p. 9. "The best Food for Children . . ."
      p. 10. "Bank of Deposit." At foot: "Summer's Cough . . .
          Lozenges."
      p. 11. "Jay's Maison de Nouveautés."
      p. 12. "Dr. De Jongh's." Below: "Parasols."

ADVERTISEMENTS (BACK)
  (1) Slip :—"A New and Beautiful Story. | . . . | Nellie of
      Truro :" 2 pp. unnumbered. (7½″ × 5″).
  (2) "Price One Shilling, Monthly. | The | Train." Verso :
      "Opinions of the Press." 2 pp. numbered on second
      page. Green paper.
  (3) "Mr. Henry Mayhew's New Work. | The | Great
      World of London." This front page is a woodcut
      design in facsimile of the monthly wrapper. 4 pp.,
      numbered on third page only. Yellow paper.

PLATES (TWO)

(No. 7) "Mr. F's Aunt is conducted into retirement." (p. 114).

(No. 8) "Little Dorrit's Party." (p. 128). Dark plate.
No. 8 is the fourth of the dark plates, and was etched in duplicate.

TEXT, WITH HEADING
"Chapter XII." pp. (97)–128.

PART 5.

FRONT WRAPPER (OUTSIDE)
Same as No. I. except "No. V. April."

FRONT WRAPPER (INSIDE)
Same as No. II.

ADVERTISEMENTS (FRONT)
"Little Dorrit Advertiser." 12 pp. numbered (1)–12.
p. (1) "No. 5.—April, 1856."
p. 2. "Travellers' and Marine." (as Part 4).
p. 3. "Medicine Chests." (as Part 4).
p. 4. ($\frac{1}{2}$ col.) "The New Novels."
p. 5. ($\frac{1}{2}$ col.) "New Serial."
p. 6. "In a few days . . . | The Lay of the Stork."
p. 7. "The Cornet-à-Pistons."
p. 8. "(Circular.) | Liverpool, 17th March, 1856." (Roberts).
p. 9. "The best Food for Children . . ."
p. 10. "Bank of Deposit." At foot : "Slack's Nickel Silver."
p. 11. "Jay's | Sponsalia."
p. 12. "Cures (without physic)." (Du Barry).

ADVERTISEMENTS (BACK)

(1) "Distinctive Peculiarities & Superiority | of | Dr. De Jongh's | Light-Brown Cod Liver Oil." 2 pp. unnumbered. Brick-brown paper.

(2) Slip :—"Re-Issue | of | Cassell's Popular Educator." Verso, blank. Blue, orange or yellow paper. ($4\frac{1}{2}'' \times 5\frac{1}{2}''$).

(3) "A Sketch | of the | Political History of the past | Three Years, | in connexion with | The Press News-

paper." Imprint (p. 1) : "London : | Press Office— 110, Strand. | 1856." Imprint on last page : "Saville & Edwards." 16 pp. numbered (1, 2, 3) — 16. ($8\frac{1}{4}'' \times 5\frac{3}{8}''$).

PLATES (TWO)

(No. 9) "Mr. & Mrs. Flintwinch." (p. 134).

(No. 10) "The Ferry." (p. 146). Dark plate.

> No. 10 is the fifth of the dark plates, and was etched in duplicate.

TEXT, WITH HEADING

"Chapter XV." pp. 129–160.

PART 6.

FRONT WRAPPER (OUTSIDE)

Same as No. I. except "No. VI. May."

FRONT WRAPPER (INSIDE)

"Waterproofs | for the Races." (Edmiston & Son).

ADVERTISEMENTS (FRONT)

"Little Dorrit Advertiser." 12 pp. numbered (1)–12.

> p. (1) "No. 6.—May, 1856."
> p. 2. "Travellers' and Marine." (as Parts 4 & 5).
> p. 3. "T. A. Simpson & Co."
> p. 4. ($\frac{1}{2}$ col.) Last advert. on page : "Schweppe's."
> p. 5. "Crystal Palace."
> p. 6. "Doctor Antonio : "
> p. 7. "Bradbury & Evans' | Periodicals for . . . May."
> p. 8. "Salt & Co.'s | India Pale Ale . . ."
> p. 9. "The best Food for Children . . ."
> p. 10. ($\frac{1}{2}$ col.) "Bank of Deposit." At foot : "The | Leader."
> p. 11. "Jay's | Sponsalia."
> p. 12. "Dr. De Jongh's," and "Parasols."

ADVERTISEMENTS (BACK)

(1) "The London | Stereoscopic Company," with woodcut on front page. Pages 3–6 in half-column measure. 8 pp. numbered (1, 2)–8.

(2) "Crystal Palace. | Season 1856. | Programme." 4 pp. numbered (1)–4.

(3) "Englishwoman's | Domestic Magazine." Verso, with woodcut. 2 pp. unnumbered. Brown-tinted paper. ($7\frac{3}{4}'' \times 5\frac{1}{2}''$).

(4) "The | Morisonian Monument," with woodcut of the Monument. At foot of page : "Morison | was the first to Protest against Bleeding, and | the Use of Poisons in Medicine." 2 pp. unnumbered. White or green paper.

(5) "The | American Sugar-Coated Pills." 4 pp. unnumbered."

PLATES (Two)
(No. 11) "The Brothers." (p. 161).
(No. 12) "Miss Dorrit and Little Dorrit." (p. 172).

TEXT, WITH HEADING
"Chapter XIX." pp. 161–192.

PART 7.

FRONT WRAPPER (OUTSIDE)
Same as No. I. except "No. VII. June."

FRONT WRAPPER (INSIDE)
Same as No. VI.

ADVERTISEMENTS (FRONT)
"Little Dorrit Advertiser." 12 pp. numbered (1)–12.
    p. (1) "No. 7.—June, 1856."
    p. 2. "New and Important Serial Publications."
    p. 3. "T. A. Simpson & Co." (as Part 6).
    p. 4. ($\frac{1}{2}$ col.) Last announcement on page, "Zibeline."
    p. 5. "New Works." (Bradbury & Evans).
    p. 6. "Nature-Printed Ferns of Great | Britain."
    p. 7. "New Work by the Author of ' Harry Lorrequer.' "
    p. 8. "Summer." (Rowlands).
    p. 9. "The best Food for Children ..." At foot : "Keating's."
    p. 10. ($\frac{1}{2}$ col.) "Bank of Deposit." At foot : "Slack's."
    pp. 11, 12. Identical with Part 6.

ADVERTISEMENTS (BACK)
(1) Norton's Camomile Pills. 4 pp. Same as Part 3.

(2) "The American | Sugar-Coated Pills." 2 pp. "Cassell's Illustrated History of England." 2 pp. In all, 4 pp. unnumbered.

> This is actually a 4-paged inset, although two distinct firms are partners in it. Being so issued, it is treated here as a single unit.

(3) "The | Morisonian Monument," with woodcut of the Monument. Following the latter, and continuing on pp. 2–4, is an article in half-measure, headed : "Reasons for the Monument : By John Fraser . . ." 4 pp. numbered (1)–4 ; printed in a range of 8 colours.

PLATES (TWO)

(No. 13) "Visitors at the Works." (p. 195). Dark plate.

(No. 14) "The Story of the Princess." (p. 215).

> No. 13 is the sixth of the dark plates, and was etched in duplicate.

TEXT, WITH HEADING
"Chapter XXIII." pp. 193–224.

PART 8.

FRONT WRAPPER (OUTSIDE)
Same as No. I. except "No. VIII. July."

FRONT WRAPPER (INSIDE)
Same as No. VI.

ADVERTISEMENTS (FRONT)
"Little Dorrit Advertiser." 12 pp. numbered (1)–12.

> p. (1) "No. 8.—July, 1856."
> p. 2. "Travellers' and Marine | Insurance Company."
> p. 3. "T. A. Simpson & Co." (as Part 7).
> p. 4. "New and Important Works."
> p. 5. "This day . . . | General Guide to the Crystal Palace. . . ."
> p. 6. "New and Important Serial Publications."
> p. 7. ($\frac{1}{2}$ col.) "Just published . . . | Consumption."
> p. 8. "Young Ladies, Young Gentlemen."
> p. 9. "The best Food for Children . . ."
> p. 10. ($\frac{1}{2}$ col.) "Bank of Deposit." At foot : "Ilkley Wells."
> p. 11. "The Sponsalia."
> p. 12. "The Optical Wonder of the Age."

ADVERTISEMENTS (BACK)

(1) "Dr. De Jongh's | Light Brown | Cod Liver Oil," with imprint of Savill and Edwards on last page. 4 pp. unnumbered. Pink paper.

(2) Slip :—"Photographic Gallery, | 224 Regent Street, London." Page 3 : "Mayall's | Photographic Gallery." 4 pp. unnumbered ; last page blank. $(7\frac{1}{4}'' \times 4\frac{1}{2}'')$.

(3) "The | General Apothecaries' Company." 2 pp., second page numbered.

PLATES (TWO)

(No. 15) "Five and Twenty." (p. 243).
(No. 16) "Floating Away." (p. 250). Dark plate.
    No. 16 is the seventh of the dark plates, and was etched in duplicate.

TEXT, WITH HEADING
"Chapter XXVI." pp. 225–256.

PART 9.

FRONT WRAPPER (OUTSIDE)
Same as No. I. except "No. IX. August."

FRONT WRAPPER (INSIDE)
Same as No. VI. with added line in middle of page :
"Knapsacks for Tourists, 18s. 6d."

ADVERTISEMENTS (FRONT)
"Little Dorrit Advertiser." 12 pp. numbered (1)–12.

    p. (1) "No. 9.—August, 1856."
    p. 2. "No more pills or any other Medicine."
    p. 3. "T. A. Simpson & Co."
    p. 4. "New Descriptive Dictionary of the Indian Islands."
    p. 5. "Household Words." Part 76.
    p. 6. "Tourists and Travellers." (Rowlands).
    p. 7. "The Granby Hotel, | Harrogate."
    p. 8. "Young Ladies, Young Gentlemen."
    pp. 9, 10. Identical with Part 7.
    p. 11. "The Sponsalia."
    p. 12. "Dr. De Jongh's," and "Parasols."

CHARLES DICKENS.

ADVERTISEMENTS (BACK)

(1) Norton's Camomile Pills. 4 pp.   Same as Part 3.

(2) Slip :—"Important Works | published by | Bradbury and Evans." Dated July, 1856. Page 4 : "The Cyclopædia of Biography." 4 pp. unnumbered. ($7\frac{1}{2}'' \times 4\frac{5}{8}''$).

PLATES (TWO)

(No. 17) "Mr. Flintwinch has a mild attack of irritability." (p. 257).

(No. 18) "The Pensioner—Entertainment." (p. 277).

No. 17 shows distinct evidence of machine ruling, but as it is not a finished example of the process, has not been included in the list of " Dark Plates."

TEXT, WITH HEADING

"Chapter XXX." pp. 257–288.

PART 10.

FRONT WRAPPER (OUTSIDE)

Same as No. I. except "No. X. September."

FRONT WRAPPER (INSIDE)

Similar to No. IX., with another added line : "Inflated Hoops for Ladies' Dresses." (Edmiston).

ADVERTISEMENTS (FRONT)

"Little Dorrit Advertiser." 12 pp. numbered (1)–12.

p. (1) "No. 10.—September, 1856."
p. 2. "Travellers' and Marine | Insurance Company."
p. 3. "T. A. Simpson & Co."
p. 4. "Household Words."   Part 77.
p. 5. "This day . . . | Popular History of England."
p. 6. "This day . . . | Cyclopædia of Biography."
p. 7. "The Grand Hotel, | Harrogate."
p. 8. "In preparation . . . | The National Magazine."
p. 9. "The best Food for Children . . ."
p. 10. ($\frac{1}{2}$ col.) "Bank of Deposit."   Last advert. : "The Capiato."
p. 11. "The Sponsalia."
p. 12. "Salt & Co.'s," and "Sangsters."

LITTLE DORRIT.

ADVERTISEMENTS (BACK)

(1) "Dr. De Jongh's." Same as Part 8, but imprint: "W. S. Johnson." 4 pp. unnumbered. Pink or yellow paper.

(2) "S. & T. Gilbert, | No. 4, Copthall Buildings." 2 pp. unnumbered; printed in red.

(3) "Specific for Rheumatism . . . | Taylor's Specific Liniment." 4 pp. numbered (1)–4.

PLATES (TWO)

(No. 19) "Society expresses its views on a question of Marriage." (p. 290).

(No. 20) "The Marshalsea becomes an Orphan." (p. 318).

TEXT, WITH HEADING

"Chapter XXXIII." pp. 289–320.

PART 11.

FRONT WRAPPER (OUTSIDE)

Same as No. I. except "No. XI. October."

FRONT WRAPPER (INSIDE)

Headed only :—"Waterproofs." (Edmiston).

ADVERTISEMENTS (FRONT)

"Little Dorrit Advertiser." 12 pp. numbered (1)–12.

p. (1) "No. 11.—October, 1856."
p. 2. "No more Pills nor any other Medicine."
p. 3. "T. A. Simpson & Co."
p. 4. "Just published . . . | Popular History of England."
p. 5. "Household Words." Part 78.
p. 6. "Kirby and Spence's Entomology."
p. 7. "New Descriptive Dictionary . . ."
p. 8. "The successful results . . . | Rowland's Macassar Oil."
p. 9. "The best Food for Children. . ."
p. 10. ($\frac{1}{2}$ col.) "Bank of Deposit," below : "The Loss of Hair."
p. 11. "The Sponsalia."
p. 12. "Dr. De Jongh's," with 12th line : "From ' The Lancet.' " Below : "Sangsters'."

ADVERTISEMENTS (BACK)

(1) Norton's Camomile Pills. 4 pp. Same as Part 3.

(2) "British College of Health, New Road, London. | Morison's Vegetable Universal Medicines." 2 pp. unnumbered. Pink paper.

(3) "Cassell's | Illustrated | Almanack, | for 1857"; p. 3 : "John Cassell's Coffees"; p. 5 : "The | American Sugar - Coated Pills"; pp. 6–8 : "Taylor's Specific Liniment." 8 pp. in all, unnumbered.

PLATES (TWO)

(No. 21) "The Travellers." (p. 325).

(No. 22) "The family dignity is affronted." (p. 344).

> Both these plates exist in two states, although it has been generally understood that only certain of the dark plates were duplicated. There is a great dissimilarity between the two sets ; one being much more highly finished and having greater detail worked in, than the other. Writer does not consider these to be duplicate plates, but rather the supersession of the inferior first by an improved second.

TEXT, WITH HEADING

"Chapter I." pp. (323)–352 ; preceded by a second half-title : "Book the Second | Riches." An unnumbered leaf, pp. (321–322).

PART 12.

FRONT WRAPPER (OUTSIDE)

Same as No. I. except "No. XII. November."

FRONT WRAPPER (INSIDE)

Same as No. XI.

ADVERTISEMENTS (FRONT)

"Little Dorrit Advertiser." 12 pp. numbered (1)–12.

> p. (1) "No. 12.—November, 1856."
> p. 2. "Travellers' and Marine | Insurance Company."
> p. 3. "T. A. Simpson & Co."
> p. 4. "Chapman & Hall's List of New Works."
> p. 5. "Publications for November, 1856."
> p. 6. "Harrow School Atlas."
> p. 7. "Immediately . . . | The Paragreens."

p. 8. "Now ready . . . | Mrs. Caudle's Curtain Lectures."
p. 9. "The best Food for Children . . ."
p. 10. (½ col.) "Bank of Deposit."   Next advert. : "Disorders of the Throat."
p. 11. "The Sponsalia."
p. 12. "Groombridge and Sons" and "Sangsters."

ADVERTISEMENTS (BACK)

(1) Dr. De Jongh's.   4 pp.   Same as Part 10.

(2) "Routledge's | Illustrated Shakespeare."   Last page : "Really useful Knowledge."   4 pp. unnumbered.

(3) Slip :—"The English Cyclopædia. | Conducted by Charles Knight."   Dated, October 27, 1856 ;   verso, blank.   Blue paper.   ($4\frac{5}{8}'' \times 5\frac{1}{2}''$).

PLATES (TWO)

(No. 23) "Instinct stronger than training."   (p. 369).

(No. 24) "Mr. Sparkler under a reverse of circumstances." (p. 373).

TEXT, WITH HEADING
"Chapter V."   pp. 353–384.

PART 13.

FRONT WRAPPER (OUTSIDE)
Same as No. I. except "No. XIII.   December."

FRONT WRAPPER (INSIDE)
Same as No. XI.

ADVERTISEMENTS (FRONT)
"Little Dorrit Advertiser."   12 pp. numbered (1)–12.

    p. (1) "No. 13.—December, 1856."
    p. 2. "No more Pills nor any other Medicine."
    p. 3. "T. A. Simpson & Co."
    p. 4. "A Double Issue of Biography this month."
    p. 5. "Sale by Auction . . . | Southgate & Barrett."
    p. 6. "Popular Edition . . . Life of Goldsmith."
    p. 7. "Christmas Presents."   (Rowlands).
    p. 8. "Fashionable | Parisian Bonnets."
    p. 9. "The best Food for Children . . ."

p. 10. ($\frac{1}{2}$ col.) "Bank of Deposit," followed by "Blair's Gout."

p. 11. "The Sponsalia."

p. 12. "Dr. De Jongh's," with line : "Opinion of A. B. Granville." Below : "Sangsters."

"Bradbury & Evans' | List of Publications for 1857." Dated, December, 1856. Running headline across pp. 2–11 : "List of Books | Published by Bradbury and Evans." 12 pp. numbered (1)–12.

Slip : (to follow plates). "Early in December will be published . . . | The | Wreck of the Golden Mary." Verso : "The | Household Words | Almanac." Green or pink paper. ($4\frac{1}{8}'' \times 5\frac{3}{8}''$).

Slip : (to follow plates). "Household Words | Almanac | for the Year 1857." Verso, blank. White paper. ($4\frac{1}{8}'' \times 5\frac{3}{4}''$).

ADVERTISEMENTS (BACK)

(1) Slip :—"New Serial Work . . . | Ask Mamma" ; verso, blank. Printed in red. ($4\frac{1}{4}'' \times 5\frac{1}{2}''$).

(2) Slip :—"Christmas | and | Winter Evening's | Enjoyment." (London Stereoscopic Company). 24 pp. numbered (1, 2, 3)–(24). ($6\frac{7}{8}'' \times 4\frac{3}{4}''$).

(3) "Publications of the London Printing & Publishing Co., Limited." This line runs along top of each page. 4 pp. unnumbered.

PLATES (TWO)

(No. 25) "Rigour of Mr. F's Aunt." (p. 402).

(No. 26) "Mr. Flintwinch receives the embrace of friendship." (p. 410).

TEXT, WITH HEADING

"Chapter VIII." pp. 385–416.

PART 14.

FRONT WRAPPER (OUTSIDE)

Same as No. I. except "No. XIV. January."

FRONT WRAPPER (INSIDE)

Same as No. XI.

LITTLE DORRIT.

ADVERTISEMENTS (FRONT)

"Little Dorrit Advertiser." 12 pp. numbered (1)–12.

 p. (1) "No. 14.—January, 1857."
 p. 2. "Messrs. W. Blackwood and Sons' List."
 p. 3. "T. A. Simpson & Co."
 p. 4. "New Atlases and Maps."
 p. 5. "New Works." (Bradbury and Evans).
 p. 6. "This day . . . | Second Series | Pictures of Life and Character."
 p. 7. "Now ready . . . | The Star and the Cloud."
 p. 8. "New Year's Gifts." (Rowlands).
 p. 9. "Mappin's Shilling Razor."
 p. 10. "Bank of Deposit."
 p. 11. "The Sponsalia."
 p. 12. "Sydenham Trousers, at 17/6," and "Sangsters."

ADVERTISEMENTS (BACK)

(1) Dr. De Jongh's. 4 pp. Same as Parts 10 & 12.

(2) " ' Stamped in Nature's Mould.' | New Era in Art. | Now Publishing, | Photographic Art Treasures." 4 pp. unnumbered : the last page having name and address of Messrs. Letts, Son & Co., ready to be folded and posted. Blue-grey paper.

(3) Slip :—(bound between the two leaves above). "Gratis. | A Catalogue | of | Letts's Diaries, Almanacks . . ." 4 pp. unnumbered. Yellow or orange paper. ($6'' \times 5\frac{1}{2}''$).

(4) "Royal Insurance Company." 2 pp. unnumbered. Printed in colours, with decorative border.

(5) "New Works and New Editions | published by | Virtue, Hall, and Virtue." 8 pp. unnumbered.

 p. (3) "Tredgold | on | The Steam Engine."
 p. (5) "Tomlinson's | Cyclopædia of Useful Arts."
 p. (8) "The History | of the | War against Russia."

PLATES (TWO)

(No. 27) "The Patriotic Conference." (p. 419).

(No. 28) "Mr. Baptist is supposed to have seen something." (p. 432).

TEXT, WITH HEADING

"Chapter XII." pp. 417–448.

CHARLES DICKENS.

PART 15.

FRONT WRAPPER (OUTSIDE)
Same as No. I. except "No. XV. February."

FRONT WRAPPER (INSIDE)
Same as No. XI.

ADVERTISEMENTS (FRONT)
"Little Dorrit Advertiser." 12 pp. numbered (1)–12.

p. (1) "No. 15.—February, 1857."
p. 2. "No more Pills nor any other Medicine."
p. 3. "T. A. Simpson & Co."
p. 4. "New Serial by the Brothers Mayhew."
p. 5. "Ask Mamma ; or, The Richest Commoner in England."
p. 6. ($\frac{1}{2}$ col.) "Works of Samuel Warren."
p. 7. "New Atlases and Maps."
p. 8. "Fashionable Parisian Bonnets."
p. 9. "To Ladies whose faces are tender . . ." (Rowlands).
p. 10. "Notice of Dividend. | Bank of Deposit."
p. 11. "The Sponsalia."
p. 12. "The | Royal Sanitary Police of Prussia." (De Jongh).
Below : "Sangsters."

ADVERTISEMENTS (BACK)

(1) Norton's Camomile Pills. 4 pp. Same as Part 3, except page 4 is headed :—"A Cure for Gout and Rheumatism."

(2) "Curiosities of London.—Third Thousand." Page 3 : "Curiosities of History." 4 pp. unnumbered.

PLATES (TWO)

(No. 29) "Missing and Dreaming." (p. 474).

(No. 30) "Reception of an old friend." (p. 476).

TEXT, WITH HEADING
"Chapter XV." pp. 449–480.

In the first issue of this number the name "Rigaud" is used instead of "Blandois." The error occurs seven times in pp. 469, 470, 472, and 473 ; and in Part 16 a slip is inserted pointing out this oversight by the Author.

It does not necessarily follow that a first issue must be scarcer than a later one, as in this particular case the corrected version is infinitely less common than the original.

LITTLE DORRIT.

PART 16.

FRONT WRAPPER (OUTSIDE)
Same as No. I. except "No. XVI. March."

FRONT WRAPPER (INSIDE)
Same as No. XI.

ADVERTISEMENTS (FRONT)
"Little Dorrit Advertiser." 8 pp. numbered (1)–8.
- p. (1) "No. 16.—March, 1857."
- p. 2. "Mappin's Shilling Razor."
- p. 3. "T. A. Simpson & Co." (Within ruled border).
- p. 4. "Important to Ladies. | . . . | The Ladies' Treasury."
- p. 5. "To Ladies whose faces are tender . . ." (Rowlands).
- p. 6. "Notice of Dividend. | Bank of Deposit."
- p. 7. "The Sponsalia."
- p. 8. "Sydenham Trousers, at 17/6."

Slip : (to follow plates). A note of correction (9 lines) respecting the use of the name "Rigaud" for "Blandois" in Part 15. ($2\frac{7}{8}'' \times 5\frac{1}{2}''$).

ADVERTISEMENTS (BACK)
(1) Dr. De Jongh's. 4 pp. Same as Parts 10, 12 & 14.
(2) "32, Fleet Street, London, 1857. | Popular Atlases and Maps, published by | George Philip & Son." 4 pp. unnumbered. Green or blue paper.

PLATES (TWO)
(No. 31) "An unexpected After Dinner Speech." (p. 489).
(No. 32) "The Night." (p. 492).

TEXT, WITH HEADING
"Chapter XIX." pp. 481–512.

PART 17.

FRONT WRAPPER (OUTSIDE)
Same as No. I. except "No. XVII. April."

FRONT WRAPPER (INSIDE)
Same as No. XI.

ADVERTISEMENTS (FRONT)
"Little Dorrit Advertiser." 12 pp. numbered (1)–12.

p. (1) "No. 17.—April, 1857."
p. 2. "No more Pills nor any other Medicine."
p. 3. "T. A. Simpson & Co." (as Part 16).
p. 4. "New Illustrated Works."
p. 5. "Part 84 of Household Words."
p. 6. (½ col.) "3 vols. . . . | Madaron ; "
p. 7. "Complete in one Volume . . . | The Butterflies . . ."
p. 8. "Salt and Co.'s | East India . . . Ales."
p. 9. "The successful results . . . | Rowland's Macassar Oil."
p. 10. "Notice of Dividend. | Bank of Deposit."
p. 11. "The Sponsalia."
p. 12. "The | Royal Sanitary Police of Prussia" (De Jongh), and "Persian Parasols."

ADVERTISEMENTS (BACK)
"Royal Insurance Company."   2 pp.   Same as Part 14.

PLATES (TWO)
(No. 33) "Flora's tour of inspection."   (p. 519).
(No. 34) "Mr. Merdle a borrower."   (p. 530).

TEXT, WITH HEADING
"Chapter XXIII."   pp. 513–544.

PART 18.

FRONT WRAPPER (OUTSIDE)
Same as No. I. except "No. XVIII. May."

FRONT WRAPPER (INSIDE)
Same as No. XI.

ADVERTISEMENTS (FRONT)
"Little Dorrit Advertiser."   12 pp. numbered (1)–12.
p. (1) "No. 18.—May, 1857."
p. 2. "Mappin's Cutlery & Electro-Silver Plate."
p. 3. "T. A. Simpson & Co." (as Part 16).
p. 4. "Works on Gardening, Botany, &c."
p. 5. "A New Tale—The Dead Secret ! "   (Household Words).
p. 6. "New Illustrated Serials for May."
p. 7. "Sound and White Teeth."   (Rowlands).
p. 8. "Ilkley Wells Hydropathic Establishment."
p. 9. "(Annual Circular.) | Royal Bank Buildings, | Liverpool, April 6th, 1857."   (Roberts & Compy.).

p. 10. "Notice of Dividend. | Bank of Deposit."
p. 11. "The Sponsalia."
p. 12. "Sydenham Trousers, at 17/6," and "Persian Parasols."

ADVERTISEMENTS (BACK)

(1) Dr. De Jongh's.   4 pp.   Same as Parts 10, 12, 14 & 16.
(2) "The | English Cyclopædia." Verso: "Knight's | Cyclopædia of Biography."   2 pp. unnumbered.   Pink paper.

PLATES (TWO)

(No. 35) "At Mr. John Chivery's tea-table."   (p. 548).
(No. 36) "In the old room."   (p. 562).

TEXT, WITH HEADING

"Chapter XXVII."   pp. 545–576.

PARTS 19 AND 20.

FRONT WRAPPER (OUTSIDE)

Same as No. I. except "Nos. XIX. & XX. June. Price 2s."

FRONT WRAPPER (INSIDE)

Same as No. XI.

ADVERTISEMENTS (FRONT)

"Little Dorrit Advertiser."   12 pp. numbered (1)–12.
p. (1) "Nos. 19 & 20.—June, 1857."
p. 2. "No more Pills nor any other Medicine."
p. 3. "T. A. Simpson & Co." (as Part 16).
p. 4. "The | English Cyclopædia."
p. 5. "Completion of Little Dorrit."
p. 6. ($\frac{1}{2}$ col.) "Now ready, at all the Libraries."
p. 7. "To Young Authors and Inexperienced Writers."
p. 8. "Ilkley Wells Hydropathic Establishment."
p. 9. ($\frac{1}{2}$ col.) "Ice, and Refrigerators . . ."
p. 10. "Notice of Dividend. | Bank of Deposit."
p. 11. "The Sponsalia."
p. 12. " 'The Lancet.' "   (Dr. De Jongh's).

ADVERTISEMENTS (BACK)

(1) "Royal Insurance Company."   2 pp.   Same as Part 14.
(2) "193, Piccadilly. | June 1, 1857. | New Serial | . . . | Davenport Dunn." Page 3:   "Cheap Edition of Carlyle's Works."   4 pp. unnumbered.

PLATES (FOUR)

(No. 37) "Damocles." (p. 595). Dark plate.

(No. 38) "The Third Volume of the Registers." (p. 624).

(No. 39) "Frontispiece."

(No. 40) Vignette Title. Dated 1857.

> No. 37 is the eighth and last of the series of dark plates. Unlike the others, it was not etched in duplicate.

TEXT, WITH HEADING

"Chapter XXX." pp. 577–625, blank (626). Imprint at foot of p. 625 : "Bradbury and Evans, Printers, Whitefriars."

PRELIMINARY LEAVES

Title-page : dated 1857. Verso, with imprint : "London | Bradbury and Evans, Printers, Whitefriars." (I., II.). See Illustration.

Dedication : (to Clarkson Stanfield, R.A.). Verso, blank. (III., IV.).

"Preface." Dated, "London, | May, 1857." 4 pp. numbered (V.), VI., VII., (VIII.) : last page blank.

"Contents." 4 pp. numbered (IX.), X., XI., XII.

"List of Plates," with 3-line "Errata." 2 pp. numbered (XIII.), XIV.

> As pp. 625 and (626) conjugated with the preliminary leaves in sig. SS, the half-title was dispensed with.

A

TALE OF TWO CITIES.

BY

CHARLES DICKENS.

WITH ILLUSTRATIONS BY H. K. BROWNE.

LONDON:

CHAPMAN AND HALL, 193, PICCADILLY;

AND AT THE OFFICE OF ALL THE YEAR ROUND,

11, WELLINGTON STREET NORTH.

MDCCCLIX.

[The above is a facsimile of a spurious title-page, of which many specimens are in circulation. It is reproduced in exact proportions, and shows an extreme page depth of 168½ mm.
in comparison with the genuine title measuring 174 mm. See note on page 342.]

A Tale of Two Cities

in

7/8 Monthly Parts,
July to December, 1859.

THIS story first appeared as a serial in "All the Year Round," a weekly journal conducted by Charles Dickens, and was later issued as a periodical in eight monthly parts. The first part was published in July, 1859, and completed in December of the same year. Price was one shilling per number except the last two (7 and 8), which as usual formed a double number at two shillings.

It is worthy of note that "A Tale of Two Cities" marks a break in the association of the Author and two parties who were important factors in the success of all the preceding works. Hablot K. Browne, for twenty-three years responsible for all the etchings which had so successfully embellished these books, produced his last drawings for the present work. The decided deterioration in the quality of his work disclosed by these plates, is painful evidence of the reason for his retirement. Bradbury and Evans, the printers of all, and publishers of five of Dickens's works as issued in monthly parts, had ceased to act in this dual capacity, after completion of Little Dorrit. The story of the disagreement between the Author and his publishers need not be enlarged upon here, but it resulted in the return of Chapman and Hall, as publishers of this and all succeeding works.

TEXT.

There are practically no "points" sufficiently outstanding to distinguish the earlier from later printings, but a copy of first issue text should have the misprinted page-number "113" instead of "213." The imprint of "C. Whiting" appears for the first time.

CHARLES DICKENS.

PLATES.

Including the vignette title-page, "Phiz" etched sixteen plates, but none of them was duplicated. Some very poor impressions are to be seen, the result of large initial printings, with only one set of plates to produce them. Even the earliest and best impressions fall much below the standard of previous work of this time-honoured artist. Except the Frontispiece and Vignette, all the plates were etched horizontally.

WRAPPERS.

The parts were bound in blue paper wrappers, with a front cover design by "Phiz"; and whatever may be the merits or demerits of the plates accompanying the parts, it can be said of the cover design that it is an excellent and attractive effort. Apart from the necessary adjustment in "Part No." and month of issue for each monthly wrapper, a slight alteration of text at the foot of Part 2 is effected, and continues so to the end of the series.

ADVERTISEMENTS.

Each of the seven monthly issues contain the "Advertiser," uniformly of eight pages. The only other advertising material appearing in the front consists of one leaf and two slips, which are found in Parts 1, 5 and 6.

Some material appears at the back of each part. A particularly scarce item is "The Cornhill Magazine," which should be present in all copies of the last number that have pretence to first issue in original state. It is a single leaf, more generally printed on reddish-brown paper, but as in the "Bruton" copy, is also printed on white paper. The inset announces the publication of No. 1, and contains an original contribution by W. M. Thackeray, signed by him, and dated Nov. 1, 1859.

PART 1.

FRONT WRAPPER (OUTSIDE)
"No. I. June. Price 1s. | A Tale | of | Two Cities | by | Charles Dickens. | with | Illustrations by H. K. Browne. | London: Chapman and Hall, 193, Piccadilly.

A TALE OF TWO CITIES.

| Agents : J. Menzies, Edinburgh; Murray and Son, Glasgow; J. M'Glashan and Gill, Dublin. | (Pointing hand). The Author reserves the right of Translation." The title is embodied in, and forms part of, the cover design all other lettering is type-set.

FRONT WRAPPER (INSIDE)
"The War | With The Sardinians." (Jay). Full page.

BACK WRAPPER (INSIDE)
"Slack's Catalogue with 350 Engravings Gratis, or Post Free." With 3 woodcuts. Full page.

BACK WRAPPER (OUTSIDE)
"Cheap Book-Stalls." (E. Moses and Son). Full page.

ADVERTISEMENTS (FRONT)
"Tale of Two Cities Advertiser." 8 pp. numbered (1)–8.

    p. (1) "No. I.—June, 1859."
    p. 2. "New Works." Chapman and Hall's list of nine works, the first :—"Northumberland and the Border."
    p. 3. "The United Libraries, | Booth's, Churton's, and Hodgson's." Full page.
    p. 4. "List of the principal | Works of the Present Season | in circulation at | Mudie's Select Library."
    p. 5. "Published by | William Blackwood and Sons." Eleven titles of works, numbered I.—XI.
    p. 6. ($\frac{1}{2}$ col.) "Joseph Gillott" ; "Gowland's Lotion" ; "Smith, Elder, and Co." ; and "Works by Mr. Charles Dickens" (Chapman and Hall).
    p. 7. "Rowland's Macassar Oil" ; "Nissen and Parker" ; and "Health and Disease—Their Laws" (Chapman and Hall).
    p. 8. "Edmiston's" with illustration of premises and vicinity, and "Parasols" with woodcut (W. & J. Sangster).
    Slip : (to follow plates). "Discontinuance of Household Words. | . . . | All the Year Round. | containing, | . . . | A Tale of Two Cities." Verso blank. Yellow paper. ($4\frac{1}{2}'' \times 5\frac{5}{8}''$).

ADVERTISEMENTS (BACK)
(1) "Dr. | De Jongh's | . . . | Light-Brown | Cod Liver Oil," with a woodcut of a medallion each side of this heading. Page 4. "Select Medical Opinions"; the first being : "The late Jonathan Pereira," and dated April 16, 1851. 4 pp. unnumbered. Yellow or pink paper.

335

(2) "The | Morisonian Monument | erected in front of the | British College of Health." Below, a woodcut of the Monument, and under this : "Reasons for the Monument : by John Fraser," which heads 18 lines in half-measure. 4 pp. numbered (1)–4. White paper only.

An alternative to the above, printed in French, is headed : "Collège Britannique de Santé | Euston Road, Londres." It is a literal translation of the address by John Fraser, and was alternatively inserted with the English version. It must be a scarce item, as only one copy has been noted out of 100 examined.

PLATES (TWO)
(No. 1) "The Mail." (Page 5).
(No. 2) "The Shoemaker." (Page 29).

TEXT, WITH HEADING
"A Tale of Two Cities. | Chapter I." pp. (1)–32.

PART 2.

FRONT WRAPPER (OUTSIDE)
Same as No. I. except "No. II. July," and in place of list of Agents is substituted a line reading : "And 'All the Year Round' Office, 11, Wellington-Street North, Strand." There is no comma after "Hall" but a semi-colon appears after "Piccadilly" instead of full-point.

FRONT WRAPPER (INSIDE)
"Family Mourning." (Jay's). Full page.

BACK WRAPPER (INSIDE)
"Fenders, Fire-Irons, and Furnishing | Ironmongery." With two woodcuts. (R. & J. Slack). Full page.

BACK WRAPPER (OUTSIDE)
"The War." (E. Moses and Son). Full page.

ADVERTISEMENTS (FRONT)
"Tale of Two Cities Advertiser." 8 pp. numbered (1)–8.

    p. (1) "No. II.—July, 1859."
    p. 2. "Mr. Charles Dickens's Works."
    p. 3. "New Works." Same as Part 1, page 2.
    p. 4. ($\frac{1}{2}$ col.) "Joseph Gillott" ; "Keatings" ; "Gowland's Lotion" ; "Rimmell" ; "Bank of Deposit" ; "Pelican Life Insurance" ; "Bartholomew Fair" ; and "Life in Victoria."

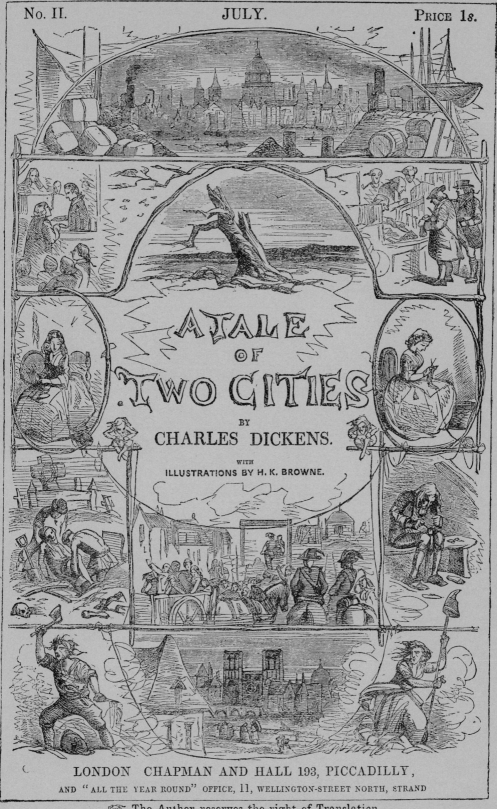

No. II.   JULY.   PRICE 1*s.*

A TALE OF TWO CITIES

BY
CHARLES DICKENS.

WITH
ILLUSTRATIONS BY H. K. BROWNE.

LONDON CHAPMAN AND HALL 193, PICCADILLY,
AND "ALL THE YEAR ROUND" OFFICE, 11, WELLINGTON-STREET NORTH, STRAND

☞ The Author reserves the right of Translation.

The Front Wrapper to the edition of "A Tale of Two Cities,"
as published in 7/8 monthly parts, 1859.   The story first appeared
as a serial in *All the Year Round*.

p. 5. "The National Review" ; Anthony Trollope's Novels, and others ; published by Chapman & Hall.

p. 6. "Mr. Carlyle's Works." Nine titles, with half-page Press notice of "The Saturday Review."

p. 7. "Rowland's Macassar Oil" ; "Allen's Patent Portmanteaus"; "Modern Domestic Medicine" and "Health and Disease— Their Laws."

p. 8. Same as Part 1.

ADVERTISEMENTS (BACK)

(1) Norton's Camomile Pills. 4 pp. numbered (1), 2, 3, (4).

p. 2. First word in first column   .. "stomach"
     Last   „ „ second „   .. "their"
p. 3. Last   „ „ first   „   .. "as-"
     First   „ „ second „   .. "sist"

(2) British College of Health. "Report of P. A. Aveilhé," dated, "Charleston, 28th February, 1859." 2 pp. un-numbered. Brick-red paper.

PLATES (TWO)

(No. 3) "The Likeness." (Page 48).

(No. 4) "Congratulations." (Page 51).

TEXT, WITH HEADING

"Book the Second. | Chapter I." pp. 33–68.

PART 3.

FRONT WRAPPER (OUTSIDE)

Same as No. II. except "No. III. August."

FRONT WRAPPER (INSIDE)

Same as No. II.

BACK WRAPPER (INSIDE)

Same as No. II.

BACK WRAPPER (OUTSIDE)

"A Tale of the Two Cities." (E. Moses and Son).

ADVERTISEMENTS (FRONT)

"Tale of Two Cities Advertiser." 8 pp. numbered (1)–8.

p. (1) "No. III.—August, 1859."
p. 2. Same as Part 2.
p. 3. "New Works." Chapman and Hall's list of Ten works ; the first : "Secret History of the Austrian Government."

p. 4. (½ col.) Same as Part 2, except "Phillipson & Co.'s New Perfume" replaces "Gowland's Lotion."

p. 5. "New Work by the Author of ' John Halifax,' " which replaces "The National Review" ; otherwise the same as Part 2.

p. 6. Same as Part 2.

p. 7. "Tourists and Travellers" (Rowlands) ; "Allen's Patent Portmanteaus" ; "Nissen and Parker" ; "The Ordeal of Richard Feveral."

p. 8. Same as Parts 1 and 2.

ADVERTISEMENTS (BACK)

(1) Dr. De Jongh's. 4 pp. Same as Part 1.

(2) British College of Health (Morison's Pills) ; with view of premises printed crosswise. 4 pp. unnumbered. White paper.

PLATES (TWO)

(No. 5) "The Stoppage at the Fountain." (Page 72).

(No. 6) "Mr. Striver at Tellson's Bank." (Page 94).

In "List of Plates" the name "Striver" is spelt "Stryver."

TEXT, WITH HEADING

"Chapter VII." pp. 69–100.

PART 4.

FRONT WRAPPER (OUTSIDE)

Same as No. II. except "No. IV. September."

FRONT WRAPPER (INSIDE)

"Millinery for Mourning" (Jay's). Full page.

BACK WRAPPER (INSIDE)

Same as Nos. II. and III.

BACK WRAPPER (OUTSIDE)

"To Sportsmen and Others." (E. Moses and Son).

ADVERTISEMENTS (FRONT)

"Tale of Two Cities Advertiser." 8 pp. numbered (1)–8.

p. (1) "No. IV.—September, 1859."

p. 2. "New Works. | Tuscany in '49 and '59" and Seven other titles ; the last, "Robert Mornay : A Novel."

p. 3. "New Works | Our Farm of Four Acres." Five other titles ; the last, "The Three Gates : in Verse."

p. 4. "Mr. Charles Dickens's Works"; "New and Complete Library Edition"; "Original Editions"; "Cheap and Uniform Editions."

p. 5. (½ col.) "Joseph Gillott" followed by "Bank of Deposit" and "A Clear Complexion." Last announcement, "Life in Victoria." Ten announcements in all.

p. 6. "Mr. Carlyle's Works" followed by "Cheap Edition of Mr. Lever's Works" and "The National Review."

p. 7. "Tourists and Travellers." (Rowlands); "Allen's Patent Portmanteaus"; "Keatings" and "Health and Disease—Their Laws."

p. 8. "Edmiston's" and "Sangster's | Silk and Alpaca Umbrellas."

ADVERTISEMENTS (BACK)
Norton's Pills. 4 pp. Same as Part 2.

PLATES (TWO)
(No. 7) "The Spy's Funeral." (Page 102).
(No. 8) "The Wine Shop." (Page 109).

TEXT, WITH HEADING
"Chapter XIV." pp. 101–132.

PART 5.

FRONT WRAPPER (OUTSIDE)
Same as No. II. except "No. V. October."

FRONT WRAPPER (INSIDE)
Same as No. IV.

BACK WRAPPER (INSIDE)
Same as Nos. II. III. and IV.

BACK WRAPPER (OUTSIDE)
"The Month of October." (E. Moses and Son).

ADVERTISEMENTS (FRONT)
"Tale of Two Cities Advertiser." 8 pp. numbered (1)–8.

p. (1) "No. V.—October, 1859."

p. 2. "New Works. | The Poems of John Milton," and Five other books.

p. 3. "New Works. | Tuscany in '49 and '59," and Six other books.

p. 4. "Works in Preparation." ("One of Them," by Charles Lever). Seven titles in all.

p. 5. (½ col.) "Joseph Gillott," followed by "Pelican" and "La Duchesse." Ten announcements in all.

p. 6. "New Works," 12 Titles, followed by "Mr. Carlyle's Works | New Edition in Sixteen Volumes," Nine Titles.

p. 7. "Sixty Years of Success." (Rowlands); "Keatings"; "Allen's Patent Portmanteaus," and "Household Words."

p. 8. Same as Part 4.

Slip: (to follow plates). "193, Piccadilly, October 1, 1859. | New Serial," verso blank. Yellow paper. ($4\frac{5}{8}'' \times 5\frac{1}{2}''$).

ADVERTISEMENTS (BACK)
Dr. De Jongh's. 4 pp. Same as Part 1.

PLATES (TWO)
(No. 9) "The Accomplices." (Page 137).
(No. 10) "The Sea Rises." (Page 150).

TEXT, WITH HEADING
"Chapter XIX." pp. 133–164.

PART 6.

FRONT WRAPPER (OUTSIDE)
Same as No. II. except "No. VI. November."

FRONT WRAPPER (INSIDE)
Same as Nos. IV. and V.

BACK WRAPPER (INSIDE)
Same as Nos. II. III. IV. and V.

BACK WRAPPER (OUTSIDE)
"Lord Brougham and the | Working Classes." (E. Moses and Son).

ADVERTISEMENTS (FRONT)
"The Story of our Lives, from Year to Year," advertising the first volume of "All the Year Round." 1 leaf, verso blank.

"Tale of Two Cities Advertiser." 8 pp. numbered (1)–8.

p. (1) "No. VI.—November, 1859."

p. 2. "New Works. | Tuscany in '49 and '59." Seven titles in all, in six paragraphs.

p. 3. "Smith, Elder, and Co.'s List. | . . . | A New Periodical. | Edited by W. M. Thackeray"; and 17 Titles of books.

p. 4. "Chapman and Hall's List of New Works | for November." Seven titles in all.

p. 5. ($\frac{1}{2}$ col.) "Joseph Gillott," with Nine other advertisements. Last in first column : "The National Review." Last in second column : "Life in Victoria."

p. 6. Same as Part 5.
p. 7. "White and Sound Teeth" (Rowlands) ; "Keating's Cough Lozenges" ; "Gowland's Lotion," and Two announcements of Chapman and Hall.
p. 8. Same as Parts 4 and 5.

ADVERTISEMENTS (BACK)
Thomas De La Rue. 4 pp. unnumbered.

p. (1) "Diaries & Almanacks | for 1860."
pp. (2 & 3) "Opinions of the Press."
p. (4) "Thomas De La Rue & Co.'s | Vegetable Parchment."

PLATES (TWO)
(No. 11) "Before the Prison Tribunal." (Page 168).
(No. 12) "The Knock at the Door." (Page 196).

TEXT, WITH HEADING
"Book the Third. | Chapter I." pp. 165–196.

PARTS 7 AND 8.

FRONT WRAPPER (OUTSIDE)
Same as No. II. except "Nos. VII. & VIII. December. Price 2s."

FRONT WRAPPER (INSIDE)
Same as Nos. IV. V. and VI.

BACK WRAPPER (INSIDE)
"Slack's Nickel Electro-Plate."

BACK WRAPPER (OUTSIDE)
"British Volunteers." (E. Moses and Son).

ADVERTISEMENTS (FRONT)
"Tale of Two Cities Advertiser." 8 pp. numbered (1)–8.

p. (1) "Nos. VII. & VIII.—December, 1859."
p. 2. "Mr. Dickens's New Work | A Tale of Two Cities." Seven other titles, each divided by rule.
p. 3. "Now ready . . . | The First Volume of | All the Year Round | Conducted by | Charles Dickens," announcing publication of "The Haunted House." Lower half of page with other announcements of Chapman and Hall.
p. 4. "New Works." Six titles : "One of Them" ; "Our Farm of Four Acres" ; "A Decade of Italian Women" ; "The Wanderer" ; "Our Engines of War" ; "The Rifle Musket."

341

p. 5. Same as Page 6, in Parts 5 and 6.
p. 6. Same as Page 5, in Part 5.
p. 7. "Christmas Presents" (Rowlands); "Keating's Cough Lozenges"; "Notice. | To induce a Trial of | South African Wines"; "Notice to the Trade. | Household Words."
p. 8. Same as Parts 4, 5 and 6.

ADVERTISEMENTS (BACK)

"One Shilling Monthly, | with Illustrations. | The | Cornhill Magazine." 2 pp. numbered on second page. Brick-red or white paper. ($8\frac{5}{8}'' \times 5\frac{3}{8}''$).

PLATES (FOUR)

(No. 13) "The double recognition." (Page 197).
(No. 14) "After the sentence." (Page 225).
(No. 15) "Frontispiece."
(No. 16) Vignette Title (undated).

TEXT, WITH HEADING

"Chapter VIII." pp. 197–254. Imprint at foot of p. 254 : "C. Whiting, Beaufort House, Strand."

Page 213 of the first impression is misnumbered 113.

PRELIMINARY LEAVES

Title-page : dated 1859, verso blank. (I. II.). (See Illustration).

Dedication : to Lord John Russell ; verso blank. (III. IV.).

Preface : dated, "Tavistock House, London, | November, 1859." Verso blank. (V. VI.).

Contents : 2 pp. numbered. (VII.) VIII.

List of Plates : with sig. "b" at foot, verso blank. (IX. X.).

The last leaf of text (pp. 253-4) which carries sig. "T" conjugates with "List of Plates" (sig. "b"). The latter signature is omitted in early re-issues.

No half-title is called for, as the preliminary leaves (I-VIII) make up a level half sheet.

Of the Title-page, a very clever facsimile exists in goodly numbers, and without a close comparison it is difficult to detect the spurious from the original. A genuine copy should show an extreme page-depth measurement of 174 mm., whilst the facsimile will pull only $168\frac{1}{2}$ mm. The letter "A" at top is also slightly larger in the genuine title.

OUR MUTUAL FRIEND.

BY

CHARLES DICKENS.

WITH ILLUSTRATIONS BY MARCUS STONE.

IN TWO VOLUMES.

VOL. II.

LONDON:
CHAPMAN AND HALL, 193 PICCADILLY.
1865.

No. 8.   DECEMBER, 1864.   Price 1s.

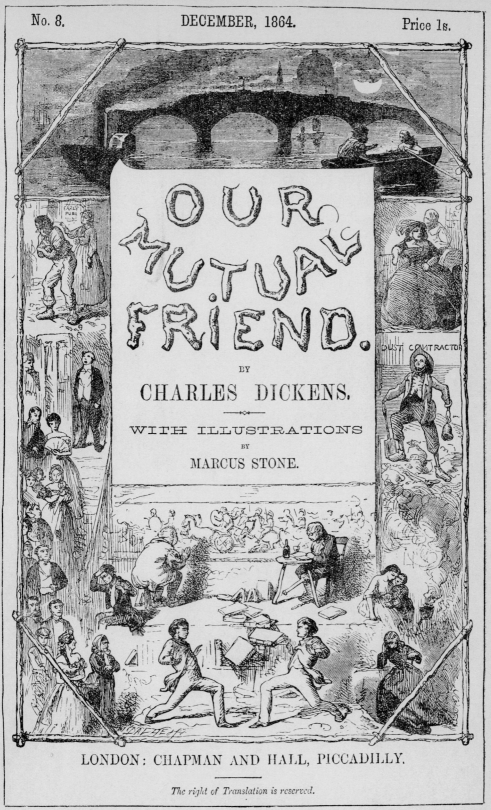

OUR MUTUAL FRIEND.

BY

CHARLES DICKENS.

WITH ILLUSTRATIONS

BY

MARCUS STONE.

LONDON: CHAPMAN AND HALL, PICCADILLY.

The right of Translation is reserved.

LONDON PRINTED BY W. CLOWES AND SONS, STAMFORD STREET, AND CHARING CROSS.

The Front Wrapper to the original edition of "Our Mutual Friend," as published in 19/20 monthly parts, 1864-1865.

Our Mutual Friend

in

19/20 Monthly Parts

May, 1864, to November, 1865.

ORIGINALLY issued in twenty numbers, bound in nineteen monthly parts, price one shilling per number, except the last two (19 and 20) which formed a double number at two shillings. The design for the front wrapper and forty wood-engravings were for the first and only time entrusted to Marcus Stone. After a lapse of some years, a return to the familiar green wrappers was decided upon; replacing blue, which had been in use for "Bleak House," "Little Dorrit," and "A Tale of Two Cities."

ADVERTISEMENTS.

The official advertising sheet has a greater volume of material than any other of the works in original parts—a total number of 320 pages occupying the front position within the covers. Each part has its quota—32 pages in Part 1, and 16 pages in each of the others. Every page is headed throughout : "Our Mutual Friend Advertiser." All the pages are foliated, although in a few copies seen of Part 10, page 13 was misprinted "31." In addition to the "Advertiser" some insets are called for; one of these is particularly scarce. This is a 4-paged inset of "The Economic Life Assurance Society," and fully described in the collation of Part 14.

No less than 89 individual insets and slips are placed within the back wrappers, each monthly part containing a proportion. The slip, "Foreign Bank Notes," should be present in Parts 19/20, but is often found wanting.

345

CHARLES DICKENS.

WRAPPERS.

In addition to the essential change of "Part No." and month of issue, one other alteration in type-setting of the front cover is effected. The first issue of Part 1 is without the imprint at foot ; but in Part 2 and following numbers, the name and address of the printers is added—W. Clowes and Sons. Below, in tabular form, are shown the variations of advertisements occupying the inside of front, and both sides of back wrappers :

FRONT WRAPPERS.

With names of Advertisers in order as printed.

Part.	1st Ad.	2nd Ad.	3rd Ad.	4th Ad.	5th Ad.	6th Ad.
1	John Harvey	B. Blake	Nevell	Philpott		
2	do.	Le Follet	do.	do.		
3	do.	Thomas's	do.	do.		
4	do.	do.	Denman	do.		
5	do.	do.	do.	do.		
6	do.	do.	do.	do.		
7	do.	do.	do.	Grant & Gask		
8	do.	do.	do.	G. Poland	Farmer & Rogers	W. Stevens
9	do.	do.	do.	Cassell	Cassell	Cassell
10	do.	do.	do.	Grant & Gask		
11	do.	do.	do.	do.		
12	do.	do.	do.	do.	W. Stevens	
13	do.	do.	do.	Family Herald	Family Herald	W. Stevens
14	do.	do.	do.	do.	W. Stevens	
15	do.	do.	do.	do.	do.	
16	do.	do.	do.	do.	do.	
17	do.	do.	do.	do.	do.	
18	do.	Denman	W. Stevens	Accidental		
19/20	do.	do.	do.	G. Poland	Accidental	

BACK WRAPPERS.

Part.	Outside.	Inside.
1	The Furnishing of Bed-rooms (Heal).	Patterns Post Free (Peter Robinson).
2	as Part 1.	as Part 1.
3	as Part 1.	as Part 1.
4	Overcoats for Riding or Driving (Nicoll).	as Part 1.
5	as Part 1.	as Part 1.
6	Fashions for the Winter Season (Nicoll).	Patterns free for selection (Robinson).
7	as Part 1.	Patterns free to any Part. do.
8	H. J. & D. Nicoll : repeated twice.	London and Lancashire Insurance Companies.
9	as Part 1.	Jackson & Graham.
10	as Part 8.	The Queen Insurance Company
11	as Part 1.	Early Spring Fabrics (Robinson).
12	Tailors to the Queen and Royal Family (Nicoll).	New Spring Fabrics. do.
13	as Part 1.	Court Trains, Silk Robes, etc.
14	as Part 12.	as Part 13.
15	as Part 1.	Silks, Fancy Dress Fabrics, etc.
16	Army and Navy Outfits (Nicoll).	2nd line :—Silks, Fancy Dress Fabrics, etc.
17	as Part 1.	2nd line :—All Summer Stocks at Greatly Reduced Prices.
18	Foreigners and Visitors to London, etc. (Nicoll).	The New Autumn Fashions.
19/20	as Part 1.	New Autumn Fashions.

ILLUSTRATIONS.

With this book, and for the first time, a departure is made from etchings on steel. The designs of Marcus Stone are engraved on wood by Dalziel (21), and W. T. Green (19), to the usual number of forty subjects. Meritorious as are these illustrations, it cannot be said they add to the embellishment of the work, as did the etchings of "Phiz" or the artists who preceded him, and it is difficult to raise an enthusiastic note in

347

their favour. They leave nothing to the imagination or research of the collector, who so keenly appreciates the fine points of precedence in "states" of the plates, and quality of impression.

PART 1.

FRONT WRAPPER (OUTSIDE)

"No. I. May, 1864. Price 1s. | Our | Mutual | Friend | by | Charles Dickens. | With Illustrations | by | Marcus Stone. | London : Chapman and Hall, Piccadilly. | The right of Translation is reserved."

The Title alone is embodied in the cover design, all other matter is set-up in type.

ADVERTISEMENTS (FRONT)

"Our Mutual Friend Advertiser." 32 pp. numbered (1)–32.

p. (1) At foot : "Part I.—May, 1864."
p. 2. "Works published by Griffith and Farran."
p. 3. "Mudie's Select Library. | Twenty-third Year."
p. 4. "The most appropriate of Memorials."
p. 5. "Hurst and Blackett's New Works."
p. 6. "New Works and New Editions." (Virtue Brothers).
p. 7. "Smith, Elder, & Co.'s New Publications."
p. 8. "The Select Library." (Chapman & Hall).
p. 9. "Messrs. Blackwood's New Publications."
p. 10. "Mr. Thomas Carlyle's Works."
p. 11. "Weekly Numbers... | Cassell's | Illustrated Shakespeare."
p. 12. "Hatchard & Co."
p. 13. "Uniform with Lord Macaulay's ' England.' "
p. 14. "New Serials." (Chapman & Hall).
p. 15. "The Family Herald ;"
p. 16. Second line : "All the Year Round for Five Years."
p. 17. "Stanford's Foreign Office Passport Agency."
p. 18. "Chapman and Hall's Standard Editions . . ."
p. 19. ($\frac{1}{2}$ col.) "The Author's Editions."
p. 20. ($\frac{1}{2}$ col.) "Sheppard's | New Model Dairy Butter."
p. 21. "Kinahan's L.L. Whisky v. Cognac Brandy."
p. 22. ($\frac{1}{2}$ col.) "Reconnoit'rer Glass."
p. 23. "Slack's Electro-Plate."
p. 24. Callaghan's | Opera, Race, Field . . . Glasses."
p. 25. "E.R. 1564 (Crown) V.R. 1864."
p. 26. "Scott Adie."
p. 27. "Important Announcement. | Joseph Gillott."

p. 28. "Cooper's | Antiseptic Carnation Tooth Paste."
p. 29. "Benham and Sons'."
p. 30. "Personal Beauty."   (Rowlands).
p. 31. "The Ondina, or Waved Jupon."
p. 32. "William S. Burton."

Slip :   (to follow plates).   "The Reader will understand the use of the popular | phrase Our Mutual Friend, as the title of this book, | on arriving at the Ninth Chapter (page 84)."   ($1\frac{5}{8}'' \times 5\frac{1}{2}''$).

ADVERTISEMENTS (BACK)

(1) "Dr. De Jongh's | Light-Brown Cod Liver Oil." This heading set-up within a fancy double-lined frame. Verso : "Consumption & Diseases of the Chest," and below, eight medical opinions set in half-measure. 2 pp. unnumbered.   Pink paper.

(2) Groombridge & Sons' Publications. pp. 1 and 2 : "The Temple Anecdotes."   8 pp. unnumbered.

(3) "A Shakspeare Memorial."   Verso : "Form of Order." 2 pp. unnumbered.   Brown-tinted paper.

(4) "Messrs. Chapman and Hall's | New Publications." Dated on first page, "April 30, 1864."   In all, 27 Authors' works are listed, each numbered 1–27.   8 pp. numbered (1)–8.

(5) "Thorley's."   4 pp. unnumbered, the first and last with full-page woodcuts.

(6) "Fry's | Iceland Moss Cocoa."   Verso :   "The Only Prize Medal."   2 pp. unnumbered.   Lemon paper. Two alternatives to this inset were used; one advertising "Homœopathic Cocoa," on pink paper, and the other "Trinidad Rock Cocoa," on orange paper.

(7) "Glenfield | Starch."   Verso : (within circle in centre of page) "Glenfield | Patent | Starch."   2 pp. unnumbered.   Brown-tinted paper.

(8) "The Queen Insurance Company," with Portrait. Verso : dated in top right corner, "Nov., 1863."   2 pp. unnumbered.   Pink or blue paper.

(9) "The Scottish National | Insurance Company."   4 pp. unnumbered.   pp. (1) and (4) printed in red and black, and pp. (2) and (3) in black only.   Cream-tinted paper.

(10) Slip :—"In ' The Churchman's Family Magazine.' "
Verso : a list of 12 books.   Yellow paper.   ($4\frac{3}{4}'' \times 5\frac{1}{2}''$).

PLATES (TWO)
(No. 1) "The Bird of Prey."   (to face title of Vol. I.).
(No. 2) "Witnessing the Agreement."   (p. 30).

TEXT, WITH HEADING
"Our Mutual Friend. | In Four Books. | Book the First.
The Cup and the Lip. | Chapter I. | On the Look Out."
pp. (1)–32.

PART 2.

FRONT WRAPPER (OUTSIDE)
Same as No. 1, except "No. 2.   June" ; and an additional
line on bottom margin :—"London : Printed by W.
Clowes and Sons, Stamford Street, and Charing Cross."

ADVERTISEMENTS (FRONT)
"Our Mutual Friend Advertiser."   16 pp. numbered (1)–16.

p. (1)   At foot : "Part II.—June, 1864."
p.   2. "Price List. | Mr. Mayall's | Photographs."
p.   3. "Macmillan and Co.'s New List."   13 Titles.
p.   4. "New Serials."   (Chapman & Hall).
p.   5. ($\frac{1}{2}$ col.) "Fourth Thousand . . . | A Manual of British
But- | terflies and Moths."
p.   6. "Mr. Thomas Carlyle's Works."
p.   7. "Chapman and Hall's Standard Editions. . . ."
p.   8. ($\frac{1}{2}$ col.) "Reckitt's Diamond | Black Lead."
p.   9. "Cooper's | Antiseptic Carnation Tooth Paste."
p. 10. " ' Reconnoiterer ' Glass 9/6 ! ! ! "
p. 11. "Important Announcement. | Joseph Gillott."
p. 12. "Scott Adie."
p. 13. "Benham & Sons'."
p. 14. "Slack's Electro-Plate."
p. 15. "Tourists & Travellers" ; and "W. & J. Sangster."
p. 16. "W. S. Burton." (Foot of 2nd column : "Baths & Toilet
Ware").

ADVERTISEMENTS (BACK)

(1) Norton's Camomile Pills ;   with illustration of a Pill
Bottle.   4 pp. numbered on pp. 2 and 3.
(2) Fry's Cocoa.   2 pp.   Same as Part 1.

(3) "The | Scottish Widows' Fund | Life Assurance Society" ; verso : same heading. 2 pp. unnumbered. Light-green paper.

(4) Slip :—"On the 31st May will be published, | ... | The Fisherman's Magazine | and | Review." Page 3 is a subscribers' form, with postal address on verso. 4 pp. unnumbered. Cream paper. ($7\frac{3}{4}'' \times 4\frac{7}{8}''$).

(5) Glenfield Starch. 2 pp. Same as Part 1.

PLATES (TWO)

(No. 3) "At the Bar." (p. 48).

(No. 4) "Mr. Venus surrounded by the Trophies of his Art." (p. 61).

TEXT, WITH HEADING

"Chapter V." pp. 33–64.

PART 3.

FRONT WRAPPER (OUTSIDE)

Same as No. 2, except "No. 3. July."

ADVERTISEMENTS (FRONT)

"Our Mutual Friend Advertiser." 16 pp. numbered (1)–16.

p. (1) At foot : "Part III.—July, 1864."
p. 2. "Mayall's | New Series of | Portraits of Eminent . . . | Persons."
p. 3. "Black's Guide Books. | 1864."
p. 4. "Chapman and Hall's | New Publications."
p. 5. ($\frac{1}{2}$ col.) "Third Edition . . . | The Old Forest Ranger."
p. 6. "Mr. Thomas Carlyle's Works."
p. 7. "Benham and Sons'."
p. 8. ($\frac{1}{4}$ col.) "The Malvern Glasses."
p. 9. "Cooper's | Antiseptic . . ." (as Part 2).
p. 10. ($\frac{1}{2}$ col.) "Reckitt's Diamond Black Lead."
p. 11. Same as Part 2.
p. 12. " ' Reconnoiterer ' Glass 9/6 ! ! ! "
p. 13. "Slack's Electro-Plate."
p. 14. "Scott Adie" ; "Kinahan's" ; and "Jaques and Son."
p. 15. Same as Part 2.
p. 16. Same as Part 2.

ADVERTISEMENTS (BACK)
(1) Slip :—"The July Number of | The Cornhill Magazine | begins a New Volume." Verso, blank. Orange paper. ($4\frac{3}{8}'' \times 5\frac{1}{2}''$).
(2) "Dr. De Jongh's | Light-Brown Cod Liver Oil." Last line on p. (1) : "much fatigue as any of his fellow sportsmen." 2 pp. unnumbered. Yellow paper.
(3) "The Directors of the | North British & Mercantile | Insurance Company." At foot of last page : "West-end Office, 8 Waterloo Place, Pall Mall." 4 pp. unnumbered. Light-green paper.
(4) "Messrs. Chapman and Hall's | New Publications." Dated on first page, "June 30, 1864." In all, 31 Authors' works are listed, each numbered 1–31. Imprint at foot of last page. 8 pp. numbered (1)–8.
(5) Glenfield Starch. 2 pp. Same as Part 1.

PLATES (TWO)
(No. 5) "The Boffin Progress." (p. 78).
(No. 6) "The Happy Pair." (p. 93).

TEXT, WITH HEADING
"Chapter VIII." pp. 65–96.

PART 4.

FRONT WRAPPER (OUTSIDE)
Same as No. 2, except "No. 4. August."

ADVERTISEMENTS (FRONT)
"Our Mutual Friend Advertiser." 16 pp. numbered (1)-16.
  p. (1) At foot : "Part IV.—August, 1864."
  p. 2. "Mayall's | New Photographic Portrait Studio."
  p. 3. "Black's Guide Books. | 1864." As Part 3.
  p. 4. "Many Thoughts of Many Minds."
  p. 5. "Cassell, Petter, and Galpin's."
  p. 6. "Chapman and Hall's | New Novels."
  p. 7. "Benham & Sons'."
  p. 8. "The Ondina, or Waved Jupon."
  p. 9. Same as Parts 2 & 3.
  p. 10. Same as Part 3.
  p. 11. Same as Parts 2 & 3.
  p. 12. Same as Part 3.

p. 13. Same as Part 3, except 3rd advert. is differently set.
p. 14. Same as Part 3.
p. 15. "Travellers & Tourists"; and "Thurston and Co."
p. 16. Same as Parts 2 & 3.

ADVERTISEMENTS (BACK)

(1) Norton's Camomile Pills. 4 pp. Same as Part 2.

(2) Slip :—"Tourists, Yachtsmen," etc. (Burrow's Field Glasses). Verso, blank. 1 leaf. Blue or pink paper. (7″ × 4″).

(3) "Tender Feet. | Angus Sleigh's | ' Salveo Pedes.' " 1 leaf. Verso, blank. Pink paper.

(4) "Facts are stronger than Theories." (Parr's Life Pills). Signed on last page :—"T. Roberts & Co." 4 pp. unnumbered.

(5) "The Queen Insurance Company." 2 pp. Same as Part 1.

(6) "The | Scottish Widows' Fund | Life Assurance Society." Dated on last page : "Edinburgh, July, 1864." 4 pp. unnumbered. Pink-tinted paper.

(7) "Glenfield Starch." Verso printed in four colours, with portrait of the Princess of Wales." 2 pp. unnumbered.

PLATES (TWO)
(No. 7) "Podsnappery." (p. 97).
(No. 8) "Waiting for Father." (p. 124).

TEXT, WITH HEADING
"Chapter XI." pp. 97–128.

PART 5.

FRONT WRAPPER (OUTSIDE)
Same as No. 2, except "No. 5. September."

ADVERTISEMENTS (FRONT)
"Our Mutual Friend Advertiser." 16 pp. numbered (1)-16.
p. (1) At foot : "Part V.—September, 1864."
p. 2. "Gounod's New Opera, ' Mirella.' "
p. 3. "Mudie's Select Library."
p. 4. "For fiction . . . | The Waverley Novels."

p. 5. "Now Ready . . . | Cassell's | . . . Edition of Goldsmith's Works."

p. 6. "Chapman and Hall's New Publications."

p. 7. "Benham and Sons'."

p. 8. "Kinahan's L.L. Whisky . . ."

p. 9. Same as Parts 2, 3, & 4.

p. 10. ($\frac{1}{2}$ col.) At foot of first column : "Dyspepsia."

p. 11. Same as Parts 2, 3, & 4.

p. 12. "By appointment . . . | Sangster's Umbrellas."

p. 13. Same as Part 4.

p. 14. "Scott Adie" and "Keen's Mustard."

p. 15. Same as Part 4.

p. 16. "W. S. Burton." (Foot of 2nd column : "Fenders, Stoves, Fire-Irons").

Slip : (to follow plates). "In No. 280 . . . | of | All the Year Round, | Never Forgotten." Verso, blank. Yellow paper. ($4\frac{5}{8}'' \times 5\frac{1}{2}''$).

ADVERTISEMENTS (BACK)

(1) Slip :—"The Tale of a Chivalrous Life." Verso : "London Society." Yellow paper. ($2\frac{1}{4}'' \times 5\frac{1}{2}''$).

(2) Dr. De Jongh's. 2 pp. Same as Part 3.

(3) Glenfield Starch. 2 pp. Same as Part 4.

PLATES (TWO)

(No. 9) "The Bird of Prey brought down." (p. 132).

(No. 10) "Mrs. Boffin discovers an Orphan." (p. 148).

TEXT, WITH HEADING

"Chapter XIV." pp. 129–160.

PART 6.

FRONT WRAPPER (OUTSIDE)

Same as No. 2, except "No. 6. October."

ADVERTISEMENTS (FRONT)

"Our Mutual Friend Advertiser." 16 pp. numbered (1)-16.

p. (1) At foot : "Part VI.—October, 1864."

p. 2. "Mr. Charles Dickens's Works."

p. 3. "Mudie's Select Library."

p. 4. "Chapman and Hall's New Publications."

p. 5. "Messrs. Blackwood & Sons | Publications." 16 Titles.

p. 6. "Just ready . . . | Tom Brown at Oxford."

p. 7. "Works published by Griffin and Co."

p. 8. "Benham & Sons'."

p. 9. "Sansflectum Crinolines."

p. 10. (½ col.) At foot of first column, "Glass Shades."
p. 11. "Scott Adie" and "Keen's Mustard."
p. 12. Same as Part 5.
p. 13. Same as Parts 4 & 5.
p. 14. "Kinahan's" ; "J. C. & J. Field" and three others.
p. 15. "Cooper's Antiseptic" and "Du Barry & Co."
p. 16. Same as Part 5.

ADVERTISEMENTS (BACK)

(1) Slip :—" ' Armadale ' ; | A new Novel by | Mr. Wilkie Collins." Verso, blank. Orange. ($4\frac{5}{8}'' \times 5\frac{1}{2}''$).

(2) Norton's Camomile Pills. 4 pp. Same as Part 2.

(3) "Liverpool & London & Globe | Insurance Company." 4 pp. numbered on pages 2 and 3. Pink-tinted or light-blue paper.

(4) "Albert | Insurance Company Limited." 1 leaf; verso, blank. Four varying tints of paper.

(5) "Mutual Life Assurance. | The Scottish Provident Institution." First and last pages printed broadside across. 4 pp. unnumbered. Grey, green, or light-blue paper.

(6) "Cramer and Co." 8 pp. unnumbered.
   p. (1) Heading as above. Imprint at foot.
   p. (3) With illustration of Pianoforte.
   p. (5) "The Orchestra, | a | Weekly Review."
   p. (7) "Debain's Harmoniums, &c."

(7) "Chapman and Hall's | Announcements." Dated on first page, " October 1, 1864." Pages 2–4 carry headline as above. In all, 23 Authors' works are listed, each numbered 1–23. 4 pp. numbered (1), 2, 3, 4.

(8) Glenfield Starch. 2 pp. Same as Part 4.

PLATES (TWO)

(No. 11) "The Person of the House and the bad Child." (p. 182).

(No. 12) "Bringing him in." (p. 186).

TEXT, WITH HEADING

"Book the Second. Birds of a Feather. | Chapter 1." pp. (161)–192.

CHARLES DICKENS.

PART 7.

FRONT WRAPPER (OUTSIDE)
Same as No. 2, except "No. 7. November."

ADVERTISEMENTS (FRONT)
"Our Mutual Friend Advertiser."   16 pp. numbered (1)-16.

    p. (1) At foot : "Part VII.—November, 1864."
    p. 2. "Chapman and Hall's New Publications."   16 Titles.
    p. 3. "In Weekly Numbers . . . | Don Quixote."
    p. 4. "Chapman and Hall's New Publications."   5 Titles.
    p. 5. "Works Published by Griffin and Co."
    p. 6. "The Ondina, or Waved Jupon."
    p. 7. "This day is published, | The Perpetual Curate."
    p. 8. "Benham and Sons' " and "Colman's Mustard."
    p. 9. "Personal Beauty" (Rowlands) and "Thurston & Co."
    p. 10. Same as Part 6.
    p. 11. Same as Part 6.
    p. 12. "By Appointment . . . | Sangster's Umbrellas."
    p. 13. "Bryant and May."
    p. 14. "Warner's | Kohinoor Lamps" ;   "Rimmel's" and three
        others.
    p. 15. Same as Part 6.
    p. 16. Same as Parts 5 & 6.

ADVERTISEMENTS (BACK)

(1) Slip :—"Kaye's Worsdell's . . . Pills."   1 leaf ; verso,
blank ; printed in green and red. $(7\frac{1}{2}'' \times 5\frac{1}{4}'')$.

(2) Dr. De Jongh's.   2 pp.   Same as Part 3.

(3) "Thomson's 'Prize Medal' Skirts."   Illustration.   1 leaf ;
verso, blank.

(4) "The | Scottish Widows' Fund | ... | Will complete
its 50th Year | on 31st December, 1864."   2 pp.
unnumbered.   Printed in blue.

(5) Slip :—Cassell, Petter, and Galpin.   4 pp. unnumbered.
$(6\frac{7}{8}'' \times 5\frac{1}{4}'')$.
    p. (1) "Don Quixote" : printed broadside across.
    p. (4) "The Quiver."

(6) Slip :—"Now ready. | Thorley's | Farmers' Almanack."
Verso, blank.   Yellow. $(5'' \times 5'')$.

PLATES (TWO)
(No. 13) "The Garden on the Roof."   (p. 212).
(No. 14) "Forming the Domestic Virtues."   (p. 218).

OUR MUTUAL FRIEND.

TEXT, WITH HEADING
"Chapter IV."   pp. 193–224.

PART 8.

FRONT WRAPPER (OUTSIDE)
Same as No. 2, except "No. 8.   December."

ADVERTISEMENTS (FRONT)
"Our Mutual Friend Advertiser."   16 pp. numbered (1)–16.
 p. (1) At foot : "Part VIII.—December, 1864."
 p. 2. "No Home complete without a Magic Lantern."
 p. 3. "Messrs. Griffith and Farran's."
 p. 4. "New Novel.   Now ready. | The Aarbergs."
 p. 5. "Christmas Gift Books."
 p. 6. "Hubbell's Gemma, or Jewel Jupon."
 p. 7. "Kinahan's L.L. Whisky . . ."
 p. 8. "Benham & Sons'."
 p. 9. "Christmas Presents" ; and "Thurston and Co."
 p. 10. (½ col.) "The Perfect Hair-Dye."
 p. 11. Same as Parts 6 & 7.
 p. 12. "Sangster's Umbrellas" ; last word on page, "packet."
 p. 13. Same as Part 7.
 p. 14. "Warner's | Kohinoor Lamps" ; and Colman's Mustard.
 p. 15. "Cooper's Antiseptic" ; "Fry's Cocoa" ; and "Brown
   & Polson's."
 p. 16. Same as Parts 5, 6, & 7.
Slip : (to precede "Advertiser").   "The | Christmas Number | of
 | London Society."   Verso, partly in half-measure : "London
 Society. | The January Number."   Yellow or brick-red paper.
 (6″ × 5½″).
Slip : (to follow "Advertiser").   "December the First . . . | The
 New Christmas Number | of | All the Year Round | . . . | Mrs.
 Lirriper's Legacy."   Verso, blank.   Yellow paper.   (4½″ × 5½″).

ADVERTISEMENTS (BACK)
(1) Norton's Camomile Pills.   4 pp.   Same as Part 2.
(2) "Chapman & Hall's List of New Books," dated
November 25th.   4 pp. numbered (1)–4.

PLATES (TWO)
(No. 15) "Pa's Lodger, and Pa's Daughter."   (p. 235).
(No. 16) "Our Johnny."   (p. 248).

TEXT, WITH HEADING
"Chapter VII."   pp. 225–256.

CHARLES DICKENS.

PART 9.

FRONT WRAPPER (OUTSIDE)
Same as No. 2, except "No. 9.   January, 1865."

ADVERTISEMENTS (FRONT)
"Our Mutual Friend Advertiser."   16 pp. numbered (1)-16.

       p. (1)   At foot : "Part IX.—January, 1865."
       p. 2. "Hurst and Blackett's New Works."
       p. 3. "Chapman and Hall's New Books."   8 Titles.
       p. 4. ($\frac{1}{2}$ col.) " ' Nulla dies sine linea.' "   (Letts's Diary).
       p. 5. "Joseph Gillott" ; and "Jaques's Games."
       p. 6. (Illustration of Seascape).   T. Roberts & Co.
       p. 7. ($\frac{1}{2}$ col.) "Osborne's | Analysed Provisions."
       p. 8. "Benham and Sons' " ; and Colman's Mustard.
       p. 9. "Christmas Presents " ; "Samuel Fox & Co." ; and "Thurston."
       p. 10. "The New Candle."
       p. 11.   Same as Parts 6, 7 & 8.
       p. 12. "Sangster's Umbrellas" ; last word on page, "neatness."
       p. 13. "Cooper's" ; "Fry's Cocoa" ; and "Brown & Polson's."
       p. 14. ($\frac{1}{2}$ col.) "The Perfect Hair-Dye." In second column appears a heading : "Dyspepsia."
       p. 15. "Chapman and Hall's | Standard Editions . . ." 34 Titles.
       p. 16.   Same as Parts 5, 6, 7 & 8.

Slip : (to precede "Advertiser").   "New Humorous Series in London Society for 1865." (Woodcut) "New Story in London Society for 1865."   Each of these words is lined separately in column form.   Verso advertises the January Number of "London Society" ; with two woodcuts.   Yellow paper.   (6″ × 5½″).

ADVERTISEMENTS (BACK)

(1) Dr. De Jongh's.   Last line on p. (1) "Debility and Diseases of the Chest."   2 pp.   Yellow paper.

(2) "Dalziels' Fine Art Gift Book for 1865."   Imprint at foot of each page : "London : Routledge, Warne, & Routledge, Broadway, Ludgate Hill."   4 pp. un-numbered.

(3) "Scottish Union | Fire (woodcut) Life | Insurance Company."   Imprint at foot of last page :—"R. & R. Clark, Printers."   4 pp. unnumbered.   Cream paper.
Copies of this inset are also printed on a white ribbed paper, and they are scarce.   Of 45 copies examined, only two were seen of this paper.

(4) "Ewer & Co.'s Musical Library." With specimen score of music, "Danish Wedding Song." Verso with score, "Fröhlicher Landmann." 2 pp. unnumbered.

(5) "Albert | Insurance Company Limited." 1 leaf. Same as Part 6.

(6) "Astra Castra. | Experiments and Adventures | in | The Atmosphere. | by | Hatton Turnor." Contains "General Summary of Contents," Chapters I. to XII., occupying pp. 2–6. List of subscribers on pp. 7 and 8. In all, 8 pp. numbered (1)–8.

(7) "Mr. S. O. Beeton's Announcements for Christmas & the New Year." Last two pages printed with "Forms of Order." 4 pp. unnumbered. Yellow or white paper.

PLATES (TWO)
(No. 17) "Miss Riderhood at Home." (p. 268).
(No. 18) "More Dead than Alive." (p. 281).

TEXT, WITH HEADING
"Chapter XI." pp. 257–288.

PART 10.

FRONT WRAPPER (OUTSIDE)
Same as No. 2, except "No. 10. February, 1865."

ADVERTISEMENTS (FRONT)
"Our Mutual Friend Advertiser." 16 pp. numbered (1)-16.

p. (1) At foot : "Part X.—February, 1865."
p. 2. "The Cestus of Aglaia. | The Art Journal."
p. 3. "The | Pall Mall Gazette."
p. 4. (½ col.) "Middle Class Education."
p. 5. "Robert Browning."
p. 6. "Chapman and Hall's | New Publications for February."
p. 7. (½ col.) "Osborne's | Analysed Provisions."
p. 8. "Benham & Sons' " ; and "Samuel Fox & Co."
p. 9. Colman's Mustard ; and "Thurston and Co."
p. 10. "White and Sound Teeth." (Rowlands).
p. 11. Same as Parts 6, 7, 8 & 9.
p. 12. Same as Part 9.
p. 13. Same as Part 9.

p. 14. Same as Part 9.
p. 15. "Kinahan's " ; "Osler" ; and "Gillott."
p. 16. Same as Parts 5, 6, 7, 8 & 9.
In a few copies seen, page 13 was misprinted "31."

ADVERTISEMENTS (BACK)
  (1) Slip :—"New Serial by Capt. Mayne Reid | . . . | On
    March 1st will be published, Part I. of The | Headless
    Horseman :" Verso, blank. Printed on either grey,
    yellow, or biscuit-tinted paper. Cut to sizes between
    $3\frac{5}{8}'' \times 4\frac{1}{8}''$ and $4\frac{3}{4}'' \times 5''$.
  (2) Norton's Camomile Pills. 4 pp. Same as Part 2.
  (3) Liverpool & London & Globe. 4 pp. Same as
    Part 6.

PLATES (TWO)
  (No. 19) "The Boofer Lady." (p. 298).
  (No. 20) "A Friend in Need." (p. 308).

TEXT, WITH HEADING
  "Chapter XIV." pp. 289–320. Imprint at foot of page
  320 :—"London : Printed by William Clowes and
  Sons, Stamford Street | and Charing Cross."

PRELIMINARY LEAVES
  Half-title : "Our Mutual Friend. | Volume I." Verso,
  blank. 1 leaf. (I. II.).
  Title-page (Vol. I.), dated 1865 ; verso, with imprint as on
  p. 320. 1 leaf. (III. IV.).
  Dedication : to Sir James Emerson Tennent ; verso, blank.
  1 leaf. (V. VI.).
  "Contents." 4 pp. Last page blank, numbered (VII.)
  VIII. IX. (X.).
  "Illustrations to Volume I." Verso, blank. 1 leaf,
  numbered XI. (XII.).

PART 11.

FRONT WRAPPER (OUTSIDE)
  Same as No. 2, except "No. 11. March, 1865."

ADVERTISEMENTS (FRONT)
  "Our Mutual Friend Advertiser." 16 pp. numbered (1)-16.

p. (1) At foot : "Part XI.—March, 1865."
p. 2. "Chapman & Hall's New Publications. | February 28, 1865."
p. 3. "Major Whyte Melvilles' " (10 Titles in all).
p. 4. (½ col.) "The Perfect Hair-Dye."
p. 5. "Family Medicine. | Parr's Life Pills."
p. 6. (½ col.) "Mr. Charles Dickens's Works."
p. 7. "Osborne's | Analysed Provisions." Next below :— "Toothache."
p. 8. Chapman & Hall's List. 15 Titles, the first : "The Life of Thorvaldsen."
p. 9. "Benham and Sons' " and Colman's Mustard.
p. 10. "Rowlands' Macassar Oil."
p. 11. Same as Parts 6, 7, 8, 9 & 10.
p. 12. "By Appointment to the Royal Family." Last word, "neatness."
p. 13. "Thurston and Co." ; "Fry's Cocoa" ; and "Brown & Polson's."
p. 14. "Major Whyte Melville's New Novel." 6 Titles on page.
p. 15. Same as Part 10.
p. 16. Same as Parts 5, 6, 7, 8, 9 & 10.
Slip : (to follow plates). "The People's Pickwick." Announcing the issue on March the 30th (1865) of Vol. I. of The Pickwick Papers in Two volumes. Verso, blank. Blue paper. (4½″ × 5½″).

ADVERTISEMENTS (BACK)

(1) Dr. De Jongh's. 2 pp. Same as Part 9.
(2) "Chapman & Hall's New Publications. | February 28, 1865." First title on p. 3 : "The Life of Thorvaldsen." 4 pp. numbered (1)–4.
(3) Slip :—"In Twenty Parts ... The Headless Horseman :" with woodcut ; verso, blank. White paper. (5¾″ × 4¼″).

PLATES (TWO)

(No. 21) "Trying on for the Dolls' Dressmaker." (p. 13).
(No. 22) "Rogue Riderhood's recovery." (p. 23).

TEXT, WITH HEADING

"Our Mutual Friend. | In Four Books. | Book the Third. A Long Lane. | Chapter I." pp. (1)–32.

PART 12.

FRONT WRAPPER (OUTSIDE)
Same as No. 2, except "No. 12. April, 1865."

CHARLES DICKENS.

ADVERTISEMENTS (FRONT)
"Our Mutual Friend Advertiser."   16 pp. numbered (1)-16.
- p. (1) At foot : "Part XII.—April, 1865."
- p. 2. "The Fortnightly Review."
- p. 3. "Chapman and Hall's | New Publications." (6th Title : "Mr. James Hutchings.—Scenes of Wonder.")
- p. 4. "Now Ready . . . | Elementary | Drawing Copy Books."
- p. 5. Continuation of page 4.
- p. 6. "The | London Season." Below :—"Great Governing Families."
- p. 7. "Humidic Copying Book."
- p. 8. (½ col.) "The New Novels."
- p. 9. "Benham & Sons' " ; and "Samuel Fox and Co."
- p. 10. "By Appointment to the Royal Family," and Colman's Mustard.
- p. 11. Same as Parts 6, 7, 8, 9, 10 & 11.
- p. 12. "Severe Coughs . . . | Spencer's Pulmonic Elixir."
- p. 13. Same as Part 11.
- p. 14. (½ col.) "The Perfect Hair-Dye." (In second column, "Treloar's" replaces "Dyspepsia.")
- p. 15. Same as Parts 10 & 11.
- p. 16. "William S. Burton." (In second column appears a headline : "Bedsteads, Bedding and Furniture.")

Slip : (to follow "Advertiser"). "In Number 313 of | All the Year Round, | Half a Million of Money." Verso blank. Yellow paper. (4½″ × 5½″).

(To follow plates). "The People's Pickwick" : with woodcut of Pickwick standing on chair. Verso blank.

ADVERTISEMENTS (BACK)
(1) Norton's Camomile Pills.   4 pp.   Same as Part 2.
(2) George Philip & Son's List of Maps. 4 pp. un-numbered.
- p. (1) "32 Fleet Street, London, 1865."
- p. (2) "George Philip & Son's List of Atlases."   10 Titles.
- p. (3) "George Philip & Son's List of Maps."   6 Titles.
- p. (4) "G. Philip & Son's Educational Works."   10 Titles.

(3) "Albert | Insurance Company Limited." 1 leaf. Same as Part 6.
(4) "The | Prospects of Policy-Holders | in the | Scottish Widows' Fund." Top line on p. 4, begins : "Agent in Limerick." 4 pp. unnumbered. White or light-blue paper.

(5) "Liverpool & London & Globe." 4 pp. Same as
Part 6. Pink only.

PLATES (TWO)
(No. 23) "Bibliomania of the Golden Dustman." (p. 37).
(No. 24) "The Evil Genius of the House of Boffin." (p. 64).

TEXT, WITH HEADING
"Chapter V." pp. 33–64.

PART 13.

FRONT WRAPPER (OUTSIDE)
Same as No. 2, except "No. 13. May, 1865."

ADVERTISEMENTS (FRONT)
"Our Mutual Friend Advertiser." 16 pp. numbered (1)-16.

>   p. (1) At foot: "Part XIII.—May, 1865."
>   p. 2. "The | Fortnightly Review." Slightly different to Part 12.
>   p. 3. "Chapman and Hall's | New Publications." (6th Title:
>   "Mr. John Forster.—Life of Oliver Goldsmith.")
>   pp. 4, 5. Same as Part 12.
>   p. 6. "The | London Season." Below: "Chlorodyne."
>   p. 7. "Dedicated . . . | The Life of Josiah Wedgwood"; at foot:
>   "This day . . . | Cawnpore."
>   p. 8. (½ col.) "Worthy Words on Marriage."
>   p. 9. Same as Part 11.
>   p. 10. "By Appointment to the Royal Family"; "Samuel Fox
>   and Co."; and "J. C. & J. Field."
>   p. 11. Same as Parts 6, 7, 8, 9, 10, 11 & 12.
>   p. 12. "Now ready, Vol. I. . . . | Our Mutual Friend."
>   p. 13. Same as Parts 11 & 12.
>   p. 14. (½ col.) "The Perfect Hair-Dye." (In second column
>   appears "Kaye's Worsdell's Pills.")
>   p. 15. Same as Parts 10, 11 & 12.
>   p. 16. Same as Part 12.

ADVERTISEMENTS (BACK)
Dr. De Jongh's. Last line on page (1): "undergoing as
much fatigue as any of his fellow sportsmen." 2 pp.
Yellow paper.

PLATES (TWO)
(No. 25) "The Flight." (p. 70).
(No. 26) "Threepenn'orth Rum." (p. 91).

CHARLES DICKENS.

TEXT, WITH HEADING
"Chapter VIII." pp. 65–96.

PART 14.

FRONT WRAPPER (OUTSIDE)
Same as Part 2, except "No. 14. June, 1865."

ADVERTISEMENTS (FRONT)
"Our Mutual Friend Advertiser."   16 pp. numbered (1)-16.

   p. (1) At foot : "Part XIV.—June, 1865."
   p. 2. "Chapman and Hall's New Publications."   12 Titles.
   p. 3. Continuation of page 2, with 5 Titles.
 pp. 4. 5, Same as Parts 12 & 13.
   p. 6. Tourists & Travellers.
   p. 7. "Dedicated ... | The Life of Josiah Wedgwood" ; at foot :
      "Now ready . . . | Our Mutual Friend."
   p. 8. "In the Press . . . | Dante's ' Inferno.' "
   p. 9. "Benham & Sons' " and "J. C. & J. Field."
   p. 10. "By Appointment to the Royal Family," and Colman's
      Mustard.
   p. 11. Same as Parts 6, 7, 8, 9, 10, 11, 12 & 13.
   p. 12. "Thurston and Co." ; "Fry's Cocoa" ; and "Brown
      & Polson's."
   p. 13. "Reconnoiterer Glass. 10/10d. ! ! ! | sent free."
   p. 14. Same as Part 13.
   p. 15. Same as Parts 10, 11, 12 & 13.
   p. 16. Same as Parts 12 & 13.
(To follow plates). " ' Mutual Friend.'—1-6-65.] | The Economic
Life Assurance Society."   The first line, with date, is repeated at
top of page (3), and on page (4) is a form of proposal.   4 pp.
unnumbered.

ADVERTISEMENTS (BACK)
(1) Norton's Camomile Pills.   4 pp.   Same as Part 2.
(2) "Mappin, Webb & Co. ; | 77 & 78, Oxford-St. ; &
71 & 72, Cornhill."   Verso : "Mappin, Webb & Co's
| Travelling & Dressing Bags & Cases." 2 pp.
unnumbered.   White paper.

PLATES (TWO)
(No. 27) "Mr. Fledgeby departs on his errand of mercy."
(p. 110).
(No. 28) "Mr. Wegg prepares a Grindstone for Mr.
Boffin's nose."   (p. 125).

OUR MUTUAL FRIEND.

Text, with Heading
"Chapter XI."   pp. 97–128.

PART 15.

Front Wrapper (Outside)
Same as No. 2, except "No. 15.   July, 1865."

Advertisements (Front)
"Our Mutual Friend Advertiser."   16 pp. numbered (1)-16.

    p. (1) At foot : "Part XV.—July, 1865."
    p. 2. "Chapman and Hall's New Publications."   3 Titles.
    p. 3. "This day is published . . . Astra Castra."
    p. 4. "Chapman and Hall's New Publications."   13 Titles.
    p. 5. "The People's Edition of the Works of | Mr. Charles Dickens."
    p. 6. "Mr. Palgrave's Travels in Arabia."
    p. 7. "Reconnoiterer Glass" ; "Jaques" ; and "Chlorodyne."
    p. 8. ($\frac{1}{2}$ col.). "Osborne's | Analysed Provisions."
    p. 9. Same as Parts 11 & 13.
    p. 10. "By Appointment to the Royal Family" ; and "John Warner."
    p. 11. Same as Parts 6, 7, 8, 9, 10, 11, 12, 13 & 14.
    p. 12. Same as Part 14.
    p. 13. "Tourists & Travellers."
    p. 14. Same as Parts 13 & 14.
    p. 15. "Joseph Gillott" ; and "Slack's Electro-Plate."
    p. 16. Same as Parts 12, 13 & 14.

Advertisements (Back)

(1) Dr. De Jongh's.   2 pp.   Final words in last line of text on first page : "and its use prescribed."   Yellow paper.

(2) Slip :—"Keating's | Persian | Insect Destroying Powder" ; the first and third lines of this heading printed in red and green respectively.   Verso, with two Testimonials.   2 pp. unnumbered.   ($7\frac{1}{4}'' \times 4\frac{3}{4}''$).

(3) "The Book of Perfumes | by | Eugene Rimmel" ; with specimen illustration : the whole enclosed within a rustic and floral designed border.   Pages 2 & 3 contain "Opinions of the Press." Imprint on last page : "Stephen Austin, Printer, Hereford."   4 pp.   unnumbered.

(4) "Scottish Union | Fire (woodcut) Life | Insurance Company." Five lines printed in red on front, and repeated on verso. 2 pp. unnumbered. Cream paper.

(5) Liverpool & London & Globe. 4 pp. Same as Part 6.

(6) Mappin, Webb & Co. 2 pp. Same as Part 14.

PLATES (TWO)

(No. 29) "Bella 'righted' by the Golden Dustman." (p. 130).

(No. 30) "The lovely woman has her fortune told." (p. 151).

TEXT, WITH HEADING

"Chapter XV." pp. 129–160.

PART 16.

FRONT WRAPPER (OUTSIDE)

Same as No. 2, except "No. 16. August, 1865."

ADVERTISEMENTS (FRONT)

"Our Mutual Friend Advertiser." 16 pp. numbered (1)-16.

p. (1) At foot : "Part XVI.—August, 1865."
p. 2. Same as Part 15.
p. 3. "In one handsome 4to Vol. . . . | Astra Castra."
p. 4. Same as Part 15.
p. 5. "Now ready . . . | Miss Carew."
p. 6. "Mr. Thomas Carlyle's Works" ; and Colman's Mustard.
p. 7. Same as Part 15.
p. 8. "Kinahan's L.L. Whisky . . ."
p. 9. "Benham & Sons' " and "Mr. Charles Dickens's Works."
p. 10. Same as Part 15.
p. 11. Same as Parts 6, 7, 8, 9, 10, 11, 12, 13, 14 & 15.
p. 12. "Thurston & Co." ; "Brown & Polson's" ; and "Our Mutual Friend."
p. 13. "The New Candle."
p. 14. Same as Parts 13, 14 & 15.
p. 15. Same as Part 15.
p. 16. ($\frac{1}{2}$ col.) "Cutlery, Warranted." (W. S. Burton).

ADVERTISEMENTS (BACK)

(1) Norton's Camomile Pills. 4 pp. Same as Part 2.

(2) Mappin, Webb & Co. 2 pp. Same as Part 14.

PLATES (TWO)

(No. 31) "In the Lock-Keeper's House." (p. 169).

(No. 32) "The Wedding Dinner at Greenwich." (p. 189).
Plate 31. In the List of Illustrations the title reads :—"The Lock-Keeper's House."

Text, with Heading

"Book the Fourth. A Turning. | Chapter I. | Setting
Traps." pp. (161)–192.

PART 17.

Front Wrapper (Outside)

Same as No. 2, except "No. 17. September, 1865."

Advertisements (Front)

"Our Mutual Friend Advertiser." 16 pp. numbered (1)-16.

p. (1) At foot : "Part XVII.—September, 1865."
p. 2. "Chapman & Hall's New Publications." 3 Titles.
p. 3. As Part 16, with : "Opinions of the Press."
p. 4. "Works published by Griffith and Farran."
p. 5. "Chapman and Hall's New Publications." 13 Titles.
p. 6. "Mr. Charles Dickens's Works."
p. 7. "Sangster's Umbrellas" ; "Kinahan's" ; and "Thomas Carlyle."
p. 8. ($\frac{1}{2}$ col.) "Osborne's | Analysed Provisions."
p. 9. Same as Parts 11, 13 & 15.
p. 10. "Scott Adie" ; and "Chlorodyne."
p. 11. "Reconnoiterer Glass" ; "Jaques" ; and "Keen's Mustard."
p. 12. "Thurston" ; "Brown & Polson's" ; and "Fry's Cocoa."
p. 13. "Soft, Delicate, White." (J. C. & J. Field).
p. 14. As Parts 13, 14, 15 & 16, except, the second line of "Treloar's" now reads : "Kamptulicon."
p. 15. Same as Parts 15 & 16.
p. 16. Same as Part 16.

Advertisements (Back)

(1) Dr. De Jongh's. 2 pp. Same as Part 15. Yellow paper.
(2) Day & Son, Limited, Printers, etc. 4 pp. un-numbered.

p. (1) Prospectus of new capital issue.
p. (2) Report and Balance Sheet.
pp. (3, 4) List of Works in preparation or lately published.

(3) "Messrs. Chapman and Hall's | New Publications."
Dated Sept. 1, 1865. Works of 22 Authors are listed
on pp. 1–6, each numbered 1–22. Last page headed :

"New Novels," with 10 Titles, of which the first is
"The Spanish Match" by W. H. Ainsworth.   8 pp.
unnumbered.

(4) Mappin, Webb & Co.   2 pp.   Same as Part 14.   Green
or yellow paper.

PLATES (TWO)
(No. 33) "The Parting by the River."   (p. 211).
(No. 34) "Better to be Abel than Cain."   (p. 224).

TEXT, WITH HEADING
"Chapter V."   pp. 193–224.

PART 18.

FRONT WRAPPER (OUTSIDE)
Same as Part 2, except "No. 18.   October, 1865."

ADVERTISEMENTS (FRONT)
"Our Mutual Friend Advertiser."   16 pp. numbered (1)-16.
    p. (1)   At foot : "Part XVIII.—October, 1865."
    p. 2. "Works published by Griffith and Farran."
    p. 3. "Mudie's Select Library."
    p. 4. "Astra Castra."   Same as Part 17, page 3.
    p. 5. "Chapman and Hall's | Announcements for October."
    p. 6. "New Publications."   9 Titles.   (Chapman & Hall).
    p. 7. "New Novels."   12 Titles.   (Chapman & Hall).
    p. 8. "New Novels to be had at all Libraries."
    p. 9. "Benham & Sons' " ; and "Fry's Cocoa."
    p. 10. "Tourists & Travellers" ; "E. G. Wood" ; and "Colman's."
    p. 11.   Same as Part 17.
    p. 12. "Thurston & Co." ; and "Chlorodyne."
    p. 13.   Same as Part 16.
    p. 14.   Same as Part 17.
    p. 15.   Same as Parts 15, 16 & 17.
    p. 16.   Same as Parts 16 & 17.
  Slip : (to follow plates).   "In Number 335 . . . | of | All the Year
    Round | . . . | At the Bar | by | Charles Collins."   Verso, blank.
    Yellow paper.   ($4\frac{5}{8}'' \times 5\frac{1}{2}''$).

ADVERTISEMENTS (BACK)
(1) Norton's Camomile Pills.   4 pp.   Same as Part 2.
(2) Liverpool & London & Globe.   4 pp.   Same as Part 6.
(3) Mappin, Webb & Co.   2 pp.   Same as Part 14.   White
or yellow paper.

PLATES (TWO)
(No. 35) "Miss Wren fixes her idea." (p. 227).
(No. 36) "Eugene's Bedside." (p. 255).

TEXT, WITH HEADING
"Chapter VIII." pp. 225–256.

PARTS 19 AND 20.

FRONT WRAPPER (OUTSIDE)
Same as No. 2, except "Nos. 19 and 20. November, 1865. Price 2s."

ADVERTISEMENTS (FRONT)
"Our Mutual Friend Advertiser." 16 pp. numbered (1)-16.

p. (1) At foot : "Parts XIX. and XX.—November, 1865."
p. 2. ($\frac{1}{2}$ col.) "A New Edition. . . | Modern Domestic Medicine."
p. 3. "The History of Gibraltar."
p. 4. "Astra Castra." Same as Part 17, page 3.
p. 5. "Chapman and Hall's New Publications." 5 Titles.
p. 6. Same as Part 18.
p. 7. "Reconnoiterer Glass" ; and "Journal of Social Science."
p. 8. "Kinahan's Whisky."
p. 9. Same as Parts 11, 13, 15 & 17.
p. 10. "Advice to Invalids."
p. 11. "White and Sound Teeth" ; "Jaques" ; and "Keen's."
p. 12. Same as Part 18.
p. 13. Same as Parts 16 & 18.
p. 14. Same as Parts 17 & 18.
p. 15. Same as Parts 15, 16, 17 & 18.
p. 16. Same as Parts 16, 17 & 18.

(To follow plates). " ' Our Mutual Friend,' Nov., 1865.] | The Economic Life Assurance Society." The first line, with date, is repeated in each succeeding page. On page 4 is a proposal form for Insurance. 4 pp. unnumbered. ($8\frac{1}{4}"\times5\frac{1}{4}"$).

ADVERTISEMENTS (BACK)
(1) Dr. De Jongh's. 2 pp. Last line of text on first page : "excellent restorative in Debility and Diseases of the Chest." Yellow paper.
(2) "The | Anthelmintic Bon Bon," printed in brown and grey. Verso : "Keating's Cough Lozenges." 2 pp. unnumbered.

(3) "Chapman and Hall's | New Publications." Dated November, 1865. First title on p. (4): "Can You Forgive Her?" by Anthony Trollope. 4 pp. numbered (1), 2, 3, (4).

(4) "The | Scottish Widows' Fund." Last words on verso: "17 South Mall." 2 pp. unnumbered. Grey paper.
This inset is entirely different to Parts 2 & 7.

(5) Slip :—"Foreign Bank Notes." (Nissen & Parker). White lettering on green ground. $(3\frac{1}{2}'' \times 5\frac{1}{2}'')$.

(6) "Boosey & Co.'s Miniature Pianoforte." Page (4): "English Harmoniums." 4 pp. unnumbered. Brick-red paper.

(7) Mappin, Webb & Co. 2 pp. Same as Part 14. Green paper.

PLATES (FOUR)

(No. 37) "Lightwood at last." (p. 258).

(No. 38) "Mr. Boffin does the Honours of the Nursery Door." (p. 274).

(No. 39) "Not to be shaken off." (p. 292).

(No. 40) "The Dutch Bottle." (Frontispiece to Vol. II.).
Plate 38. In the List of Illustrations, the word "Honours" is printed "Honors," and "Mr. Boffin" reads "Mrs. Boffin."

TEXT, WITH HEADING

"Chapter XII." pp. 257–306; with "Postscript" and Imprint, 4 pp. (307–310); and 1 leaf, "Mr. Charles Dickens's Works"; verso blank (311 & 312). Imprint p. (310) same as Part 10, p. 320, except in 3 lines instead of 2 lines.

PRELIMINARY LEAVES

Half-title: "Our Mutual Friend. | Volume II." Verso, blank. 1 leaf. (I. II).

Title-page (Vol. II), dated 1865; verso, with 2-line imprint as Part 10, p. 320. 1 leaf. (III. IV.).

"Contents" and "Illustrations to Volume II." 4 pp. numbered (V.) VI. VII. (VIII.).

THE MYSTERY

OF

EDWIN DROOD.

BY

CHARLES DICKENS.

WITH TWELVE ILLUSTRATIONS BY S. L. FILDES.
AND A PORTRAIT.

LONDON:
CHAPMAN AND HALL, 193 PICCADILLY.
1870.

The Mystery of Edwin Drood

in

6 Monthly Parts

April to September, 1870.

ORIGINALLY published in six monthly parts, price one shilling per number, except the last, which was issued at eighteenpence. The first number appeared in April, 1870, and was completed in September of the same year.

When Dickens died on June 9, 1870, he had completed only enough of his manuscript to make up six instalments, leaving unfinished a work which had commanded the widest attention for its opening numbers, and which promised to be one of his most effective and popular books. Although only three parts had been issued prior to his death, publication of the work continued, and on completion with Part 6 of all available material, the vast army of readers was left high and dry as to "The Mystery." The design for the front cover was by C. A. Collins (brother of Wilkie Collins), and therein are depicted eight incidents of the story, which it is frequently suggested have a bearing on the eventual solution. The Author during the writing of the story never disclosed the ultimate development of his plot, but on the other hand took especial precautions to guard the *dénouement*. This, however, has not prevented many "solutionists" from reading into the cover design, the lines upon which the story was intended to run—with what success it would be futile to hazard a guess.

WRAPPERS.

Green covers were again adopted, and as usual carry advertisements printed upon the insides, and outside of back cover. The earliest issue of Part 6 should have a slip "Eighteenpence" pasted over the originally printed "One Shilling"—in re-issues the slip is dispensed with, the price figure being corrected when the wrapper was reprinted.

ILLUSTRATIONS.

These comprise fourteen designs by Luke Fildes, and are engraved on wood by Dalziel, C. Roberts and others.

ADVERTISEMENTS (FRONT).

Each part contains the "Edwin Drood Advertiser," and every page throughout is so headed. All are paginated, except the first in each. No other insets at the front are called for.

ADVERTISEMENTS (BACK).

Some insets or slips appear in each number. Part 2 should contain the "Cork Hat" slip, which consists of a thinly split piece of real cork printed upon both sides. This latter was not included in later bound copies.

PART 1.

FRONT WRAPPER (OUTSIDE)
"No. I.] April, 1870. [Price One Shilling. | The | Mystery | of | Edwin Drood. | by | Charles Dickens. | With Illustrations. | London : Chapman & Hall, 193, Piccadilly. | Advertisements to be sent to the Publishers, and Adams & Francis, 59, Fleet Street, E.C. | [The right of Translation is reserved.]"
The Title, Author, and "With Illustrations" are embodied in, and form part of the cover design. All other matter is type-set.

FRONT WRAPPER (INSIDE)
"Chappell's New Pianoforte Rooms" ; with illustration of Pianoforte. Two lines at foot, beginning :—"A liberal Discount for Cash."

BACK WRAPPER (INSIDE)
    Upper half of page: "John Brogden's 18-carat Gold Chains"; 12 lines in all. Lower half: "Caution.—The Pall Mall Jewel Case"; 15 lines in all, with only one word in last line—"application."

BACK WRAPPER (OUTSIDE)
    "10,000 Presents, 5s. to £5. | Parkins & Gotto." Last line: "The new square cut envelopes." (No illustrations).

ADVERTISEMENTS (FRONT)
    "Edwin Drood Advertiser."   36 pp. numbered (1)-36.
        p. (1) At foot: "Part I.—April, 1870."
        p.   3. (Two lines of Press Notices.)   "Pompeian Studio."
        p.   5. "Griffith and Farran's New Works."
        p.   7. "The Athenæum."
        p.   9. "Messrs. Blackwood's New Publications."
        p. 11. "Centenary Edition. | The Waverley Novels."
        p. 13. "New Works."   (Smith, Elder & Co.)
        p. 15. "Educational Works of Dr. Cornwell, F.R.G.S."
        p. 17. "Monarch Insurance Company."
        p. 19. "Mr. Thomas Carlyle's Works."
        p. 21. (Illustration) "In the Spring Parr's Life Pills . . ."
        p. 23. "1869. | The ' Vowel ' Washing Machine."
        p. 25. "Great Sale of Ladies' Underclothing ! ! "
        p. 27. "J. L. Denman, 20, Piccadilly, London, W."
        p. 29. "Naldire's Tablet."
        p. 31. "Jenner and Knewstub."
        p. 33. "Elegant Presents . . . | Macmichael's Monograms."
        p. 35. "284, Regent Street, London, W."
    Odd numbered pages only are quoted for this part, as in no instance do the clues recur in the corresponding pages of the other 5 parts.

ADVERTISEMENTS (BACK)
    (1) "Dr. De Jongh's | Light-Brown | Cod Liver Oil." The whole of this heading together with two medals, are set in a fancy frame-work design, in shape almost square. Last words of text on p. (1): "his fellow-sportsmen." 2 pp. unnumbered. Yellow paper.
    (2) "Mutual Life Assurance. | The Corporation of | The Scottish Provident | Institution." Foot of last page

with address of Dublin office. 4 pp. unnumbered. Mauve paper.

(3) "Cassell, Petter, and Galpin Publications." 4 pp. unnumbered.

    p. (1) 1st Title : "Cassell's Magazine for April."
    p. (3) 1st Title : "Cassell's Gulliver's Travels."

(4) Chapman & Hall's Publications. 8 pp. unnumbered. Yellow.

    pp. (1, 2, 3). "The Select Library of Fiction." 172 Vols. enumerated. Dated on p. (1) March, 1870.
    p. (4) "Standard Authors. | One Shilling."
    p. (5) "Jane Austen's Novels. | Author's Edition."
    p. (6) "Charles Lever's Works."
    p. (7) "Anthony Trollope's Works."
    p. (8) "Charles Lever's Works | Library Edition."

(5) "Henry Brett & Co. ; | Distillers and Importers." Verso blank, as also page (3). On back page : "Eau de Vie | Pure | Pale Brandy | 18/- Per Gallon." 4 pp. unnumbered.

PLATES (Two)
  (No. 1) "In the Court." (p. 1).
  (No. 2) "Under the Trees." (p. 20).

TEXT, WITH HEADING
  "The Mystery | of | Edwin Drood. | Chapter I. | The Dawn." pp. (1)–32.

PART 2.

FRONT WRAPPER (OUTSIDE)
  Same as No. I. except "No. II. May."
    Some copies have no full point after "II"

FRONT WRAPPER (INSIDE)
  Same as No. I. except three substituted lines at foot : "Chappell's Musical Magazine for May."

BACK WRAPPER (INSIDE)
  Same as No. I. except there are seven words in last line.

No. II]   MAY, 1870.   [Price One Shilling.

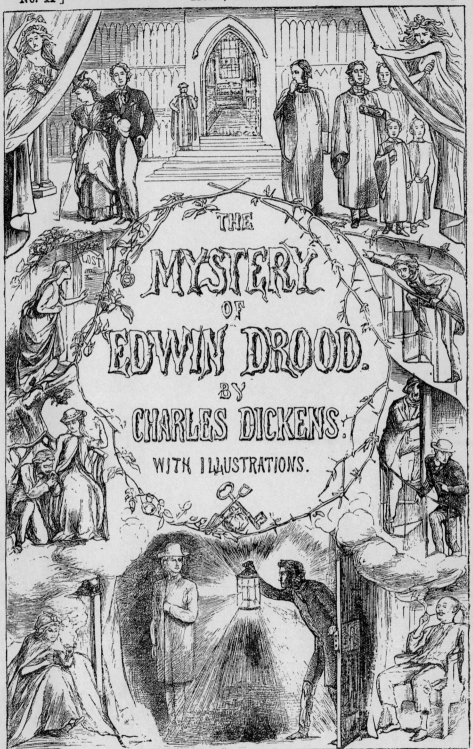

THE MYSTERY OF EDWIN DROOD.

BY CHARLES DICKENS.

WITH ILLUSTRATIONS.

LONDON: CHAPMAN & HALL, 193. PICCADILLY.

Advertisements to be sent to the Publishers, and ADAMS & FRANCIS 59, Fleet Street, E C

[The right of Translation is reserved.]

The Front Wrapper to the original edition of "Edwin Drood,"
as published in six monthly parts, 1870. The story was left
unfinished at the time of death of the Author, in June, 1870.

THE MYSTERY OF EDWIN DROOD.

BACK WRAPPER (OUTSIDE)
Same as No. I.

ADVERTISEMENTS (FRONT)
"Edwin Drood Advertiser."   20 pp. numbered (1)–20.

      p. (1) At foot : "Part II.—May, 1870."
      p. 2. "Howard & Sons."
      p. 3. "Will shortly be published . . . | A Scholar's Day Dream."
      p. 4. "Lessey's Marking Ink."
      p. 5. "The London Season."   (No illustration).
      p. 6. "Fender and Fire-Irons. | Slack's."
      p. 7. "1869. | The ' Vowel ' Washing Machine."
      p. 8. "Monarch Insurance Company."
      p. 9. "The Hydronette."
      p. 10. "28s. per Dozen. | Santorin Port . . ."
      p. 11. "Nunn's Marsala or Bronte Wine."
      p. 12. "New Music. | Vocal Music. | Pianoforte Music."
      p. 13. "Waterproofs for India."
      p. 14. "Bragg's Vegetable Charcoal."
      p. 15. "A. Sedley & Co."   Below : "George Hobson."
      p. 16. "The Surplice Shirt."
      p. 17. "Elegant Presents . . . | Macmichael's Monograms."
      p. 18. "Cricket Marquees."   With illustration.
      p. 19. "Birmingham. | The | New Great Western | Hotel."
      p. 20. "A Cup of Coffee in one minute."

ADVERTISEMENTS (BACK)

(1) "To Whom it may Concern ! "   At foot of last page : "Wilcox & Gibbs Sewing Machine Co."   4 pp. unnumbered.

(2) Gaimes, Sanders & Nicol, London.   "Cork Hats."
This consists of a thin sheet of actual cork ; split to the substance of ordinary news-paper, on both sides of which is printed the publicity matter, including a representation of "George Peabody | MDCCCLXIX," seated in chair which rests on a plinth. ($5\frac{1}{2}'' \times 4''$).

PLATES (TWO)

(No. 3) "At the piano."   (p. 44).

(No. 4) "On dangerous Ground."   (p. 50).

TEXT, WITH HEADING
"Chapter VI."   pp. 33–64.

CHARLES DICKENS.

PART 3.

FRONT WRAPPER (OUTSIDE)
Same as No. I. except "No. III. June."

FRONT WRAPPER (INSIDE)
Same as No. 2, except at foot : "June" for "May."

BACK WRAPPER (INSIDE)
Same as No. 2.

BACK WRAPPER (OUTSIDE)
First two lines same as No. I. with line : "Dressing Bags &
Dressing Cases" above two illustrations of these articles.

ADVERTISEMENTS (FRONT)
"Edwin Drood Advertiser."   20 pp. numbered (1)-20.
- p. (1) At foot : "Part III.—June, 1870."
- p. 2. "Howard & Sons."   Same as Part 2.
- p. 3. "The Guelph Reversible Sewing Machine."
- p. 4. "Lessey's Marking Ink."   Same as Part 2.
- p. 5. "The London Season."   With woodcut.
- p. 6. "Slack's Electro-Plate."
- p. 7. "The ' Vowel ' Washing Machine."   Same as Part 2.
- p. 8. "28s. per Dozen. | Santorin Port . . ."
- p. 9. "John Richard Wace & Co."
- p. 10. "Chapman & Co.'s | Entire Wheat Flour."
- p. 11. "Waterproofs for India."
- p. 12. "New Music."   (No other headings as in Part 2).
- p. 13. "Mr. Thomas Carlyle's Works."
- p. 14. "The | Fortnightly Review | for May."
- p. 15. "A. Sedley & Co."   Below : "Hobson's Choice ! ! !"
- p. 16. "The Surplice Shirt."
- p. 17. "Elegant presents . . . | Macmichael's Monograms."
- p. 18. "Bragg's Vegetable Charcoal."
- p. 19. "Birmingham. | The | New Great Western | Hotel."
- p. 20. "Dunn & Hewett's."   Below, in half measure : "The ' Watteau.' "

ADVERTISEMENTS (BACK)
(1) Dr. De Jongh's.   2 pp.   Same as Part 1.
(2) Slip :—"New Series | of | All the Year Round, | . . .
    | Two Serial Stories | . . . | The Doctor's Mixture ;
    | . . . | In that state of Life."   Verso, blank.   Yellow.
($4\frac{5}{8}'' \times 5\frac{1}{2}''$).

(3) "Chapman & Hall's | Recent Publications. | . . . | On May 31st will be published . . . Part III. of | 'The Mystery of Edwin Drood." Each succeeding page has running headline: "Chapman and Hall's Recent Publications." 8 pp. numbered (1)-8. Imprint on p. 8: "Bradbury, Evans, and, Co. Printers, Whitefriars."

(4) "Chapman & Co.'s | Entire Wheat Flour." Last page: "Orlando Jones & Co. | Original Patent | Rice Starch." 4 pp. unnumbered. Yellow paper.

(5) "Cassell, Petter, and Galpin Publications." 4 pp. unnumbered.

p. (1) "The Doré Don Quixote | Re-Issue."
p. (2) Section of a full-page Engraving by Gustave Doré.
p. (3) 1st Title: "Cassell's Book of Birds."
p. (4) "How to make the most of everything."

PLATES (Two)

(No. 5) "Mr. Crisparkle is Overpaid." (p. 72).

(No. 6) "Durdles Cautions Mr. Sapsea against Boasting." (p. 88).

TEXT, WITH HEADING
"Chapter X." pp. 65-96.

PART 4.

FRONT WRAPPER (OUTSIDE)
Same as No. 1. except "No. IV. July."

FRONT WRAPPER (INSIDE)
Same as No. 3, except at foot: "July" for "June."

BACK WRAPPER (INSIDE)
Upper half, same as Part 1. Lower half headed: "Messrs. Howell, James, & Co."

BACK WRAPPER (OUTSIDE)
Same as Part 3, except the line "Dressing Bags & Dressing Cases" is below the two illustrations.

CHARLES DICKENS.

ADVERTISEMENTS (FRONT)

"Edwin Drood Advertiser." 24 pp. numbered. (1)-24.

p. (1) At foot: "Part IV.—July, 1870."
p. 2. "Howard & Sons." Same as Parts 2 & 3.
p. 3. "Allen's | Patent Seamless | Portmanteaus."
p. 4. "Lessey's Marking Ink." Same as Parts 2 & 3.
p. 5. "Arundel Society."
p. 6. "New Music." Partly in half measure.
p. 7. "Visitors | to | the Sea-side."
p. 8. "Fender and Fire-Irons. | Slack's."
p. 9. "Bradford's Patent Washing Machinery."
p. 10. "28s. per Dozen. | Santorin Port . ."
p. 11. (Two lines of Press Notices). "Charles Dickens. | (The last portrait ever taken of this great Author."
p. 12. "Chapman & Co.'s | Entire Wheat Flour."
p. 13. "Waterproofs for India." Same as Part 2.
p. 14. "Chapman & Hall's New Publications." 15 Titles.
p. 15. "A. Sedley & Co." Below : "George Hobson." (No woodcuts).
p. 16. "The Surplice Shirt."
p. 17. "Mutual Life Assurance. | The Scottish Provident . . ."
p. 18. "New Novels." (Chapman & Hall). 26 Titles.
p. 19. "On the First of Every Month . . . | Bradshaw's ' Through Service ' Guide."
p. 20. "John Richard Ware & Co."
p. 21. "Bragg's Vegetable Charcoal."
p. 22. "Cricket Marquees." With two illustrations.
p. 23. "Birmingham. | The | Great Western Hotel."
p. 24. "A Cup of Coffee in one minute."

ADVERTISEMENTS (BACK)

(1) Wilcox & Gibbs. 4 pp. Same as Part 2.

(2) "Reasons for Insuring | in the | Scottish Widows' Fund | Life Assurance Society." Below : "First Reason." Pages 2, 3 and 4, headed : "Second," "Third," and "Fourth Reasons" respectively. 4 pp. unnumbered. Light-blue paper.

(3) "Chapman & Co.'s | Patent Prepared | Entire Wheat Flour." 2 pp. unnumbered. White paper.

In about 10 per cent. of the copies of Part 4 which have been under examination, there appeared the Chapman & Hall 8-paged

THE MYSTERY OF EDWIN DROOD.

"Recent Publications," intended for, and inserted in Part 3. The inset in its placing here is one month out of date, and obviously is a "remainder."

PLATES (Two)
(No. 7) " 'Good-bye, Rosebud, darling ! ' " (p. 98).
(No. 8) "Mr. Grewgious has his suspicions." (p. 120).

TEXT, WITH HEADING
"Chapter XIII." pp. 97-128.

PART 5.

FRONT WRAPPER (OUTSIDE)
Same as No. 1. except "No. V. August."

FRONT WRAPPER (INSIDE)
Same as No. 4.

BACK WRAPPER (INSIDE)
Same as No. 4.

BACK WRAPPER (OUTSIDE)
"Parkins & Gotto" with illustrations of four articles. Last words on page : "(Croquet sets made up.)"

ADVERTISEMENTS (FRONT)
"Edwin Drood Advertiser." 20 pp. numbered (1)-20.
p. (1) At foot : "Part V.—August, 1870."
p. 2. "Howard & Sons." Same as Parts 2, 3 & 4.
p. 3. Allen's Portmanteaus. Same as Part 4.
p. 4. "Lessey's Marking Ink." Same as Parts 2, 3 & 4.
p. 5. "New Music."
p. 6. "Slack's Electro-Plate."
p. 7. "Visitors | to | the Sea-side." Same as Part 4.
p. 8. "Mr. Charles Dickens's Works."
p. 9. "Bradford's Patent Washing Machinery." Same as Part 4.
p. 10. Santorin Port. Same as Part 4.
p. 11. " G R I P."
p. 12. "Chapman & Co.'s | Entire Wheat Flour."
p. 13. "Waterproofs for India." Same as Parts 2 & 4.
p. 14. "New Patent . . . | George Kent."
p. 15. "A. Sedley & Co." Below : "George Hobson" with two woodcuts.

CHARLES DICKENS.

p. 16. "The Surplice Shirt."
p. 17. "John Richard Wace & Co."
p. 18. "The Imperial Hotel, | Exmouth."
p. 19. "Birmingham. | The | Great Western Hotel."
p. 20. "Dunn & Hewett's." Below, in half measure : "The
| ' Bag of Bags.' "

PLATES (Two)

(No. 9) "Jasper's Sacrifices." (p. 149).
(No. 10) "Mr. Grewgious experiences a New Sensation."
(p. 157).

TEXT, WITH HEADING
"Chapter XVII." pp. 129-160.

PART 6.

FRONT WRAPPER (OUTSIDE)
Same as No. 1, except "No. VI. September," and a printed
slip, "Price Eighteenpence," pasted over the already
printed "Price One Shilling."

FRONT WRAPPER (INSIDE)
Same as No. 1, except four lines at foot, beginning :
"Harmoniums and American Organs."

382

THE MYSTERY OF EDWIN DROOD.

BACK WRAPPER (INSIDE)

Same as Nos. 4 & 5.

BACK WRAPPER (OUTSIDE)

Similar to Part 1, except last words on page read : "(Orders quickly Executed.)" (No illustrations).

ADVERTISEMENTS (FRONT)

"Edwin Drood Advertiser." 18 pp. numbered (1)–18.

p. (1) At foot : "Part VI.—September, 1870."
p. 2. "Howard & Sons." Same as Parts 2, 3, 4 & 5.
p. 3. Allen's Portmanteaus. Same as Parts 4 & 5, except the fourth line of second advertisement reads : "By Nicholas Michell."
p. 4. "Lessey's Marking Ink." Same as Parts 4 & 5.
p. 5. "New Music."
p. 6. "Fender and Fire-Irons, | Slack's."
p. 7. "Visitors | to | the Sea-side." Same as Parts 4 & 5.
p. 8. "28s. per Dozen. | Santorin Port . . ."
p. 9. "Bradford's Patent Washing Machinery." Same as Part 4.
p. 10. "A. Sedley & Co."
p. 11. "Walter Savage Landor."
p. 12. "Chapman & Co.'s | Entire Wheat Flour."
p. 13. "Waterproofs for India."
p. 14. "Naldire's Tablet."
p. 15. "John Richard Wace & Co."
p. 16. "The Surplice Shirt."
p. 17. "Birmingham. | The | Great Western Hotel."
p. 18. "A Cup of Coffee in one minute."

ADVERTISEMENTS (BACK)

(1) Wilcox & Gibbs. 1st page : "Concerning Stitches." pp. (2 & 3) have eleven illustrations of lock stitching. 4 pp. unnumbered.

(1A) Wilcox & Gibbs. 1st page : "A New World at Home | for busy people." 4 pp. unnumbered. The above two insets are seen alternatively in copies of this part, and in about equal proportions.

(2) Slip :—"Chapman & Co.'s | Entire Wheat Flour." Identical with Part 5, except date is "September 1, 1870." 4 pp. Yellow paper. ($7\frac{3}{4}'' \times 5\frac{3}{8}''$).

CHARLES DICKENS.

PLATES (FOUR)
(No. 11) "Up the River." (p. 173).
(No. 12) "Sleeping it off." (p. 183).
(No. 13) Vignette Title.
(No. 14) Portrait of Charles Dickens, with facsimile signature, and date "1870." Imprint : "Engraved by J. H. Baker from a Photograph taken in 1868, by Mason & Co."

TEXT, WITH HEADING
"Chapter XXI." pp. 161–190, plus 2 pp. (191–192) unnumbered, announcing various editions of the Author's Works. Imprint at foot of p. 190 : "London : Printed by William Clowes and Sons, Stamford Street and Charing Cross."

PRELIMINARY LEAVES
Title-page, dated 1870 ; verso, with imprint as p. 190 in two lines. (I. II.).

Publishers' note, 11 lines, and date 12th August, 1870. Verso blank. (III. IV.).

Contents, and Illustrations, 4 pp. numbered. (V.) VI. VII. (VIII.).

Raithby, Lawrence & Co., Ltd., Printers, Leicester and London.